Contents

KT-454-540

6 Contents

Foreword

One of the commonplace yet probably essential characteristics in the development of any new body of knowledge are the competing values of those who generate and use that knowledge. The new field of organizational behaviour is no exception to this trend. Those who are attracted to new areas of study are generally dissatisfied with the conventional wisdoms of more established disciplines. For the most part this is all to the good; new problems can be defined, new people encouraged to tackle them and new concepts and methodologies refined to meet the challenges of the new situations.

Difficulties start to occur, however, when the products of some of these new endeavours are communicated to the world at large. This applies not only amongst researchers and teachers, but between the whole community of students. The problems lie not only at the level of what is acceptable knowledge, though this should not be underestimated, but also in the form of how one presents this material in a way which meets the needs of varying audiences. In the context of the study of organizations this is likely to mean teachers and students at the undergraduate, post-graduate and post-experience stages. But overlaid on top of the problem of multiple audiences lies the significant question of knowledge for what purpose? There is a major difference between communicating ideas and presenting information in such a way that it is credible and can inform action.

Understanding Organizations meets some of the demands of these educational problems. This book emphasizes the importance of diagnostic skills in understanding organizations. Diagnosis of oneself and one's own personal style of relating to people and organizations, diagnosis of others, their motivations, personalities and role problems, the varying factors which determine behaviour in groups and the differences between organizational forms. In this way it is hoped to carry the reader from a state of familiarity with himself and his organization to a more active awareness of his links with people and organizations.

The diagnostic theme in the book is aided by an interpretative writing style, where the emphasis is less on comprehensiveness and more on the elucidation of a coherent set of concepts. The other main theme of the book attempts to deal with the problem of knowledge for what purpose. Connections are drawn between the concepts and a set of current organizational problems, not only in Part Two of the text but also as the diagnostic material is being presented. As with all communications in the written form, however, the final responsibility for making connections between the concepts and the reader's world lies with the reader's active involvement.

Andrew M. Pettigrew
London Graduate School of Business Studies

Part One
The Concepts

1 About This Book

1.1

I came to the study of people in organizations expecting certainty and absolute knowledge in the behavioural sciences. I anticipated that I would find laws governing the behaviour of people and of organizations as sure and as immutable as the laws of the physical sciences. I was disappointed. I found concepts and ideas abounding. I found, too often, ponderous confirmation of the obvious and weighty investigation of trivia. But the underlying unalterable laws were not there, organizations remained only patchily efficient, and the most exciting of the ideas did not always work.

This disappointment initially brought dismay and disillusionment. But then I came to realize that, perhaps with some exceptions in physiological psychology, the study of people in organizations is not to do with predictive certainty – for two very good reasons:

1 The multiplicity of variables impinging on any one organizational situation is so great (Figure 1 suggests over sixty) that data on all of them sufficient to predict the precise outcome of that multiple interrelationship would never in practice be forthcoming.

2 What seems to be the inherent ability of the human being to override many of the influences on his behaviour.

Organizational phenomena, I realized, should be explained by the kind of contextual interpretation used by an historian. Such interpretation would allow us to predict 'trends' with some degree of confidence. To add precise quantities to those trends, as in the physical sciences, would, however, be inappropriate and unrealistic.

As individual human beings we should take delight in this lack of certainty since it carries with it a guarantee of ultimate independence. As managers, or potential organizers of people, we can take comfort in the facts that:

1 Most of the variables remain constant most of the time.

2 Most individuals do not override the influencing factors most of the time.

3 Most interpretations will be valid for the future as well as the past.

Box 1.1

Until well into the seventeenth century, surgery was performed not by doctors but by barbers who, untaught and unlettered, applied whatever tortures they had picked up during their apprenticeship. Doctors, observing a literal interpretation of their oath not to inflict bodily harm, were too 'ethical' to cut and were not even supposed to watch. But the operation, if performed according to the rules, was presided over by a learned doctor who sat on a dais well above the struggle and read what the barber was supposed to be doing aloud from a Latin classic (which the barber, of course, did not understand). Needless to say, it was always the barber's fault if the patient died, and always the doctor's achievement if he survived. And the doctor got the bigger fee in either event.

There is some resemblance between the state of surgery four centuries ago and the state of organization theory until recently. There is no dearth of books in the field; indeed, organization theory is the main subject taught under the heading of 'management' in many of our business schools. There is a great deal of importance and value in these books – just as there was a great deal of genuine value in the classical texts on surgery. But the practising manager has only too often felt the way the barber must have felt. It is not that he, as a 'practical man', resisted theory. Most managers, especially in the larger companies, have learned the hard way that performance depends upon proper organization. But the practising manager did not as a rule understand the organization theorist, and vice versa.

From Drucker, *The Practice of Management*, 1954

4 Prediction tends to improve as the object of study turns from individuals to collections of individuals.

1.2

Figure 1 is a schematic way of illustrating why the study of organizational effectiveness is likely to be complicated. Over sixty different variables are listed there. Most managers could suggest a few more or would group them differently. Looking at this complexity one can begin to understand why the organizational theorist will tend to focus on one group of variables, e.g. the motivation to work, in an attempt to get hold of *something*, and why the pragmatic manager will respond to the academic's theories by saying 'Yes, that's all very well but it doesn't help my particular situation'.

The diagram should also reveal the dangers of the lure of the familiar. Because we know what to do about competition, for instance, or about

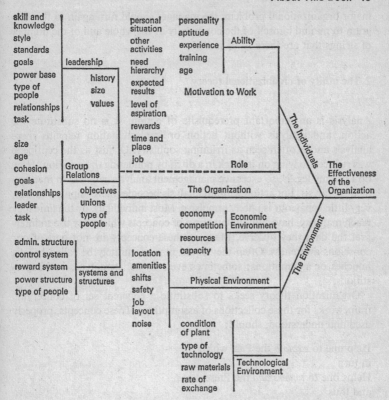

Figure 1 Some factors affecting organization effectiveness

unions, we selectively focus on that variable or group of variables in any problem situation. Unfortunately selective focusing, if done by habit, also unfocuses a lot of other variables. I have often myself been swept up in enthusiasm for a new form of training (group dynamics is one example), only to find in the cold light of practice that it deals with only one aspect of a much more complex situation. The consultant firm that links its prestige to dealing with one set of variables (e.g. systems and structures) because that is where its operational experience lies, runs the risk of doing a superlative job on an irrelevant issue. It is of little use regulating the clocks when the house is burning down.

Before reading any chapter of this book, indeed before dealing with any major organizational problem, the manager should turn again to this diagram to remind himself of the complexity of the whole and of the number of strings that are there to be pulled.

2 The utility of organizational theory

2.1

Analysis is an important prerequisite of action. It is no substitute for action, and analysis without action or implementation remains mere analysis and is often seen as irritating sophistry. Or just as the centipede was reduced to lying on its back in a ditch by pondering the question 'How do I use my legs?', so excessive management analysis can lead to management paralysis. But action without analysis becomes mere impulse. In fact, very little behaviour is purely impulsive. Most individuals, by the time they reach maturity, have built up an array of concepts which they use to interpret the data they observe. Many of these concepts are not part of our conscious awareness. Often they could more accurately be called beliefs, hunches or assumptions; sometimes even myths, stereotypes and superstitions.

Organization theory seeks to substitute a coherent set of conceptual frameworks for these collections of assumptions. These concepts, properly used and understood, should:

Help one to *explain* the Past which
in turn
Helps one to *understand* the Present
and thus
To *predict* the Future which leads
to
More *influence* over future events
and
Less *disturbance* from the Unexpected.

2.2

Do not underrate the value of the conceptual understanding of the present. One of the stereotyped assumptions of our culture is that man is master, or should be, of his environment. When anything goes wrong, or goes in an unexpected direction, we are apt to blame the individual – ourselves or someone else. This tendency towards individualism has, in my experience, caused a great deal of unnecessary trauma and personal anxiety in organizations. In fact, as Figure 1 demonstrates, the individual and his abilities are only one part of many forces bearing on a situation. A proper understanding of the relevant concepts of organization theory has brought much comfort to individuals in tension as well as allowing them to carry out the analytical task of the manager, which is:

To identify the key variables in any situation;
To predict the probable outcomes of any changes in the variables;
To select the ones he can and should influence.

Even if this yields only knowledge of the negative, that it will be useless to do such and such in such and such a situation, the manager will benefit. For in organizations, as in life, we progress as much by knowing what *not* to do as by recognizing what we must do.

Box 1.2

Some among management will scorn their colleagues who express an interest in mental health. These are the men who will say that human relations efforts in industry have failed, that a concern for the health of people is a form of 'softness' not appropriate in industry. If, however, we look closely into situations where human relations practices are alleged to have failed, we see invariably that what passed for human relations was manipulation. The allegation really means that those who sought to manipulate others failed in the effort, and when the psychological confidence game failed, they gave up altogether. Psychological *understanding* cannot fail. Although there is yet much to be learned and understood, there is already a significant body of psychological and social science knowledge. Management fails when it tries to substitute make-believe for the understanding which can come from this knowledge.

Harry Levinson *et al.*, *Men, Management and Mental Health*, 1962

2.3

This book contains:

Some of the conceptual frameworks that I have found most useful in the interpretation of organizational phenomena;
A discussion of their application to particular types of organizational problems.

This book is eclectic. It is not a comprehensive review of all the ideas that have been put forward, though ideas for further study are suggested in Part Three. But it is a coherent set of concepts. The concepts are interpretative devices, not precise definitions in the tradition of the physical sciences. Many of them will, and should, accord with the intuitive assumptions and beliefs of successful managers.

I am reminded of a student on a management development programme. He had made half-a-million pounds by his own efforts by the time he was 35. 'Why are you coming here as a student?' I asked him. 'With your success record you should join the faculty.' 'Not so,' he replied, 'I have come to find out why I was so successful.' He understood that if he could not explain his success he could not repeat it.

So it is with the interpretative devices of organization theory. Organizations have existed for thousands of years. Many have succeeded. Many have failed. The aim of organization theory is to explain the difference. To conceptualize and understand what works well so that it can be repeated. To generalize from the particular and to perceive the common thread in the tangled skein of individual incidents. If this book, therefore, can help the individual reader to re-interpret his own experience so that he can better understand it and generalize from it, then it will have achieved its aim. To distort Pope's dictum about wit

> Theory is Nature to advantage dressed,
> What oft was thought, but ne'er so well expressed.

2.4

The theme of this book could be said to be that diagnosis lies at the heart of effective management. There are lucky managers, of course; those whose favourite remedy just happens to be appropriate for the organizational malaise; those who find an organization in the bloom of health and vitality when no pill can harm or help; those few who, by force of will and personality, drag a sick constitution through to health. Most of us, however, would do better to rely on an accurate reading of the interplay of variables in Figure 1. To do this we need understanding, or theories, of the way the variables affect each other. We need to know those which we can alter and how by altering them we shall change the total situation.

This book should help towards that understanding. It will suggest some linking mechanisms, some charts for reading the signs of difficulty or success in organizations and for relating them to possible causes. But although understanding helps the diagnosis, gives better predictive ability and more power to influence the future, it nevertheless remains true that to understand all is not to resolve all. Diagnosis brings dilemmas. It is seldom possible to optimize on all the variables. What is good for the organization is not always good for all its members. Not all the variables are equally susceptible to change. 'Effectiveness' too is an umbrella-word. It leaves 'effectiveness for what or for whom?' unanswered, although the nature of goals and objectives feeds back into the set of influencing factors (see Figure 1 again).

There is no theory that unlocks these dilemmas. Diagnosis clarifies but seldom solves. This remains a question of judgement – the ultimate justification of the managerial role. Do not look, therefore, in this book or in organization theory for detailed advice on how to manage. Look rather for interpretative schemes to clarify your organization dilemmas.

Box 1.3 Diagnosis or functional myopia?

As director of a general management programme I was once in search of a so-called multi-disciplinary problem which would help the participants to understand the interlinking nature of the functional areas of management. It seemed to me that the recent much-publicized failure of a nationally-known firm would provide a good example. I suggested this to my colleagues on the teaching staff of the programme.

'Excellent idea,' said the economist, 'a classic example of the failure to forecast a peaking of the demand curve.'

'Of course,' said the accountant, 'this organization has never understood the concept of cash-flow – an excellent case-study.'

'I should be delighted to be involved,' said the organization theorist, 'it only goes to show how inflexible a centralized organization can become.'

'It's a bit too obvious, that's the only trouble,' said the marketing man, 'with their distribution system and pricing policy disaster was inevitable.'

If all were right, I wondered, could any one of them be more right than the others?

---

3 The nature and history of organization theory

The study of people in organizations is no new phenomenon. Confucius was an expert, so were the Greeks and all civilizations who discovered how to organize large numbers of men fruitfully. Aristotle had insights into organization theory which should not be ignored.

In more modern times the study of the functioning of organizations has been approached from roughly three different perspectives:

The individual;
The organization and its form;
The systems and interactions within the organizations.

This specialization of interests is necessary if any detailed understanding of the phenomena is to be achieved. But specialization can lead to isolation.

These three perspectives obviously affect one another but the specialized studies have not always been able to take this into account.

Organization Theory seeks to take a more realistic view of the people in organizations. This book in particular endeavours to recognize the multiplicity of factors impinging on organization effectiveness, *some* of which are suggested in Figure 1.

In considering organizations I have found it useful to regard them:

(a) As collections of individuals;
(b) As political systems.

Individuals have separate personality characteristics, separate needs, and ways of adapting to roles. *Political systems* are all systems which have:

Defined boundaries (so that the membership is known);
Goals and values;
Administrative mechanisms;
Hierarchies of power.

'Political' is often used of the people interested in the methods used to change or control the hierarchies of power. I want to use the word 'political' in its wider connotation without any of its pejorative overtones.

I have further found it useful to regard these two conceptual frameworks as being joined together by a third which I would call 'power and influence'. Power is a key concept in political systems and is much to do with people. Indeed the three conceptual sets of people, power and politics are very much interwoven and intertwined as Figure 2 demonstrates. I find it helpful, however, to separate power out as a linking mechanism before lumping it back in again with the two base sets.

Figure 2 is a device to display the topics and concepts discussed in Part One of this book. The organizing concepts of people, power and politics are not precise and I have no rigorous definitions for them. One could dispute the precise placement of the topics within the conceptual sets. For my purposes these exactitudes are not important. What is important is the realization that organizations are political systems, not simply collections of individuals; that the relationships which I have grouped under power are the principal linking mechanisms which turn those collections of individuals into purposive systems. People, power and politics is a mnemonic clue to the book's approach to the workings of organizations. Books have to be written in sequence and Part One of this book will cross the diagram of Figure 2 from left to right. The reader should remember, however, that the sequence is artificial.

This, therefore, is not a psychological approach, nor a sociological approach nor even a political-theory approach. It is very much a personal, but I hope integrated, anthology derived from all these sources and a few others. It is intended to be helpful to those who work in and with organizations. I can find no better description of it than 'A Managerial Approach to Organization Theory'.

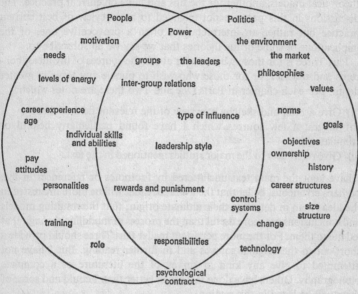

Figure 2   The relationship between people, power and politics

4 How to use this book

4.1

Part One contains a set of models, or frameworks, for the better understanding of people and organizations. I have selected seven, the seven which I have found most useful. Some of them, like 'motivation' and 'leadership' are topics common to all books on organizations. Others, like 'power and influence' and 'politics' are strangely rare. The frameworks overlap. It is not possible to talk about leadership without talking about motivation, or about politics without mentioning groups. Different models, sets of concepts, can be used to describe the same phenomena. This is as it should be. There are different angles from which we view the world. The view will be slightly different from each, the truth will be a combination of all.

Part Two looks at some key and current organizational issues in the light of the concepts introduced in Part One. Part of the intention is to demonstrate how the theories can be applied to the practices. Too often the two are kept in watertight compartments. One bookcase for the theoretical models, another for the tips and hints on current practice. The discussions in this part are not intended to be a review of best current practice but rather an interpretation, often a provocative one, of the implications of some of the theories that we say we all subscribe to.

Part Three is for those who wonder about the sources of my ideas, concepts and theories, or for those who wish to pursue any topic in greater depth. For each chapter in Parts One and Two there are notes which:

(a) Give a brief and sketchy overview of the relevant field of theory;
(b) Suggest a few sources which I have found particularly helpful or stimulating;
(c) Give references to the major studies mentioned in the text.

I have kept the main text uncluttered by footnotes or references in the, perhaps erroneous, belief that the average reader will be more interested in the ideas than in detecting their ultimate origin; that the resulting models and conclusions are more useful than the process of muddling through that led me to them. For the more persistent reader Part Three should provide a short-cut to the original sources and to further reading. But I have not attempted to give any kind of survey of the literature or a complete bibliography. Others have done this much better than I could and some of them will be listed in this section.

I have attempted to keep the matter, the layout and the style of Parts One and Two as concise as possible. The leisurely style of the Russian novel must be inappropriate for the busy student of organization theory. And I would rather that the extra time should be spent in mulling over the ideas, in re-reading them, in seeking to apply them to personal experience, than in marvelling at the length of my learning or the number of my examples.

4.2 How to learn from this book

This book has been written in the belief that a better understanding of organizations and the way they work will help to lead to more effective organizations. But it would be naïve to believe that this understanding will result merely from the reading of the text. Were that to be so then the plethora of books, journals and newspapers must by now have produced a much wiser and more understanding world than the one we observe today.

The process of understanding, or learning, is more complicated than that. There is some general agreement that it consists of four main stages.

Exploration. The individual begins to ask himself – is there a problem? What kind of a problem? What do I need to know in order to be able to deal with it? Without some form of exploration the individual will be reduced to taking it on trust that the dogma of the teacher is both apposite and useful. In the words of chapter 5 he will react in terms of compliance or identification rather than internalization. In all likelihood learning without exploration will be short-lived and under-utilized. It will be more akin to ritual or rote than true re-appraisal. Children will learn the verses of a poem one evening for repetition the next morning only to forget them by evening, for their learning had not been preceded by exploration.

Conceptualization. The nature of the problem having once been explored, the individual must conceptualize it. He must learn how to set this one experience of the problem in a more general context or framework. If he does this he will be able not only to explain the first problem but all others like it. Conceptualization elevates the particular to the universal. Without concepts the isolated experience becomes mere anecdote, an experience talked of but not learnt from. Only if the next experience is *precisely* the same as the preceding one can the lessons of the first be applied to the second.

Experimentation. The thesis of chapter 1 has been that better understanding leads to better prediction which could lead to more effective action. It is this action consequent on conceptualization that is here called experimentation. Here the individual as scientist is testing his hypothesis. Having intuitively formulated the general law of gravity as little children, we are constantly experimenting from it as a base. These acts of experimentation test out the conceptualization and, if successful, implant the concepts more firmly in one's mind. If we do not experiment with the concepts they will remain remote theory, of as much use as hieroglyphs to the average man.

Consolidation. This is the final stage. The concepts are internalized and begin to mesh in one's mind. The experimental phase is past, and the new hypotheses become the basis for future action. They have become part of one, so that habitual behaviour is altered and affected. The lesson has been learnt.

For a self-developing individual such consolidation is but the start of a new exploration, a fresh cycle of understanding. But without the consolidation phase the conceptualization and the experimentation together become mere interesting suppositions, not useful in practice. Throughout this book the reader should continually push himself through this cycle of learning. Some of the boxes contain exercises which may help.

The 'Boxes' in Parts One and Two are not crucial to the text except when the text specifically refers to them. They are intended to flesh out the rather bare bones of the main text by providing examples, fuller definitions of key concepts, and interesting research studies. They have been boxed in order to keep the supporting material out of the way of the main argument. Read them for interest rather than from vital necessity.

The book is most sensibly read from beginning to end, since the language of Part Two is explained in Part One. But the index should lead you to a discussion of any particular topic or problem.

Finally: only some of my intellectual debts are acknowledged in Part Three. No one can study and teach in this area, can work in and with organizations and their managers, without unconsciously picking up other people's amendments to one's own views. The original sources of many ideas get lost in time. The evidence for some new insight may be recalled but its provenance forgotten. In these and other ways, many unnamed, unknown or forgotten people have contributed to this work. In particular my colleagues at the London Business School, my critical but stimulating students, the many managers and executives that I have known, have all had more of a share in shaping the ideas in this book than they were aware of or I can keep tally of.

2 On the Motivation to Work

1 Introduction

The hermit sitting in his mountain cell and confronted one day with the Sunday newspaper might be pardoned for wondering why all those people were doing all those things. Why this eager striving to be President of the United States? Why this restless urge to merge, or, with fortunes made, to return again to the fray of business and create yet another empire? Why do all these people buy and sell their houses so ardently, enriching the middlemen, but disrupting families? Why do they change their jobs, divorce their wives, chase the sun or sue their neighbour? Why do they work so hard? Why do they work when they do? Why, come to that, do they work at all?

There must be many pressures and facts which can be called upon to explain any particular set of circumstances. But is there any one set of forces, any general mechanism *within* the individual which pushes him one way or the other? Can we, by looking at the *internal decision process*, answer those questions about work for any given individual or set of individuals? Is man at work dominated by sexuality and aggression, or is he engaged on an endless pursuit of happiness? The body of knowledge about this internal decision process carries the generic title of motivation theory.

'Motivate' is one of those ambiguous words. The dictionary calls it a transitive verb. It normally has a subject and an object. X motivates Y, Y is motivated by X. But is X a thing or a person? Can *you* motivate someone? Or is it only money, or hunger, or status, or need for affection? Are you motivated by a lack of something, in the sense that thirst equals lack of liquid, or only by the thing, e.g. water? Or is it a mixture? We use the word ambiguously. Does this mean we are unsure of what we really mean by it?

If we could understand, and could then predict, the ways in which individuals were motivated we could influence them by changing the components of that motivation process. Is that manipulation – or management? Certainly such understanding could lead to great power since it would allow the control of behaviour without the visible and unpopular trappings of control. Early work on motivation was indeed concerned to find ways by which the individual could be 'motivated' to apply more of his effort and his talent to the service of his employer. It is only fair to add that many of these theorists were also concerned to find an answer to the problem that was consistent with the essential dignity and independence of the individual.

We should perhaps be relieved that no guaranteed formula of motivation was found. But there is now a much better understanding of the process by which the individual reaches decisions on the general question of the apportionment of his time, energy and talent. The decision is often unconscious or instinctive, physical as when we go in search of food, or more psychological, as when we seek security under threat; or it may be a conscious and deliberate decision to leave or join a firm, to satisfice or to optimize. The process, we shall discover, is complex and particular. Particular to individuals and to situations. Thus no general formula can be guaranteed to work, but understanding of the process will help to explain some of the problems and difficulties of people at work.

Understanding of the process should help to better decisions affecting people in organizations, better decisions in the sense that they are taken with more knowledge of the implications and likely outcomes.

It is this kind of understanding that this chapter seeks to provide. It will start with a review of the earlier approaches to motivation, each of them with a grain of truth, but none of them sufficient in themselves. *Early motivation theories* will then suggest *another approach* and a look at *the psychological contract – its application*, and finally *a summary and implications*.

Box 2.1

All men seek one goal; success or happiness. The only way to achieve true success is to express yourself completely in service to society. First, have a definite, clear, practical ideal – a goal, an objective. Second, have the necessary means to achieve your ends – wisdom, money, materials, and methods. Third, adjust your means to that end.

Aristotle, 384–322 B.C.

---

2 Early motivation theories

2.1

These approaches can be categorized under three headings.

Satisfaction theories. The assumption here is that a satisfied worker is a productive worker.

Incentive theories. The assumption of these theories is based on the principle of reinforcement, what might crudely be called the 'carrot' approach. Individuals will work harder given specific reward or encouragement for good performance.

Intrinsic theories. Man is not an animal, say these theorists. He will work best if given a worth-while job and allowed to get on with it. The reward will come from the satisfaction in the work itself.

2.2 Satisfaction theories

There is very little evidence that a satisfied worker actually works harder. However there is strong support for the suggestion that a satisfied worker tends to stay in the same organization. There is also evidence that correlates satisfaction positively with mental health. This suggests that paying attention to conditions of work and worker morale will reduce turnover and absenteeism but will not necessarily increase individual productivity. Herzberg's findings (summarized in *3.2*) suggest a reason for this.

Under this heading can be grouped those theories that hold that men work best when they like their leader, or are satisfied with their work group.

It has been suggested that where satisfaction does correlate with productivity, it may be the productivity that caused the satisfaction rather than the other way round. (See chapter 6, section *3.1*.)

2.3 Incentive theories

Incentive theories suggest that the individual will increase his efforts in order to obtain a desired reward.

Although based on the general principle of reinforcement most of the studies in this area have concentrated on 'pay' or 'money' as a motivator. To some extent this concentration is justifiable in that money acts as a 'stand in' for many other rewards such as status and independence. This situation may, however, be more true of America, where most of the studies were done, than of Europe.

Incentive theories undoubtedly *can* work if:

(a) The individual perceives the increased reward to be worth the extra effort;
(b) The performance can be measured and clearly attributed to the individual;
(c) The individual wants that particular kind of reward;
(d) The increased performance will not become the new minimum standard.

Box 2.2

Nancy Morse and Robert Weiss interviewed a random sample of 401 employed men in the USA in the early 1950s to explore the function and meaning of work.

Question: If by some chance you inherited enough money to live comfortably without working, do you think you would work anyway or not?

	Total	Age 21–34	35–44	45–54	55–64	64+
would keep working (%)	80	90	83	72	61	82
would not keep working (%)	20	10	17	28	39	18

Question: Why do you feel that you would work?

	Interest or accomplishment	To keep Occupied	Other
professional/managerial (%)	44	37	19
working class (%)	10	71	19
farmers (%)	18	64	18

Question: Suppose you didn't work, what would you miss most?

the people I know through work, friends, contacts (%)	31
feeling of doing something, would be restless (%)	25
the kind of work I do (%)	12
feeling of doing something important, worth-while (%)	9
regular routine (%)	6
feeling of interest, being interested (%)	5
other (%)	6
nothing (%)	6

Question: How satisfied are you with your job?

	Very satisfied	Satisfied	Dissatisfied
professional/managerial (%)	42	37	21
working class (%)	27	57	10
farmers (%)	29	56	15

From Morse and Weiss, 'The function and meaning of work and the job', *American Sociological Review*, 1955

These theories often work well for the owner-manager or, at the worker level, in unit or small-batch manufacturing. If, however, any of the first three conditions does not apply, the individual will tend to see the reward as an improvement to the general climate of work and will react as under *Satisfaction theories*. Condition (d) of course, if violated, will only create a serious credibility gap.

2.4 Intrinsic theories

These theories derive their *raison d'être* from some general assumptions about human needs along lines originally advocated by Maslow. Maslow categorized human needs as follows:

Self-actualization needs;
Esteem needs;
Belonging and love needs;
Safety needs;
Physiological needs.

He postulates that needs are only motivators when they are unsatisfied. He further suggests that these needs work, roughly, in the kind of hierarchy implied by the listing above. The lower-order needs (physiological and safety) are dominant until satisfied, whereupon the higher-order needs come into operation. There is considerable intuitive support for this conceptualization. If you are starving, your needs for esteem or status will be unimportant; only food matters. When adequately warm, further heat will not motivate you, i.e. the need does not operate as a motivator.

The assumption of the intrinsic theorists (e.g. McGregor and Likert) is that the higher-order needs are more prevalent in modern man than we give him credit for. In particular that an individual can gain a lot of satisfaction from the job itself, provided that it is *his* job, i.e. he has some degree of freedom in determining what his job is and how he will do it. This approach would say that involvement or participation will in general tend to increase motivation, provided that it is genuine participation. Rewards tend to lie in the task itself or in the individual's relations with his group. The ideal is to create conditions where effective performance is a goal in itself rather than a means to a further goal. The manager is a colleague, consultant and resource, rather than a boss.

These theories are appealing but there is evidence to suggest that they do not work too well when:

The technology prevents the individual from having control over his job design, i.e. at shop-floor level in process, mass or large batch production;

Box 2.3

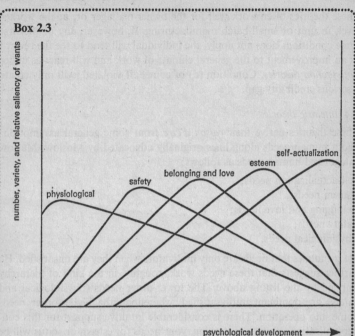

Schematic portrayal of the progressive changes in relative saliency, number and variety of wants as described by Maslow. Note that the peak of an earlier main class of wants must be passed before the next 'higher'want can begin to assume a dominant role. Note also that as psychological development takes place, the number and variety of wants increase.

The individual does not have strong needs for self-actualization, or alternatively likes authoritarian masters.

One would expect therefore to find these intrinsic theories working best where men of intelligence and independence were working on challenging problems, e.g. in R and D laboratories or in some consulting firms. The evidence supports this supposition.

2.5 Underlying assumptions

These theories all stem from some underlying assumptions about man. To a large extent unproven, they tend to represent the dominant mood or climate of opinion at that time. Schein has classified them as follows, and it

Box 2.4

Theory X and Theory Y

Douglas McGregor in the 1950s enunciated two sets of propositions and assumptions about man in the organization.

Theory X

1 The average man is by nature indolent – he works as little as possible.
2 He lacks ambition, dislikes responsibility, prefers to be led.
3 He is inherently self-centred, indifferent to organizational needs.
4 He is by nature resistant to change.
5 He is gullible, not very bright, the ready dupe of the charlatan and the demagogue.

The implications for management are:

1 Management is responsible for organizing the elements of productive enterprise – money, materials, equipment, people – in the interest of economic ends.

2 With respect to people, this is a process of directing their efforts, motivating them, controlling their actions, modifying their behaviour to fit the needs of the organization.

3 People must be persuaded, rewarded, punished, controlled, their activities must be directed.

Theory Y

1 People are not by nature passive or resistant to organizational needs. They have become so as a result of experience in organizations.

2 The motivation, the potential for development, the capacity to assume responsibility, the readiness to direct behaviour towards organizational goals, are all present in people. It is a responsibility of management to make it possible for people to reorganize and develop the human characteristics for themselves.

3 Management is responsible for organizing the elements of productive enterprise in the interest of economic ends, but their essential task is to arrange the conditions and methods of operation so that people can achieve their own goals best by directing their own efforts towards organizational objectives.

From McGregor, *The Human Side of Enterprise*, 1960

is interesting to note that the categories follow each other in a sort of historical procession, starting from the time of the industrial revolution.

Rational–economic man. Man is primarily motivated by economic needs. He is essentially a passive animal to be manipulated, motivated and controlled by the organization. His feelings are essentially irrational; organizations must be so organized that these feelings and unpredictable traits are controlled (McGregor's Theory X Assumptions). *But*, fortunately, not all men are like this. There are those who are self-motivated, self-controlling and in charge of their emotions. This group must assume responsibility for the management of the others.

Social man. Man is essentially a social animal and gains his basic sense of identity from relationships with others. As a result of the necessary rationalization of work much of the meaning has gone out of work itself and must be sought in the social relationships of the job. Management is only effective to the extent that it can mobilize and rely on these social relationships. Issues of leadership style and group behaviour are therefore of great importance.

Self-actualizing man. Man is primarily self-motivated and self-controlled. He seeks to be mature on the job and is capable of being so. External controls and pressures are likely to be seen as reducing his autonomy and therefore will affect his motivation. Given a chance, man will voluntarily integrate his own goals with those of the organization.

Complex man. Schein comes down in favour of what he calls 'complex man'. Man is variable. He has many motives which have at any one time a hierarchy, but the particular hierarchy may change from time to time and situation to situation. He does not necessarily have to find fulfilment of all his needs in any one situation. He can respond to a variety of managerial strategies. Whether he will or not, will depend upon his view of their appropriateness to the situation and to his needs.

Psychological man. This is a category suggested by Levinson, following Jacques and Zaleznik. Man is a complex, unfolding, maturing organism who passes through physiological and psychological stages of development. Man evolves an ego ideal towards which he strives. The most powerful motivating force in man, over and above such basic drives as hunger, sexuality, aggression, is the need to bring himself closer to his ideal. The greater the gap between our perception of ourselves in reality and our ego ideal the more angry we are with ourselves and the more guilt we feel. Work is part of a man's identity, his ego ideal, and opportunities must be provided for man to work towards his ego ideal in work if he is to be 'motivated'.

2.6

The kind of theory that a man subscribes to will colour all his views about management and people in organizations. Satisfaction and incentive theories, assumptions that man is rational–economic, will lead to a bargaining approach, to preoccupation with the extrinsic conditions of work, money and fringe benefits. Believers in intrinsic theories, in self-actualizing or psychological man, will be more concerned with creating opportunities for the individual to develop and realize his talents, with providing the right climate for work and the right type of work.

At this point it might be helpful to the reader to pause and reflect upon his own assumptions about man and the appropriate theory of motivation. For we are now going to complicate the whole issue, to pour more variables into the mix than are assumed even by Schein's complex man or Levinson's psychological man. Working from a basic model of a man's decision-making process we shall proceed piecemeal towards a better and fuller understanding of how people answer the three questions posed at the beginning of this chapter. The resulting picture will be complicated and intricate. This is only in line with the intricacies of reality, but for most operational purposes psychological reality is too complex. We are reduced to thinking in stereotypes or over-simplifications in order to get anything done and to avoid the paralysis of analysis. This process of reduction is, however, a better base for action if we understand the underlying complexity and if we confront our other prejudices, assumptions and stereotypes along the way.

3 An alternative approach

3.1

Faced with the variety of all the approaches to motivation it is possible to begin to build up an admittedly theoretical model but a model which seeks to explain some of the apparent contradictions or lack of support in the research studies, and pull together the various strands of the different theories.

The bare bones of the basic model are set out in Figure 3. In this form the model is most understandable if it is regarded as the way the individual deals with *individual* decisions, to do or not to do something, to go or not

Box 2.5

What motivates scientists and engineers?

Fred Landis in 1968 made an extensive survey of 1311 engineers and scientists from twelve engineering firms.

Question: What motivates you to do a good job? (first choices)

achievement needs	38%
monetary rewards and recognition	7
non-monetary recognition	10
challenging work	15
nature of work	11
responsibility/personal growth	9
relations with superiors	7
relations with associates	0·5
working conditions	0·1
company image	2·4

Question: What are your most important goals?

Under 30	35–39	45–49
1 Work on projects requiring new technical learning	1 Live in a desirable location	1 Help company increase its profits
2 Live in a desirable location	2 Have employment stability	2 Live in a desirable location
3 Become more involved in decision-making process	3 Work on projects requiring new technical knowledge	3 Have employment stability

Question: What are the principal 'bother factors'? (In order of importance.)

1 Too little time to keep up with new developments.
2 Insufficient manpower to do the job.
3 Scope and responsibility of the job not clearly defined.
4 Too much paperwork.
5 Insufficient support by other groups in the company.
6 Lack of recognition and encouragement.
7 Too many conferences.
8 Poor working conditions.

From Landis, 'What Makes Technical Men Happy and Productive?', *Research Management*, 1968

go, to apportion or not to apportion his time, energy and talents. This approach is based on the idea that man is a self-activating organism, and can, to some degree, control his own destiny and his own responses to pressures, that he can select his goals and choose the paths towards them. Some versions of this approach have in fact been given the name of path–goal theories (Georgopoulos).

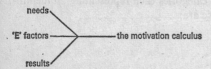

Figure 3   The individual decision

The model in this form merely states that each individual has a set of *needs* and of *desired results*. That he decides how much 'E' (which stands for effort, energy, excitement, expenditure, etc.) to invest by doing a calculation. The process of calculation is not often as cold-blooded or deliberate as this description would suggest, but more of that anon. Let us first add some flesh to the model.

3.2 Individual needs

Almost all theories of motivation make some assumptions about individual needs, or drives. They have been categorized, listed, and titled in a variety of ways. Some of the most useful lists are:

1 Maslow's hierarchy of needs.
2 Roethlisberger and Dickson amplify Maslow. They add on to physiological and safety needs the following:
   Friendship and Belonging Needs;
   Needs for Justice & Fair Treatment;
   Dependence – Independence;
   Needs for Achievement.
3 Herzberg's two-factor theory. Herzberg maintains, on the basis of his research studies, that in any work situation you can distinguish between the factors that dissatisfy and those that satisfy. The interesting thing is that they are not the opposites of each other. Dealing with the dissatisfying factors does not turn them into satisfying or motivating factors. In general, the dissatisfying factors are things to do with conditions of work – company policy and administration, supervision, salary, interpersonal relations and physical working conditions. He called these the *hygiene* or *maintenance* factors. They are the necessary conditions of successful motivation. The

satisfiers are achievement, recognition, work itself, responsibility and advancement. These he called the *motivators*. Good hygiene deals with the question 'Why work here?', only the motivators deal with 'Why work harder?'

4 McClelland. McClelland and his co-workers have looked at the way people think, in many cultures and many sections of society. They have grouped the responses into three categories each representing an identifiable human motive or need. These are:

Need for affiliation;

Need for power;

Need for achievement.

Most people have some of each in their thoughts, but seldom in the same strength.

The need for power. Most managers have a high need for power (as defined by McClelland's tests). High need for power by itself will often lead to unconstructive authoritarianism. Combined with, in particular, need for achievement it can lead to productive and satisfying results. Some degree of need for power seems to be a *necessary* condition for managerial success. Having it, however, does not guarantee success!

The need for affiliation. The individual with a high need for affiliation *alone* will tend to be more concerned with developing and maintaining relationships than with decision-making. These sort of people are often seen as ineffective helpers, probably because they are not task-oriented enough. However, some need for affiliation is probably present in most. It is present but is seldom dominant in successful individuals.

The need for achievement. The individual with high scores on this need will like personal responsibility, moderate and calculated risks, feedback on how he is doing. Unless moderated by other needs the high need-achiever may tend to become too individualistic to be very successful in any organization where other people's contentions need to be harnessed.

5 Robert Ardrey, working from his observations of animal populations arrived at three basic needs (*identity*, *security* and *stimulation*) in his book *The Territorial Imperative*.

These categories of needs should not be thought of as exclusive. Anyone can add to these lists. Nor need he feel confined to lists of three or five. My own list embraces all the needs mentioned above since they all seem to operate at one time or another. One psychologist, Murray, listed thirty needs which perhaps is too wide a spread to be useful in analysis. The valuable aspect of most of these particular lists is that ways have been developed of measuring them. The really important points to remember about needs are:

That each individual has his own set, sets that may differ widely;
That the relative importance of each need in the set can change over time. For instance, in times of redundancy, the security needs suddenly come to the fore so that there is little point in relying on self-actualization as a motivator.

It is interesting to speculate on the origins of particular need hierarchies, or individual differences. This would lead us deeper into personality and behaviour theory than would be appropriate in this section. But at least we can list the influencing factors that must be thought of in any consideration of an individual's set of needs.

Heredity/early environment. Recognized by all theorists as crucially important, it is notoriously hard to disentangle the effect of one from the other. Physical talents are more easily attributed to heredity, aspiration levels and ego ideals to environment.

Education. By changing an individual's set of models through his educational surroundings the priority rating of his needs can be changed. McClelland has also applied an educational approach to the raising of levels of need for achievement.

The individual's self-concept. The individual's assessment of his personal capacities, of his place in society, of his degree of aspiration, will affect the strength of each need. The self-concept itself is largely the result of early environment, education, and the people he has chosen to model himself on – parents, teachers, friends.

Experience. The individual's experience in life, his age, the degree to which he has in the past satiated some needs, will all affect his current need set. Needs not satisfied by experience at the appropriate stage in life can often remain dominant unnaturally long. The forty-year-old adolescent may never have had the opportunity in adolescence to satisfy the needs for play and rebellion appropriate to that age.

3.3 The motivation calculus

This calculus is the heart of the whole problem. It is the mechanism by which we decide how much 'E' we expend on any particular activity or set of activities.

Most motivational theories have been concerned with the expenditure of *effort*. This word has perhaps too narrow a connotation. There do appear to be a whole set of words, characterized by the fact that they start with 'E', which help to widen the application of motivation theory. They include for instance, the word 'energy'. There is some ground for believing that we have finite quantities or levels of energy – whether or not this is true we can certainly decide how to apportion our own individual stock of energy and we do so decide. Motivation theory has to explain that decision. So too it must be with excitement, enthusiasm, emotion, expenditure of time, expenditure of money, expenditure of passion.

The calculus is different for each individual. We have all seen instances where, when everything seems the same to everybody, one man appears to decide to invest all his energies and efforts while the rest of us hang back. For each individual the calculus has three separate elements:

(a) The strength or *salience* of the need;
(b) The *expectancy* that 'E' will lead to a particular result;
(c) The *instrumentality* of that result in reducing the need in (a).

To give an example: a man who has a high need for power if given a task to do and promised promotion at the end of it will expend energy on the task to the degree that he believes:

That good performance will lead to promotion (expectancy);
That promotion will satisfy his power needs (instrumentality).

If either of these conditions do not apply he will not expend energy over and above that needed to keep him employed (assuming that his need for security is operating). This example brings out two other important elements of the calculus:

It is *subjective*. The individual makes it himself and no one else's guess is necessarily right.
The relationship between strength of need, expectancy and instrumentality is *multiplicative*, i.e. if one is zero the whole sum is zero.

There are two further aspects of this calculus that are worthy of note:

1 The act of calculation can range from unconscious all the way to totally conscious or deliberate. The unconscious we label 'instinct', the conscious

'calculating'. When the calculus is unconscious or instinctual the individual will react to the most immediate need. The desire for another drink, although irrational, will prevail if the calculus is kept at the instinctual level. The time-span covered by the calculus can vary from the immediate to decades of years. That is, the calculus can take into account results over the next half-hour or over the following day, or following year. The longer the period the more the needs that have to be considered, e.g. desire for health versus need for a drink.

It is possible that psychological maturity in an individual shows up in a more conscious calculus and in a lengthening time-span for the pay-off of expenditure. Small children appear to make almost instinctive calculations aimed at almost immediate results. As they grow up the calculus seems to become more conscious, and often as a result more complicated, and their time-span for pay-off rather longer. Occasionally, for the highly analytical or the emotionally insecure, the possible variations of 'E', of obtainable results, and of differing time-spans, result in a paralysis of the calculus, which shows up as inertia, withdrawal or breakdown. In such cases it may help the individual to cut down the available alternatives, or to reduce the time-span, thus permitting the calculus to function again (holidays, for instance, often have this effect).

Let no one think, however, that life is an endless series of such calculations. No thinking man would ever get out of bed in the morning if that were so. Most decisions in life are based on precedent. Similar situations call forth similar reactions without the need for a deliberate activation of the calculus. We are concerned here with the precedent-setting decisions, the new decisions, the decisions to change or to do something for the first time, to leave or join a group, to double one's efforts or cease trying.

3.4 Results

It should be clear that the calculus becomes difficult if not impossible if the anticipated results are unclear. In such a situation the individual must either make up his own mind about the probable outcome or, more usually, will make no calculation at all. It is in the light of this that we should look at the principles underlying such managerial *desiderata* as 'management by objectives' and participative management. If an individual is given some say in deciding on the desired results he will at least be able to complete his personal calculation. The model also explains, however, the finding that if an individual is *rewarded* according to his performance against those same results he will normally set the standard lower than if rewards are *not* tied to performance against standards, i.e. management by objectives *can* lower performance. 'Obviously so,' the calculus would say, 'why expend energy to achieve higher results when the instrumentality (i.e. the likelihood of getting rewarded) is greater with lower results?' *Ergo*: set the results lower. Interestingly, high-need achievers, who get their satisfaction from job performance, set only moderately high standards. Interestingly, too, the most common finding on objective-setting is that the one most important factor in raising performance is the setting of any objectives at all. Without knowledge of *intended* results it is impossible to complete the calculus. Further, without knowledge of actual results there is no check that the calculations were correct or justified. Leavitt and Mueller (1951)

Box 2.6

Does aspiration breed success and/or satisfaction?

Some research findings

Hoppe found that success in a problem-solving exercise led to a rise in the level of aspiration for 69 per cent. However, for 24 per cent of the cases the individual ceased the activity altogether. Failure in the same exercise led 50 per cent of the persons to lower their aspirations, whilst 27 per cent ceased altogether.

Lewin pointed out as long ago as 1936 that 'success' is only meaningful if there is a chance of failure and failure is only recognized if there was a chance of success. Unattainable goals are not accepted by the individual. 'Acceptable' levels of aspiration are often fixed largely by one's colleagues or peer groups, i.e. a high-aspiration group will raise the aspirations of all its individuals.

Lewin also discovered that those who 'gave up' after success, or failed to raise their aspirations even higher, were usually those who had a previous history of failure. If you have failed before and then succeed you are content to leave it at that.

Rao and Russell demonstrated in an experimental 'game' situation that constant failure to achieve targets resulted in individuals ultimately setting lower targets for themselves than when they were reasonably successful in meeting their targets, i.e. the unobtainable gradually lowers aspiration levels.

Gebhard demonstrated that continued success, as against aspiration levels, increased the desirability of the task.

Stouffer, in his study of the American soldier, noted that the men who were most dissatisfied with the promotion system were in the branches that had the highest rates of promotion. The most satisfied individuals were the Military Police with the lowest rates of promotion.

amongst others have demonstrated that performance improves in relation to the quantity of feedback or knowledge of results. They also observed that absence of any knowledge of results was accompanied by high hostility and low confidence. On the other hand, a high level of feedback, no matter whether it was good or bad, brought with it high confidence and friendly attitudes. To set objectives and then forget about them is only going to produce frustration. To use an analogy, the golfer who does not count his shots is only there for the walk. Without knowledge of the score the motivation calculus will soon dry up.

3.5

The basic model is now more complicated, and looks like Figure 4.

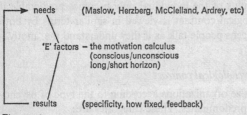

needs (Maslow, Herzberg, McClelland, Ardrey, etc)

'E' factors — the motivation calculus
(conscious/unconscious
long/short horizon)

results (specificity, how fixed, feedback)

Figure 4

No one, it must be repeated, goes through this calculus every time he takes a decision. It is useful to remember it only because it is the ultimate and underlying decision-making mechanism. *Each calculus, however, operates within the limits of a contract, a psychological contract* that each individual has with each group that plays any part in his life.

4 The psychological contract

Just as in most work situations there is a legal contract between the organization and the individual which states who gives who what in consideration for what, so there is an implied, usually unstated psychological contract between the individual and the organization, be it work organization, social organization or family. This psychological contract is essentially a set of expectations. The individual has a set of results that he expects from the organization, results that will satisfy certain of his needs and in return for which he will expend some of his energies and talents. Similarly the organization has its set of expectations of the individual and its list of payments or outcomes that it will give to him.

Three important things follow from this:

1 Most individuals belong to more than one kind of organization. They will have more than one psychological contract. It is not necessary for an individual to seek to satisfy all his needs under any one contract and few do. You cannot assume, for instance, as a manager that all your workers have put their self-actualizing or achievement needs into their contract with you.

2 A contract which is not perceived identically by both parties becomes the source of trouble, conflict or litigation. The organization's view of the psychological contract, for instance, is often more all-embracing than the individual's. This may lead to a feeling of exploitation by the individual, or, by the organization, to a feeling of lack of co-operation or involvement on the part of the individual.

3 The motivation calculus of the individual only becomes predictable if and when the psychological contract is viewed in similar terms by both parties. When this happens people talk as if they understand the 'motivation' of the individual.

4.1 The appropriate psychological contract

It is possible to categorize organizations according to the type of psychological contract which predominates. These categories are:

Coercive;
Calculative;
Co-operative.

4.2 Coercive contracts

Organizations where this kind of contract predominates are prisons, concentration camps, coercive unions, custodial mental hospitals. The individual is held as a member against his will, by forces beyond his control. The psychological contract is not therefore voluntarily entered into. The method of control is rule and punishment, power is in the hands of a small group, the individual's task is to conform and to comply in return for which he will avoid punishment. These organizations strengthen their control by depriving the individual of much of his personal identity (through uniforms, numbers, lack of contact with the outside world) and by emphasizing conformity. It is unfortunately true that some institutions, e.g. some schools and hospitals and even factories, can today fall under this heading. If this is the dominant psychological contract the expectation of any 'E' forces must be limited to those which can be called forth by fear of punishment.

4.3 Calculative contracts

In these organizations the contract is a voluntary one. There is usually a fairly explicit exchange of goods or money for services rendered. The control is retained by the management of the organization but is expressed mainly in their ability to give desired things to the individual. 'Desired things' include not only money, but promotion, social opportunities, even work itself. Studies have shown that the vast majority of people would go on working even if they had no economic need to do so, so that the availability of a place to work over and above the material rewards is a desired reward under this type of contract. Most industrial organizations have this as the dominant psychological contract for most of their employees. It is a perfectly realistic form of contract, but increases in 'E' under this contract have to be paid for by the organization in some way or other. If the organization seeks to get more 'E' for the same pay (by, for example, threatening to remove the availability of work from an individual) the contract will seem to the individual to have become a coercive one and he will tend to adjust his side of the contract accordingly.

4.4 Co-operative contracts

Under this type of contract the individual tends to identify with the goals of the organization and to become creative in the pursuit of those goals. In return, in addition to just rewards, he is given more voice in the selection of the goals and more discretion in the choice of means to achieving them. The management relinquishes a large amount of day-to-day control but retains ultimate control partly through the right of selection of people, partly through the allocation of financial resources which gives it a power of veto on certain of the goals.

There is a distinct trend on the part of many managements to move the psychological contracts of their organizations in this direction. They are on occasions surprised and offended when these kinds of gestures are rebuffed. What is often not realized is that:

1 Organizational goals which are meaningful to the management and worthy of commitment may not seem so meaningful lower down in the hierarchy.
2 Sharing responsibility for goals and decisions brings cares as well as delights. Not all individuals will want those cares as part of their psychological contract for that part of their life.

In short, you cannot impose a psychological contract on anyone without it coming to be seen as coercive. Freedom of entry into the contract is one of the prerequisites of the co-operative contract.

Box 2.7 What subordinates want in a job compared with their superiors' estimates (%)[a]

	As men	As foremen		As general foremen	
	Rated the variables for themselves	*Estimated men would rate the variables*	*Rated the variables for themselves*	*Estimated foremen would rate the variables*	*Rated the variables for themselves*
Economic variables					
steady work and steady wages	61	79	62	86	52
high wages	28	61	17	58	11
pensions and other old-age security benefits	13	17	12	29	15
not having to work too hard	13	30	4	25	2
Human-satisfaction variables					
getting along well with the people I work with	36	17	39	22	43
getting along well with my supervisor	28	14	28	15	24
good chance to turn out good-quality work	16	11	18	13	27
good chance to do interesting work	22	12	38	14	43
Other variables					
good chance for promotion	25	23	42	24	47
good physical working conditions	21	19	18	4	11
total					
number of cases[b]	2499	196	196	45	45

[a] From Kahn, 'Human relations on the shop floor' in Hugh-Jones (ed.), *Human Relations and Modern Management*, 1958
[b] Percentages total over 100 because they include three rankings for each person

4.5 *The application of the psychological contract*

The psychological contracts that apply in different organizations are seldom as clear-cut as the categorization above would imply. Furthermore, there is likely to be more than one type of contract operating in one organization, perhaps even a different contract for each manager. This variety can well be confusing to the individual at the other end of the contract when he finds that different parts of the organization have differing expectations of him.

It is often appropriate for the contract to change as the task changes. The contract in R and D for example might well differ from the contract on the shop floor. Often, however, the contract changes because the individual manager has different *assumptions about the nature of man in general*, and the way man goes about his motivation calculus. These are the stereotypes and over-simplifications referred to earlier (this chapter, section 2.5) which colour so much of our approaches to people and their management.

5 Summary and implications

5.1 *A summary of the principal arguments thus far may be helpful*

Early theories of motivation were either:

Satisfaction theories;
Incentive theories;
Intrinsic theories.

Although each worked in some situation, none was universally valid. They were based on underlying assumptions about the nature of man:

Rational–economic man;
Social man;
Self-actualizing man;
Complex man;
Psychological man.

Figure 5 is a model of the way motivation affects our decision.

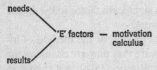

Figure 5

This decision model operates within a psychological contract which can be:

Coercive;
Calculative;
Co-operative,

but is likely to be a mix of all three, with one dominant. The nature of the contract operating within any one group will often depend on the manager's assumptions about man in general.

5.2 The implications

We have suggested:

That each individual has a motivation calculus mechanism which is used for precedent-setting decisions;
That this mechanism operates within the limits of a psychological contract implied between an individual and the group or organization;
That 'motivation' will happen when the psychological contract as viewed by the organization and by the individual is the same, irrespective of the actual nature of the contract;
That therefore there is no 'right' theory of motivation, but only the individual and the particular circumstances.

What are the implications of this? Have we not torn down some admittedly simplistic views of man and motivation but ones that were at least operational, and left behind a model too complicated and variable to be usable?

There is that danger. But the over-simplified views with their stereotyped assumptions did not seem to be leading to better or more effective organizations. Complexity has its problems but at least some general implications are clear:

1 Managers need to think more deeply and more clearly about their view of the psychological contract operating in their organization. What one asks of people, how one controls people, how one organizes people, how one rewards people, all depend on the psychological contract. If out of line with that contract they will work less well and may produce unintended effects.
Moral: The psychological contract will be a significant factor in the choice of leadership style and the organization of work.
2 If managers wish to change the method of control or the method of influence in their organization they must be aware that they are changing the psychological contract. For instance, decentralization involves a change in the responsibility levels for many people. You cannot just *assume* that this is desired by everyone for its own sake.

Moral: The psychological contract often lies at the heart of any change problem.

3 If the desired outcome of a decision reached by means of the motivation calculus is not working out, i.e. if the individual finds that his expectancy calculation is wrong and 'E' does not lead to the expected results, he experiences what is called 'dissonance'. 'Dissonance' is the discrepancy between what is and what you would like to be. It is for most people a form of psychological discomfort or stress. If not resolved, all the symptoms of stress will emerge. (These will be discussed in chapter 3.) To resolve the dissonance the individual can:

Increase 'E';
Re-calculate the expectancy, i.e. lower the target result;
Re-calculate the instrumentality, i.e. decide he does not need the result after all.

Dissonance will be more fully discussed under the heading of *Attitude change* in chapter 5. Here we must note that this sort of dilemma can be seen in objective or budget setting all the time. The motivation calculus model explains how it is that the individual can behave in one of the above ways. If he is to choose the 'increase E' alternative he will only do so if he feels committed to the results level. In other words 'budgets' will tend to work as a device to raise performance only if implemented under a certain type of psychological contract. Under other contracts they will be seen as a control device and the individual will resolve any dissonance by one of the other methods.

Moral: The motivation calculus explains much of the trouble about budgets.

6 Money

It would be inappropriate to write a chapter on motivation without some discussion of the role of money or pay as a motivating agent. Unfortunately, as one recent review concluded 'Although it is generally agreed that money is the major mechanism for rewarding and modifying behaviour in industry . . . very little is known about how it works'.

The reason should be obvious. The value of money as a motivator will depend upon the individual calculus, the salience of the needs affected by money, the expectancy that any 'E' will lead to more money, and the instrumentality of money in meeting the need.

A full review of the role of money is impossible here, but some important points need to be made.

Money is all-embracing. None of the well-known categorizations of needs include money. Money is often, however, assumed to be instrumental in satisfying each and every one of the needs, from hunger to self-actualization. But the extent to which this is true will vary from individual to individual and probably from culture to culture. Most self-reported lists of needs do not put money top of the list, though this too may represent a cultural bias ('money is bad but the things that money buys are all right').

Money is the basis for comparison. Money can be measured precisely. Most other motivating agents cannot be. Therefore money is uniquely useful as a measure of comparison. Comparison with the past, comparison with other organizations, comparison with other people. Since money accompanies increases in status, responsibility, success, independence, or security, money is the element that is measured and talked about, not the underlying factor. It has been frequently observed that we are more concerned about comparisons in our disfavour than we are pleased about comparisons in our favour. In other words, we use money as a comparative measuring stick. When *any* of the comparisons are unfavourable, inequitable, we are dissatisfied. When they are favourable we put it down to 'luck'. In a sense it is not money that is a hygiene factor, as Herzberg argues, but 'equity'. The absolute levels of pay are not often an issue but the equitable level, in relation to others, to one's own pay curve, to future expectations and self-concept. Jacques' idea of using 'time-span of discretion' as a basis for equity will be discussed in Part Two. Many union arguments are about equity, not money as such. Lawler's finding that in the absence of information we overestimate our colleagues' pay and *then* are dissatisfied, reinforces the argument that it is equity not money that matters.

Money as reinforcement. We know from research with animals that reinforcements of some desired object if given at *regular* periods have little effect as motivators. Pay, therefore, given in annual increments, is likely to be seen as a condition of work rather than related to particular effort. Only entrepreneurs and insurance salesmen, among executives, experience money tied to particular pieces of effort. They are known to be highly motivated by money.

Incentives, tied to piece-rates, often work well, for a time, but there is some evidence that it is the variety and control over output that is as motivating as the extra money. Moreover, piece-rates bring feelings of insecurity if tied to the individual, but are too spread out in their effect if tied to a group.

In spite of all the difficulties it will be argued in Part Two that pay is a much simpler, and ultimately less costly, way of *rewarding* people in some parts of the organization than security, status or job satisfaction. But the implications for equity, or perceived inequity, have to be considered.

7 In conclusion

Having got this far in an overview of motivation theory the reader may perhaps be experiencing, as I did, a sense of disappointment with much of the work in this field. I had hoped that motivation theories would reveal to me the true purpose in my life and my *raison d'être*. I expected that I would be able to answer and deal with the perplexities of the hermit described in the opening paragraph. Instead man is treated as a semi-conscious mechanism responding to a variety of impulses in a partly predictable way. This wasn't me, I cried, although I could recognize many of my colleagues in the model along with those hordes of imagined but anonymous workers out there in organizations.

From this position of disappointment I came to recognize that motivation theory is useful as a way of understanding how most individuals, *given who they are*, go about taking the short and medium-term decisions in their life. In organizations these are the important decisions for anyone seeking to activate the 'E' forces or to direct them towards any specific objective. But the proviso is important, for motivation is a process that works within me as I am. But 'me', the essential identity that is 'me', *that* must be explained in other terms. The result, however, is crucial to the working of motivation processes in that my 'self' is the case within which the process operates. 'I' *am* one party to each psychological contract, 'I' *do* have a set of needs of varying salience, but how did this come about? Through the chance accident of heredity or environment? Did I have any say in it, or was I a powerless victim?

7.1 The self-concept

This problem of the 'self', of the self-concept, of the ego-ideal and how it is formed underlies all the work on motivation. Levinson indeed has suggested, as mentioned previously, that the pull of the ego-ideal, of one's vision of what one could be, is the basic motivating drive. Karen Horney has argued that the central core of neurosis lies in the tendency of the neurotic to judge himself in terms of an unattainable ideal, that feelings of worthlessness and self-hatred come from setting one's ego-ideals too high – a thing that high need-achievers are careful not to do. Without being quite so prescriptive as Levinson it is easy to understand how one's notion of what one ought to be can affect the salience of different needs. When I changed my career from that of an organization executive to educationalist and academic I found myself that my revised self-concept had forced me to downgrade some materialist needs and to resurrect others, such as the respect of my colleagues.

Box 2.8 Tolstoy on reinforcing the self-concept

Whatever a man's position may be, he is bound to take a view of human life in general that will make his own activity seem important and good. People usually imagine that a thief, a murderer, a spy, a prostitute, knowing their occupation to be evil, must be ashamed of it. But the very opposite is true. Men who have been placed by fate and their own sins or mistakes in a certain position, however irregular that position may be, adopt a view of life as a whole which makes their position appear to them good and respectable. In order to back up their view of life they instinctively mix only with those who accept their ideas of life and their place in it. This surprises us when it is a case of thieves bragging of their skill, prostitutes flaunting their depravity or murderers boasting of their cruelty. But it surprises only because their numbers are limited and – this is the point – we live in a different atmosphere. But can we not observe the same phenomenon when the rich boast of their wealth, i.e. of robbery; when commanders of armies pride themselves on their victories, i.e. on murder; and when those in high places vaunt their power – their brute force? We do not see that their ideas of life and of good and evil are corrupt and inspired by a necessity to justify their position, only because the circle of people with such corrupt ideas is a larger one and we belong to it ourselves.

From Tolstoy, *Resurrection*

We understand only a little about the formation of the self-concept. Some of its aspects are:

1 The self-concept comes largely from our selection of models in life. Adolescence and early adulthood are often times when we are rejecting old models and seeking new ones. Parents get discarded, and sometimes re-instated. Individual teachers can have an importance out of all proportion to either their salary or their status in society. The boy brought up in the same village all his life, a member of the village school group, will have a constantly consistent set of models and will have little difficulty in arriving at a self-concept. The boy lifted by his intelligence into another class of models has a difficult choice to make. Richard Hoggart in *The Uses of Literacy* has described how the grammar-school boy from a working-class home uses two different accents, one at school, one at home, to separate out the two influences on his life. It is hard for parents to bear their rejection as models, to have little influence on the self-concept of their own flesh

and blood, yet the increasing mobility and flexibility of our society is bound to present more young people with more possible models.

2 The self-concept is not formed without trauma. Adolescence is a difficult time. As the shepherd in *A Winter's Tale* comments: 'I would there were no age between ten and three-and-twenty, or that youth could sleep out the rest: for there is nothing (in the between) but getting wenches with child, wronging the ancientry, stealing, fighting. . . .'

3 The formation (by the mass media perhaps?) of what has come to be called a youth culture with its own norms, values and symbols, has presented young people with another, and very powerful, model for their self-concept. The generality of young people becomes what is called a 'reference group'. We may have different reference groups for different things; in one study by Miles adolescent girls chose their peer group reference group (other girls) as most important in matters of taste in clothes, books, etc., but parents were preferred as a reference group in more important matters. For example, faced with the problem of which of two boys to date when she liked them both equally, only one-third accepted the recommendations of friends rather than parents.

4 The influence of the peer group may be over-emphasized, but certainly the difficulty of choosing models or reference groups can result in much alienation, withdrawal, and rebellion which is hard to deal with. Ken Loach's 1971 film, *Family Life*, based on the work of Laing, is an excellent record of one family's experiences of this problem.

5 As we grow older we tend to fix on a self-concept. We then tend to find ways of protecting that selection by surrounding ourselves with people whose self-concept is roughly the same and who confirm ours as being sensible. So we go to live amongst similar kinds of people, select newspapers which reflect our values, join clubs and go on holidays where our self-concepts will not be challenged. Criticisms of our chosen self-concept can be ignored, either by rejecting the source of it ('he's only an old fool') or by physically avoiding the chance of incurring it, e.g. by not mixing out of one's chosen group. But a different and/or traumatic experience can often cause us to revise our ideal self-concept, our ego-ideal. For many people the war was such an experience – they found a new set of models and after the war changed the direction of their lives completely. A sabbatical, a big educational programme, a stay in hospital or in prison, can have a big effect on an individual's concept. This is not always comfortable. It may involve a whole change of life since the psychological contract no longer works the same way – the things that you liked about the job, the security, the regular hours, are now perhaps examples of what you don't want to be. A girl who marries out of her own *milieu* is often confronted by a new set of

models with resulting changes in her self-concept which may take years to re-settle itself. The publicity given to Women's Lib can be seriously unsettling to many women if it presents new models for their self-concept.

Box 2.9 Does commitment freeze the self-concept?

Howard Becker has suggested that commitment in any situation forces us to behave in a consistent manner, which, over time, becomes part of our self-concept. One view of the process of becoming adult is to view it as a process of acquiring a variety of commitments – a profession, a family, a job – which constrain our behaviour within certain accepted bounds and thus push us towards defining ourselves according to the way we behave.

If this view is followed people with fewer commitments, single and jobless perhaps, are likely to have less stable self-concepts. A society which encourages lower commitment in terms for instance of higher divorce rates, greater job mobility, less personal responsibility to dependants, will find an increasing number of people with unstable self-concept. In organizational situations commitment, which often accompanies responsibility, will promote a stable self-concept and therefore more predictable and consistent behaviour and performance.

Also see Becker, 'Notes on the concept of commitment', *American Journal of Sociology*, 1960

The parts, or roles, that we take on in life are in part determined by our self-concept but they in their turn can influence it. And just as 'one man in his time plays many parts' sequentially, so too can we live separate lives simultaneously. So the dictatorial manager can be the docile husband, or the governor of a Nazi concentration camp have a contented home life. This interaction of roles and its effects will be discussed more fully in the next chapter; here let us only take notice of the fact that we can 'flow into' a role, which really means that we alter our self-concept so as to have a better fit between the requirements of the role and the way we see ourselves to be.

7.2 Psychological success

It has been suggested, particularly by Argyris, that an individual seeks continually to increase his self-esteem, or to enhance his self-concept. He does this by searching for psychological success. Psychological success is experienced by us if:

We set a challenging goal for ourselves;
We determine our own methods of achieving that goal;
The goal is relevant to our self-concept.

The experience of psychological success makes us feel more competent, gives us a more competent identity. In general the more competent someone feels the more likely he is to take risks in areas important to himself, and the less he feels the need to go around protecting his self-concept in the ways described earlier.

Psychological failure on the other hand leads to a lowering of goals, an urge to protect one's self-concept and avoid exposing it to possible damage. Failure tends to breed future low achievement just as success tends to breed further success. The man accustomed to failure, when he does succeed, tends to 'quit while he is ahead'.

It is an important aspect of psychological success that the individual should feel that it is due to his efforts or energy that the goal was achieved. If the achievement was fortuitous, or the means were decided for him, then the feeling of success is reduced. Vice-versa, the experience of psychological failure is reduced if the blame can be laid at the door of fortune, the system, or another colleague.

The theory then is that psychological success becomes one of the needs, if not the main need, for the individual. If you believe this the consequences for the motivation calculus are big:

If a goal is not relevant to an individual's self-concept, i.e. does not meet his need for psychological success, the whole sum of the calculus will be reduced and less 'E' will be expended;

If the means of achieving the goal are not chosen by the individual the goal will not satisfy his need for psychological success and again the whole sum of the calculus will be reduced.

In other words we need to know not only the need profile of an individual in any psychological contract but we must also have a picture of his self-concept and the directions in which he wishes it to move. However, although we may well agree that psychological success is a need to be found in all individuals we might well want to dispute its pre-eminent position in Everyman's need hierarchy. For some of us, psychological success may no longer be, or never have been, very important, whilst for others it may be *the* crucial need.

In conclusion, therefore, let us recognize that the motivation calculus gives some understanding about the process by which individuals decide to apportion 'E'. But the things that influence that calculus, that affect the salience of the needs, are many and various. The self-concept of the individual, the role that he is in, his psychological contract, his perceptions of the situation are all involved. We need to go much further than the process of motivation to understand the behaviour of people in organizations.

Box 2.10 Your psychological contract

Think of two different groups to which you belong. Answer the following questions in respect of both of them.

1 What do they expect from you? List as many expectations as you can.

2 Rank order these expectations, starting with 1 as top priority, in terms of their importance to (a) the group, (b) yourself.

3 What do you expect from them? List as many expectations as you can.

4 Rank order these expectations in terms of their importance to (a) yourself, (b) the group.

   Does this tell you anything about the psychological contracts you have with these groups? How could the contracts be different? Who would change them?

3 On Roles and Interactions

1 Introduction

Think of all the roles that you, or any individual, carry in life. Perhaps, executive, father, son, husband, gardener, golfer, Yorkshireman, scapegoat, go-between. Which of them is most essentially you? Or, remove them all and what of you is left? Ask the ten people who know you best to write a description of you. Will they differ very much? Who are you? Are you the same person in all your roles, or would your daughter not recognize you in your office? Are you anything over and above a collection of role performances? Should you be?

Many novels have been built around this problem of identity. Much has been suffered by individuals in sorting out the confusion of their ideas. Would you be different now if you had been cast in different roles in life – female instead of male or vice-versa, teacher not manager, chemist not clerk? To what extent does one's role shape the kind of person one is? Does the situation make the man or the man make the situation?

Motivation theory gives us some clues as to why people behave as they do. But not enough. Role theory, the study of the individual and his roles, will provide a few more clues. Or, rather, it will provide another language, another framework, to help us understand why the world is not as easy a place to manage as it should be, why individuals suffer stress and strain, why organizations breed misunderstandings and conflict. It will provide one way of linking theories about individuals to theories about organizations.

It has been argued that the main result of all the improvements in communications, in social mobility, in education, in affluence and opportunity, has been to make a lot more roles available to each and any of us. No longer, born into a community, will we take over our father's occupation, live in his house and marry down the street. Who knows now where our children will live, marry and work, or what they will be? Pre-determined roles may have been boring, or restrictive, but they led to certainty and to security, to a consistent self-concept. Role variety, role opportunity, role diversity are no doubt desirable, but they bring in their train complexity and uncertainty, insecurity and strain. Within organizations, the size and complexity of their operations, the rate of change and speed of impact, have made more complex the roles of the individual. The dominance of the work organization has increased in our society, bringing with it the problems of combining the work role and the family role, the career role and the social role. The individual is the crunch point in all these pressures. How does he react? Can it be predicted? Can he be helped? How do organizations help or hinder? These are the concerns of this chapter.

It will in turn discuss *the concepts of role theory, role stress, the implications of stress*, and will then turn to the implications of role theory in considering:

individual *perceptions* of other people;
individual *interactions* with other people.

1.1

Any individual, in any situation, occupies a role in relation to other people. His performance in that role will depend on two sets of influences:

The forces in himself – his personality, attributes, skills;
The forces in the situation.

To a degree, these two sets of influences are interactive. A personality is influenced by the situations to which it is exposed. The situation in its turn depends to a degree on the personalities involved. Much argument in psychology centres around the effect that the situation or the environment can have on behaviour or personality. Much of the argument in leadership theory (discussed in chapter 4) centres on the influence that an individual can exert on the situation. In this chapter, the focus will be largely on the effects of the situational forces – how can the concepts of role theory help us to understand and predict the behaviour and performance of individuals?

2 The concepts of role theory

2.1 Role set

The particular individual with whom one is concerned in the analysis of any situation is usually given the name of *focal person*. He has the *focal role* and can be regarded as sitting in the middle of a group of people, with all of whom he interacts in some way in that situation. This group of people is called his *role set*. For instance, in his family situation, a man's role set might be as shown in Figure 6.

The role set should include all those with whom the individual has more than trivial interactions. There are usually more people involved in any role

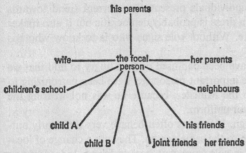

Figure 6

set than one initially expects, which is one reason why it is often a salutary experience to draw one's own role set in a given situation.

2.2 Role definition

The definition of any individual's role in any situation will be a combination of the *role expectations* that the members of the role set have of the focal role. These expectations are often occupationally defined, sometimes even legally so.

The role definitions of lawyers and doctors are fairly clearly defined both in legal and in cultural terms. The role definitions of, say, a film star or a bank manager, are also fairly clearly defined in cultural terms, too clearly perhaps.

Individuals often find it hard to escape from the role that cultural traditions have defined for them. Not only with doctors or lawyers is the required role behaviour so constrained that if you are in that role for long it eventually becomes part of *you*, part of your personality. Hence there is *some* likelihood that all accountants *will* be alike or that all blondes are similar – they are forced that way by the expectations of their role (see Box 3.3).

It is often important that you make it clear what your particular role is at a given time. The means of doing this are called, rather obviously, *role signs*. The simplest of role signs is a uniform. The number of stripes on your arm or pips on your shoulder is a very precise role definition which allows you to do certain very prescribed things in certain situations. Imagine yourself questioning a stranger on a dark street at midnight without wearing the role signs of a policeman if you need any further understanding!

In social circumstances dress has often been used as a role sign, to indicate the nature and degree of formality of any gathering, and occasionally the social status of individuals present. The current trend towards blurring these role signs in dress is probably democratic but it also makes some people very insecure. Without role signs who is to know who has what role?

We must all at times have been confused or even angry to find that we have not recognized some important personage, have been patronizing to the Chairman or rude to the Minister, because he was not wearing the appropriate kind of dress or uniform.

Place is another role sign. Managers often behave very differently outside the office and in, even to the same person. They use a change of location to indicate a change in role from, say, boss to friend. Indeed, if you wish to change your roles you must find some outward sign that you are so doing or you won't be permitted to change – the subordinate will continue to hear you as his boss no matter how hard you try to be his friend. In very significant cases of role change, e.g. from student to graduate, from N.C.O. to Officer, from bachelor to married man, the change of role has to have a very obvious *sign*, hence *rituals*. It is interesting to observe, for instance, some decline in the emphasis given to marriage rituals. This could be taken as an indication that there is no longer such a big change in role from bachelor to married man, and therefore no need for a public change in *sign*.

In organizations, office signs and furniture are often used as role signs. These and other perquisites of status are often frowned upon, but they may serve a purpose as a kind of uniform in a democratic society. For roles without signs often lead to confused or differing expectations of the role of the focal person.

2.3 Role ambiguity

Role ambiguity results when there is some uncertainty in the minds, either of the focal person or of the members of his role set, as to precisely what his role is at any given time. One of the crucial expectations that shape the role definition is that of the individual, the focal person, himself. If his conception of his role is unclear, or if his conception of his role differs from that of the others in his role set, there will be a degree of role ambiguity. Is this bad? Not necessarily, for the ability to shape one's own role is one of the freedoms that many men desire, but the ambiguity may lead to role stress which will be discussed later on. The virtue of job descriptions is that they lessen this role ambiguity. Unfortunately job descriptions are seldom complete role definitions except at the lower end of the scale. At middle and higher management levels they are often a list of formal jobs and duties that say little about the more subtle and informal expectations of the role.

The result is therefore to give the individual an uncomfortable feeling that there are things left unsaid, i.e. to *heighten* his sense of role ambiguity.

Box 3.1 Role ambiguity and the manager

In a study by Norman Maier and two colleagues, a number of vice-presidents in several organizations were each asked to select an immediate subordinate with whose work they were thoroughly familiar, and to define his role (including major responsibilities, priorities among these, and qualifications required by the job). The subordinates were then requested to define their own roles independently but with respect to the same variables. The agreement between the members of the pairs was of the order of 35 per cent.

Adapted from Maier, Read and Hoover, 'Breakdowns in boss–subordinate communication', Foundation for Research on Human Behaviour, 1959

The four most frequently cited instances of role ambiguity in a work situation are:

Uncertainty about how one's work is evaluated;
Uncertainty about scope for advancement;
Uncertainty about scope of responsibility;
Uncertainty about others' expectations of one's performance.

Looking at role ambiguity from the other side, from the point of view of the members of the role set, lack of clarity in the role of the focal person can cause insecurity, lack of confidence, irritation and even anger among members of his role set. One list of the roles of a manager identified the following:

Executive, planner, policy-maker, expert, controller of rewards and punishments, arbitrator, exemplar, representative of the group, scapegoat, counsellor, friend, teacher.

If it is not clear, through role signs of one sort or another, which role is currently the operational one the other party may not react in the appropriate way – he may in fact hear quite another message if the focal person speaks to him, for example, as a teacher and he hears him as an executive. The section on interactions spells out this problem in more detail.

2.4 *Role incompatibility*

Role incompatibility results when the expectations of the members of the role set are well-known but are incompatible as features of the same role.

For instance, an individual's superior may make it clear that he wants a tight structured rule-oriented form of leadership, while his subordinates want a loose, relaxed, friendly style. The expectations of a man's line superior and his staff superior are another frequent source of role incompatibility.

Perhaps, however, the most difficult form of role incompatibility is that which results from a clash between other people's expectations of one in one's role and one's own self-concept. The most clear-cut examples exist in the ethical issues, where company practice and standards may differ from a man's personal standards. More subtle, but more intrusive, are the pressures that result when a man feels that the role requirements or expectations are 'just not him', when he is forced to act in a way which, in a psychological rather than an ethical sense, gives the lie to his personal identity. Some research has indicated that successful managers have a strong definition of their identity, are, in a sense, self-centred, yet it is also clear that to succeed in the middle layers of large organizations it is usually necessary to be organization-centred. This suggests that many successful managers must, at some time in their careers, go through a period of this particular form of role incompatibility. The consequences and methods of dealing with it will be discussed under *role stress*.

2.5 Role conflict

Role conflict results from the necessity for a person to carry out one or more roles in the same situation. The expectations of each role may be quite clear and the expectations be compatible for each role, but the roles themselves may be in conflict. The career woman, for instance, often finds that she is expected to fulfil at one and the same time the expectations attached to being a woman and the expectations attached to a male stereotype of successful executives. The two roles are in conflict. All managers have a variety of roles from amongst those listed in 2.3. Many of these roles are in conflict. Many successful executives find that the role of husband/father and the role of manager are in conflict. Although in different role sets the roles can encroach on each other in such a way as to cause conflict, both cannot be done well at the same time.

It is useful to separate role conflict (conflicting roles) from role incompatibility (conflicting expectations) but the end result is the same – *role stress*.

2.6 Role overload

Another form of role conflict is what can best be described as *role overload*. Most people can handle some measure of role conflict. That is a collection

Box 3.2   Role conflict in the Mikado

Ko-Ko: Pooh-Bah, it seems that the festivities in connection with my approaching marriage must last a week. I should like to do it handsomely, and I want to consult you as to the amount I ought to spend upon them.

Pooh-Bah: Certainly. In which of my capacities? As First Lord of the Treasury, Lord Chamberlain, Attorney-General, Chancellor of the Exchequer, Privy Purse, or Private Secretary?

Ko-Ko: Suppose we say as Private Secretary.

Pooh-Bah: Speaking as your Private Secretary, I should say that as the city will have to pay for it, don't stint yourself, do it well.

Ko-Ko: Exactly – as the city will have to pay for it. That is your advice.

Pooh-Bah: As Private Secretary. Of course, you will understand that, as Chancellor of the Exchequer, I am bound to see that due economy is observed.

Ko-Ko: Oh! But you said just now 'Don't stint yourself, do it well'.

Pooh-Bah: As Private Secretary.

Ko-Ko: And now you say that due economy must be observed.

Pooh-Bah: As Chancellor of the Exchequer.

Ko-Ko: I see. Come over here, where the Chancellor can't hear us. [They cross the stage.] Now, as my Solicitor, how do you advise me to deal with this difficulty?

Pooh-Bah: Oh, as your Solicitor, I should have no hesitation in saying, 'Chance it'.

Ko-Ko: Thank you. [Shaking his hand.] I will.

Pooh-Bah: If it were not that, as Lord Chief Justice, I am bound to see that the law isn't violated.

Ko-Ko: I see. Come over here where the Chief Justice can't hear us. [They cross the stage.] Now, then, as First Lord of the Treasury?

Pooh-Bah: Of course, as First Lord of the Treasury, I could propose a special vote that would cover all expenses, if it were not that, as Leader of the Opposition, it would be my duty to resist it, tooth and nail. Or, as Paymaster-General, I could so cook the accounts that, as Lord High Auditor, I should never discover the fraud. But then, as Archbishop of Titipu, it would be my duty to denounce my dishonesty and give myself into my own custody as First Commissioner of Police.

Ko-Ko: That's extremely awkward.

W. S. Gilbert, *The Mikado*

of roles that do not precisely fit. There comes a time, however, when the number of roles that one person has to handle becomes just too much. He then experiences role overload. This is not the same as work overload. Work overload can often mean that there is just too much to do in one role. It has its own problems – often of weariness resulting in stress – but is of a different order from role overload which is concerned with variety as well as quantity.

The transition from executive to manager is often accompanied by a change in the problem of work overload into one of role overload. Overtime is a feasible strategy for dealing with work overload, but it may be, and often is, an inappropriate strategy for role overload. This can be confusing to the individual who has successfully employed this strategy as an executive only to find it fail as a manager.

2.7 Role underload

A neglected but very real problem in the lower parts of the organization is *role underload*. This form of role conflict arises when an individual feels that the role definition is out of line with his self-concept – out of line, that is, in terms of his capacity to handle a bigger role or a greater set of roles. It occurs, for instance, when the recruiting arm of an organization takes on a new graduate and, by means of their talk about opportunities, can even enlarge the individual's self-concept. This concept then suffers a rude shock when the recruit is given a job which, in the opinion of the individual, is well below his capacities. Whether it is or not becomes irrelevant – it is the individual's perception that causes role underload. Individuals placed in auditing roles in organizations – quality control, part of the finance department, some computer sections – often suffer from role underload. Indeed they are placed in positions where, if all goes well, they should not be needed!

Delegation often, when first practised, creates a feeling of underload. The delegating manager feels naked and un-needed. Role underload is the form of role conflict which perhaps most seriously threatens an individual's self-concept. As will be seen it is the most insidious, but most ignored, perverter of organizational efficiency.

3 Role stress

It is now pertinent to look at the implications of these varieties of role problems and to examine some of the ways of dealing with them.

3.1 Role stress

All of them, role ambiguity, incompatibility, conflict, overload and under-load, lead to role stress. Stress can be good, stress can be bad. Most people need some form of stress to bring out their best performance, but if the stress is of the wrong form, or too much, it becomes damaging. One of the major tasks of management in organizations is to control the level of stress.

For convenience we shall define beneficial stress as *role pressure* and harmful stress as *role strain*. Unfortunately there is no clear way of dis-tinguishing between them except by their effects.

3.2 Symptoms of role strain

When role strain exists for the focal person, he will normally exhibit some of the following symptoms:

Tension. Often expressed by irritation, excessive preoccupation with trivia, great attention to precision, or periods of sickness. Tension focuses atten-tion on the immediate, polarizes situations into 'black' and 'white' extremes, leads to stereotyped responses and increases sensitivity to rumours and group pressures.

Low morale. Often expressed as low confidence in the organization, expres-sions of dissatisfaction with the job, or a sense of futility.

Communication difficulties. Often the individual is hard to talk with or even breaks off communication entirely. He becomes silent and withdrawn. Absenteeism is an extreme form of this symptom.

You cannot, of course, assume that the reverse is true, that because these symptoms appear there must be role strain. There are other forms of organization diseases that will cause these symptoms. But if role strain seems to underly those behaviour patterns the next step is to identify the types of role problem. This can sometimes be done by looking at the mechanisms employed by the individual to ease the strain.

3.3 Strategies for dealing with role strain

There are some general strategies which could be better described as coping rather than solution strategies:

1 *Repression.* The individual refuses to admit that there is any problem,

although all the symptoms are there. Laughter or jocular behaviour is often a symptom of repression.

2 *Withdrawal*. The individual retreats behind a psychological barrier, or leaves the organization.

3 *Rationalization*. The individual decides that the conflict is inevitable and that he must live with it.

If the problem is one of *role ambiguity*, the individual will attempt to clarify his role definition either:

By enforcing his expectations on other members of his role set;
By asking for clarification, either specifically or by precedent, from key members of his role set – particularly his line and staff superiors.

Role incompatibility problems can be resolved for the individual:
By deciding privately to give preference to the more important or salient of the members of his role set and down-grading the expectations of the others. He will decide, for instance, between his line and his staff superior, usually in terms of their political importance for him;
By asking for a resolution of the incompatibility from the affected parties. (He may not always be in a position to do this.)

Role conflict is eased for someone:
By reducing the salience or importance of one of the roles so that poor performance in that role is no longer a bother to himself, e.g. reduce the salience of the father role and therefore allow himself to opt out of it;
By an agreed compartmentalization of his life so that the roles do not overlap and by setting up rules and procedures to maintain those compartments and their relative priorities, e.g. week-ends kept for the family.

Role overload can be reduced:
By downgrading the importance of some of his roles and turning in low performance in those areas, but accepting that as consistent with the reduced importance of those goals;
By an agreed re-assignment of role responsibilities and priorities.

Role underload can be made easier for the individual:
By exerting his irritant powers (described as *negative power* in chapter 5) to increase his visibility and felt presence in the organization;
By taking on someone else's role in addition to his own.

Looking at these solution strategies it will be seen that in each case the first strategy is always a unilateral strategy. Sometimes this involves the unilateral re-definition of priorities (one way of resolving dissonance), in other cases it means the unilateral re-definition of responsibilities and scope of the job. Unilateral strategies invite retaliation from others involved, and are often only steps to an escalation of the problem. Unfortunately under conditions of strain (which often means tension or withdrawal) unilateral strategies come more naturally to mind than co-operative ones.

The second set of strategies are (with the exception of role underload) all co-operative ones. There is good evidence that close and positive interpersonal relationships with members of one's role set can mediate substantially the effects of role problems. A given degree of role conflict is experienced as carrying less strain when there are positive relations with the others involved. Unfortunately role problems work to cause deterioration in inter-personal relations. Decreased trust, liking and respect for fellow-workers often follows role incompatibility or role conflict. This tendency leads on to unilateral solutions which tend to be self-defeating.

In the case of role underload there appears to be no co-operative strategy that the individual can initiate, apart from asking for an enlargement of his role – a strategy seen as presumptuous or arrogant. The first unilateral strategy – the use of his negative or irritant power – is so tempting that it is hard to resist trying it. Most individuals find that they are in a position to initiate new systems, rules or procedures which will effectively give them more prominence in the organization and so re-define their role. These strategies are all legal, indeed since they often appear to be synonymous with a desire for increased efficiency, they are even approved of. But if originating from role underload they effectively act to hamper the natural workings of the organization.

The second strategy, take-over, can seldom be done co-operatively and therefore results either in inter-personal conflict or duplication of effort – or both.

Since role underload is so potentially harmful to the self-concept of the individual it is hard to resist the individual's attempts to enlarge his own job. Indeed, put that way, it might seem actually beneficial. But in fact most people in underload positions can *only* enlarge their jobs by encroaching on the roles and responsibilities of others since they will tend to be in the middle or lower reaches of the organization.

4 The implications of stress

4.1

Stress can be either stimulating (pressure) or harmful (strain). The dividing line will depend partly on the situation and the role problems it creates, partly on the individual and the degree to which he can tolerate and even gain benefit from stress.

4.2 Situations leading to stress

There are three organizational situations that are likely to create role problems, and therefore stress, for the individual:

1 *Responsibility for the work of others.* The role ambiguity, incompatibility and conflict that are inherent in the typical 'management' situation have already been touched upon. In a sense, a manager's task is always to reconcile overlapping or conflicting objectives – of groups and organization, of groups and individuals, of self and superiors. One study has shown that role stress increases as rank in the organization increases.

2 *Innovative functions.* The major role problem encountered by people responsible for innovative activities is that of conflicting priorities. In general the power centres in the organization are in favour of the *status quo* – this will impart a high degree of role ambiguity to the manager of an innovative function – is he or is he not supposed to innovate? He will also find considerable conflict between the routine administrative aspect of his job and the creative side – two types of work with different psychological demands, hard to combine in the one individual.

3 *Integrative or boundary functions.* The role of the co-ordinator, linkman or outside contact man appears to be particularly stressful. This is perhaps due to the lack of control that he has over their demands or their resources. He often becomes the focal point for inter-group conflict either within the organization or between the organization and its environment.

4.3 Stress – personality variables

It is obviously important for the organization to choose people for inherently stressful roles who will be able to tolerate the stress. Several personality variables are known to be involved in the management of stress. These are:

1 *Sociability.* The person who builds strong inter-personal bonds finds stress more tolerable than the independent individual who develops relationships which, while often congenial, are seldom deep-rooted enough to withstand conditions of tension. The independent or autonomous person often withdraws from inter-personal relationships when things get tough and resorts to unilateral methods of resolving role problems.

2 *Emotional sensitivity.* People who are emotionally sensitive tend to feel more tension in any given conflict or ambiguous situation than those with lower sensitivity. Complete insensitivity will tend to produce bad interpersonal relationships, so the 'happy mean' is required here.

3 *Flexibility/rigidity.* There is evidence that members of a role set will apply

pressure where it is seen to be effective. Thus people seen to be flexible will tend to have more pressure applied to them than those whose steadfastness has already demonstrated the futility of pressure.

In general, the strong-minded relatively insensitive individual *feels* less tension. The individual with deep inter-personal relationships can *withstand* more tension. Alas, the former leads to independence which is undesirable in promoting the latter. The tough executive will better survive the pressures of organizational life, but at the cost of damaging the inter-personal relationships which should make the organization more effective and more tolerable.

4.4 Stress – implications for organizations

Role problems are inherent in organizations, particularly for those in key managerial roles. Too often, the reactions to the stress resulting from these problems are:

To carry the strain outside the organization (the home can often become an emotional litter-bin for work problems);
To adopt the unilateral solution. This can be detrimental to the individual and the organization.

Those with overall responsibility need to endeavour:

So to design the organization that role problems are not exaggerated, with particular reference to role underload;
To pay particular attention to the selection of individuals for inherently stressful situations;
To help individuals encountering role problems to find co-operative strategies for resolution (it is easier for the superior to initiate meetings or discussions on role problems than the individuals directly concerned).

5 Perceiving people

5.1

Role theory is the key to the tricky area of how we perceive other people. If we know someone very well, a friend, a relation or a close colleague, then we tend to know them as a person, with all their individual differences. E. M. Forster has differentiated between flat characters and round characters in novels. 'The test of a round character is whether it is capable of surprising in a convincing way. If it never surprises, it is flat. If it does not convince it is a flat pretending to be round. It has the incalculability of life in it.' He went on to label most of the characters in Dickens as flat in comparison with those of Tolstoy and Jane Austen. Those people that we know well become round characters, but a great amount of time in organizations is spent with people who, to us, are flat since we shall never get to know them well enough to know their hidden depths.

In interacting with someone that we do not know in the round we have to make some assumptions as to what kind of person they are, what their motives are, what their likely reaction or behaviour is going to be in any situation. In order to do this we:

Box 3.3 The effects of occupational roles

Terman and Miles examined personality differences between the sexes in the American culture and concluded:

The males directly or indirectly manifest the greater self-assertion and aggres-siveness; they express more hardihood and fearlessness, and more roughness of manner, language and sentiments. The females express themselves as more com-passionate and sympathetic, more timid, more fastidious and aesthetically sensi-tive, more emotional in general, ... severer moralists, yet admit in themselves weaknesses in emotional control and (less noticeably) in physique.

Waller did a study of 'What Teaching Does to Teachers'. He summarized his impressions:

There is first that certain inflexibility or unbendingness of personality which is thought to mark the person who has taught. That stiff and formal manner into which the young teacher compresses himself every morning when he puts on his collar becomes, they say, a plaster case which at length he cannot loosen. ... One who has taught long enough may wax unenthusiastic on any subject under the sun. ... The didactic manner, the authoritative manner, the flat, assured tones of voice that go with them, are bred in the teacher by his dealings in the classroom. If these traits ... are found among the generality of teachers, it is because these traits have survival value in the schools of today. If one does not have them when he joins the faculty, he must develop them or die the academic death.

Merton commented about the impact of performing the bureaucratic role on the occupant of that role:

The bureaucrat's official life is planned for him in terms of a graded career, through the organizational devices of promotion by seniority, pensions, incre-mental salaries etc., all of which are designed to provide incentives for disci-plined action and conformity to the official regulations. The official is tacitly expected to, and largely does, adapt his thought, feelings and actions to the prospect of this career. But these very devices ... also lead to an over-concern with strict adherence to regulations which induce timidity, conservatism and technicism.

Collect data;
Fit the information into categories;
Make some predictions.

Categories. Let us first consider the categories. Categories are a way of organizing material and as such are very useful. But they have their dangers, for with those categories go a certain set of assumptions or predictions. 'Professors are absent-minded', 'Blondes are willing', 'Chinese are superstitious', 'Brown-skinned men are violent', 'Older men are less ready to change'. These are stereotypes. Stereotypes we know to be inaccurate. We cannot preface any of the above statements with 'All' for we know there to be exceptions to each of them. However, stereotyping does happen to be an easy way to think. If we can fit someone into a stereotyped category then he becomes predictable and easier to deal with. Box 3.9 shows how pupils, given a slightly different stereotype of a teacher, reacted quite differently to the same behaviour, influenced by the prediction they had made from the stereotype. Knowing the role of an individual, that he is a doctor, or a professor, or a steelworker lets us make all sorts of quick assumptions about him.

Data. In order to place someone in a category we need information about them. This information may be public reputation, published fact or private hearsay. All of this data would be prior information which would allow you to build up a picture of the individual and make some assumptions about him before he arrives. But we also use clues – dress, speech, actions, gestures. It used to be said that by the time an Englishman had entered a room and greeted his hostess every other Englishman would have decided where he came from, where he was educated, how much he earned and how

---

Box 3.4   Roles and symbols

Farr's Law of Mean Familiarity... can be expressed as a curve, but is much clearer set down as follows: The Guv'nor addresses:

Co-director Michael Yates as *Mike*;
Assistant director Michael Yates as *Michael*;
Section manager Michael Yates as *Mr Yates*;
Second assistant Michael Yates as *Yates*;
Apprentice Michael Yates as *Michael*;
Night-watchman Michael Yates as *Mike*.

From S. Potter, *One-Upmanship*

he earned it. Role signs are, of course, a very useful source of data. If escaping criminals were to use the role signs of priests by donning clerical collars and dark suits, they would be trying to suggest a particular stereotype, and all the assumptions about behaviour that go with that stereotype. Most people are, however, remarkably unscientific in their collection of perceptual data. For instance:

1 We collect very little. The outcome of most interviews appears to be decided in the first three minutes. We form a stereotype from the first available perceptual information and regard that as adequate. For some people, the simple information that X is a Jew, or coloured, or a student at L.S.E., is enough to enable them to make a whole range of predictions about their behaviour, many of which will be false. The students in Box 3.9 needed only a change of one adjective to change their stereotype.

2 We are very prone to the sin of *selective perception*. We only perceive what we want to perceive. We look for data to support our initial assumptions, and neglect or do not notice contradictory evidence. Since we cannot register all the data that our senses can bring us, we focus on what we want to see and ignore, do not see, things or behaviour that do not fit our categories. Confronted with the same shop-window, the housewife may easily 'see' a quite different collection of objects from that 'seen' by her husband. In a management game used at the London Business School the instructions for the groups included, for one group, the words 'You report to the head of group X'. In nearly every exercise this group did not realize their supposedly subordinate position. They had not ignored or disobeyed the instruction, they literally did not perceive it. They 'selected it out' of their perceptual screen.

3 The order in which the data is collected is important. Box 3.6 offers some evidence to support the view that the earlier information, if received, colours that which comes after it. In part this is probably due to rapid stereotyping based on very little information.

4 Our own roles colour our perceptions. The same set of facts viewed from different angles will look different. This is another kind of selective perception.

Dearborn and Simon conducted an experiment on this theme with a group of executives who represented different functional areas of business. These areas included sales, accounting, production and others. The executives were given a description of a management situation and asked to identify the principal problem of the company described in the case. The case was designed to encourage them to take a company-wide view. The majority of the executives identified the principal problem as one related to their own functional role. Thus 83 per cent of the sales executives mentioned sales as the most important problem facing the company while only 29 per cent of the non-sales executives did so. Another experiment, of a different type but on the same theme, was by Bagley. Mexican and U.S. schoolteachers were given stereoscopes (binoculars which project a different image to each eye). They were all presented with the same two pictures simultaneously – one of bullfighters and one of baseball players. Most of the Mexicans saw the bullfighters, most of the U.S. teachers saw only the baseball players. National roles had coloured their perception.

Box 3.5   Manager response to tension

Job-related tension index items	All managers indicating item as a pressure inducing item (%)	Top managers only (%)	Middle managers only (%)	Difference (%)
having to decide things on the job that affect the lives of individuals, people you have come to know	88	83	90	7
feeling unable to influence your immediate superior's decisions and actions that affect you	85	67	90	23
thinking that you'll not be able to satisfy the conflicting demands of various people over you	81	67	85	18
fact that you can't get the necessary information needed to carry out your job	77	67	90	23
feeling that you have to do things on the job that are against your better judgement	73	67	75	8
feeling that you have too little authority to carry out the responsibilities assigned to you	69	50	75	25

Box 3.5 – *contd*

Job-related tension index terms	All managers indicating item as a pressure inducing item (%)	Tap managers only (%)	Middle managers only (%)	Difference (%)
feeling that you have too heavy a work load, one you can't possibly finish in an ordinary work day	66	66	66	0
being unclear on just what the scope and responsibilities of your job are	65	33	75	42
feeling that you may not be liked or accepted by the people you work with	61	33	70	37
not knowing just what the people you work with expect of you	58	34	65	31
feeling that your job tends to interfere with your family life	50	50	70	20
feeling that you're not fully qualified to handle yourself	50	33	65	32
not knowing what your supervisor thinks of you or how he evaluates your performance	46	50	70	20
not knowing what opportunities for advancement or promotion exist for you	39	17	45	28
thinking that the amount of work you do may interfere with how well it gets done	23	33	20	13

Adapted from Miller, 'Using behavioural science to solve organization problems', *Personnel Administration*, 1968

5.2 Implications of role perception

The implications of the way we perceive other people and their roles are various and important. Some of the more interesting ones are mentioned below.

The snares of stereotyping. In *She Stoops to Conquer* Charles Marlow is under the impression that he is staying at an Inn and that Mr Hardcastle is the innkeeper. Marlow therefore treats Hardcastle according to his stereotype of the role of a landlord. In reality, however, Hardcastle is Marlow's prospective father-in-law and he behaves in the manner appropriate towards a future son-in-law. The ensuing bewilderment and frustration on the part of the two characters who receive data that so vehemently conflicts with their stereotypes of the other's role is great entertainment for the audience who are party to the role confusion.

Box 3.6   First impressions count

Asch read the following list of traits to a group of subjects: intelligent – industrious – impulsive – critical – stubborn – envious. A second list of subjects was given the same list of traits, but in the reverse order. For Group A subjects the trait list opens with the desirable qualities of intelligence and industry but proceeds to the less desirable (stubbornness and envy). For Group B subjects the progression is from negatively valued qualities to the positively valued ones.

When the groups were asked to write brief characterizations of the individual possessing these traits, the two groups produced very different portraits, despite the fact that the lists were identical in everything except order. For example, a member of Group A wrote:

The person is intelligent and fortunately he puts his intelligence to work. That he is stubborn and impulsive may be due to the fact that he knows what he is saying and what he means and will not therefore give in easily to someone else's idea which he disagrees with.

In contrast, a member of Group B, who had received the trait list with the negative qualities first, wrote:

This person's good qualities such as industry and intelligence are bound to be restricted by jealousy and stubbornness. The person is emotional. He is unsuccessful because he is weak and allows his bad points to cover up his good ones.

Adapted from Asch, 'Forming impressions of personality', *Journal of abnormal and social psychology*, 1946

If individuals do not give clear data on their role they run the risk of either confusing, or antagonizing, those with whom they come in contact, or, more often, of being stuck with a stereotype which they did not want.

I recall my first experience of unwanted stereotyping. Participating for the first time in a group learning experience in the U.S.A., I said nothing at all for the first three hours, feeling that the others, who were all American, had more to contribute than I. I was therefore astonished in a feedback session to discover that in spite of saying nothing they still had a clear impression of me as a social snob, intellectually arrogant, conservative, narrow-minded, unfriendly and effeminate! In not providing them with any contrary data they had stuck me with their, largely unfavourable, stereotype of the Englishman. Thereafter, in new encounters, I went to some lengths to provide early data to offset the initial stereotyping!

Unilateral decisions to behave differently from one's role stereotype are not always popular. The manager who does not behave as a manager, the parson who leaves off his collar in the pub, will initially cause role confusion which will be resented. The experiment recounted in Box 3.8 shows what happens in families when the children unilaterally re-define their role. The consultant, in industry, often suffers from role confusion. Seeing himself as a helper he is often perceived as a spy, disrupter of established order, or advance redundancy man. If unused to the experience he may be surprised at the antagonisms aroused by this alternative stereotype of his role.

In general, it is wise to remember that people have to place other people in roles and stereotypes in order to make predictions about them. They will act on whatever information is available, be over-influenced by what they receive first and will be hard to sway from their first impressions. If anyone is not content with the stereotype likely to be provided by existing information he would do well to provide alternative data, or clearer role signs, as quickly as possible.

The halo effect. There is a strong tendency for people to conform to other people's perceptions of them. The bishop tends to behave as bishops are expected to behave, the father begins to conform to the stereotype of a father. The children who are perceived to be bright do in fact become bright (see Box 3.7). Those who are thought to be malcontents tend to become malcontents. If you wish your children to be clever, treat them as if they were clever. If you desire your subordinates to become responsible, behave to them as if they already were responsible. The timid new officer finds himself demonstrating unsuspected bravery in action, because that is part of the role requirement.

There appear to be two reasons for this readily observable pheno-menon:

1 People tend to enforce their expectations on the role occupier. The teacher applies higher standards and more encouragement to the pupils he or she regards as talented, thus making them reach ever higher. The officer is forced by his N.C.O. to give orders and take command in certain situations. The Cabinet Minister finds his car waiting for him, the speaking engagements arranged, the appointments set up. It is usually easier in the short-run to conform to the expectations of the role than to change the

---

Box 3.7 Role expectations and the self-fulfilling prophecy

There have been a number of studies of the self-fulfilling prophecy in educational contexts, but the most famous study is that of Robert Rosenthal and Lenore Jacobson, social psychologists at Harvard University. Rosenthal is concerned with the positive self-fulfilling prophecy which states that if children are predicted to improve they will do so, although the *negative* form, whereby pupils deteriorate in work or behaviour as a result of the teacher's expectation, is obviously of at least equal educational significance. The results of Rosenthal's experiment are very complicated in detail, but the main findings can be briefly summarized.

The pupils of an American elementary school were given the 'Harvard test of inflected acquisition'. The teachers were told that this test would single out those pupils who could be expected to make dramatic academic progress. Actually the test was simply an intelligence test. Rosenthal selected *at random* 20 per cent of the pupils, who, the teachers were informed, were the spurters. After the teachers were given the names of the alleged spurters no further action was taken until the pupils were all re-tested for intelligence one year later. If the teachers believed that the alleged spurters would indeed bloom academically, then they might so influence events that the prediction would come true. The results supported such an interpretation. After one year the children nominated as spurters did make marked gains in intelligence. Spurters in the first grade gained on average fifteen IQ points more than did other pupils and in the second grade the spurters gained on average nine IQ points over the others. In these two grades one-fifth of the pupils not nominated as spurters gained over twenty IQ points whereas almost half the spurters did so. The spurters also made marked gains in reading as assessed by the teacher. Rosenthal was able to show that more teacher time was not devoted to the spurters and attributes the result to the quality of the teacher-student interactions.

Reported by Hargreaves in *Interpersonal Relations and Education*, 1972

role. Not living up to role expectations is regarded either as failure or deviancy. Deviant behaviour unaccompanied by demonstrable success is regarded as failure. Only a very self-confident man will be deviant, i.e. overthrow the role expectations. It is often easier for the child to bring his performance up to the teacher's expectations than to change the expectations.

2 Most individuals do not like ambiguity. A new role has lots of ambiguity. Joining a firm, moving into a new level of management, going away on secondment to another institution, are all situations fraught with ambiguity. Explicit role expectations by the 'significant others' (people who matter to the occupant of the role) are one way of resolving the ambiguity. Thankfully, the newcomer does all that he is asked or expected to do. The best way to make a newcomer feel insecure, in a university, in a graduate entry scheme, after mergers or on transfer, is to provide no structure, no rules, no role prescriptions. On the other hand, a detailed programme, instructions on when to eat, how to get things done, the provision of a very competent secretary, will induce feelings of security and compliance. Educational institutions discovered long ago that busy students are contented students, at least as long as they are busy.

The implications of the halo effect are considerable. Self-fulfilling prophecies of a positive or negative kind can readily be created by treating people as if they already are what you want them to become. Assumptions that men are animals lead to treating them like animals and to them behaving like animals, thus justifying your assumptions. Positive self-fulfilling prophecies do not work so infallibly as the negative kind. The basic ability has to be then called out. In Rosenthal's experiment on IQ levels (Box 3.7) not all the supposed spurters prospered. One child had regressed six IQ points by the end of the year. But when people talk of the job making the man, they are pointing to an individual living up to his role expectations. It is probable that not enough people find their role expectations hard to attain – the negative prophecy is more prevalent than the positive, for positive prophecies require faith and trust. Yet if, as has been asserted, the average individual during his lifetime uses only 20 per cent of his talents, it is stimulating to reflect what a burst of 'E' forces could be released in most of us by the use of revised role expectations.

6 Interacting with people

6.1

Our interactions with people are affected to a large extent by the way we perceive them, the things they say and what they do. Our perceptions are in turn affected by our roles *vis-à-vis* them and our view of their roles. Personality, inter-personal skills, the structure of the situation, the qualities of the leader are other factors that affect our interactions. Here we are concerned with the intervening effect of roles and the perception of roles on the behaviour of individuals. We shall consider the interactions of an individual with another individual and the interactions of an individual in a group.

6.2 Interacting with individuals

We have seen that the first thing that anyone does in a new interaction is to place the other individual in some sort of role. The kind of role may vary. It may be occupational (the personnel manager), or social (a worker), or behavioural (a drunkard), or mixed (a snobbish banker). In this way we can make predictions about how they will react and the attitudes they will carry.

When the roles are unclear, the individuals will probe, like two strangers at a cocktail party, to find categories and structures into which they can fit the other. Unless they can find some congruent way of defining the situation, communication will be impaired. If the personnel manager sees himself as advising, but is regarded as telling, he will be resented and will not understand the resentment. This need for an agreement on the relative roles within any particular situation can be illustrated by thinking of each individual as being in one of the metaphorical roles of *parent, adult, child*. If the individual X intends to relate to the individual Y as Adult to Adult, but is heard by Y as a Parent speaking to a Child, the interaction will result in misunderstanding and possibly resentment. When my wife says to me 'Where did you put the scissors?' my reaction to her simple question will vary depending on which of the relationships depicted in Figure 7 seems to me to be operating. If I hear her speaking to me as a mother to

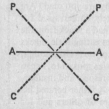

Figure 7

a naughty child I might reply, resentfully, 'I haven't the slightest idea, you used them last.' If I hear her as an inefficient child looking for help, I could reply, 'Don't you know that they are always in the top left-hand drawer.' If, however, it's Adult to Adult I might reply in the same vein, 'I think I left them on the sitting-room table.'

We can also use the need for role classification to influence the situation in the way we want it. Amidst a group of strangers at a party a friend deliberately created ambiguity and even hostility by answering 'nothing' to the repeated question 'What do you do?' When they said 'Oh, you're self-employed, are you?' he replied, 'No, I do nothing.' This blocking response gave them no way of placing him and thus frustrated further communications. Others will experiment with new roles, allowing people to mistake them for a television personality, or claiming to be a distinguished author. The role definition will colour the whole interaction. Or you can force a role definition on someone. 'You are well-known, Sir, for your knowledge of . . .' is an approach that casts the other in the role of expert. He may find the role definition so pleasing that he will carry out the role requirements.

Many of the rituals of greetings – introductions, indications of appropriate dress or degree of informality, the separation of the sexes after dinner – are ways of clarifying role situations, of saying who is who and

---

Box 3.8 Confused role expectations in the family

Garfinkel once asked some of his students to behave in their own homes as if they were lodgers and to report back the results:

. . . family members were stupefied. They vigorously sought to make the strange actions intelligible and to restore the situation to normal appearances. Reports were filled with accounts of astonishment, bewilderment, shock, anxiety, embarrassment and anger, and with charges by various family members that the student was mean, inconsiderate, nasty or impolite. Family members demanded explanations: What's the matter? What has got into you? Did you get fired? Are you sick? What are you being so superior about? Why are you mad? Are you out of your mind or just stupid? One student acutely embarrassed his mother in front of her friend by asking if she minded if he had a snack from the refrigerator. 'Mind if you have a little snack? You've been eating little snacks around here for years without asking me. What has got into you?' One mother, infuriated when her daughter spoke to her only when she was spoken to, began to shriek in angry denunciation of the daughter for her disrespect and insubordination and refused to be calmed by the student's sister. A father berated his daughter for being insufficiently concerned for the welfare of others and for acting like a spoiled child.

Adapted from Garfinkel, *Studies in Ethnomethodology*, 1967

who is expected to do what and when. But in addition to our attempts to define the role relationships we also look for cues as to how they are behaving in those roles. Are they warm and friendly, or suspicious, or threatening? I once worked in a large open-plan office. One morning the manager came in and walked quickly through to his partitioned office in the corner. As he went past he said 'Good morning, Tony' to my neighbour but said nothing to me. As soon as he had entered his office, Tony turned to me. 'I wonder what was the meaning of that,' he said, 'is he softening me up for a body-blow later this morning, or does he have it in for you and is warning you by ignoring you?' The alternative explanation, that the man was in a hurry and had not noticed me, was too superficial to satisfy Tony's needs for cues as to his boss's feelings.

Non-verbal communication is in fact as important, if not more so, than the actual words used. Non-verbal cues are often the best ways we have of ascertaining the goals, intentions and expectations of the other party in the interaction. Anyone who has the opportunity should study or record an interaction with the sound turned off (videotape can be used effectively for this purpose). He will be surprised at the amount that he will uncover about the overtones in the interaction. Detailed studies have been done of eye contact, of physical proximity and of features in interactions in order to demonstrate the ways we have of communicating without words. Mime is a crucial element in the training of actors for this sort of reason. An awareness of the non-verbal cues we give to people is certainly a useful piece of knowledge for anyone who has a lot of interactions with relative strangers.

Like dogs in a garden, our aim in sniffing each other out in interaction situations is to find answers to the following questions:

What is the other's role?
How does he perceive his role?
What are the other's goals?
What does he expect to gain from the interaction?
What are his immediate intentions?
How is he going to behave towards me?

The answers to these questions can result in quite false outcomes. Laing has identified three levels of complication: the direct perspective (my thoughts), the metaperspective (what I think you think of me), and the metametaperspective (what I think you think I think). To make it clearer let us look at one of Laing's examples:

Box 3.9 Reputations matter

Harold Kelley conducted an experiment to test the effect of prior impressions on perception and behaviour. At the beginning of a psychology class some students at the Massachusetts Institute of Technology were informed that their usual instructor was out of town and that a substitute would take his place. The students were then given, in the form of a note, some information about the replacement instructor:

Mr ... is a graduate student in the Department of Economics and Social Science here at MIT. He has had three semesters of teaching experience in psychology at another college. This is his first semester teaching EC.70. He is 26 years old, a veteran and married. People who know him consider him to be a rather cold person, industrious, critical, practical and determined.

For half the students in the class this prior information contained the words 'very warm' instead of 'rather cold'. At the end of class the students were asked to rate the instructor on a number of traits and it was found that those students who received the 'warm' information rated the instructor as more considerate, more informal, more sociable, more popular, better natured, more humorous and more human than did the students who received the 'cold' information.

Furthermore, since the class took the form of a discussion group, Kelley was able to record the number of times any student initiated verbal interaction with the instructor. 56 per cent of the students with the 'warm' information participated as against only 32 per cent of those with the 'cold' information.

Adapted from Kelley, 'The warm-cold variable in first impressions of people', *Journal of Personality*, 1950

Direct Perspective

John does not love Mary   Mary does not love John

Metaperspective

John thinks Mary loves   Mary thinks John loves
him   her

Metametaperspective

John thinks that Mary   Mary thinks that John
thinks that he loves her   thinks that he loves her

Neither wants to hurt each other; rather than resolve the misunderstanding, they might well get married.

Manager–subordinate relationships can easily get into this kind of tangle. If a manager thinks (falsely) that a favourite subordinate dislikes him he can easily behave in such a way that the subordinate begins to think the manager dislikes him. In this way they both are convinced of the other's dislike although the apparent dislike is only a reaction to their interpretation of the other's feelings. If Laing's systematization of the problem appears complicated it is nothing to the complications that underlie many of the role relationships in real life.

Box 3.10 Cross-cultural metaperspectives

We were negotiating with our French partners. The moment of agreement on intentions had arrived. The Frenchmen immediately pushed a document across the table asking us to sign our agreement to our stated intentions in quadruplicate. Reacting like typical Englishmen we regarded this request for a signature at this stage as somehow reflecting on our integrity. After all we had *said* that we agreed to their suggested course of action and at this stage no legal documentation was necessary. Clearly the other side did not trust us. Huffily we replied that signatures were not necessary. So, thought the French, reared in a bureaucratic tradition, they will not sign. What does this mean? Clearly they do not trust us and want to retain room for manoeuvre. It is common practice to record the process of negotiations by signature at each stage.

The meeting was rescued from this cross-cultural misperception only by the intervention of an American who was able to discern that cues were being misinterpreted.

The problem of perspective and the dangers of misperception become heightened when there is a mix of cultures. The cultures can be the obvious national ones, as in Box 3.10, or the less obvious ones of staff and line, professional and manager. A piece of behaviour that means one thing to you may be interpreted quite differently by the other person inducing a false metaperspective. What is a *salient* characteristic of the role in my view may not be salient to you. Englishmen who have been brought up to associate articulate ability with intelligence are prone to think inarticulate people stupid. This has led them into difficulties when they encounter the inarticulate scientist, or the silent but efficient engineer and mistakenly write them off as unintelligent. In perceiving and being perceived it is necessary to find out what the other person regards as salient clues to any role.

6.3 Interacting with groups

The working of groups is discussed in a later chapter. Here it needs to be recognized that group situations confront the individual with considerable role problems and identity problems, which in turn cause problems for organizations.

The problem for organizations. Individuals must be organized in groups in order to make most effective use of their mix of skills and abilities, but *too much* emphasis on the group may blunt the individual contribution; whilst too much emphasis on the autonomous individual may hinder the development of group identities.

The problem for individuals. Groups, or families, are desirable psychological homes. Without them individuals can become too egocentric to be effective in organizational situations and can deprive themselves of the richness of interpersonal relationships. To submerge oneself in a group too far may involve the sacrifice of some of one's individuality.

Only those who have worked or lived in a small group can fully understand the force of group pressures on an individual. The group pressures need not be explicit, they can be implicit, in that merely being 'out of line' with the group can be itself a pressure towards conforming. Groups tend to develop an identity of their own. The general nature of group pressure is to require the individual to share in this identity, to be one of the group, even if this means subordinating some part of his identity (see Box 3.3).

In simplistic terms this means conforming to the group norms, its customs and standards. Individuals have the choice of:

Complying as a matter of convenience but without real conviction (compliance);
Fully accepting the group norms (internalization);
Rejecting the norms, or the group, or both (counter-conformity).

There is good evidence that group pressure towards conformity or acceptance of norms is strong on the individual, particularly:

When the issue is ambiguous, not clear-cut;
When the individual is in prolonged physical proximity to the other members of the group;
When the individual lacks support for *his* views or behaviour.

Individuals differ in the degree to which they are affected by group pressure to conform. In particular:

More intelligent people conform less readily;
Conformists tend to be more anxious and to lack spontaneity;

Box 3.11   Group pressures for conformity

Crutchfield devised an experimental way of testing these pressures. Five subjects at a time are seated in individual booths, screened from one another. Each booth has a panel with a row of numbered switches which the person uses to signal his judgements on items presented on a screen. Also displayed on his panel are signal lights which indicate what judgements the other four members are giving to the item. No one is permitted to talk during the session.

In fact the subjects are being deceived by the experimenter. There are no electrical connections between the five panels. The signals to each individual are in fact given by the experimenter from a master panel so that he can present any combination of four choices to each individual before that individual makes his choice. The individual can then follow the majority (conform) or remain independent. In a one hour session as many as fifty items can be presented to the five subjects, items of fact or logic, opinion or attitude. Some of the general findings are:

1 When two figures, one a third larger than the others, are presented a large proportion of people will go along with a majority which appears to say that the smaller figure is in fact larger. In a sample of fifty military officers 46 per cent conformed.

2 Among the military officers not a single one, questioned privately, agreed with the statement 'I doubt whether I would make a good leader'. Under group pressure in the test situation 37 per cent expressed agreement.

3 There are large individual differences in degree of conformity.

4 Over an hour-long session some individuals grow more conforming, some grow more independent, though the overall average remains fairly constant.

5 When re-tested privately afterwards, some but not all of the conformity was reversed. The amount retained varied widely for individuals.

From Crutchfield, 'Conformity and Character', *American Psychology*, 1955

Conformists lack self-confidence;
Autonomous people conform less readily;
Conformists tend to be conventional in their social values.

In order to preserve some of his identity the individual will seek for a role in the group. There are numerous ways of classifying the possible roles. We shall list only two of them here, as illustrations.

[1]Some, following Wallen, take a behaviourist view in stating that everyone could choose between the roles of:

Friend and helper;
Strong fighter;
Logical thinker.

In fact, in any group situation, we probably opt for a mixture of all three. But we are likely to have a characteristic pattern of behaviour, whether recognized by us or not, which can be diagrammatically represented by placing ourselves within a triangle formed by putting these three styles at the assumed points, as in Figure 8. It is worth reflecting how much vari-

Figure 8

ability there is in fact in your behaviour, whether your colleagues would agree on your assessment, and whether that style is that whicht he group needs for its particular task. Most groups need a combination of all three; lacking one, they may force an individual into an unaccustomed role, as when the staff adviser finds that, as temporary leader, he has to abandon his favourite stance of 'logical thinker' and become a 'strong fighter'.

Every group needs some admixture of the three elements if it is to (a) do its task, (b) maintain itself as a group. Who provides which element will be in part determined by the organizational roles and in part by the personalities of the individual. A new form of role problem can arise:

If individuals are competing for one of the categorizations;
If an individual's behavioural role is out of line with his organizational role (e.g. staff assistant is a strong fighter).

[2]More whimsical lists include the following roles.

The comedian. He is valuable in relaxing tension, in providing a willing butt for other members of the group and in particular the chairman. When, however, the task becomes dominant the comedian is often discarded as being no longer necessary. People who are insecure often can find this role a quick way of establishing an identity within a group. It brings popularity – is threatening to no one. Unfortunately, the comedian's role is a hard one to escape from. Many people are overlooked in groups because they initially seized on this role.

The organizer. Usually taken by an extrovert character at the outset when the group is relieved that any leader should emerge. He establishes his identity within the group by becoming their spokesman or leader on anything that does not call for the presence or action of the formal leader. Physical arrangements, social activities and a lot of chore-like jobs come his way and are willingly taken on.

The commentator. Not a popular role since it involves some threat to the other members. The occupant, often clever but disillusioned, takes it upon himself to maintain an occasional commentary on the proceedings, e.g. 'By my reckoning we have now spent one hour discussing the opening paragraph of the report ...' This activity is often useful but is seldom seen to be so by the other group members.

The deviant. One way to establish one's identity is to exploit any differences that there may be between you and the group. For instance, a reputation for always asking for definitions can be exploited, sometimes humorously, to give someone an early role in a group. Others make a role out of always opposing anything. To become a common enemy is a sure way of attracting attention. Members of minority groups, Jews or Negroes or Irishmen, often use this fact to gain the role of legitimate deviant.

There are other group roles – the bully, the cynic, the politician. Eric Berne in *Games People Play* has built a semi-serious analysis of group games around role caricatures such as the Rapist, Frigid Women, etc. The names of the roles are immaterial. The point to remember is that roles allow people to acquire an identity in a group. The danger is that they then cannot change that identity. The commentator is not allowed to contribute, only to comment. The deviant is never taken seriously. A mature group allows people to switch roles and does not seek to suppress individuality in favour of group conformity, which is another way of saying that the group identity takes precedence over that of the individual.

7 Summary and implications

7.1

This chapter has introduced the concepts of role theory as a way of understanding the dilemmas and problems of individuals as members of organizations, groups and pairs. The concepts were:

Role set – the people with whom the *focal person* interacts;

Role definition as a result of *role expectations*;
Role ambiguity – unclear role expectations.

Role conflict – conflicting or overlapping roles;
Role overload – too many roles;
Role underload – too few roles.

In the organization, role problems manifested themselves in:

Individual tension;
Low morale;
Poor communications.

Strategies for resolving these problems were either:

Coping mechanisms – repression, withdrawals, rationalization;
Unilateral strategies;
Co-operative strategies.

Role stress is inherent in organizations:

It can be healthy (role pressure) or unhealthy (role strain);
It occurs mainly in management, innovative or integrative areas;
Some personalities have a higher tolerance for stress than others.

Roles are important to interactions since they provide *categories* into which we can fit data about people and make some assumptions. In seeking for role clarification we often rely on inadequate information, reject conflicting evidence, and are biased by early impressions. This can lead to:

The problem of role confusion;
The halo effect.

When interacting with individuals, separately or in groups, we continually seek for *role clarification* since lack of congruence between the role perceptions of the interacting parties will lead to misinterpretations.

In group interactions, roles are a way of protecting the individual and his identity from the undoubted pressures towards conformity exerted by a group.

7.2 The implications of role theory

Role theory is much better at explaining situations than predicting them. But, as chapter 1 emphasized, explanations lead to understanding; and understanding, even if it cannot lead to prediction in all cases, does lead to increased tolerance and, perhaps, sympathy for the individual who is the fulcrum poised between large group and small group, between work group and family group, between individual and individual.

Strain is a big factor in our society. Mental illness perhaps should not be so termed, but the symptoms of strain that are often diagnosed as mental illness are becoming increasingly common in all sectors of society. The stress of being an adolescent, of being a successful manager, of ceasing to be a successful manager, too often result in strain. The problem of society, not just of organizations, is the management of stress, that is does not become strain. Role theory is one way of looking at stress, at individuals under stress, at situations that cause stress.

Organizations and individuals need to do more to:

1 Compartmentalize roles appropriately, particularly between work and family. The involvement of the wife in the husband's work too often only creates role strain for her without relieving his. Holidays, respites after foreign travel, sacrosanct week-ends, all are ways of compartmentalizing family from work but they can only be done with the organization's consent.

2 Prepare for role transition. More attention needs to be paid to ways of learning a new role, as opposed to a new set of techniques or tasks. Successful managers tend to change positions every two years. No specific time is allocated to role definition, role expectations, or role relationships. The mere act of changing position is stressful enough. Complicate it with fostered ambiguity and stress can easily become strain.

3 Encourage the second career as a way out of the role underload problem of the sideways-shunted executive. Often, an individual can no longer contribute to an organization in proportion to his status and salary expectations. There should therefore be no implication that he cannot contribute to another type of organization or another type of work. He should be encouraged to make the big role transition from a manager to adviser, or from organization man to lone wolf, or from businessman to local government official. The alternative is security, but often accompanied by a particularly denigrating form of role underload. This role underload of the older executive is becoming an important problem for society which only the co-operation of government and organizations can solve.

4 Remember that many of the problems in organizations arise from role strain, misconceptions about role, role underload, or bad communications because of false role expectations. Often, discussion of the problem in terms of role theory clarifies it out of existence. 'There is nothing so practical as a good theory' said Kurt Lewin years ago.

So much of our time is spent in interactions, at home with our families or our friends, with colleagues at work, or strangers in the street, that it seems strange that we give ourselves or our children so little formal training in it. There is now developing a corpus of training methods in this area, but most of them focus on the operational end of interactions, the actual act of communication. Yet roles and the perceptions of roles underlie all interactions between individuals. More understanding of role perception and of the part that roles play in interactions would surely help to reduce the misunderstandings so common with all of us. This book is not the place for a complete discussion of all the aspects of individual interactions. There are suggestions in Part Three for further reading in this interesting area.

4 On Leadership

1 Introduction

Leadership as a topic has rather a dated air about it. It smacks of trench warfare and imperial administration. It implies setting one man up above another, raises spectres of élites and privileged classes. 'Why is leadership necessary?' asked a group of undergraduates. 'Surely a group of intelligent, well-meaning individuals can tackle any problem without the need for a leader?' Yet, call him chairman or co-ordinator, representative or organizer, there is a need in all organizations for individual linking-pins who will bind groups together and as members of other groups represent their groups elsewhere in the organization.

Anyone who has ever been responsible for organizing or co-ordinating the work of others, who has sought to get things done through other people, has encountered some of the problems of the management of groups. But the management of people is like driving a car or, perhaps, making love. Most of us do it at some time or other. Most of us do it at least adequately though perhaps we worry from time to time that we might do it better. But we are certainly not going to admit it openly, certainly not going to ask for lessons in it, hardly prepared to discuss it except in a jocular vein. For the management of people is something that all able-bodied men can take in their stride.

Or is it? Is leadership, for want of a better word, an innate characteristic? Are leaders born or made? Can anyone be a leader, or only the favoured few? Is there a particular trick to it or a particular style, something that, if we could learn it, would transform our lives? Are there models we should imitate, great men we can learn from? Do you have to be popular to be effective? Or is it the other way round: is it impossible to be both well-liked and productive?

Assumptions about the nature of leadership have affected not only particular institutions and organizations, but the whole design of the political system in individual countries, the design of the educational system and the management of the government. In Britain, for instance, the belief that leaders had certain basic characteristics which were given them by birth or early environment, led to a caste of leaders with educational systems geared to developing those features thought most desirable in leaders. The Second World War was probably a milestone in a continuing trend in that it demonstrated that all sorts of people from all sorts of origins and educational backgrounds could be effective leaders. The redesigned selection procedure for officers in the army was a formal recognition of this. Since this war the whole issue of leadership has been thrown wide open, with consequences for education, for admission procedures to government service, for the management of industrial enterprises.

But the scene remains one of confusion. Can anyone be an effective leader? Or are the traditionalists right and it is bred into you? The search for the definitive answers to the leadership problem have prompted hundreds of studies and as many theories, many of them seeking a justification for their view of the proper nature of society. Theorists have speculated that the secret lay in the style of the leader, or in the nature of the task and the situation or indeed in the characteristics of his personality.

Let it be said at the outset that, like motivation, the search for the definitive solution to the leadership problem has proved to be another endless quest for the Holy Grail in organization theory. There is no secret trick. But, again, better understanding of the nature of the overall problem may lead to better solutions of individual situations. This is the aim of this chapter.

Approaches to the problem of leadership have usually fallen under one of three general headings: *trait theories*, *style theories* and *contingency theories*. Each of these seems to contain some elements of truth but has always in the final analysis failed to explain enough of the difference between effective and ineffective leadership to be generally useful in a variety of situations. The theories will be briefly discussed and reviewed. A more complex, but potentially more realistic, model for understanding leadership situations will then be suggested and its implications discussed.

2 Trait theories

2.1 The findings

These theories rest on the assumption that the individual is more important than the situation, that if we can identify the distinguishing characteristics of successful leaders we shall have the clue to the leadership problem, that if we cannot *make* good leaders we will at least be able to *select* good leaders. By 1950 there had been over 100 studies on this kind of basis. Unfortunately, when looked at *en masse* only 5 per cent of the traits identified were common throughout. In part, this diversity probably reflected the differing biases of the researchers who inevitably tailored their interviews and research instruments towards the particular qualities or traits that they expected to find. In part, however, the diversity suggests that good leaders can come from a wide variety of sources, that the traits that lead to success may differ according to the situation. Most studies single out the following traits:

Intelligence should be above average but not of genius level. Particularly good in solving complex and abstract problems;
Initiative. Independence and inventiveness, the capacity to perceive a need for action and the urge to do it. Appears to correlate quite well with age, i.e. drops off after 40;
Self-assurance. Implies self-confidence, reasonably high self-ratings on competence and aspiration levels, and on perceived ultimate occupational level in society.

Recent studies in a large international company added another:
The helicopter factor. The ability to rise above the particulars of a situation and perceive it in its relations to the overall environment.

Box 4.1   A leader's prayer

Dear Lord, help me to become the kind of leader my management would like to have me be. Give me the mysterious something which will enable me at all times satisfactorily to explain policies, rules, regulations and procedures to my workers even when they have never been explained to me.

Help me to teach and to train the uninterested and dim-witted without ever losing my patience or my temper.

Give me that love for my fellow men which passeth all understanding so that I may lead the recalcitrant, obstinate, no-good worker into the paths of righteousness by my own example, and by soft persuading remonstrance, instead of busting him on the nose.

Instil into my inner-being tranquillity and peace of mind that no longer will I wake from my restless sleep in the middle of the night crying out 'What has the boss got that I haven't got and how did he get it?'

Teach me to smile if it kills me.

Make me a better leader of men by helping develop larger and greater qualities of understanding, tolerance, sympathy, wisdom, perspective, equanimity, mind-reading and second sight.

And when, Dear Lord, Thou has helped me to achieve the high pinnacle my management has prescribed for me and when I shall have become the paragon of all supervisory virtues in this earthly world, Dear Lord, move over.   Amen.

In addition most successful leaders appear to:

Have good health;
Be above average height or well below it;
Come from the upper socio-economic levels in society.

Other studies mention *enthusiasm, sociability, integrity, courage, imagination, decisiveness, determination, energy, faith,* even *virility* (Dueu).

2.2 The criticisms

In general, these theories have been criticized because:

Possession of all the traits becomes an impossible ideal (see Box 4.1);
There are too many exceptions, people who do not have the major traits but are notably successful as leaders;
If reduced to the useful minimum, the top three, they become at best necessary but not sufficient conditions, i.e. good leaders have these qualities but possession of them does not always make one a good leader;
The traits are so ill-defined as to be useless in practice.

There is, however, a danger that these very real disadvantages of trait theory may have led to its undeserved demolition in leadership studies. In practice most managerial selection schemes work on some assumed, and often unspecified, trait basis, i.e. what traits are most effective or most necessary in what conditions.

To some degree the fade-out of trait theory in favour of style or contingency theory may be a function of a democratic culture. For the implied assumption behind these latter theories is that anyone can be an effective leader provided he behaves in the right way, or at least in the way appropriate to the situation, whereas trait theories seemed to imply an élite officer corps of managerial talent who had inherited or acquired the requisite characteristics.

3 Style theories

3.1

The assumption behind these theories is that employees will work harder (and therefore more effectively) for managers who employ given styles of leadership than they will for managers who employ other styles. The styles usually compared are the *authoritarian* and *democratic* dimensions. The major differences between these styles resides in the focus of power. In the extreme authoritarian style power resides with the leader; authority for decision-making, arbitration, control and reward or punishment is vested in the leader who alone exercises this authority. In the democratic style, on the other hand, these powers and responsibilities are shared with the group in some way or other. It is commonly assumed that people will produce more under democratic conditions than under authoritarian conditions. One would like to add 'other things being equal' but not all the studies or theories do add this qualifying factor.

One theoretical base for this belief is that participation in these areas of responsibility will tend to satisfy the self-actualization and esteem needs of the individual and will therefore release more effort. Another set of theories holds that participation affects one's need for stimulation and variety in one's work, and thereby releases more effort.

3.2 A classification

Several theories of leadership style, or whole theories of management, have rested on this assumption. Often given proprietary labels to distinguish them, they can be very broadly classified under authoritarian or democratic, although their authors would rightly claim that there is more to them than that one dimension.

	Authoritarian	Democratic
McGregor	theory X	theory Y (see Box 2.4)
Likert	system 1	system 4
managerial grid	9·1	9·9 (see Box 4.3)
Ohio State studies	initiating structure	consideration

Since the words 'authoritarian' and 'democratic' can have an emotive connotation, and since the other descriptions carry the overtones of their particular creators, we shall, in this book, when wishing to refer to these styles, generically talk of *structuring* and *supportive* styles.

Box 4.2 Wishful thinking

Douglas McGregor, on leaving Antioch College, of which he had been President, said:

I believed, for example, that a leader could operate successfully as a kind of advisor to his organization. I thought I could avoid being a 'boss' . . . I thought that maybe I could operate so that everyone would like me – that 'good human relations' would eliminate all discord and disagreement. I couldn't have been more wrong. It took a couple of years, but I finally began to realize that a leader cannot avoid the exercise of authority any more than he can avoid the responsibility for what happens to his organization.

Box 4.3

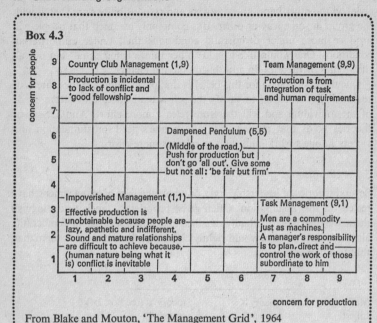

From Blake and Mouton, 'The Management Grid', 1964

3.3 The evidence of style theories

There is evidence that supportive styles of leadership:

Are related to subordinate satisfaction;
Are related to lower turnover and grievance rates;
Result in less inter-group conflict;
Are often the preferred styles of subordinates.

There are also many instances where supportive styles of leadership were found to be associated with higher-producing work groups. But:

1 On average, over all the studies, the productivity differential has only been 15 per cent – a figure well below what some theorists would lead one to expect.
2 It has been suggested that it could be more effective working that leads to (or permits) more supportive styles – i.e. the causal relationships might be the other way round than that supposed.
3 Experimental studies, where the style of leadership has been deliberately manipulated as an experimental variable, have failed to reproduce the evi-

dence on improved productivity. Out of six available studies, four report no difference in productivity between the styles, one reports the structuring style to be more effective and one reports the supportive style to be more effective.

4 It has been shown that some people prefer to be directed and structured – in particular individuals with low needs for independence and in cultures where participation with the leader is not 'legitimate'.

5 In repetitive or routine work, a structured style of leadership leads to higher productivity in the short term, although usually accompanied by lower morale. (It is arguable, but unproven, that this lower morale will eventually lead to reduced productivity.)

3.4 The conclusion

The research findings suggest that style alone is not the answer to effective leadership, nor indeed would many of its principal prophets today maintain that it was. However, there are good indications that, where the psychological contract encourages it, a supportive style of management will lead to a higher degree of contentment and to greater involvement with the work group. This is not necessarily the cause of higher productivity but it is a good base to build on. Overall effectiveness, however, is clearly dependent on more than style alone. Hence, what are called *contingency* theories.

Box 4.4 Intelligence levels and leadership style

The effects of leadership style and members' intelligence upon 'group performance' in Twenty Questions game.

Intelligence of members	Leadership style	Median number of questions asked per problem	Problems solved (%)
bright	supportive	15·5	100
bright	directive	18·5	87·5
dull	supportive	31·0	37·5
dull	directive	24·5	75·0

From Calvin et al., 'The effect of intelligence on group problem-solving behaviour', *Journal of Social Psychology*, 1957

4 Contingency theories

4.1

Contingency theorists take more specific account of the other variables involved in any leadership situation, in particular the task and/or the work group and the position of the leader within that work group.

4.2 Fiedler's theory

Fiedler, in particular, concentrated upon (a) the relationship between the leader and his group, and (b) the structure of the task, as determinants in the choice of the most effective style of leadership. His conclusions are interesting. After looking at leadership situations in a wide range of organizations he found that a structuring style was most effective when the situation was either very favourable to the leader or very unfavourable. When the situation was only moderately favourable then the supportive style worked best. By 'situations favourable to the leader', Fiedler meant situations where:

(a) The leader was liked and trusted by the group;
(b) The task to be done was clearly laid down and well defined;
(c) The power of the leader in respect to the group was high, i.e. he could reward and punish and had organizational backing.

Of these the leader–group relationship (a) was, in Fiedler's view, the most important. His findings are, in general, in agreement with much practical

---

Box 4.5 The psychologically distant manager

Fiedler has shown that the leaders of more effective groups, when evaluating subordinates, indicate that they maintain greater psychological distance between themselves and their subordinates than do leaders of less effective groups. The explanation for this appears to be that a manager cannot properly control and discipline subordinates if he is too close to them emotionally: likewise if a manager is emotionally dependent on a subordinate.

An ingenious technique has been developed for measuring psychological distance. The manager is asked to rate his most preferred and least preferred subordinates on various psychological traits. The greater the difference between these two ratings, the more psychologically distant the manager was considered to be. Thus the psychologically distant manager (PD manager) rejects those with whom he cannot work easily while the

Box 4.5 – *contd*

psychologically closer (PC manager) is more tolerant of his subordinates, or he accepts or rejects subordinates on some criterion other than his ability to work with them. It has been suggested that the PD manager 'has many acquaintances, but few friends: he likes to be with others but he does not want to become emotionally dependent on them'.

Fiedler has shown in his study of the management of small consumer co-operatives that the PD manager was a 'task specialist'.

1 The PD manager tended to be considerably more role-oriented in his dealings with superiors and inferiors.

2 The PD manager saw himself as a professional administrator who held regular staff meetings with his inferiors.

3 The PD manager demanded and got considerable freedom from his superiors.

In contrast the PC manager was more of a 'human relations' specialist.

1 The PC manager saw his job primarily in terms of ensuring smooth inter-personal relations with his superiors and inferiors.

2 The PC manager had a strong trend to close informal ties with people. Some of the attitudes which Fiedler found characteristic of PC managers suggested a need of dominating and possessing people.

3 The PC manager held few formal meetings.

The PD leader is effective in achieving greater productivity from the group only when he is informally accepted by the members of the group. If this condition is not met, then the group will not 'listen to' him and he cannot influence their behaviour. In conclusion it can be stated, subject to the above qualifications, that PD managers are more efficient on task problems and that in contradistinction to PC managers they tend to formalize role relations.

Fiedler illustrates this emphasis on the task and the formalizing of the role

... by the experience of one airforce officer in command of an air base who systematically varied his psychological distance from his chief subordinates. When he had very close relations with these officers, they seemed to feel secure and they did not worry overly about the efficiency of their units. As soon as he became more reserved and role-oriented, his sub-commanders began to worry whether anything had gone awry, they became less sure of their standing in the organization, and channelled their anxieties into paying more attention to their work. As a result, there was a noticeable increase in the efficiency of the base.

Summarized by Kelly in 'The organizational concept of leadership', *International Management*, 1970

experience. When the task is clearly defined and the leader strong and well-respected he is expected to get on with the job and to be fairly directive. When the task is ambiguous and he is in a weak position *vis-à-vis* the group his best strategy is still to be directive or structuring – to involve the group would then be seen as total abdication of leadership. On the other hand an ambiguous task confronted by a respected leader calls for a more supportive approach, if he is to draw out from his group all the contributions they can make. Fiedler's general conclusion is that organizations could do much more to help the individual leader by either (a) structuring the task, or (b) improving the formal power *vis-à-vis* his group, or (c) changing the composition of the group in order to give the leader a more favourable climate to work in. He suggests that this approach is perhaps more practicable than hoping for the leader to adapt himself to changing circumstances.

4.3 In conclusion

Fiedler's contingency approach to leadership is useful. Apart from anything else, it is good to be reminded of the situations in which a structuring style is effective. However, the reality of leadership situations is more complex than even Fiedler would have it.

5 The 'best fit' approach

5.1 A description

In any situation that confronts a leader there are four sets of influencing factors that he must take into consideration:

The leader – his preferred style of operating and his personal characteristics;
The subordinates – their preferred style of leadership in the light of the circumstances;
The task – the job, its objectives and its technology.

These three factors and their fit will in their turn all depend to some extent on:

The environment – the organizational setting of the leader, his group and the importance of the task.

The 'best fit' approach maintains that there is no such thing as the 'right' style of leadership, but that leadership will be most effective when the requirements of the *leader*, the *subordinates* and the *task* fit together. This fit can be measured on a scale that runs from 'tight' to 'flexible'.

tight   flexible
_____

There is no fixed measuring device for this scale – it is a low-definition subjective tool of analysis. The suggestion is that the three factors in any situation can be roughly placed along this scale. For instance:

tight   flexible
_____

leader   ——
subordinates   ——
task   ——

In this situation you have a leader whose preferred style is fairly structuring, working with subordinates whose preference is to have more control over their work, on a task which is loosely defined with no tight time parameters. In this situation the task and the subordinates 'fit' but the leader is out on a limb.

In any situation such as this there will be a tendency for the three factors to move towards each other along the scale. If they remain too far apart

---

Box 4.6 Morale, productivity and popularity

Irving R. Weschler, Murray Kahone and Robert Tannenbaum of the Institute of Human Relations, University of California, Los Angeles, collaborated in a study of the effect of leadership on job productivity and morale.

Two divisions – A and B – of the same scientific department in a naval research laboratory were studied. Division A consisted of twenty-eight members; division B, of thirty-eight. The leaders of the two divisions differed in their style of leadership: 'Division A ... was headed by a brilliant young scientist, who directed the division along restrictive lines. Division B was headed by an older man, a fatherly type, who directed his division along permissive lines.'

All members of these divisions were asked (a) to rate the level of productivity and of morale of their own work group, of their division and of the laboratory as a whole; (b) to specify their choices for research and administrative leaders of their division and their choices for best-liked person. Morale and productivity were rated on five-point scales which ranged from 'very high' (scale value 1) to 'very low' (scale value 5).

Seven members of the top administrative staff of the laboratory who were familiar with the two divisions then appraised the level of job satis-

Box 4.6 – *contd*

faction, morale and productivity of the two divisions. The following table shows the ratings by these seven superiors and the ratings by the division members themselves.

| | Productivity | | Morale | |
Division	Superiors	Members	Superiors	Members
A	2·71	3·22	3·43	3·42
B	2·86	2·37	2·00	1·95

In the view of the superiors, Division A, with low morale, was doing a better job in productivity than Division B, and a better job than the low-morale members gave themselves credit for. The permissively led group, B, with high morale, overrated their productivity when checked by the ratings of the superiors.

The sociometric data, summarized in the following table, show that the leader of division A was chosen as a competent research worker (in 39·3 per cent of the choices), but was not perceived as a good administrator and was not liked. The members of division B made a much smaller percentage of choices outside their division for 'best administrator' and 'best liked' than did division A. This finding is further evidence that the permissively-led division was more cohesive and integrated than the restrictively-led division.

Chosen persons	Best researcher (%) Division A	Division B	Best administrator (%) Division A	Division B	Best liked (%) Division A	Division B
division head	39·3	15·8	7·2	26·4	0·0	31·6
other	39·3	50·0	71·4	57·8	92·8	52·6
unspecified	21·4	34·2	21·4	15·8	7·2	15·8

The permissive leadership of the older scientist promoted higher morale than did the restrictive leadership of the brilliant younger man, but did not result in greater productivity. Morale and productivity do not necessarily go hand in hand.

From Weschler, Kahone and Tannenbaum, 'Assessing organizational effectiveness: job satisfaction, productivity and morale', in Tannenbaum, Weschler and Massaryk, *Leadership and Organization*, 1961

the group will cease to function as a group or the task will not get done. In the situation described above a powerful leader will often pull the subordinates and the task towards him as far as he can. In the process he may breach the psychological contract with his subordinates and impair the optimum performance of the task. Alternatively he may adjust his style to the requirements of the other two factors. Whether he can do this without losing credibility will depend on the organizational setting – the environment. Before analysing any further the way this scale works let us look in more detail at the three factors.

5.2 The three factors

The leader. For the leader tight or flexible can be interpreted as structuring or supportive. His preferred place on the scale will depend on:

1 His value system. To what degree does he feel that subordinates should be involved in planning, deciding, controlling? How does he *in general* define a leader's job? How much importance *in general* does he give to organizational efficiency, subordinate satisfaction, personal success?

2 His confidence in his subordinates. If he feels that they are technically competent and can be trusted he is more likely to give them control over the work.

3 His habitual style. Though most people hope that they can be flexible they usually have a way of operating in which they feel most comfortable – this becomes their habitual style.

4 His assessment of his personal contribution. If he feels that his contribution to the group is vital he will tend to want to be more structuring and controlling.

5 His need for certainty. A leader who relinquishes control of a situation reduces the predictability of the outcome. If he has a high need for predictability, a low tolerance for ambiguity, he will tend towards the 'tight' end of the scale. Similarly, a low risk-taker will be less willing to relinquish control.

6 Degree of stress. Stress and tension will usually lead to a tighter style.

7 Age. Older men seem to be more structuring.

These forces in the leader will often conflict with each other. However, the net result will be to place him somewhere along the tight–flexible continuum in relation to a particular group. This will be his personal starting point in considering any particular task or objective. The degree to which he is able to move from that point on the scale will be considered shortly.

Box 4.7   Leadership and popularity at school

Hargreaves has vividly described the life and culture of the fourth-year pupils in downtown Lumley Secondary School. In particular there was a wide difference between the A and C streams. The A stream was the academic, hard-working stream, C the anti-academic, anti-school stream where the academic pupil was a deviant, delinquency the norm and the main aim was to 'have fun'.

One of the principal values of this group was fighting ability. The boy with the greatest fighting ability was given the title 'cock'. Clint was able to maintain this position by his swaggering, threatening display as being 'hard' or tough and by the lack of challenge to his supremacy from other boys. Being the cock, Clint exercised the most influence. But although this fighting ability gave him social power, it did not elicit liking from other boys. Most boys secretly disliked him. Other resources were required for this second dimension of status and these Clint lacked. Indeed, his cold vindictive personality and his arbitrary aggressive outbursts alienated the boys who succumbed to his influence, for to do so would be to incur his hostility. They were influenced through fear. Thus, Clint's power, unlike that of Adrian, can be regarded as coercive and illegitimate. His followers expressed this by calling him, though not to his face, a 'bighead'. Had he been challenged and beaten in a fight, the others would have been glad. Unfortunately, the only potential pretender to the title of cock was Don, who being the sociometric star of the lower streams, was aware of the difficulties in being a popular cock and never issued a challenge. It was thought that Don could beat Clint in a fight. Clint seems to have thought this too, for he scrupulously avoided antagonizing Don.

Adapted from Hargreaves, *Social Relations in a Secondary School*, 1967

The Subordinates. Their preference for a particular type of leadership (structuring or supportive) will be influenced by:

1 Their estimate of their own intelligence and competence. The more competent and professional they feel the more control they will normally want.

2 Their psychological contract with that group and that leader. Does the contract specify involvement or is it a satisficing contract?

3 Their interest in the problem and their view of its importance. They will not want lots of involvement in trivia.

4 Their tolerance for ambiguity or their need for structure.

5 The past experience of the group. Have they been used to involvement? Are they used to working together and do they have respect for each

other's competence? New, inexperienced or distrustful people tend to need structuring leadership at the start.

6 Cultural factors. Younger people, more highly educated and perhaps more permissively reared, tend to want more involvement. Democratic norms in most societies reinforce this tendency. People in creative situations (R and D, and marketing) tend to want more responsibility for their own work.

The task. Should it be programmed and structured or should it be left open-ended? This will depend on:

1 The kind of task. Is it decision-making or implementing? Does it require initiative or obedience? Is it a routine administrative function? Is it creative (e.g. R and D), or problem-solving (e.g. consultancy), or pioneering (e.g. new product marketing)? In general if it is a problem with an open-ended solution it will tend towards the flexible end of the scale. Closed or finite problems tend towards the tight end.

2 The time-scale. Participation takes time. Short time-horizons drive one towards the tight end of the scale.

3 The complexity. This can go either way. Technical or conceptual complexity will usually push the task towards the flexible or open-ended portion of the scale. Organizational complexity will push it to the structuring or tight end.

4 Do mistakes matter? (a) In a creative or problem-solving task the more brains the better – but such involvement will take time. A more structured approach may be less perfect or less creative. Does a 60 per cent solution matter? Or is it desirable? (b) In an executive or controlling function tight controls may be necessary to prevent any possibility of error, e.g. in the manufacture of manned space rockets.

5 The importance of the task. Unimportant tasks do not merit time or attention, i.e. should be tightly structured.

5.3 Analysis of the 'fit'

For any given situation the three factors should be plotted very roughly along the scale tight–flexible. In practice this will normally be done by the leader himself, and one must recognize that his analysis is likely to be biased. The aim of all analysis is to remove bias and substitute objectivity. Clearly the more objective the leader can be, the more useful will be the analysis.

In many situations there will not be a perfect fit. To some degree one can generalize about the nature of the misfits:

1 In many middle-management situations the comparative youth and high educational level of both manager and managed pushes their preferred styles towards the supportive or flexible end. But in many such situations the task requirements, as they are normally defined, are for structure and tight control mechanisms.

2 Top management, on the other hand, is inclined by age and by middle-management task experience towards the tight end of the scale, but is confronted by open-ended problem-solving tasks which need a more flexible approach.

3 Sales executives, developed in a job with a fairly high degree of structure and control, and promoted to posts of marketing responsibility with numbers of staff marketing experts reporting to them, often find the new and more 'flexible' requirements of task and subordinates a big challenge to their habitual style.

4 The effect of technology and computers is often to tighten up the job in order to achieve better predictability. This can be at variance with any wish for more flexibility on the part of men or management.

5.4 Achieving the best fit

Confronted with a lack of fit the leader must consider which of the three factors to adjust in order to achieve a fit. Theoretically, it is easiest for him to alter his own style – particularly if the other two factors already have a degree of fit between themselves. This explains why there is emphasis on *leadership style* in literature on the subject.

However, although the leader's style is theoretically the easiest to alter in the short term, there are often long-term benefits to be achieved from re-designing or re-defining the task (e.g. job-enlargement) or from developing the work group.

5.5 The environment

The fourth element, the *environment* must now be considered. The leader, his subordinates and the task do not occur in a vacuum. The setting of the situation will have a big bearing on the degree of freedom which the leader has to adjust any of the three factors. There are six key aspects of the environment:

The power position of the leader in the total organization;
The relationship of the leader to his group;
The organizational norms;
The structure and technology of the organization;
The variety of tasks;
The variety of subordinates.

These aspects of the environment can best be considered in pairs:

The power position of the leader in the organization;
The relationship of the leader and his group.

These two elements – two of those considered by Fiedler – are best regarded as conditioning the freedom of the leader to adjust his style and the task. Variability in leadership style can lead to unpredictability and to lack of confidence, credibility and trust in the subordinates unless the leader is already trusted and respected by them. Power based on expertise and achievement gives the leader more freedom than purely legal power. Most organizational tasks are not isolated tasks – they have some impact on other parts of the organization. The re-definition of any task, in terms of time-span, complexity, scope or implication will therefore require the ability of the leader to negotiate this re-definition with the affected parts of the organization. Hollander coined the phrase 'idiosyncrasy credit' to explain a leader's degree of freedom. If the leader has piled up lots of credits with the group (for conformity in the past, for success, for status) he can spend them on deviant behaviour. If, on the other hand, he has no credit then he has nothing to lose by doing the unexpected or unwanted and everything to gain if he makes it work. It is the leader in the middle, with middle status with the group, who has to be careful and conform to the group:

The organizational norms;
The structure and technology of the organization.

A leader is never completely free in an organization to behave as he would want to behave. There are organizational requirements, such as hours of work, reports and returns; and organizational norms, such as methods of reward and punishment, mode of address to subordinates. Neil Rackham and his colleagues, for example, discovered that in the U.S. division of one corporation effective leaders were expected to be critical of their subordinates, whereas in the U.K. there was no such expectation. Conformity to these organizational norms is to some degree required of all managers and supervisors, particularly those low in position power in the organization. Organizations also have formal structures and procedures. Not only does this mean that work cannot easily be re-defined in isolation but re-definition of work may involve a change in the structure of the organization. Decentralized or project-type organizations allow more scope for individual managers to redefine their style and task but decentralized organizations are not possible in certain technologies (e.g. process manufacturing):

Variety of tasks;

Variety of subordinates.

Most managers find that the task of achieving a best fit is complicated by two further factors:

(a) They have a wide variety of tasks to perform, ranging from complex long-range assignments, through more intangible tasks such as building a team or developing subordinates, to the day-to-day routine. The best fit for each task may well be different. To manage variety through adaptability requires a very good relationship with the group but,

(b) the membership of work groups is constantly changing, partly because the actual work group may be re-defined for differing purposes (one committee for this, another for that) and partly because individuals move in and out of groups as their lives and careers progress.

Given this complexity, it is understandable if managers give up the attempt to find a best fit and merely impose their habitual style upon the task and the subordinates.

The emphasis in the literature of management theory upon the importance of group relationships is at least partially justified in that an individual leader's ability to adapt is very largely governed by his relationship with his group. Given the changing nature of that group he needs to allocate a considerable amount of his managerial energy to building the required relationship.

The 'building of a relationship' is often seen as a supportive 'style' when it can perhaps be better described as a base for a flexible style.

Thus, one set of studies concluded that the basic dimensions of leadership are:

Support – behaviour that enhances subordinates' feelings of personal worth;

Interaction facilitation – behaviour that encourages members of the group to develop mutually satisfying relationships;

Goal emphasis – behaviour that stimulates a desire for excellent performance;

Work facilitation – such activities are scheduling, co-ordinating and planning resources.

6 The problem complicated

6.1

So far this chapter has looked at the leader in his role as mobilizer and activator of groups. This is how the problem of leadership is normally viewed. But this is, unfortunately, an over-simplification of the role of leader. His job is more complex – he also has the roles of *ambassador* of the group and *model* to the group.

6.2 Ambassador

As ambassador he represents the group to people and groups:

(a) above him in the organization;
(b) horizontally connected with his group.

The effectiveness of his group will be very largely determined by the way the leader performs his role as ambassador. There is a human tendency to interpret all data in the light of its source. If the leader conveys to those above him an impression of a group that is responsible, keen and effective most data will be interpreted in that light. As a result:

1 He will be left alone. An interesting study of managerial succession in an automobile plant is described in Part Three. It appears to demonstrate the effectiveness of a more supportive managerial style, but the success of the new manager was undoubtedly helped by the fact that, unlike his predecessor, he was trusted by senior managers and allowed to develop his own ideas without interference.
2 He will find it easier to get required resources – in the way of finance, people or facilities, often in competition with other groups in the organization.

It is naïve these days to regard organizations as composed of isolated groups arranged in some hierarchical descending order. The horizontal interactions are usually more numerous and more important. The ability of the leader to represent his group and to negotiate arrangements and solutions that are fair and equitable but that do not unduly constrain his group will contribute very largely to the effective working of the group. A study by Petz has shown that groups where the leader was seen by his subordinates to have more influence with his superiors, tended to be the more effective groups.

In general, a leader's ambassadorial role consists in representing his group and in filtering out the organizational strains so that the internal workings of the group are facilitated.

6.3 Model

A leader is a model. A large amount of learning in life takes place through modelling. As young children we have our models thrust upon us in the form of our parents. A part of adolescence consists in the search for new models. Organizational learning is only partly technical or intellectual. A considerable part involves the individual finding relevant people to use as models. The leader of his group is in a position slightly analogous to that of a parent. He is the most obviously available model, to be accepted or rejected as such by his subordinates. Maturity perhaps implies having no further need of models but if that be so it comes to most people fairly late in life. Meantime the importance of group leaders in management development is not so much the time they spend on performance appraisal with their subordinates but rather the degree to which they are regarded as desirable models by those subordinates.

The conscientious developer of men will often be less successful in training good subordinates than the manager who spends no formal time on such activities. If nature seems unfair the answer lies in modelling. The latter manager could well be the more effective model in that organization.

We cannot avoid the role of model once we have any importance in the world. Since modelling is thrust upon us it would be well for us to consider what forms of behaviour, what attitudes and values, we represent. If we are seen as effective then these behaviours and values will be imitated, if ineffective they will be shunned. Either way we influence behaviour.

7 Summary

This chapter has reviewed the main theories on leadership and suggested a more integrative way of looking at the subject.

The approaches reviewed were *trait theories*, *style theories* and *contingency theories*. The approach suggested was an extension of the contingency theories called *best fit approach*. This approach requires that the style preferences of the *leader*, *subordinates*, and the demands of the *task* be ranged along a scale from *tight* (or structured) to *flexible* (or supportive).

The suggestion is that for effective performance the requirements of the three factors have to 'fit' together on the scale. The way the fit is achieved, i.e. which factors will adapt or be adapted, will depend on *the environment* (or organization setting) which includes:

The power or position of the leader;
The relationship with his group;
The organizational norms;
The structure and technology;
The variety of tasks;
The variety of subordinates.

In addition the leader has two roles – *ambassador* and *model* – which are vital to the effective performance of his group. The leadership of groups or divisions is a vital part of organizational effectiveness but results in role complexity, incompatibility, conflict, ambiguity, and therefore stress. To help manage this complexity there are things that:

Organizations need to know and understand;
Organizations need to *do*;
Individuals need to *do*;
Individuals *and* organizations need to *do*.

These *desiderata* are spelt out in the next section.

8 General conclusions on leadership

8.1 The desiderata

The modern trend in organization theory has been to play down the importance of the individual and the group leader in favour of things like structure, control systems and climate. Later chapters in this book will however suggest that trends in these areas are beginning to highlight once again the importance of the individual as an 'integrator' or a 'linking-pin' or a 'catalyst'.

Whatever words are used, the leadership of groups within organizations is always going to be a vital ingredient in the effectiveness of organizations. The discussion in this chapter should have made it apparent that the role of leader is a complex one, riddled with ambiguity, incompatibility and conflict. The analytical model should make the complexity more understandable though it will not always make it more resolvable. For that to happen:

1 Senior managers need to develop a better understanding of the complexity of the role of group or divisional manager. Lack of understanding can lead to stereotyping which in turn can lead to a unified set of models for leaders in the organization, often based on narrow 'trait' definitions. Better understanding of the complexity and variety of leadership situations should lead to better differentiation between situations and leadership requirements.

2 Senior Managers need to help individual leaders to reduce the complexity of their roles by:

(a) Clearer role definitions;

(b) Creating less variety in the composition of the work groups;

(c) Allowing more freedom to individuals to pursue a style different from the norm. One of the hardest tasks of management is to allow your subordinates to behave in a different style from yourself;

(d) Judging effectiveness by ends not means, i.e. by performance and not by style;

(e) Giving an individual time to produce results, i.e. not moving him every eighteen months.

3 Individuals need to learn to:

(a) Live with the complexity of the role, i.e. handle the role incompatibility and conflict with a co-operative strategy;

(b) Adapt their behaviour to the role requirements;

(c) Build up the trust and respect of their group so that they have the essential conditions to allow them to adapt their style to the contingency requirements;

(d) Remember that successful performance of their ambassadorial role is essential if they are to have freedom to behave as they think best within their group;

(e) Remember that they represent the organization to their subordinates and should practise all the precepts enjoined on the senior managers (above).

4 Individuals and organizations should bear in mind that the individual who meets the above requirements will tend to:

(a) Have high tolerance for ambiguity and be good at handling open-ended problems;

(b) Be good at differentiating – between people and between situations;

(c) Have a clear self-concept which will tend to go with self-confidence;

(d) Have a high reservoir of the 'E' factors, in particular, energy;

(e) Be prepared to set moderately high standards for himself and his co-workers and to give and receive feedback on performance.

8.2 The differentiated trait approach

All this adds up to what might be called a differentiated trait approach to leadership. For although the personality and style cults have been overthrown in favour of a more complex model, all experience tells us that there are, nevertheless, individuals who are in general better leaders than others. Research is beginning to suggest that it is those who have the characteristics listed in the previous paragraph, because those are the kind of people who can handle the complex model described in this chapter.

In particular situations, particular characteristics or particular styles will be effective because they will be appropriate. In that sense almost everyone can be an effective leader by finding the circumstances that suit him.

Organizations can also do far more to fit the job to the man and so make better use of their available talent.

But organizations will always have a need for the 'manager', the leader who is effective in a variety of situations. They need criteria for selecting them. The criteria listed above will provide a starting-point. They have affinities with the early traits of intelligence, integrity and helicopter factor – but are capable of more precise definition and measurement and can be related to the requirements of particular situations. The criteria will be altered or added to in each organization depending on its culture (see chapter 7) and its particular leadership requirements. In one part of one organization, Rackham and his colleagues found that the desired characteristics included:

Checking that people understood communications;
Giving specific objectives;
Admitting when things are not going well.

8.3 In conclusion

How can individuals improve their leadership abilities? How can organizations help them to do so? This will be discussed in more detail in a later chapter. The characteristics listed in 8.1 cannot be taught in the classroom. To some extent they will be there, or not be there, by the time the individual reaches maturity and joins the organization. Early environment and education clearly have a lot to do with them. The individual and the organization can, however, build on what is already there. The only effective way of doing this is to:

Place the individual in situations, real or artificial, where the principal characteristics will be tested;
Help him to understand how these characteristics could be improved, by particular examples.

This will involve the organization in:

Devising 'leadership learning' situations, even if this distorts the short-term efficiency of the organization structure;
Paying more attention to the 'coaching role' in organizations. It is unrealistic to leave this to the immediate superior since the 'coaching role' and the 'leader role' are not easy ones to combine. Under pressure the coaching role is too easily forgotten or postponed in favour of the decision-making role. Someone other than the immediate superior can often be more objective and more helpful to a junior struggling in a leadership

situation. Perhaps this 'uncle role' needs to be more formally recognized and legitimized in organizations.

Box 4.8   Two leaders

Think of two individuals you have known whom you would describe as successful leaders. Write a short description of each, then answer the following questions:

(a) What did they have in common?
(b) In what did they differ?
(c) Were there any features of the situation that should be taken into account?
(d) Were there any features of the task that need to be considered?

Does this analysis support or contradict any of the suggestions of this chapter?

---

5 On Power and Influence

1 Introduction

Motivation theory, role theory, leadership theory are all ways of describing why people behave as they do and how it is that others can set them to behave as they do. It is time now to look at this problem in a more general way, at the overall problem of power and influence.

Power and influence make up the fine texture of organizations, and indeed of all interactions. Influence is the process whereby A modifies the attitudes or behaviour of B. Power is that which enables him to do it. Organizations can be looked at as a fine weave of influence patterns whereby individuals or groups seek to influence others to think or act in particular ways. If we are to understand organizations we must understand the nature of power and influence for they are the means by which the people of the organization are linked to its purpose. Yet they are unfashionable words, words that we shun in daily discourse. Perhaps because they imply levels, one man over another. Yet we recognize that hierarchies are inevitable in groups or societies of any size at all. Perhaps because power and influence in some way implies the infringement of some individual's freedom over his actions. But if so then only the ostrich among us can survive modern organizational life with his ideals of individual freedom intact. Complete individual freedom is the perquisite of the hermit and the recluse; today perhaps only the solitary artist or poet, the tramp or the hippie can enjoy that luxury. For part of any psychological contract with any group, family, firm or society is an exchange of some individual freedom in return for the rewards of belonging. All interactions, Homans would maintain, involve an exchange of something for something in return. But how much individual freedom should one give up? And how defined, in what areas? Who shall influence me, and whom shall I influence? Which methods will be tolerated, and which will not? What ways are there of resisting influence, what of gaining it? These questions lie bedded in the true reality of organizational life. Anyone who would wish to understand organizations must try to deal with them.

The power to influence is something that most people would like more of, in some respect, even if they do not want the responsibility that may go with it. Thus, many research studies show that individuals in organizations would like more influence over their work. There is also some evidence that the man who feels he exercises influence gives more of himself to his job, takes more interest, is more involved. The responsibility of influence creates a stake in success or failure – even to the extent of illness. (More managers tend to have psychosomatic disorders than workers.) Likert has shown that groups where individuals feel they each have more influence tend to be more productive.

I have distinguished between power and influence. Not everyone does so in ordinary life. When people talk of having influence they mean, in my terminology, having the power to influence. This confusion between influence and potential influence can cause a lot of misunderstanding in ordinary conversation. We will therefore always distinguish here between *influence* (an active process) and the *ability* to influence or *power* (a resource).

If A is to influence B he must first have some understanding of B, of his motivation calculus, his psychological contract, his role. Only then can he know what things are likely to influence B. These we have already explored in the early chapters. He, A, must then understand what methods of influence are available to him in that situation, and the sources of power that underlie them. This is the immediate concern of this chapter. The particular exercise of influence that is involved in the formal leadership of groups was discussed in chapter 4. But formal leadership is only one aspect of individual influence, only one expression of an influence system in an organization. Individuals, in any role, in any organization, have some power, some capacity to exert influence. When we speak of argument or persuasion, threats or blandishments, love or hate, we are talking of individual influence. When we talk of group pressure or conformity, socialization or propaganda, education or development, we are talking of organizational or group influence.

The study of influence and power has proved to be for social scientists 'a bottomless swamp' (Dahl). There are many piecemeal studies of various bits of the field – it is hard to pull them together into any coherent picture. This chapter will attempt to do just that. First we shall describe various *sources of power* which underlie the *methods of influence*. The use of any particular method of influence will involve *implications* about the individuals involved, the situation and the response mechanisms. Two particular aspects of influence will then be discussed: *socialisation* and *attitude change*.

2 Power as a source of influence

2.1

There have been various categorizations of power in social or organizational settings. The one used here is a variety of that proposed by French and Raven. The possible sources of individual power which give one the ability to influence others are physical power, resource power, position power, expert power and personal power.

Before describing these particular sources of power there are some general considerations which we shall need to bear in mind throughout the discussion.

1 The relativity of power. If A's power source has no salience for B then that source of power is ineffective in that situation: A will have no ability to influence B. The group that overawes one man with its prestige and renown looks ludicrous to another. The guns that silence one will only stimulate another. Bribes will sway some but repulse others. The effective amount of power that anyone has will constantly ebb and flow as the constituency in which it is exercised changes its membership.

2 The balance of power. Most influence situations, most relationships, come to that, are balanced on a power equation. Power is seldom one-sided. Even the prisoner can hit back. The power to disrupt, for instance, or 'negative power' as it is termed later in this chapter, is always available in some form to everyone. Power seems most blatant and most extreme when the power equation is most unbalanced. It follows that the possession of a power source does not automatically mean that you can influence someone. It depends on what power he can put into the balance, remembering always that one type of power can offset another. Money has been known to overrule expertise.

3 The domain of power. Few sources of power are universally valid over all constituencies. Many of the arguments and haggles about power in organizations are to do with the domain of a particular power source. Individuals wish to extend the scope of their own power, to limit the scope of others' power. When we speak of someone's power or influence as legitimate we mean that the domain has been prescribed, the conditions under which and over whom it can be exercised have been laid down. But we do not always wait for official sanction. Custom is a strong legitimizer, since power is often regarded as legitimate until challenged. Once challenged the effect may not be to destroy that power but only to constrict the domain. The computer expert, at one time the organizational wizard,

has over the years had his domain progressively restricted although his expertise has seldom been called in question.

2.2 Physical power

This category of power is self-explanatory. It is the power of superior force. The bully or the big man has it. The tyrant or the commander of the army has it. In many developing nations physical power is ultimately more important than the will of a majority of the people. Prisons and the enforcement of law rest ultimately on physical power. For, of course, in order to be effective as a basis for influence physical power does not have to be used. Its existence, or the belief in its existence, is enough.

In few work organizations is physical power the source of any individual's influence. Ultimately no organization, save those supposed guardians of public safety, the prisons and some mental hospitals, have the right to detain an individual by force. Some schools may claim the right, a few pupils question their headmaster's physical power, but most adult organizations are in essence organizations which the individual is *physically* free to leave.

This is not to deny, however, that in individual transactions the threat of physical coercion may not seem temporarily a very potent source of influence. Bullies are not confined to schools. Picket lines have often held a distinct element of coercion in their attitudes. The physical presence of a dictatorial boss can often seem like coercion to his quavering subordinates. Whilst physical power is less respectable in our society than all other power sources there are signs that it is increasingly becoming the power of last resort when the other sources appear ineffective or too closely balanced against opposing sources. Ulster, lock-outs, mass demonstrations are all examples of this phenomenon.

2.3 Resource power

Possession of valued resources is a useful basis for influence. Reward power is another term for it, preferred by French and Raven. It is the power source implicit in most calculative contracts. For resource power to be effective (a) there must be control of the resources, and (b) those resources must be desired by the potential recipient. (These are rather obvious conditions but ones not always remembered.) For instance, in union negotiations if the union negotiator does not have control (i.e. cannot commit or withdraw the labour of his members), or if his resources are not desired by the employers (i.e. there are other sources of labour) then he will have very reduced power. The union movement's attempts to create labour monopolies are simply an effort to increase their resource power. Govern-

Box 5.1 Perceptions of the bases of authority in three public service organizations

Bases of authority	Police department (%)[a] (N = 33)	Welfare office (%)[b] (N = 23)	Elementary school (%)[c] (N = 20)
Authority of legitimacy			
Generalized legitimacy	12	9	10
Law, state legislation, city ordinances, the state, county, city	15	17	15
Administrative codes, rules, regulations, manuals	0	17	0
Governing boards, policies of board	0	0	10
Authority of position			
Top *external* executive or executives, organization as a whole	0	17	15
Top *internal* executive, ranking officers, administration as a whole	27	13	30
Immediate supervisor	9	39	0[d]
Inherent in position or job characteristics	30	26	15
Authority of competence			
Professional or technical competence, experience	15	22	45
Authority of person			
Personal characteristics or way in which authority is exercised	42	13	15
Other sources	6	4	0
No source specified	18	22	15

[a] Percentages total more than 100 per cent because some respondents indicated more than one base of authority

[b] The category of 'top *external* executive' included the chief executives of the parent organizations; for example, the county manager, director of public welfare, city manager, and school superintendent

[c] The category of 'top *internal* executive' included the police chief, the district director, and the principal

[d] Coded as 'top *internal* executive' in the case of the elementary school

From Peabody, 'Perceptions of organizational authority', *Administrative Science Quarterly*, 1962

ments' attempts to match this with the ultimate threat of legal enforcement of physical power is an interesting but perhaps unresolvable conflict between two types of power, the resource power of organized labour and society's ultimate sanction of physical imprisonment. A manager often has resource power to the extent that he can give promotion or pay increases to his subordinates. If the subordinate does not want promotion the manager may find himself in the position of the harassed father whose bribe of ice-cream is met with the rejoinder, 'I don't like ice-cream today!' The codification of pay, the bureaucratization of promotion – as in teaching institutions, civil service departments, hospitals – is an effective reduction in the power of the individual manager since it reduces his control over these desired resources.

Resources do not have to be material. They can consist, for instance, of grants of status, the equivalent of a key to the executive washroom. Belonging, the admission to a select group, is another valued resource to many people. But one must beware of overrating the attractions to others of the things one values oneself. A friend's attempt, in undergraduate days, to form an exclusive dining-club, foundered when no one else saw it as exclusive. The kind of exclusivity over which he had control was not valued by anyone else. Power is always relative to the constituency in which it is exercised. Resource power is not usually popular. People do not like to be reminded that they can, in effect, be bought. Paternalistic organizations are sometimes surprised when their occasional bountiful distributions receive only grudging thanks. Maybe without meaning to, they are seen to be needlessly re-emphasizing their power base.

2.4 Position power

This has been called 'legal' or 'legitimate power'. It is the power that comes as a result of the role or the position in the organization. The occupancy of a role entitles one to all the rights of that role in that organization. The manager is by right allowed to order people to do so-and-so. The inspector is by right allowed to inspect other people's work. When theorists distinguish between power and authority, position power is usually equated with authority as being legitimized power, or power residing in the position rather than in the individual.

The value of position power as a source of power depends ultimately on the value placed on the guarantor of the position. Position power has to be ultimately underwritten by either physical power or resource power. If the occupant of a particular role either (a) does not receive backing from the organization, or (b) the organization is not seen as controlling any desired or coercive resources, then the occupant of the position will find that his influence attempts will fail, because his power source is invalid. The occupant of a position, it should be made clear, does not himself have to have resource power, but the organization guaranteeing or establishing that position has to have it. The secretary of a voluntary organization, a post which is unpaid and of not very high status, will have position power but only to a limited degree. Once the guaranteeing power source is withdrawn the position power is minimal or illegitimate or both. The ambassador of a deposed government turns into a dispossessed citizen. The chairman's secretary is just another person when the chairman is deposed.

Position power gives to the occupant potential control over some *invisible assets*. Principally these are:

1 *Information*. A flow of information often belongs as of right to a 'position' in the organization. If it does not already belong it can often be originated as a necessary input to that position. This can be horizontal information, i.e. information, often of a technical nature, from the same level of the organization: vertical information, from above or from below but potentially trapped in the particular 'position' and to be dispersed with the agreement of the occupant. Information, above all else in life, seems to display the essential features of synergy. The whole is so often much more meaningful than the sum of individual parts. An informational jig-saw, even though all the pieces are separately available, is nothing until put together. A 'position' can be, or can be made to be, simply by function of its position, a junction-box for information.

2 *Right of access*. A position gives its occupant the right of access to a variety of networks. Some networks are of course informal, or professional, and membership depends on 'expert' or 'personal' power. But many organizational networks are initially recruited from the occupants of specified positions. Most committee memberships, for instance, are *ex officio*. This right of access not only leads to more information, the other invisible asset, but also lends propinquity. It is hard to apply influence without access to the bodies to be influenced. The right of access to individuals and to networks is an indispensable invisible asset.

3 *The right to organize*. As will be seen later under the discussion of ecology as a method of influence, the way in which work is organized, the physical and social environments, the flow of communication, the right to decide, these factors are all potent ways of influencing behaviour. The occupant of a position has this right should he choose to exercise it and regard it as a hidden asset.

It is not, therefore, without reason that titles and places on organigrams are so valued in organizations. Status has only a small part to do with it.

Official positions in bureaucracies carry with them these hidden assets. Organizations that like to do away with organigrams and formal position descriptions have usually very good reasons for doing so. It must be recognized, however, that they are eliminating one potent type of power within the organization. The fact that the assets accruing to a position are unspoken of and therefore largely invisible should not detract from their potency. Indeed some writers (e.g. Pettigrew) regard them as principal power resources. I feel it easier to classify them as potential assets that stem from position power. The word 'asset' is used because assets are still potentially productive whether or not they are activated. The invisible assets of position power do not, of course, have to be activated to make them exist.

Box 5.2 Machiavelli's thoughts on a choice of power

From this arises the following question: whether it is better to be loved than feared, or the reverse. The answer is that one would like to be both the one and the other; but because it is difficult to combine them, it is far better to be feared than loved if you cannot be both. One can make this generalization about men: they are ungrateful, fickle, liars, and deceivers, they shun danger and are greedy for profit; while you treat them well, they are yours. They would shed their blood for you, risk their property, their lives, their children, so long, as I said above, as danger is remote; but when you are in danger they turn against you. Any prince who has come to depend entirely on promises and has taken no other precautions ensures his own ruin; friendship which is bought with money and not with greatness and nobility of mind is paid for, but it does not last and it yields nothing. Men worry less about doing an injury to one who makes himself loved than to one who makes himself feared. The bond of love is one which men, wretched creatures that they are, break when it is to their advantage to do so; but fear is strengthened by a dread of punishment which is always effective.

The prince should nonetheless make himself feared in such a way that, if he is not loved, at least he escapes being hated. For fear is quite compatible with an absence of hatred; and the prince can always avoid hatred if he abstains from the property of his subjects and citizens and from their women. . . .

So on this question of being loved or feared, I conclude that since some men love as they please but fear when the prince pleases, a wise prince should rely on what he controls, not on what he cannot control.

From Machiavelli, *The Prince*

2.5 Expert power

Expert power is the power that is vested in someone because of his acknowledged expertise. It is, for many, the least obnoxious of the sources of power. In a meritocratic tradition people do not resent being influenced by those whom they regard as the experts. It is, furthermore, a power base that requires no sanctions. The specialist departments of an organization, if acknowledged to be expert, will find their suggestions or instructions readily implemented. Only if their expertise is questioned will they have to fall back on other sources of power to implement their wishes. Too often the personnel departments of organizations are forced to rely on position or resource power when their expert power proves to be unrecognized. For expert power is hedged about by one major qualification; it can only be given by those over whom it will be exercised. This is not to say that you cannot claim expert power for yourself in some field, and have your claim recognized. But until that claim is recognized, explicitly or implicitly, the power will not really be yours. Because this power source is the most socially acceptable it is also the most sought after and will bring out many spurious claimants. Their bluff, if bluff it is, may well work, but if discovered the dethroned expert will find that he has created a credibility gap that may well contaminate future attempts to claim expertise for himself.

Expert power is comparative – anyone is an expert who knows more than anyone else around. This works both ways. It means that even a small differential in expertise can give one man great power over his fellows if that expertise happens to be in great demand. But it also means that he will lose all his power to another arrival if that other has even a small degree of further expertise. In the country of the blind the one-eyed man is king – until he with two eyes comes.

2.6 Personal power

Sometimes called *charisma*, sometimes popularity, sometimes sociometrically central. This power resides in the person and in his personality. It can be enhanced by his position or by his expert status, so that a Prime Minister loses some of his charisma when he leaves office, and the sports star fades when dropped from the team. For charisma is brittle. It is elusive, is fanned by success and by self-confidence and can evaporate in defeat. Like expert power, personal power only comes from those who will be exposed to it, from beneath it in a sense. Because it is tied to the individual rather than to a position, a role or a block of resources, personal power is much sought after. Many a manager will attribute his degree of influence to his charisma rather than to his position, only to be disillusioned when, having been removed from his position, he finds that no one invites him to meetings, consults him or seeks him out.

2.7 Negative power

It is necessary at this stage to point out that all of these sorts of power can be used both legitimately and illegitimately. If used in the agreed manner in the agreed constituency, i.e. in its appropriate *domain*, the power is regarded as legitimate. If used contrary to accepted practice or outside the domain the power is regarded as disruptive and illegitimate. We shall call this the *negative* use of power.

Negative power is the capacity to stop things happening, to delay them, to distort or disrupt them. The clerk who sorts the incoming mail has little power to initiate, but he can misdirect, mislay or destroy important documents. His power to block or distort, his negative power, is quite out of proportion to his position. On a higher level, staff people in organiza-

---

Box 5.3   The case of the missing factory

Jim was only 29 but he was the envy of many of his friends. His job, in the Head Office of a large international organization, carried the title of Manufacturing Co-Ordinator – Mediterranean. Under 'Mediterranean' fell all the countries that bordered that sea, including France and Italy, all of them with their own companies, reporting to Head Office in London, and most of them with their own manufacturing facilities.

What Jim did not tell his friends outside the organization was that he was not permitted to visit any of these countries and that his formal job description defined his authorities as 'Approval of incidental expenses up to a limit of £10.' Jim, in fact, in spite of his grand title, was essentially a post-box in the Head Office organization, with the processing of and occasional analysis of, incoming manufacturing problems, and proposals from the Mediterranean countries. Decisions were taken from above him in the organization and he was never involved, rarely consulted.

One day, when life had been particularly tedious and unexciting, Jim received from the Italian company a proposal for a large new integrated factory in southern Italy. He decided to test his powers. Without consulting anyone he sent back the proposal to the Italian company asking for further details and raising some questions. In due course they replied. He queried some of their responses and asked for their comments on possible political implications. In all, it was six months before Jim felt obliged to pass on the factory proposal to those above him, but with the proposal went six months' worth of supplementary information. Jim had thoroughly enjoyed exercising his role as filter. Did he do well?

tions tend to be used as expert filters. Filters have a lot of latent negative power: they can cease to filter, or filter arbitrarily. All subordinates are, in a sense, gate-keepers to their bosses. They screen out information and activities, they do completed staff work and operate under management by exception. All this means that the boss only sees what they want him to see. They have a high degree of latent negative power.

Negative power is latent; it does not operate all the time. It operates at times of low morale, irritation, stress, or frustration at the failure of other influence attempts. The disgruntled bus conductor on a rainy evening who allows no more passengers on to a half-full bus is activating his negative power out of resentment against his employers or the world or his wife. Successful, high morale organizations see little negative power. Discontented, low-utilization (e.g. role underload) organizations bring out negative power. The use of negative power breeds lack of trust by the superior for the subordinate. The superior then sets up checking procedures and alternative information channels to thwart the use of negative power. This is seen by the subordinates as job diminution and further provocation to activate his negative power!

In one of its aspects negative power is the ability to filter or distort information, instructions, or requests from one part of the organization to another. At an extreme it is the ability given to even the meanest of employees to throw a wrench into the assembly line or to fuse the computer. It is this power latent in all positions that allows individuals and groups of individuals to exert influence laterally and upwards in organizations. The distortions that result from the exercise of negative power have much to do with the politics of organizations, to be discussed in chapter 8.

3 Methods of influence

3.1

These bases of power allow one to use one or more methods of influence. These methods of influence can be usefully divided into two classes: *the overt* and *the unseen*. Although attention has been paid to the sources of power by social scientists not much description has been recorded of the influence methods, particularly the unseen ones. A rough table will relate the methods of influence to the sources of power.

Power source:	physical	resource	position	expert	personal
(Overt methods):	force	exchange	rules and procedures	persuasion	
(Unseen methods):				ecology	magnetism

These will now need to be described in their turn.

3.2 Force

This is the crudest of the methods. It derives from physical power or, occasionally, from resource power. A applies force, or the *threat* of force, to influence B to do what he wants him to do. Physical bullying, hold-ups, armed raids, are examples of force. Whole systems, such as some prisons or concentration camps, are based on force as a method of influence. Individual instances of force are found in business or government organizations but they are rare, are usually related to a particular individual, and tend to be short-lived. The supervisor who threatens physical force, the boss who loses his temper, the strike leader who hints at violence in the picket lines, are all relying on force. But though the immediate effects are usually very satisfactory to A, who is doing the influencing, the longer term fall-out is sufficiently damaging to make it a tactic of last resort in situations of any permanency. In other words, if you are not going to see the person again, and are big enough, bullying will get you what you want. Economic force, or the threat of economic force, is a little more common. It is found in some Union situations, or, with individuals, when one person is totally dependent on another. Sometimes concealed as exchange influence, the effects of economic force are the same as for physical force, effective and short-lived.

3.3 Rules and procedures

A vast amount of influence in our society, from childhood to old age, is exerted through *rules* and *procedures*. A can influence B to do something by laying down a rule that the something must be done by all people in B's position. It need not necessarily be an influence attempt on B specifically, but on all people in B's position (e.g. nobody may smoke in the factory). Alternatively it is used as an indirect way of influencing B personally by implying that it is a genuine, all-embracing, rule and not A trying to impose his will on B. If A is going to use rules and procedures he must have:

The perceived right to institute these rules and procedures;
The means and will to enforce them, i.e. the appropriate power base.

Without these two provisos the influence attempt will fail, as many parents of adolescents have found. Rules and regulations therefore derive largely from position power, backed by resource power. Experts, however, in functional organizations, can well give expression to their wishes through a series of rules or required procedures. Provided that the power source is adequate this is a very acceptable method of influence.

Michel Crozier has argued, and demonstrated in a study of some French organizations, that the way to increase one's power in an organization is to circumscribe your opponent with rules and regulations whilst retaining the maximum degree of uncertainty relating to your own position. This is a tactical use of influence which will be discussed under politics in chapter 8, but it is one example of the use of rules and procedures as a method of influence.

Their usage does not, however, always have to be so blatantly political. Provided that the appropriate power base exists this is a very efficient way of getting B to do X. In the majority of cases B is not going to make an issue out of following a procedure. Few people revel in constant petty decisions. It is usually called inefficiency. Rules and procedures are one very sensible way of reducing the number of one-off decisions. Rules protect liberty as well as restrict it. Rules sanction behaviour as well as prohibiting it. Rules are in themselves non-evaluative. They are a convenient way of influencing behaviour.

3.4 Exchange

Call it bargaining, negotiating – even cajoling or bribing in some situations. A agrees with B to give him something in return for desired behaviour. Sweets to a child, tips to the dustman, promotion to the executive are obvious examples. Less obvious, but perhaps more common, are friendship and favour, inclusion in a group, approval and status. Exchange methods can follow from any power source, depending on what is offered. But resource and position are the most frequent bases.

If exchange methods are going to work A has to offer something that B desires, and the payment has to be worth the effort or expenditure. Obvious perhaps, but too often the exchange is only implicit not explicit and the expectations of B are unreal and he is destined to be disappointed. Homans and other exchange theorists would argue that all influence can be regarded as an exchange transaction. Homans suggests that in every transaction there are rewards and costs. A gives something (maybe help) to B. In return B gives gratitude or respect. Ideally both parties make a profit, i.e. both parties give something they can well afford (advice or respect) and get that which they desire more (respect or advice).

Exchange methods very often, like incentive theories of motivation, are self-cancelling. Once the reward for certain desired behaviour has been paid that transaction has been completed. The new bargain then often becomes 'A will withdraw the reward if B does not continue the behaviour'. This is still an exchange method of influence but one that is much less pleasing to B who may see it either as rules and procedures or, ultimately, as economic force.

Exchange methods, if based on correct assumptions about the individual to be influenced and if made explicit, can be very effective in the short term. They do, however, carry some longer term implications, since the 'rewards' get progressively less desired by the recipient as he gets more used to them. Thus, again like incentive schemes, the exchange gets more and more highly priced until, ultimately, a bargain may be impossible.

3.5 Persuasion

The least value-laden of the methods of influence – this method relies supposedly on logic, the power of argument and the evidence of the facts. It is the preferred method of influence of most people and is usually the method of first resort. However, in practice, it nearly always gets contaminated by one of the other methods. A manager who genuinely attempts to reason with a subordinate may not be heard as persuading but as telling, i.e. using rules and procedures as a method of influence.

The arguments advanced in any cause gain most of their validity and much of their weight from their source. Therefore the evaluation of the source by the recipient is a vital part of any assessment of persuasion as a method of influence. Expert or personal power, acknowledged, it will be recalled, by the recipient, are the foundations for this method. Like all other methods, it is only as strong as its sources.

These four – force, exchange, rules and persuasion – are the most obvious, or overt, methods used to get another to do something. Many of the leadership issues can be explained by the typology thus far. A leader whose power is based only on his position will be wise to maintain a psychological distance from his subordinates and to adopt a fairly formal style based on rules and regulations. Democratically elected leaders, or those appointed with the support of their group, can assume that they have some degree of expert power and can therefore safely resort to persuasion, or participation, methods of leadership. Dictatorial styles will be effective, even if not enjoyed, when the leader owns the outfit or has effective control over the allocation of rewards, i.e. has resource power. Good teachers, with recognized expert power, can afford to be more liberal and relaxed than bad teachers who have to rely on rules upheld by the authority of their position.

But there remain two ways of influencing people which are not normally discussed under the heading of influence because they are, in a way, unseen and unperceived. Nevertheless they are very effective and the first in particular, *ecology*, is a method available to, often neglected by, and sometimes abused by, every manager.

3.6 Ecology

Ecology is the study of the relationship between an environment and its organisms. As politicians are discovering in the wider context of government we neglect ecology at our peril. So with the ecology of the organization, or the relationship of the environment to individual behaviour or attitudes. Behaviour and attitudes occur within an environment, a physical, a psychological, a sociological environment. That environment has its effects upon them. For instance, in the physical environment we know that:

Noise tends to impair performance on complicated tasks;
Variety relieves monotony, provides stimulation and contributes to improved performance;
Seating patterns tend to affect interaction patterns;
Open-plan offices are popular and improve communications when the work is routine;
Segregation prohibits communication;
Dangerous surroundings increase tension and lower productivity.

In the psychological and sociological environments, we know for instance that:

Small groups are easier to participate in than large groups;
Specific, challenging but attainable targets tend to produce commitments irrespective of their specific content (people can get committed to morally unacceptable tasks for this reason);
Increased interaction leads to increased sentiments – either favourable or hostile;
Participation increases commitment if the individual considers participation worth-while and legitimate.

All behaviour takes place in an environment. To ignore the influence of the environment is implicitly to accept constraints and conditions, to take a negative decision about influence. To adjust the environment in order to remove constraints or facilitate some aspect of behaviour is indirect influence. The understanding of ecology is necessary to an understanding of behaviour. The use of ecology is a powerful means of influencing behaviour, or at the very least, of allowing other methods of influence to work. To call ecology 'manipulation' is to libel it. It is powerful because often unrealized, only if abused does it become manipulation. This book in a sense is a guide to the ecology of organizations. The design of work, the work, the structure of reward and control systems, the structure of the organization, the management of groups and the control of conflict, are all ways of managing the environment in order to influence behaviour. Let us never forget that although the environment is all around us, it is not unalterable, that to change it is to influence people, that ecology is potent, the more so because it is often unnoticed.

This idea of ecology, or environmental control, as a method of influence is unusual. It is more normal to think of influence as a direct interaction between A and B, with A and B being either groups or individuals. Most behaviour, however, in organizations is conditioned more by the way things and people are organized than by the more obvious forms of influence. Much of this we know is not deliberate conditioning. People do not create large committees in order deliberately to cause frustration. Assembly-lines were not designed to cause apathy. Autonomous groups in R and D laboratories were not designed as a deliberate attempt to promote commitment. At least not usually! The environment is often created for other reasons and is accepted by most of us as one of those so-called 'facts of life'. It is not, however, unalterable. One can change behaviour by changing the environment, changing the way in which things are done as well as the physical and social atmosphere. The practitioners of O.D. (organization development) talk of improving the 'climate' of organizations. They refer to the human climate – one aspect of the environment. Chapter 7 describes the different cultures of organizations and how these cultures encourage certain types of behaviour.

The suggestion of this chapter is that attention to the way things are done, ecology, is one way of eliciting desired behaviour from individuals. To a very large extent, ecology consists in seeing that environmental aspects *do not prevent or obstruct normal behaviour*. Participation takes time. If you want it you must allocate the time. Mini-jobs promote apathy. If you do not want apathy you must enlarge the jobs. If you want innovative behaviour, set selection criteria that capture innovative people. Conflicting objectives bring conflicting groups. If you wish to remove a principal cause of conflict the responsibilities must be so re-arranged that objectives do not conflict. On an opposing tack, responsibility is only effective if all the information is available. If you wish to curtail someone's responsibility the easiest method is to cut off information.

The concept of ecology is similar in many senses to what two famous writers on organizations, March and Simon, have called the 'vocabulary' of the organization. By this they mean things like the structure of communication, rules and regulations, standard programmes (e.g. for stock control or material purchasing), selection and promotion criteria. This 'vocabulary' forms the premises for decision-making and is, they claim, easier to change than the process of decision-making itself.

In short, ecology sets the conditions or premises for behaviour. Inattention to ecology will make things difficult if not impossible. Similarly ecology can be used to create impossible conditions for other people, if you are so minded. Before you plant an azalea you check that the soil and climatic conditions are suitable. Similarly the manager in an organization will check the environment before he acts. If unsuitable for his purpose he will alter it, using, in general, those hidden assets of position power, the right to organize, the right of access, and information.

But just as the weather is only a subject for conversation in poor climates, so ecology is often only mentioned when it does not work:

'The fact that the division was spread over seven counties accounts for the lack of co-ordination';
'Putting two groups on the same site with no indication of overall ranking was bound to result in conflict';
'Separate car-parks for production and marketing certainly created a "them" and "us" feeling from the first day at the new site';
'With a committee of fifteen when only two were needed, of course there was frustration'.

It is a pity if ecological considerations are only taken into account after the event rather than before. The size of the group, the facilities, the time available, the method of decision-taking, are all within the scope of the manager to change, no matter how weak his power base.

3.7 Magnetism

The invisible but felt pull of a stronger force, *magnetism*, is the application of personal power. We have all felt, at some time, the perhaps illogical, often inexplicable, attraction of an individual, the desire to work with and for him whenever he called. Not easily measurable by social scientists and therefore more frequently mentioned in novels than in textbooks, this way of influencing people cannot be ignored. Since it depends on personal, or sometimes expert, power, it is very much, like beauty, in the eye of the beholder. Most open to abuse, because perhaps it has no obvious mechanism, it is the favourite method of demagogues, some salesmen, guerrilla leaders and faith healers.

Magnetism, however, has its other aspects. We are often influenced by someone not so much because of his personality but rather because we trust or respect him. Such a man does not have to persuade us, or to give us rules. We will follow him and be pulled towards him, because we are convinced of his ability, or of his principles, or of his loyalty to us. This pulling power, this magnetism of trust can stem from expert power at least as frequently as from personal power, for we will trust those whom we dislike if we respect their competence.

Empathy, the feeling of being pulled towards someone because you share the same views or convictions, because you suffer with them or rejoice with them, is another manifestation of magnetism. In its strongest form, that of love, it can influence people to abandon rationality.

Love, though not unknown, is infrequently found in organizational relationships. But the other aspects of magnetism, the unseen drawing-power of one individual, are found all the time. Trust, respect, charm, infectious enthusiasm, these attributes all allow us to influence people without apparently imposing on them. The invisibility of magnetism is a major attraction as is its attachment to one individual. Each of us in some way is a magnet to someone, but the magnetism is unique, special to ourselves.

All the aspects of magnetism stem from particular sources of power, usually personal or expert power. Magnetism is therefore only as effective as its sources, to increase it we must work on those sources, to maintain it we must be careful to nourish those sources. Trust, for instance, is easily fractured by one false step, and hard to mend – like a pane of glass.

4 Implications

4.1

Where does this leave us? What are the major lessons to be learnt from this categorization of methods of influence and sources of power?

4.2 The choice of method

Anyone contemplating, or involved in, a process of influence needs to reflect upon his source of power, and thence the range of methods of influence that it suggests. In particular he needs to remember that the source of power, and the method of influence, will depend as much on the individual recipient and his perceptions as on the person applying the influence. The perception of the individual will be very largely coloured by the nature of his psychological contract with that group.

In a coercive environment, expert power is of little avail. Calculative contracts are good for those whose power is based on resources or position. In a co-operative environment expert or charismatic power works best and position power is less effective. Thus in a voluntary organization (co-operative) the secretary is useful but has little influence. In consultancy firms (usually co-operative), expertise is valued more than length of service. In Universities (co-operative) the experts, the faculty, have a lot of influence. The administrators with only position power have little influence. Hospital administrators might sympathize, as they see their position power outflanked by the expert power of the consultant.

A prophet is without honour in his own country, the expert often without influence in his own family because his power base has changed. The prophet has exchanged expert power for nothing, the expert position power and expert power for resource power (money and affection). Professional men, one has noticed, often have very undisciplined children. Whether it be educationally sound or not is one matter, the reason for it often lies in the nature of influence. In their working lives professional men are used to relying on expert power, or using persuasion as their preferred method of influence and finding it effective. In the family situation they have no expert power. Reasoning and argument seem not to prevail. They are reluctant to invoke physical power, resource power, or parental position power and, therefore, find themselves without influence and baffled by their recalcitrant families.

There are two general considerations underlying the choice of a method of influence:

1 *Credibility*. The relativity of power has already been stressed. Your power source, under normal circumstances, is only as good as it is believed to be. This applies totally to expert and personal power. It applies partially to the other sources. If you have to demonstrate your resource power you have probably already failed to use its latent ability to influence. Credibility comes from many sources: a record of prior success, the reports of respected colleagues. A lot of credibility credits can stem from one's observed behaviour, e.g. a willingness to see what is important or salient in the situation for the other party, or evidence that your objectives are consistent with theirs, or a low-key, low-threat approach. These will all enhance your credibility.

In any situation one should ask oneself how many credibility credits one has with that particular constituency and to what power sources do they pertain, remembering always that what works in one constituency may not work in another. The Nobel Prize-winner may have little credibility in the factory, however influential he may be in the laboratory.

2 *Multiplex or Uniplex*. A relationship which has only one strand in it is usually weaker than a multi-strand one. The lawyer who only sees his client in a formal legal situation can only relate to him in that role. If he is a friend as well, or a colleague in another venture, the relationship will be harder to break. Similarly an influence attempt backed by more than one sort of power is likely to be harder to resist. The specialist who relies only on his expert credentials without establishing any personal rapport with

his line counterpart will find his attempts at persuasion that much more difficult.

4.3 The individual response to influence

The recipient of an influence attempt can always reject it, ignore it or rebel. But if we accept it, we have in some way to justify to ourselves the fact that we have been influenced. We have to reduce the dissonance between what we are now doing and what we would, uninfluenced, be doing. The individual recipient of influence responds to influence assuming it is effective, in psychologically different ways. There are three psychological mechanisms for adjusting to influence:

Compliance;
Identification;
Internalization.

1 *Compliance*. The recipient agrees to the influence attempt because it is worth his while to do so. Force, rules and procedure and some exchange methods will usually result in compliance.

The implication of compliance is that the individual is doing what he is doing because he has to do it. The onus for seeing that he does what he is supposed to do remains with the initiator of influence.

2 *Internalization*. The recipient adopts the idea or proposal as his own, he internalizes it so that it becomes one of his possessions.

3 *Identification*. The recipient adopts the idea of proposal because he admires or identifies with the source, the initiator of influence.

Each mechanism carries some consequences in its train. The outcome of influence cannot be predicted without some understanding of the likely response mechanism at the other end.

Compliance. If you have the necessary power source, you can usually make sure that your attempt at influence is accepted. It will be accepted because the recipient acknowledges your power, but it will be accepted grudgingly since the act of acceptance is seen as a denial of his choice. If the influence is received freely, then the psychological adjustment mechanism will be either identification or internalization. Compliance always implies 'has to'. It may well be that the individual would have accepted the influence willingly if he had had the choice; it is the implicit denial of that choice from the outset that produces the grudging nature of the acceptance. Compliance therefore has its advantages for the person with power. It is reliable in the short term (if his assessment of his power source is correct), and it is usually quick. The impatient father enforcing his instructions with 'because I say so' is going to get his way and soon, but with compliance rather than internalization. The manager who uses his position to enforce his preferences on a subordinate will be obeyed, but probably reluctantly. For the costs of compliance as a way of responding to influence are clear enough. Firstly, the order or request will be carried out grudgingly, with less than full commitment. Secondly, some mechanism must be available to back up the influence, if necessary. Influence attempts which assume compliant responses need maintenance. Those attempts which rely on identification or internalization are self-maintaining – if they succeed. Compliance and trust do not go together, compliance and checking do. Internalization and identification imply choice on the part of the recipient, the right to reject as well as to accept. Compliance carries no such implication. Often a manager will start off by using persuasion or some form of magnetism in an attempt to influence and hope for a free and accepting response. When his attempt is rejected he will fall back on position or resource power and ensure that his views are adopted. The result will be compliance, meaning lowered commitment and no guarantee that what he wants to happen will continue to happen unless he enforces it.

In many parts of organizations, choice, or the right to reject an idea or request, cannot be admitted without the possibility of chaos. Fair enough, but the inevitable outcome will be compliant responses to orders, rules and requests, meaning lowered commitment and the need for maintenance or checking.

Identification. This is the most pleasurable to the person exerting influence. It is nice to be identified with, to exert magnetism, or even to have your group or its task exert magnetism. But such magnetism has to be maintained; it can too easily disappear. More importantly, identification makes the recipient of influence dependent on the source of magnetism. Dependency is nice but it carries responsibilities and costs. The source of magnetism becomes indispensable, thus reducing flexibility. The dependent person is also more inclined to obey than to initiate (charismatic leaders are often surrounded by followers rather than by other leaders). Identification, therefore, while attractive to the individual exerting influence, is not usually favoured by the organization. Commando leaders, in organizations, while often very effective, tend to be regarded as a glamorous nuisance because their magnetism has resulted in identification and thus reduced flexibility. They have made themselves indispensable to the effective performance of their group.

Identification with a group or a task carries the same problems. It is a very effective form of commitment, but change the group or the salience of the task, and the commitment will vanish. Identification does not maintain itself. Initial enthusiasm for a project can evaporate. The magnetism will need constant re-charging.

Internalization. This is the form of commitment most desired by organizations. It is commitment that is self-maintaining and independent of the original source of influence. But it is the hardest to obtain and takes the longest time. In addition, if internalization is truly desired, then no pressure must be put on the individual to accept influence. He must be totally free to argue about it and even to reject it if he is to regard it as his own. If he is *forced* to accept it, his response, whatever he may say, will really be one of compliance or identification. If the source of influence is respected or liked, the individual will respond out of goodwill for that source (identification); if the source is not respected but can enforce the influence, the response will be compliance. Since organizations cannot always spare the time for full discussion or easily tolerate individuals independently rejecting influence, it is not common to find internalization responses except at the highest levels.

Internalization also means that the individual recipient of influence adopts the idea, the change in attitude or the new behaviour, as his own. Fine. He will act on it without pressure. The change will be self-maintaining to a high degree. But he will also tend to believe that the change was his idea and no one else's. He will in a sense deny that influence took place. This matters not at all in terms of the desired result, but if you are the person exerting influence it is remarkably hard to let the recipient take all the credit for himself. The successful psychotherapist is the one whose patients all believe they cured themselves – they internalized the therapy and it thereby became truly an integral part of them. Consultants suffer much from the dilemma of the psychotherapist – the problem of internalization. If they wish the client to use the right solution with full and lasting commitment then they must let him believe it is *his* solution. But in that case they won't get the credit – or the goodwill. Commitment through identification is more profitable for consultants, and staff experts. The report is stamped with their name and they lend their prestige to support it. Internalization is as hard for a boss to endure as it is for a consultant, but it's better for the organization.

Internalization, then, is the most lasting. Identification is the most pleasant. Compliance is the quickest. But each has its costs.

Interestingly, ecology, being indirect or unnoticed, is a method of influence that requires no response mechanism from the recipient. Should he, however, suspect that he is being deliberately manipulated, should ecology be uncovered, then he is likely to see ecology as concealed force and to respond with the compliance mechanism. But most ecological mechanisms are not seen as deliberate manipulations. Groups have to be organized in some way, meetings chaired, offices sited, tasks defined. To ignore ecology is stupid, to boast about it is folly.

Box 5.4   The grasshopper study

'Too nice is too easy'

Army reservists undergoing training at an Army Reserve centre were asked by Smith under the guise of a study of survival in emergency situations, to eat grasshoppers. They were told by the experimenter, who was introduced to them as someone doing research for the Army Quartermaster, that in the 'New Army' small units would have to be more mobile and possibly live off the land more. Therefore the researchers were going to find out 'what your attitudes and reactions are towards an unusual food that you might have to eat in an emergency. This food is grasshoppers.'

All subjects were given a pre-questionnaire, which included an attitude scale on their liking for grasshoppers as food. Then with half of the subjects the experimenter acted in a friendly, warm, permissive manner throughout the experimental period (the positive communicator condition). He smiled frequently, referred to himself by nickname, sat on the counter, said that the subjects could smoke if they wished, that they should relax and enjoy themselves. The other half of the subjects (the negative communicator condition) were treated throughout in a formal, cool, official manner. The men were ordered rather than requested; they were told that they could not smoke; the experimenter never smiled; he stood in a stiff pose and replied in a sharp manner to all questions.

After the subjects in both conditions had been induced to eat at least one grasshopper (encouraged by the offer of 50 cents) they were permitted to go ahead and eat as many as they liked. Subjects in the two conditions ate on average almost exactly the same number of grasshoppers. After eating they filled out the attitude questionnaires again.

It was found that the subjects in the negative communicator condition showed more increase in liking for grasshoppers than those in the positive communicator condition. This seems to show that the more negative the characteristics of the influencing agent the greater the dissonance between active and earlier attitudes and the greater the pressure to change one's views.

Adapted from Smith, 'The power of dissonance techniques to change attitudes', *Public Opinion Quarterly*, 1961

5 Two applications of influence

5.1 Socialization

Socialization is the process by which an organization seeks to make the individual more amenable to the prevalent mode of influence. It can best be described by listing its principal forms:

1 *Schooling.* Formal instruction in the history and traditions, in the language and the technology, in the practices and the structures of the organization. Schooling (often titled 'induction programme' or 'training') usually takes place within the organization but can be done outside if required on a large enough scale, or if the individual organizations are too small. Medical and Law Schools are examples of extra-organizational schooling, although they link it to apprenticeship.

2 *Apprenticeship.* The individual is assigned to another individual or small group of individuals to learn their skills, their values and to acquire, if possible, their judgement and expertise. It is found particularly in craft industries or in occupations where the skills cannot easily be written down but have to be learnt by supervised practice. Merchant banks, consultancy organizations, commodity trading firms today practise apprenticeship in an informal way.

3 *Co-option.* Individuals are made members of progressively inner groups in the organization. Because of the desirability of the in-group (see the discussion on territory in chapter 8) the individual adapts his behaviour and attitudes to resemble those of the desired group. By the time he becomes a member he is likely to be fully in tune with the names and customs of the group; since he prizes his membership he is likely to want to continue their names and customs.

4 *Mortification.* The individual is harassed, deprived of his identity and forced into conformity by punishment, obloquy or ridicule. Those who get through will tend to feel close identity with the norms of the institution and will seek to enforce them themselves. (An example of mortification is provided in Box 5.5.)

Most organizations use a mixture of all four methods, but usually one will predominate. If the preferred method of influence is rules, regulations, or exchange then schooling will be the most appropriate. But where, as in medicine or law, there are values and standards to be acquired, apprenticeship must be included. If the preferred method of influence is force then mortification will be most appropriate; if magnetism is the prevailing method, apprenticeship will be found more suitable.

Box 5.5   Socialization in a military academy

Experience in the Coast Guard Academy starts with the suppression of former affiliations. The new cadets, called swabs, are not allowed to leave the base or to interact with outsiders. All swabs wear the same uniform. They are not permitted to receive money from home, and discussions of family background are taboo. This initiation produces a low-status peer group, without any outside sources of prestige.

The cadet is subject to two sets of rules; the 'regulations' and the 'traditions'. One function of the regulations is to punish violation of the traditions. This is done by labelling any offence against the traditions as a breach of the regulations. The traditions are norms enforced by peers, or by student superiors, rather than by instructors. Although described as 'unwritten rules' they are presented to new cadets in writing in the orientation manual. When there is a conflict between the regulations and traditions, the traditions win. For example, when a swab violates the regulations by carrying out the orders of an upperclassman, and receives demerits, the upperclassman continues to excuse him from other official rule violations until his demerit account has been balanced.

The form classes in residence at any one time constitute a hierarchy, with the first class having almost complete control over the rest of the students and the classes in the middle having the responsibility (for so it is defined) of harassing, called hazing, the swabs. The first class insists that hazing takes place and has the power to enforce this demand on the other classes by giving demerits. In the face of the unpleasant and protracted experience of hazing, swabs develop very strong peer-group sentiments, some of which interfere with the programme of classroom instruction. For example, if a cadet is unable to answer a question addressed to him, no other member of the class will answer. Together with the system of hazing and its *prescribed* infractions of the regulations goes a system of fraternization, which amounts to a *prescribed* violation of the traditions. This fraternization, whereby the hazers apologize for the aggressiveness they are compelled to display towards the swabs, is one element in the development of officer solidarity. Other elements are orientation to a common career and stereotyped antagonisms towards enlisted men, reservists and civilians.

Adapted from Dornbusch, 'The military academy as an assimilating institution', *Social Forces*, vol. 33, 1953

In all these instances we have defined the initial mode of socialization, but co-option will increasingly become used in all situations as the individual rises to the top of an organization where his values and norms may have to change once again.

Individuals will, again, either reject the influence attempt and withdraw either physically or psychologically from the organization, or will use one of the three response mechanisms:

Compliance will go with schooling and mortification;
Identification will go with apprenticeship and co-option – the individual will model himself on his advised superiors. Pre-identification (or anticipatory socialization) is quite common, as when a would-be member of an organization starts to adopt its values and norms before he ever joins, e.g. the aspiring doctor or soldier, the would-be architect or lawyer. In a sense he is preparing himself psychologically for what he instinctively knows will be a systematic influence attempt.

Socialization will not normally result in internalization until the individual has had some hand in shaping the values and norms and practices, i.e. has reached the upper reaches of his organization. Identification and compliance require maintenance. Without maintenance or re-socializing cynicism and rejection may set in. The disillusioned middle manager, the jaundiced cynics of the professions, the jaded detractors of bureaucracies are often those who feel that they were duped by socialization. The reality did not live up to the image, the socialization was not self-maintaining and was not maintained. On the other side of the coin, the top administrators, the doyens of professions, who occasionally appear victims of their own propaganda, are often cases where socialization has been internalized, and has perhaps been too effective.

The rights and wrongs of socialization – of softening up for influence – are an important issue in society and will be discussed in Part Two. Suffice it here to say that as always, a tool must not be rejected as immoral or wrong because it is sometimes used for immoral or wrong purposes. Socialization is a powerful pre-condition of influence and needs to be better understood by those responsible for it.

5.2. Attitude change

Getting people to change their behaviour is relatively easy compared with changing their attitudes. We are not here concerned with brainwashing or indoctrination although these are, of course, systematic and powerful ways of changing attitudes. Mortification methods of socialization, and indeed socialization in general, are examples of deliberate and systematic attitude change. In this section we shall be considering the milder types of change, the attempts that every individual makes from time to time to get people to change their minds. Is the salesman seeking to get the customer to switch brands, the wife to induce her husband to give up smoking, the manager to arouse enthusiasm for his new system? All these are examples of attempted attitude change. Let us not at this stage debate the morals of attempts to change attitudes, but look rather for a better understanding of what happens when A tries to change B's attitude.

The concepts of dissonance theory are a useful framework for looking at the whole question of attitude change. This theory states that when two cognitive inputs to our mental process are out of line, are dissonant, we experience psychological discomfort. We like our world to be balanced, so that when, for instance, we consider university education to be an unnecessary frivolity and a waste of money while all of our most admired friends regard it as key to the future of their children and very valuable, then our cognitive inputs are out of balance. In order to bring them into balance we can either change our views so that we are now in line with our friends, or we can cease to admire our friends so that their dissonant input is no longer of importance. The worst thing an engaged man can do is to ask a friend his opinion of his fiancée. For if the friend expresses an adverse view then the poor man must either change his own view or reduce the importance of his relationship with his friend. Perversely, a favourable opinion is often discounted as pure politeness! Those who lose their friends after marriage, and after arguments, are showing that they cannot handle dissonance. And although we have varying capacities for handling dissonance none of us is very good at coping with extreme dissonance on subjects close to our heart. A strategy often adopted to avoid dissonance is that of separation. If you suspect that some information might be dissonant, you avoid collecting it, even avidly search for the non-dissonant information. Those who have recently bought a new car, or gone to live in a new locality, perhaps marginally inferior to the one they would have preferred, will recall how greedily they pick on any advertisement or anecdote that supports their final choice, how carefully they avoid exposing themselves to dissonant information.

The easiest way to get rid of dissonance is not, usually, to change one's own views or behaviour because this creates another sort of dissonance – that between your previous behaviour or attitude and your present one – but to find some reason to explain away the dissonance, by perhaps downgrading the source of the discrepant information, or by arguing that the situation was irregular, that you were not thinking or were compelled or over-persuaded. In line with this thinking the research on dissonance has thrown up some interesting findings, for instance:

If the source of dissonant information is not highly regarded the dissonance will not be experienced as uncomfortable and the recipient will not need to change his views.

Box 5.6 Attitudes are not bought

Under the guise of a general survey, thirty students at Yale were asked to write an essay in favour of the actions of the local police force. This issue was chosen because, just before the study, there had been student riots at Yale with widespread accusations of police brutality. Every student was hostile to the police force and the essay topic would therefore involve them in writing something opposed to their normal attitudes. They were asked to write the 'strongest, most forceful, most creative and thoughtful essay you can, unequivocally against your own position and in favour of the police side of the riots'. A differential reward element was then introduced. The researcher said 'as part of our study we have some funds available and we are prepared to pay you $. . . . All groups were told exactly the same thing, except that some were offered $10, some $5, some $1 and some 50c.

All essays were unequivocally in favour of the police, with little distinction between the groups. However, after writing the essays, all the groups, plus a control group who had not written any essays, were asked to complete an opinion scale asking 'Considering the circumstances, how justified do you think the New Maren police actions were in the riot?'

The results are shown in the table below. The higher the score the more positive the attitudes towards the police. The highest possible score was 7, the lowest 1.

Attitudes towards police actions

Control Group	2·70
$10 Group	2·32
$5 Group	3·08
$1 Group	3·47
50c Group	4·54

Adapted from Brehen and Cohen, *Explorations in Cognitive Dissonance*, 1962

Aronson, for example, in an experiment told a class of girls that someone else disagreed with their evaluation of a poem. The dissonance in this case was, as experienced by them:

1 I think this poem is very poor;
2 X thinks very highly of it.

When the girls were told that T. S. Eliot, whom they revered, was X the dissonance was high, and most of them changed their evaluation of the poem to resolve it. On the other hand when told that X was another student, not revered as a critic, there was little dissonance and no change in view. To put it another way, persuasion as a method of influence only works when expert power is very high.

The more you pay people to induce them to change their views the less they need to change them. They may change their behaviour, but they can explain the dissonance that results from acting contrary to their belief by pointing to the reward. Cohen's experiment reported in Box 5.6 shows that those who were paid less changed more – they had less excuse for their dissonance, so had to change their views. Large bonus percentages will get formal agreement to change from method A to method B but will not necessarily mean that the men agree with the principle – 'We might as well go along with them' would be the response. To put it another way, use of resource power results in compliance, not internalization.

Public commitment produces more dissonance than private listening. In research studies those who were asked to instruct others in a new point of view showed more change than those who merely listened. Any form of public commitment results in an admission of ownership which it is hard for them to disclaim unless there are very obvious mitigating factors (e.g. forced confessions from prisoners-of-war). The best way to avoid ownership, and therefore dissonance in public pronouncements, is to ascribe the views or ideas to someone else as in, for example, 'The chairman has asked me to tell you . . .' Teachers and writers can do this by describing other people's views rather than their own. Students can avoid learning by merely repeating other people's writings without working through theirs to make them their own. To put it another way, ownership results in internalization.

The tougher the price for something, the more those who pay it value what they get.
Studies show that the tougher the initiation, or the more difficult the experience, the more the outcome is valued. If something is made easy, it is not valued when attained. The dissonance between paying a high price for what seems to be worthless can only be resolved by increasing to one-self the value of what one has bought. Hence the rationale for mortification as a method of socialization. Those who stick it out will value the resulting membership of the institution very highly. Old-timers will speak most appreciatively of the learning they gained from their years 'on the shop floor' or 'on the road'. The tougher the educational programme, the more highly it is likely to be rated at the end.

Discussion groups are a two-edged weapon. Although it is often held that discussion, as a way of participating, will get change accepted, dissonance theory shows that it can work two ways. If the majority or the key part of the group is in favour of A, the new attitude, then the minority will experience dissonance and will either change their views or leave the group.

However, if the majority do *not* favour A, then the group becomes a way of resisting rather than promoting change. One study showed that when Catholics were placed in a group and made aware that it was an all-Catholic group, they were much more orthodox in their views than Catholics put into a similar group but not made aware of the other members' affiliations.

The essential message of dissonance theory is that an individual will only change his attitude or view or belief if (a) the topic is of little importance or centrality to him, or (b) there is no other way of reducing the dissonance between his original attitude and what he does or says.

Behaviour change does not imply attitude change. Compliance is quicker but internalization lasts longer. Dissonance theory, unfortunately, cannot predict precisely how an individual will resolve his dissonance but some general precepts can be enunciated:

Box 5.7 'Obedience'

Stanley Milgram has examined the tendency to obey. Milgram focused his work on destructive obedience – obedience to demands which injure others. The basic experiment involves a naïve subject who administers what he believes are extremely severe electric shocks to another 'subject' who is in fact a confederate of the experimenter. The subject believes that he is participating in an experiment which involves the effect of punishment on learning. He is instructed to raise the shock level administered after each error which the victim makes in a learning task involving the pairing of words. The simulated generator which the subject uses is extremely convincing; it is marked with voltage designations from fifteen to 450 which are accompanied by verbal designations of slight shock, moderate shock, strong shock, very strong shock, intense shock, extreme intensity shock, danger: severe shock, and two more positions ominously marked XXX. When the naïve subject pulls the generator switch, the generator lights and buzzes but, unknown to him, no shock is actually transmitted.

In Milgram's original experiment, the victim-confederate was in an adjacent room providing answers by pushing buttons. At the 300-volt level and again at the 315-volt level, he was instructed to pound on the wall and, thereafter, provide no more answers. Subjects typically turned to the experimenter at that point who advised them to treat no response as an incorrect response and to proceed with the shock schedule. If the subject asked about injury to the victim, the experimenter replied, 'Although the shocks can be extremely painful, they cause no permanent tissue damage.'

The results of this experiment are startling. Of the forty subjects, all proceed past the strong and very strong shock readings and none break off before reaching 300 volts. Even more startling, twenty-six of the forty reach

Box 5.7 – *contd*

the maximum level of 450 volts – the XXX category. Such behaviour is clearly not sadism. Subjects are under considerable stress and manifest it by sweating, stuttering, uncontrollable laughing fits, trembling, and other manifestations of extreme tension. Milgram (1963, p. 377) quotes one observer:

I observed a mature and initially poised businessman enter the laboratory smiling and confident. Within twenty minutes, he was reduced to a twitching, stuttering wreck who was rapidly approaching a point of nervous collapse. He constantly pulled on his earlobe and twisted his hands. At one point, he pushed his fist into his forehead and muttered 'Oh, God. Let's stop it.' And yet he continued to respond to every word of the experimenter and obeyed to the end.

Why do subjects continue to honour a presumed obligation to an experimenter whom they do not know, to accomplish goals which are at best vague and obscure to them, and which at the same time involve virtually gratuitous injury to another human being whom they have no reason to dislike? Variations of the experiment point to the fact that the strength of the obligation is heavily influenced by the physical presence of the experimenter. In one condition with forty fresh subjects, the experimenter leaves after presenting the initial instructions and gives subsequent orders over the telephone. Where twenty-six of forty were fully obedient when the experimenter was present, only nine of the forty subjects were fully obedient when the orders were conveyed over the phone. In a number of cases, the subject lied to the experimenter, saying that he was raising the shock level when he was in fact using the lowest level on the board. If the experimenter appeared in person after the subject refused over the telephone, he was sometimes able to re-activate compliance with the simple assertion, 'The experiment requires that you continue.'

Adapted from Milgram, 'Behavioural study of obedience', *J. Abnorm. Psych.*, 1963

The example of repeated models is useful. Do not assume that a manager is necessarily a good model for people other than managers. Other comparable work groups may be better.

Seduction can be rationalized as manipulation. Do not provide too many possible excuses for a change of behaviour.

Public commitment helps. Lectures and memoranda do not involve any commitment on the part of the recipient.

Study the group norms before you advocate group discussion of a new idea. Argument (see chapter 8) can help to clarify issues and to bring commitment, but the pull of the group may offset the benefits of argument.

6 Summary of the model

6.1

Let us now reassess this complicated process of influence. The full model looks something like this:

Source of
power: physical resource position expert personal

Method of
influence: force   exchange   rules   persuasion
                     ecology   magnetism

Psychological
contract: alienative calculative co-operative

Method of
adapting: compliance   internalization   identification

Method of
socialization: mortification schooling co-option apprenticeship

The positioning of the words is important, particularly in relationship to the source of power. From that all else tends to follow.

Thus we can see that motivation theories, the psychological contract and the motivation calculus, ultimately depend on the source of power, as it is perceived by the individual. It is hard indeed for the dictator truly to use persuasion as a method of influence, no matter how sincere he may be. The recipient will always detect the iron hand inside the velvet glove. Magnetism is nice – but can you assume that you have it?

6.2 The implications

Your role, and the role relationships between you and those you wish to influence, will tend to determine the methods of influence open to you. The most that you can do is to be honest in your predictions, to understand, for instance, that whatever you may pretend it is actually exchange or ecology methods which you are using, methods which will result in compliance or at best identification, which are not self-maintaining states. A meeting that ends with the chairman saying 'So I take it that we are all agreed?' (expecting the answer 'Yes') is seldom an example of a completed influence attempt which will be self-maintaining. The 'false consensus' is an influence attempt that failed, usually because the chairman thought he was using persuasion when in fact he was using the dynamics of the meeting, i.e. ecology backed by his position power, to obtain an unreal agreement. When ecology is uncovered, as when individuals leaving the meeting are heard to comment 'I didn't like to say it in there, but I cannot see how this scheme will work in view of . . .', then ecology uncovered becomes manipulation, results in compliance, and compliance only works when the initiator uses his coercive or resource power. So it will be that, unless the chairman demands implementation, the first meeting will be followed by a second meeting which will pretend that the conclusion of the first meeting never happened.

As the formal leader in the group, your estimate of your source of power in relation to your group will affect your positioning of your leadership behaviour on the tight–flexible continuum. Similarly your group's assessment of the proper source of power for your role will condition their preferred position on that continuum. Participative management implies expert power sources, influence by persuasion, and response by internalization. Great if it works. But as we have seen the likelihood of this method of influence working properly in the hustle and bustle of organizational life is very unlikely. In situations where resource power is evenly spread, where there are no time pressures, where individuals are free to refuse influence, where there is respect for expert power, then participative management might be expected to flourish and authoritarian (rules and procedures) management to fail. Where does this happen? Sometimes in universities, occasionally in R and D laboratories, often in the advisory units (e.g. corporate planning, investment analysis, market analysis) of functional areas. Hardly on the assembly line, in the accounting office or the typing pool as their work is normally organized.

Persuasive influence, expert power, are more compatible with contemporary feelings about the essential rights of the individual, about society as a contractual system, about freedom to say 'No' in all situations. They are more compatible with rising standards of education with the changing role of women – from 'female' to 'person'. They will tend to move the preferred management style of subordinates well down towards the flexible end – more control to the subordinates, i.e. more freedom to reject influence. But this form of influence, this source of power, is not obviously compatible with the emerging forms of the giant corporation, is not compatible with the task requirements of most managerial roles in the organizations of today, or of tomorrow.

We have therefore another way of looking at the organizational dilemma of today. How to select and implement an appropriate source of power that will reflect the trends in society and still get the work done? Nor is this a purely idealistic dilemma – how to be rich but good – it is a very practical problem of the short-term long-term variety. The psychological contract, the preferred method of influence, the ultimate source of power, are hygiene factors. If they are not right, then individuals will leave the organization, good individuals will not join the organization. Turnover will go up, talent will go down. You may get this year's task done with rules and procedures but you may not be around next year to get any task done. Do we then have to think of re-designing the tasks and structures of our corporations, accepting lower economic returns perhaps, raising output prices perhaps, in order to take account of changing values on influence and power? Is the assembly-line doomed? Not because it is inefficient in the normal sense, but because the assumptions it makes about influence and the sources of power are no longer acceptable in our society? Must we de-systemize our work, break up the large units, decentralize our control system even if it costs more in order to realize the structure in line with new conceptions of power and influence?

This chapter has not looked in any detail at the tactics of power and influence. It is not automatic that the possessor of power can proceed to influence his target population. There are tactics that one can use to resist influence and there are tactics to counter those tactics. The tactics, the application of power and influence to social and organizational systems is, in this book, called politics. These topics will, therefore, be dealt with in chapter 8. Here in chapter 5 we have been concerned to develop a diagnostic framework for the analysis of the pattern of influence and reactions to it. Without understanding, action becomes merely instinctive – the constant theme of this book.

6 On the Workings of Groups

1 Introduction

If a camel is a horse put together by a Committee, why then do people spend so much of their lives in groups? On average, managers spend 50 per cent of their working day in one sort of group or another. Senior managers can spend 80 per cent.

There are more myths, more stereotypes, about groups and committees than about most subjects in organizations. There are the individualists, to whom groups and committees are an encumbrance and a nuisance. There are the team men, who want participation and involvement by all concerned. Does it matter? Are groups a fashion or a necessity?

What is a 'group' anyway? They vary from the formal – a work group, a project team, a committee, a board – to the informal – the *ad hoc* meeting or discussion, the luncheon group, the clique, the cabal. They are permanent or temporary. They are liked by their members or regarded as a waste of time. They can be a most effective device for blocking and obstructing new ideas, or the best way of putting them into practice.

What is the truth about groups? Is there any better understanding that we can gain about this universal phenomenon? Is there a diagnostic framework that we can apply to the workings of groups which will allow us to understand more fully this part of organizational life?

In this chapter we shall look first at *the purposes of groups* – what they are used for, and by whom, what they are good at and when. We shall then consider *the determinants of group effectiveness* and conclude with some *conclusions and implications*.

2 The purposes of groups

2.1

We shall first need to define the types of group rather more precisely. A group, first of all, is any collection of people who perceive themselves to be a group. If this seems to be dodging the issue, reflect a minute. A dozen individuals in a pub by random chance are not a group, although they may be interacting (talking), have a common objective (drink and socialization), and be aware of each other. (These are some other definitions of groups.) But put those same people in an emergency situation, let them be trapped by fire in the saloon bar, then that random collection of people will become a group, will start to have some collective identity, because they will start to perceive themselves as a group, with another sort of objective and with needs for other sorts of interaction. All of us, at some time, must have experienced the formation of a group from random individuals, when danger seems to threaten, when the bus is marooned by snow, when the yacht loses its rudder, even in power cuts when one is trapped in the lift. Then we suddenly perceive ourselves to be members of a group. Common objectives, defined membership criteria, predetermined hierarchies, these are not enough without this self-perception by the members. So you will find that when the numbers get too large the members, perceiving themselves to be no longer a group but a crowd or an association, will start reforming into smaller collections. So it is that a name, even a jocular name, for the group becomes an important part of acquiring a perceived identity. Put random collections of people into groups – for instance on a management training programme – and they will, if they wish to be a group and it is important for them to be a group, start to find a name, or a private territorial sign, or a ritual, which will give them an independent identity. If they do not do this, it often means that membership of such a group is not important to them, that they are happy to remain a random collection of individuals.

2.2 The organizational purposes

Organizations use groups, or teams and committees for the following major purposes:

1 For the distribution of work. To bring together a set of skills, talents, responsibilities, and allocate to them their particular duties.

2 For the management and control of work. To allow work to be organized and controlled by appropriate individuals with responsibility for a certain range of work.

3 For problem-solving and decision-taking. To bring together a set of skills, talents and responsibilities so that the solution to any problem will have all available capacities applied to it.

4 For information processing. To pass on decisions or information to those who need to know.

5 For information and idea collection. To gather ideas, information or suggestions.

6 For testing and ratifying decisions. To test the validity of a decision taken outside the group, or to ratify such a decision.

7 For co-ordination and liaison. To co-ordinate problems and tasks between functions or divisions.

8 For increased commitment and involvement. To allow and encourage individuals to get involved in the plans and activities of the organization.

9 For negotiation or conflict resolution. To resolve a dispute or argument between levels, divisions or functions.

10 For inquest or inquiry into the past.

Some of these functions may well be combined. Some will overlap. It should become clear from the discussion in this chapter that groups will behave differently and will need to be organized differently, managed differently, for each of these functions. Some of the major difficulties with groups arise because the same group is expected simultaneously to perform two different functions. A management meeting, for instance, which starts as a negotiation between functions will not proceed very satisfactorily to a discussion of the long-term plan of the organization. This does not mean that the same collection of individuals cannot perform two or more different functions. But they need to see themselves as a different group in order to do so. Thus the functions need to be separated by time, or place, or title. There is more sense than might appear in the comedian's stereotype of the small town functionaries who flit from committee to committee where all the participants are the same, and only the name of the committee changes.

2.3 The individuals' purposes

Individuals use groups for one or more of the following purposes:

1 A means of satisfying their social or affiliation needs; to belong to something or to share in something.

2 A means of establishing a self-concept. Most people find it easier to define themselves in terms of their relationship to others, as members of a role set with a role in that set.

3 A means of gaining help and support to carry out their particular objectives, which may or may not be the same as the organization's objectives.

4 A means of sharing and helping in a common activity or purpose which may be making a product, or carrying out a job, or having fun, or giving help, or creating something.

Again these purposes often overlap. They may also conflict. As many studies have shown, the social functions of work groups can get in the way of the productive functions. Rate-setting is the use of a group to set standards, achieve objectives, which may be contrary to the organization's objectives. The individual who is satisfying his affiliation needs through

Box 6.1 Bull dogs and red devils

In 1949 Sherif and Sherif designed an experiment to demonstrate group formation, in conditions that were as far as possible controlled. Their work is an excellent example of experimental method outside the laboratory. They selected a sample of twenty-four boys for an eighteen-day summer camp in Connecticut, U.S.A. So that grouping among the boys should be determined only by experimental factors, and not by differences in factors outside the experiment like previous friendships or different ages, such possible influences had to be ruled out. This was done by selecting boys the same or nearly the same in:

Age (about twelve);
Social origin (lower-middle-class American families);
Educational experience and opportunity;
Religion (Protestant families);
Intelligence (middling test results);
Normal boyhood (no 'behaviour problems');
Being unknown to one another beforehand.

Intrinsic personality differences and shared interests which might create personal likes or dislikes had still to be eliminated. So for the first three days at the camp the boys were left to sort themselves out spontaneously into small groups of new pals. Then they were officially divided into two groups for the purpose of the experimental stage, the division deliberately splitting up these incipient friendships so that within the two arranged groups spontaneous attractions would be minimized.

The camp organizers closely watched the boys' behaviour, and made notes of significant happenings when they were out of sight, but the boys were not aware that the control exercised was for any purpose beyond that of the usual summer camp. Sherif himself took the role of a caretaker. Records compiled included charts of who chose to sleep in adjacent bunks, to sit together at meals, to take part in games, etc. The conditions having been set, the experimental stages could begin, namely – *Stage 2: experimentally determined forming of groups*, and *Stage 3: experimentally determined forming of the relationship between groups.*

Stage 2: the forming of groups (five days). After the division into two lots of twelve boys, each half was assigned an identifying colour, red and blue, and each chose a separate bunkhouse for itself. Straight away they were sent off on hikes in opposite directions, to counteract any resentment at new buddies being parted and to begin the experimental conditions. All activities were henceforth organized separately. Eating was at separate tables, camp chores done on alternate days, separate camping trips and swimming arranged.

Box 6.1 – *contd*

The effect was striking. Two collections of twelve boys turned into two close-knit groups. They chose group names, the Bull Dogs and the Red Devils. Each group found its own 'secret' hide-out in the woods, and its swimming place. Each preferred certain songs, each preferred particular ways of doing things, like making lanyards. Each tended to refer to its bunkhouse as 'home'. Certain boys took the lead in each group, and enforced types of punishment peculiar to each: for example, offenders among the Bull Dogs were made to remove stones from the group's swimming pool, a sanction utilized by their leader and accepted as fair by the group. Moreover, the incipient friendship choices of the first three days were often completely reversed. The boys were given questionnaires asking which other boys out of the whole twenty-four they now liked best, so that the sociometric pattern of choice could be compared with what it was before.

Table *Friendship choices*

	Choices made by	Choices (%) received by	
		eventual in-group	eventual out-group
end of stage 1	eventual Red Devils	35·1	64·9
(first three days)	eventual Bull Dogs	35·0	65·0
		in-group	out-group
end of stage 2	Red Devils	95·0	5·0
(five days)	Bull Dogs	87·7	12·3

These results show the overwhelming concentration of choice within the boundaries of each group, former likings for boys now in the other groups having been largely forgotten. Indeed, comments were beginning to be heard in each group about 'their lousy cabin', or 'our pond is better'.

Stage 3: The forming of relationships between groups (five days). To test whether inter-group friction could be created, a series of competitive games and contests between the Bull Dogs and the Red Devils was now announced: in fact, some boys had been asking for this. Each day began with a tug-of-war, there were ball games, and so on. The overall winners were to receive twelve four-bladed knives as prizes. At first there was 'good sportsmanship' and cheers for the other team, but soon '2–4–6–8–, who do we

Box 6.1 – *contd*

appreciate' became '2–4–6–8–, who do we appreci-hate'. Name-calling began, the losing Red Devils labelling the winning Bull Dogs as 'dirty players', 'cheats', and worse. The Bull Dogs showed increased pride in their group; but the Red Devils became frustrated and a little disorganized. But later attacks by the Bull Dogs produced a freshly cohesive rallying of the Red Devils.

Finally, when the Bull Dogs won the inter-group prize, the experimenters proposed a party in the evening to let 'bygones be bygones'. Refreshments were set out in the mess hall, half of them delectable and the other half crushed and unappetizing. By careful timing the Red Devils were allowed to arrive first. They took the good half and tucked in. The Bull Dogs arrived. Shocked by the situation as it appeared to them, they refrained from hurling their crushed cake at the Red Devils only when they realized it tasted good anyway. But the meal broke up in a series of fights. Next morning after breakfast the Red Devils deliberately dirtied their table, it being the Bull Dogs' turn to clear up; so the latter retaliated by making a bigger mess and leaving it. At lunch the two groups were soon lined up throwing food and crockery at each other.

Here the experiment finished as such. But it took two days' exhortation and discipline from the staff to stop open fighting: and efforts to unite the camp by mixing the groups in games and activities and in a softball game against an outside team were only partially successful by the time the camp ended.

Adapted from Sherif and Sherif, *An Outline of Social Psychology*, 1956; and Rohrer and Sherif (eds.), *Social Psychology at the Crossroads*, 1951

membership of that group, must pay the price of conformity or be expelled.

The famous Hawthorne Studies in the Western Electric Company of Chicago demonstrated above all that the membership of a group is important to most individuals and that the norms and objectives of the group will have a very large say in the norms and objectives of the individual who belongs to it.

The optimum, of course, is to see that the objectives and purposes of the individual, the group and the organization all coincide.

2.4 Group effectiveness

In general, can we say anything about groups and the things they are good at? There are some things:

1 They are necessary in order to provide a psychological home for the individual. They are essential to organization effectiveness in that they provide the cells within the honeycomb. If they weren't required for the organization of work they would be formed by the individuals. (See Box 6.1.) Individuals will usually look to the work group, as a place of first resort, to satisfy their needs. Only if this fails will they turn elsewhere.

2 Groups produce less ideas, in total, than the individuals of those groups working separately. So much for the stereotype of brainstorming! But groups, though producing less ideas in total, produce better ideas in the sense that they are better evaluated, more thought through. A group will often produce a better solution to a quiz than the best individual in the group, since it can add the missing bits to the best performer. As we shall see, size and the organization of the group are factors that can stop this happening.

3 Groups, rather surprisingly, take riskier decisions than the individuals comprising them would have done if they had been acting independently. Nobody is quite sure of the reason for this but it is either that:

Groups give a sense of shared responsibility; or risk-taking, within limits, being 'a good thing', we tend to behave more adventurously in groups than in private, where we do not have to live up to any public standard.

3 The determinants of group effectiveness

3.1

As with most features of organizations, the answer to the question 'what makes an effective group?' is 'it depends'. In the first place, it depends on the answer to the question 'effective for whom?' We have to remember that productivity and member satisfaction are two possible outcomes of group activity which may or may not be in double harness.

A point however worth stressing: although satisfaction does not necessarily lead to productivity, productivity can often lead to satisfaction. The pride and sense of achievement that comes from being a member of an effective group can lead to satisfaction if the individual values the group and the work that it is doing. This has been called a sense of competence, and 'competence motivation'.

We shall divide the determinants of group effectiveness as follows:

the givens the group   the task   the environment
the intervening factors   leadership style, processes and procedures, motivation
the outcomes productivity, member satisfaction.

The implication behind this division is that there are some aspects of the situation which will affect the outcome but which are 'given'. They can be altered in the long or medium term but in the short term they are constraints within which the group has to operate. The intervening factors are determinants of effectiveness which can be changed in the immediate present. The division is not absolute. Aspects of the group or of the task can often be altered in the short term, can become intervening factors. No one should assume that 'the givens' are given for all time. The successful man is the man who constantly appraises and challenges his constraints. The management of the 'givens' is one example of influence through ecology – and a very important example of it. As a starting point for analysis let us accept the ecology as fixed for the medium term.

3.2 The group

Under this heading we shall briefly examine *size*, *member characteristics*, *individual objectives* and *stage of development*.

Size. There are two, fairly obvious, conflicting tendencies in group size: (a) the larger the group, the greater the diversity of talent, skills and knowledge and (b) the larger the group, the less chance of an individual participating.

In fact, under (b), participation does not diminish uniformly. Some people talk more easily than others in groups, individuals have different thresholds of participation. One man finds no difficulty in speaking in a group of twenty strangers, another will find a group of ten too large unless he knows them well, or has some official role in the group. Studies have shown that those who participate most in a group are perceived as having the most influence. This means that as a group gets larger the influence pattern will get distorted in favour of those with low thresholds of participation. This distribution of influence may not be in accordance with the distribution of knowledge or experience. The 'neglected resource' is a common feature of groups; the retiring expert whose views are never heard or never noticed because his participation level is so low.

The size of the group is therefore a trade-off. For best participation, for highest all-round involvement, a size of between five and seven seems to be optimum. However, in order to achieve the requisite breadth of knowledge or the requisite representation, the required size may be considerably larger. If that is so then the leader or chairman must be particularly aware of the participation–influence problem.

In work groups, size tends to be related to cohesiveness, which in turn is positively related to member satisfaction. Large work-groups tend to

Box 6.2   The Hawthorne studies

In the late 1920s a group of girls who assembled telephone equipment were the subjects of a series of studies undertaken to determine the effect on their output of working conditions, length of the working day, number and length of rest pauses, and other factors relating to the 'non-human' environment. The girls, especially chosen for the study, were placed in a special room under one supervisor and were carefully observed.

As the experimenters began to vary the conditions of work, they found that, with each major change, there was a substantial increase in production. Being good experimenters, they decided, when all the conditions to be varied had been tested, to return the girls to their original poorly-lit work benches for a long working day without rest pauses and other amenities. To the astonishment of the researchers, output rose again, to a level higher than it had been even under the best of the experimental conditions.

At this point, the researchers were forced to look for factors other than those which had been deliberately manipulated in the experiment. For one thing, it was quite evident that the girls developed very high morale during the experiment and became extremely motivated to work hard and well. The reasons for this high morale were found to be several:

1 The girls felt special because they had been singled out for a research role; this selection showed that management thought them to be important.
2 The girls developed good relationships with one another and with their supervisor because they had considerable freedom to develop their own pace of work and to divide the work among themselves in a manner most comfortable for them.
3 The social contact and easy relations among the girls made the work generally more pleasant.

A new kind of hypothesis was formulated out of this preliminary research. The hypothesis was that motivation to work, productivity and quality of work are all related to the nature of the social relations among the workers and between the workers and their boss. In order to investigate this more systematically, a new group was selected. This group consisted of fourteen men: some wired banks of equipment which others then soldered, and which two inspectors examined before labelling it 'finished'. The men were put into a special room where they could be observed around the clock by a trained observer who sat in the corner of the room. At first the men were suspicious of the outsider, but as time wore on and nothing special happened as a result of his presence, they relaxed and fell into their 'normal' working routines. The observer discovered a number of very interesting things about the work group in the bank-wiring room.

Box 6.2 – *contd*

Result 1. Though the group keenly felt its own identity as a total group, there were nevertheless two cliques within it, roughly corresponding to those in the front of the room and those at the back. The men in front felt themselves to be of higher status and they thought that the equipment they were wiring was more difficult than that of the back group. Each clique included most of the wiremen, soldermen and inspectors in that part of the room, but there were some persons who did not belong to either clique. The two cliques each had its own special games and habits, and there was a good deal of competition and mutual ribbing between them.

Result 2. The group as a whole had some 'norms', certain ideas of what was a proper and fair way for things to be. Several of these norms concerned the production rate of the group and could best be described by the concept of 'a fair day's work for a fair day's pay'. In other words, the group had established a norm of how much production was 'fair', namely 6,000 units, a figure which satisfied management but well below what the men could have produced had fatigue been the only limiting factor. Related to this basic norm were two others: 'one must not be a rate-buster', which meant that no member should produce at a rate too high relative to that of the others in the group, and 'one must not be a chiseller', which meant that one must not produce too little relative to the others. Being a deviant in either direction elicited kidding rebukes, social pressure to get back into line, and social ostracism if the person did not respond to the pressure. In that the men were colluding to produce at a level below their capacity, these norms taken together amounted to what has come to be called 'restriction of output'.

The other key norm which affected working relationships concerned the inspectors and the supervisor of the group. In effect, the norm stated that 'those in authority must not act officious or take advantage of their authority position'. The men attempted to uphold the assumption that inspectors were no better than anybody else and that, if they attempted to take advantage of their role or if they acted officiously, they were violating group norms. One inspector did feel superior and showed it. The men were able to play tricks on him with the equipment, to ostracize him, and to put social pressure of such an extent on him that he asked to be transferred to another group. The other inspector and the group supervisor were 'part of the gang' and were accepted for this reason.

Result 3. The observer discovered that the group did not follow company policy on a number of key issues. For example, it was forbidden to trade jobs because each job had been rated carefully to require a certain skill

Box 6.2 – *contd*

level. Nevertheless, the wiremen often asked soldermen to take over wiring while they soldered. In this way, they relieved monotony and kept up social contacts with others in the room. At the end of each day, each man was required to report the amount of work he had done. Actually the supervisor was supposed to report for all the men, but he had learned that the men wished to do their own reporting and decided to let them do it. What the men actually reported was a relatively standard figure for each day, in spite of large variations in actual output. This practice produced a 'straight line output', a standard figure for each day. Actually, however, the output within the group varied greatly as a function of how tired the men were, their morale on any particular day, and many other circumstances. The men did not cheat in the sense of reporting more than they had done. Rather, they would under-report some days, thus saving up extra units to list on another day when they had actually under-produced.

Result 4. The men varied markedly in their individual production rates. An attempt was made to account for these differences by means of dexterity tests given to the men. Dexterity test results did not correlate with output, however. An intelligence measure was then tried with similar lack of success. What finally turned out to be the key to output rates was the social membership in the cliques. The members of the high-status clique were uniformly higher producers than the members of the low-status clique. But the very highest and very lowest producers were the social isolates, who did not belong to either group. Evidently the individual output was most closely related to the social membership of the workers, not to their innate ability.

The output rates were actually one of the major bones of contention between the two cliques because of the pay system: each man got a base rate plus a percentage of the group bonus based on the total production. The high-status clique felt that the low-status one was chiselling and nagged them about it. The low-status group felt insulted to be looked down upon and realized that the best way to get back at the others was through low production. Thus, the two groups were caught in a self-defeating cycle which further depressed the production rate for the group as a whole.

From the original researches of Roethlisberger and Dickson, *Management and the Worker*. Summarized by Schein, *Organizational Psychology*, 1965

have more absenteeism and lower morale. Large in this context, however, seems to be twenty or over.

Member characteristics. First and most obviously, the members must have the requisite skills and abilities to do the job. So must the leader. But other things are known about the mix of characteristics and personalities.

People who are similar in their attitudes, values and beliefs tend to form stable enduring groups. Homogeneity tends in general to promote satisfaction. Heterogeneous groups tend to exhibit more conflict, but most studies do show them to be more productive than the homogeneous groups. However, as one might expect, these groups were heterogeneous only in certain specific characteristics. One study pinpointed radicalism, adventuresomeness and character integration as the variables which should vary amongst group members. Variety in sensitivity, suspiciousness and aggressiveness impeded productivity. Variety but compatibility was the conclusion of another study, i.e. too many potential leaders was bad, groups with a mixture of assertive and dependent people were effective, for they had variety, but variety which could be organized.

Study of the teams playing a year-long business game at Carnegie Institute of Technology has shown that those groups where there was the greatest differentiation of influence among team members were highest in morale and also performed best. That is, teams whose players saw themselves as all about equally influential were less satisfied and made less profits than teams whose players agreed that some particular individuals were a good deal more influential than others.

There have been many studies concerned with compatibility in groups. It was found that compatibility became more crucial as the task became more complex. With simple routine tasks characteristics of the individuals could be as heterogeneous as you liked. Not so with complex tasks where interaction between group members is required. Compatibility can be achieved in various ways. An assertive leader with dependent followers makes for a compatible group. When the individuals all rate highly on warmth and affection it will contribute to compatibility. One common thread stands out. The need for consensus on a focal person, or leader. Two potential leaders do not make for compatibility in a group.

Individual objectives and roles. It is only common sense to assert that if all members of a group have the same objectives the group will tend to be that much more effective. Nevertheless most people bring hidden agendas to groups. These hidden agendas are a set of personal objectives, which often may have nothing to do with the declared objectives of the group. Hidden agendas can include:

Protecting the interests of one's sub-group;
Impressing one's boss;

Box 6.3   The prisoner's dilemma

Two subjects are questioned separately by the district attorney. They are guilty of the crime of which they are suspected, but the D.A. does not have sufficient evidence to convict either. The state has, however, sufficient evidence to convict both of a lesser offence. The alternatives open to the suspects, A and B, are to confess or not to confess to the serious crime. They are separated and cannot communicate. The outcomes are as follows. If both confess, both get severe sentences, which are, however, somewhat reduced because of the confession. If one confesses (turns state's evidence), the other gets the book thrown at him, and the informer goes scot-free. If neither confesses, they cannot be convicted of the serious crime, but will surely be tried and convicted for the lesser offence. The matrix of negative outcomes (years in prison), with those of A shown in the upper right and those of B in the lower left corner of each cell, have the following form:

	A's choice: confess	A's choice: not confess
B's choice: confess	−8 / −8	−10 / 0
B's choice: not confess	0 / −10	−1 / −1

It is evidently to the joint advantage of the two prisoners not to confess and get off with a light sentence of only one year each in jail (lower right cell), but rational calculation of self-interest makes it impossible to achieve this end. A realizes that should B confess he would be better off if he also confessed (eight years in prison) than if he does not (ten years), and should B not confess he again would be better off if he himself confesses (no sentence) than if he does not (one year). In terms of his self-interest, therefore, A must confess, since doing so is to his advantage whether B confesses or not, and as the same considerations apply to B, his self-interest too demands that he confess. Hence both must confess, with the result that each gets an eight-year sentence, which is the worst joint outcome and clearly much more disadvantageous than the one-year sentence they would have received had both kept silent.

Only if each prisoner should use as the criterion of his decision what is in the collective interest of both rather than his own individual interest will the collective optimum result be achieved. In replications of this exercise nearly two-thirds of all subjects, however, make the selfish or distrustful choice.

Adapted from an exercise described by Blau in *Exchange and Power in Social Life*, 1964

Scoring off an opponent;
Making a particular alliance;
Covering up past errors.

In most group situations it is not possible to satisfy all the individual and group objectives simultaneously. There has to be a trade-off. The exercise of 'the prisoner's dilemma', described in Box 6.3, is a specific example of this kind of trade-off problem. In order to achieve the best combined result each individual has to (a) take a risk, (b) accept a less than optimum outcome for himself. Only in certain conditions will this happen:

If the participants can agree on a common objective;
If they trust each other.

These conditions will normally only happen if:

The individuals are given a chance to communicate about objectives;
The individuals are allowed to prove that trust is justified by putting it to the test in some other instance.

The exceptions are:

When there is a 'common enemy' – an objective so obviously common to each that it makes clear sense to make the trade-off;
There are clear group rules or norms, e.g. a prisoner never confesses.

In most organization situations the exceptions do not apply. Unless, therefore, the individuals in a group make specific efforts to agree on common objectives and to prove a level of trust, they will tend to promote their own interests at the expense of the group. Naturally they will not normally do this to the extent of destroying the group or ensuring their own eviction from it – they will only promote their self-interest up to a point, a point where the group's performance 'passes', e.g. is not over budget.

Times of emergency, of crisis and mutual peril, tend to make us all sink our differences. Then it is that the 'common enemy' is dominant, groups become much more cohesive and productive. It is a pity that we have to rely on outside events to produce this change in the individual calculus. It might not have to be so if more attention were paid to the collective purpose and more time devoted to improving the trust relationship. Arising out of his objectives, each individual will assess his role in the group. This topic has been touched on in chapter 3. He will decide to assume some combination of the roles of:

Box 6.4 Behaviour analysis in a group

date: 24 March 1971   observer: SBT
group: C   task: 14

name	JEAN	MIKE	JOHN	MARK	PETER	Jim		total
supporting	ℍℍ III	ℍℍ ℍℍ ℍℍ II	II	IIII	IIII	ℍℍ		
disagreeing		ℍℍ III	II	I	I	IIII		
building		ℍℍ III	IIII	IIII	IIII	ℍℍ I		
criticising		II			II	I		
bringing in	IIII	ℍℍ III				ℍℍ		
shutting out	II	IIII	II	III	II	II		
innovating		III				II		
solidifying	III	II	I	III		ℍℍ I		
admitting difficulty		II	I			I		
defending/ attacking		II						
giving information	ℍℍ ℍℍ II	ℍℍ ℍℍ ℍℍ ℍℍ ℍℍ I	ℍℍ ℍℍ ℍℍ II	ℍℍ ℍℍ III	ℍℍ ℍℍ ℍℍ III	ℍℍ ℍℍ ℍℍ ℍℍ I		
seeking information	ℍℍ II	ℍℍ ℍℍ ℍℍ ℍℍ I	I	ℍℍ ℍℍ I	II	ℍℍ II		
other								

From Rackham, Honey and Colbert, *Developing Interactive Skills*, 1971

Strong fighter;
Friend and helper;
Logical thinker.

In making this implicit or explicit decision about his behaviour in the group he is going to have to answer for himself three questions:

1 Who am I in this group? What is my occupational role here? What are the role expectations of me? Am I here to listen or to lead? Am I repre-

sentative or present in my own right? Who is judging me on my role performance?

2 What is the influence pattern? Who has the power? What kind of power is it? Do I want to change the influence pattern? If so, how do I do it?

3 What are my needs and objectives? Are they in line with the group? Should they be? What do I do about them if they are not? If one of these needs is to be liked and accepted, how important is that for me?

In addition to the three roles outlined earlier, the individual in the group has another choice – to play no role, to withdraw. This withdrawal phenomenon often occurs as a result of:

Strain. The role conflict or ambiguity in the group situation is too great;
Apathy. The salience of the task is so low that the individual is not prepared to pay the cost of contributing to the group.

You cannot assume, without investigation, that the symptom of withdrawal is always caused by apathy although that is the frequent assumption by group leaders. The result of all these role considerations will show up as individual behaviour characteristics. One way of classifying these is shown in Box 6.4.

Stage of development. Groups mature and develop. Like individuals they have a fairly clearly defined growth cycle. This has been categorized as having four successive stages:

1 *Forming.* The group is not yet a group but a set of individuals. This stage is characterized by talk about the purpose of the group. The definition and the title of the group, its composition, leadership pattern, and life-span. At this stage, too, each individual tends to want to establish his personal identity within the group, make some individual impression.

2 *Storming.* Most groups go through a conflict stage when the prelimi nary, and often false, consensus on purposes, on leadership and other rol es, on norms of work and behaviour, is challenged and re-established. At this stage a lot of personal agendas are revealed and a certain amount of inter-personal hostility is generated. If successfully handled this period of s torming leads to a new and more realistic setting of objectives, procedures and norms. This stage is particularly important for testing the norms of trust in the group.

3 *Norming.* The group needs to establish norms and practices. When and how it should work, how it should take decisions, what type of behaviour, what level of work, what degree of openness, trust and confidence is appropriate. At this stage there will be a lot of tentative experimentation by

individuals to test the temperature of the group and to measure the appropriate level of commitment.

4 *Performing*. Only when the three previous stages have been successfully completed will the group be at full maturity and be able to be fully and sensibly productive. Some kind of performance will be achieved at all stages of development but it is likely to be impeded by the other processes of growth and by individual agendas. In many periodic committees the leadership issue, or the objective and purpose of the group, are recurring topics that crop up in every meeting in some form or other, seriously hindering the true work of the group.

When the task is very important, when the individuals are highly committed to the group, or when individual and group objectives are identical then these stages may become almost perfunctory. Certainly the group will 'grow up', will mature very rapidly and reach its optimum performance level. More often the issues are not dealt with specifically and the group's maturing process is driven underground, particularly the 'storming' stage. When this occurs you have the backstage covert politicking, the hidden agendas, the abuse of negative power. In other words, the storming, not culturally acceptable in the open, goes on all the same but often in a much more disruptive manner, concealed under the heading of *performance*. Box 6.5 gives a set of scales for assessing group effectiveness.

Box 6.5   Rating group effectiveness

A: Goals

poor   1 2 3 4 5 6 7 8 9 10   good

confused; diverse;   clear to all; shared
conflicting; indifferent;   by all; all care about
little interest   the goals; feel involved

B: Participation

poor   1 2 3 4 5 6 7 8 9 10   good

few dominate; some   all get in; all are
passive; some not listened   really listened to
to; several talk at once or
interrupt

C: Feelings

poor   1 2 3 4 5 6 7 8 9 10   good

unexpected; ignored or   freely expressed;
criticized   emphatic responses

Box 6.5 – *contd*

D: Diagnosis of group problems

poor　　　　1　2　3　4　5　6　7　8　9　10　*good*

jump directly to
remedial proposals;
treat symptoms rather
than basic causes

when problems arise the
situation is carefully
diagnosed before action
is proposed; remedies
attack basic causes

E: Leadership

poor　　　　1　2　3　4　5　6　7　8　9　10　*good*

group needs for
leadership not met;
group depends too
much on single
person or on a few
persons

as needs for leadership
arise various members
meet them ('distributed
leadership'); anyone
feels free to volunteer
as he sees a group need

F: Decisions

poor　　　　1　2　3　4　5　6　7　8　9　10　*good*

needed decisions don't
get made; decision made
by part of group; others
uncommitted

consensus sought and
tested; deviates appreciated
and used to improve
decision; decisions when
made are fully supported

G: Trust

poor　　　　1　2　3　4　5　6　7　8　9　10　*good*

members distrust one
another; are polite,
careful, closed,
guarded; they listen
superficially but inwardly
reject what others say;
are afraid to criticize
or to be criticized

members trust one
another; they reveal
to group what they
would be reluctant
to expose to others; they
respect and use the
responses they get; they
can freely express negative
reactions without fearing
reprisal

H: Creativity and growth

poor　　　　1　2　3　4　5　6　7　8　9　10　*good*

members and group
in a rut; operate
routinely; persons
stereotyped and rigid in
their roles; no progress

group flexible; seeks
new and better ways;
individuals changing
and growing; creative;
individually supported

From Schein, *Process Consultation*, 1969

If group members were to rate themselves, as a group, on these scales they would have an overall indication of their level of maturity as a group.

Low ratings would indicate that one or more of the stages of development had not been fully worked through.

Whether a particular group needs to be fully mature to do its job will, of course, depend on the importance of that job. In many instances the cost of developing a group to maturity, in sheer time, the displacement of other priorities, the displacement of other groups in importance to the individuals, will not be worth the increased gain in effectiveness. But in many instances – the start-up of a new operation for the top management team, or a new group resulting from a re-organization – it is worth spending time specifically to build a group. Many organizations now recognize the benefits in doing this. There are known techniques built around the theories of Group Dynamics which can help. Essentially these techniques help the group to analyse and improve its 'process', as opposed to its work on particular tasks, and to hasten its maturity by focusing specifically on each of the stages of development. Process consultation, T-groups, Coverdale training are some of these techniques.

Box 6.6   For 'self' or for 'group'

Fouriezos, Hutt and Guetzhow studied the effects of low 'group task motivation' upon group productivity in the seventy-two conference groups in the Conference Research Project of the University of Michigan. The groups were rated on the extent to which the members expressed self-oriented needs, i.e. motives resulting in behaviour 'not necessarily directed towards a group's goals, or ... a solution of group's problems' but 'primarily toward the satisfaction of the need itself, regardless of the effect on attainment of the group goal'. The experimenters found that the amount of such self-orientated behaviour correlated negatively with measures of member satisfaction. In other words, groups in which there was a high frequency of self-orientated behaviour were relatively dissatisfied with the meeting as a whole, with the decisions arrived at, with the procedures used to reach decisions, and with the chairmanship. These 'self-oriented' groups were also high in the amount of conflict they exhibited.

Finally, measures of productivity showed significant inverse relations with amount of self-oriented behaviour. For example, groups rated high on such behaviour tended to complete fewer items on the agenda, although their meetings lasted longer.

Abridged from Fouriezos, Hutt and Guetzhow, 'Measurement of self-oriented needs in discussion groups', *J. Abnormal Soc. Psych.*

3.3 The task

The 'givens' that must be looked at under the heading of the *task* are *nature of the task*, *criteria for effectiveness*, *salience of the task* and *clarity of the task*. The implications of these are straightforward, but they must not be ignored.

The nature of the task. The types of task for which groups or committees are used have been listed in 2.2. Obviously, the type of task will affect the kind of group you can have. Information dissemination permits a larger group size than problem-solving. Task allocation allows a structured approach, idea formulation needs a more supportive style. The point was made in 2.2 that to confuse two tasks in the one group is inadvisable. In particular this is so when the change in tasks involves a change in role for individuals. For instance in work allocation or in an inquest situation the individual will be wearing his departmental, ambassadorial hat. For problem-solving or creativity he is expected to don his overall company apparel and to forget departmental politics. The switch in roles is not easy. The departmental hat will stay on. The creativity discussion will bog down in departmental quibbles. The individual will be castigated as narrow-minded and short-sighted. The group will be ineffective. Essentially it was a different group. The people were the same but the roles were different. A different group needs a different identity – fixed by title, place or time. Agendas or meetings could usefully be split by type of task, rather than all items lumped together in the order they were received by the secretary.

The criteria for effectiveness. In addition to the type of task, one has to consider the *urgency* with which results are required. Pressures of time or competition legitimize more structured forms of working, allow less freedom to develop a group or to deal with individual needs. As a result, the work will often be less accurate, or worse in terms of possible quality. One needs therefore to reflect upon the required *standards*. How, in short, is the effectiveness of the result to be measured? In quantity? In quality? In speed? In cost? In profit? The criteria for assessing performance is going to be a big determining factor on the way the group can operate as well as on what is meant by effectiveness at the end of the day.

Salience of the task. This aspect has already intruded into the discussion of individual objectives. The more important the task to the individual the more committed he is going to be to the group, the less concerned about his own objectives.

The more important the task to the organization the more attention they are likely to pay to the group's performance. If this attention takes the form of setting high expectations on effectiveness it will tend to increase the salience of the task for the individuals. If, however, the increased attention is accompanied by increased monitoring or controls then the implication is of lack of trust and confidence in the group. The group will then experience the pressure of control rather than the pressure of expectation. Pressure by control is demotivating. It is also expensive.

In general, the more salient the task is, the more you can demand of the group. But salience that leads to increased control will only cause strain within the group and within individuals.

Clarity of the task. The less ambiguous the task the more structured the leadership can be. A precise detailed and compartmentalized task implies no requirements in the way of homogeneity or compatibility. A precise task will assist the group through the forming and norming stages of development.

But not all tasks can or should be described so precisely. Ambiguous, open-ended assignments or objectives increase complexity, bring increased demands for compatibility, for time, for supportive leadership. Ambiguity increases stress, and therefore has implications for the kind of individuals required in the group and particularly in the leadership roles.

3.4 The environment

All groups work within an environment, usually the environment of the total organization. The environment imposes certain conditions or constraints on the way they operate. The principal 'givens' in this area are *the norms and expectations, the leader position, inter-group relations* and *the physical location.*

Norms and expectations. The degree of salience that the task has for the organization, and the implications of that for the work group, has already been discussed (3.3).

In addition, however, every organization has some norms about ways of working, style of meeting, methods of reporting and co-ordinating. It is not always possible for a group or a committee to avoid conforming to these norms whether or not they are the most appropriate in their circumstances.

Leader position. The power position of the leader has been discussed in the chapter on leadership. The view taken there was that the more powerful the leader in the organization as a whole, the greater freedom he had to be flexible in his style.

It is also true that a powerful leader has a positive effect on the morale of his work group. People like working under a respected chief. Just as civil servants appreciate a Minister who is effective in cabinet, so in all organizations the leader who is effective in his ambassadorial role will do most to help, not only the ultimate effectiveness of the group, but also its internal *esprit de corps*. A leader who cannot give effect to, cannot sell, the product of the group or the committee is often sufficient grounds for the group members to turn the group into a social or casual group, rejecting the task goals as unrealistic.

Research studies support these common-sense conclusions. Studies have shown that in high-producing groups the leader is seen by his subordinates as possessing more influence with his superiors than the leader of the low-producing groups.

Inter-group relations. The standing of the group or the committee as a whole will affect its productivity and its morale. The degree to which the group is accepted as important, as helpful, as co-operative to the overall goals of the organization; the influence wielded by the group with key figures in the organization; the degree to which it is perceived to influence events in the organization or outside; these factors are all important. No one wants to spend whole mornings in committees whose conclusions will never be noticed, or will be overruled.

The ambassadorial role of the leader has a big bearing on this. But so does the status of the individual members. The marginal group, the low-status group, the unnoticed group, is under a big temptation to activate their latent *negative power*.

Membership of a group which appears to make no difference to anyone will cause dissonance for most individuals. There are two possible ways for someone to resolve that dissonance, and bring his wishes into accord with reality:

1 He can reduce the importance of the group to himself. He can cease attending, or cease contributing.
2 He can activate the negative power of the group, its blocking or nuisance value, so that more people notice it. Its salience in the organization is then increased, if not its popularity.

This irritation factor in committees will always tend to arise if the committee is low in *centrality* in the organization, is not perceived to be useful or necessary or high in status by other groups.

The physical location. The simplest of the 'givens' but one very often ignored. There are certain specific aspects of the physical location of the group and the members of the group that must be considered:

1 Physical proximity increases interaction. One study showed that a flight of stairs interposed between the offices of members of one group reduced interaction of all types by 30 per cent.

2 Interaction normally increases co-operative feelings. In the exceptional instances, where interaction leads to increasing dislike, divorce ensues and interaction ceases. Studies in a housing project showed that people whose doorways faced each other were more likely to become friends than others.

3 Physical barriers can prevent groups from forming. Assembly-lines inhibit the formation of social groups at work. This is a drawback to workers and one reason for their forming other groups, e.g. strike committees, purely social groups, etc. Concentration camps and prisons use the technique of isolation very effectively to prevent the formation of groups and to deprive the individual of a psychological home.

4 The location of a meeting gives out signals. The Managing Director's office reinforces his role. If it is off-site, in a hotel in the country, the signal is that people can forget their ambassadorial role for the time being, and be themselves, be individuals.

5 Shared facilities, even shared discomfort, does much to help group identity. Luncheon and coffee facilities, meeting places and conference rooms can be used deliberately for this purpose. The 'Nissen Hut' experience, groups crowded uncomfortably together, will often produce high cohesion. An isolated location, where all facilities have to be shared, will tend to create involvement in the group.

3.5 *The intervening factors*

These are the aspects of group work that can be changed or adapted in the short term, taking account of the 'givens', to improve group productivity or member satisfaction. They fall under the headings of:

Leadership style;
Process and procedure;
Motivation.

Leadership style. This has already been discussed in chapter 4. The 'best fit' approach, the need to adapt the style to the task, the requirements of the subordinates, and the natural preference of the Leader should have been underlined by all the foregoing discussion.

Box 6.7 The ineffective management committee

The organization was having trouble getting its top management committee to act as a *management* group. It was composed of the senior divisional and functional managers. The M.D. complained that they could only think in departmental terms and in the short term. He could not get them to take a long-term, company-wide view. He attributed this to their personal incapacities. Investigation revealed that:

1 The committee meetings usually started with some form of 'inquest' which forced the managers into departmental roles. They found it hard to exchange these roles for company ones for the next item, which was usually of a different 'type'.
2 Decision was by authority rule. Discussion therefore was peripheral and mainly concerned to pinpoint departmental pit-falls.
3 The agenda was lengthy, the time available was short. Interjections therefore had to be short and factual. Philosophical discussions were not encouraged.
4 The offices of the departmental managers were all in the centres of their departments. This enhanced their ambassadorial or departmental role.
5 The meetings were run on a 'wheel' basis – thus accentuating the power of the chairman and providing the basis for authority rule.
6 Two of the members of the group were not trusted or respected by their colleagues. Everyone, including the two, was aware of this but the formality of the proceedings prevented its coming into the open.

Changes were made:

1 The committee was re-organized and re-named to exclude the two 'unrespected' members.
2 The offices of the others were then all situated on the fifth floor away from their departments. This not only changed their view of the role but also cut down their day-to-day interaction ('interference' said subordinates) with their departments.
3 The agendas were shortened, and the items divided by type.
4 The meeting times were lengthened.
5 The smaller number permitted the interaction pattern to change from the wheel to all-channel. The decision mechanism changed to consensus.

All agreed that the committee worked much more effectively and more like a management group. Levels of mutual trust went up. The M.D.'s appraisals of his managers were revised – upwards.

Process and procedures. For any group to be effective there is a set of processes or functions that have to be done by some person or persons in the group at some time or other. It is the ultimate responsibility of the leader to see that they are done – his choice of style will determine whether he does them, or whether the processes are shared out amongst other individuals. In certain types of group it would be quite appropriate for all the members at some point to perform each of these functions.

The processes or functions are usually grouped under two broad headings – *task functions* and *maintenance functions* – and comprise the following:

task	maintenance
initiating	encouraging
information seeking	compromising
diagnosing	peace-keeping
opinion-seeking	clarifying summarizing
evaluating	standard-setting
decision-managing	

Task functions. Particularly in any problem-solving situation all the listed processes ought to happen. Furthermore, they ought to happen in the order in which they are listed. Too often group discussions leap from initiating through rudimentary opinion-seeking to evaluation. The chairman states the problem, a solution is proposed, it is evaluated and a decision taken. The separation of information from opinion, of diagnosis from evaluation, greatly improves the quality of the solution. Evaluation is, at its heart, a comparative process. It compares one solution against other available solutions. To be well done it is therefore important that all solutions are known before any are evaluated. The stages of opinion-seeking, or idea generation, and evaluation should be separated. A mechanism for recording these ideas is also important – a blackboard, or large sheet of paper, some public recording device so that all members have available to them all possibilities before evaluation starts.

It has been shown in experimental studies that groups who attack a problem systematically perform better than groups who 'muddle through' or 'evolve'. The decision-making procedure is also of great importance. Will it be:

Decision by authority;
Decision by majority;
Decision by consensus;

Decision by minority;
Decision by no response?

The last two are usually only negative. That is, an idea is suggested: either no one responds and it is dropped, or a minority bloc exercises its veto. Most group decisions are negative decisions and as such often pass unnoticed as decisions. If ideas are evaluated separately it can easily happen that each idea receives a veto or negative decision, the meeting then becoming totally unfruitful and very dispiriting to all present.

The kind of task procedure to adopt and in particular the decision-making process are two of the things that the group has to make up its mind on in the 'norming' stage of its development. The leader, by virtue of his position power, has great influence over choice of procedure (ecology), although he does not have to perform all of the functions himself.

Maintenance functions. Effective groups, be they problem-solving or producing, need maintenance. There are neglected resources in groups, they need encouraging; there are often opposing factions, they must be helped to compromise, to resolve or manage their conflict; individuals too often do not listen in groups, each man intent on preparing his own contribution; someone must clarify and summarize so that there is a common awareness of all that has happened. Lastly, the performance of the group will be vastly influenced by the kind of standards that it is aiming at. Someone has to set those standards and have them adopted by the group. Groups without standards will satisfice at the lowest level. Standards without groups, not accepted by the group as realistic for them, are meaningless.

Again, the leader does not have to perform all these functions himself, but they need doing. Groups in which these tasks and maintenance functions were observed to happen have been entitled co-operative groups. They were found, in one study by Deutsch, in comparison with 'competitive' groups to:

1 Be more productive in quantity.
2 Produce higher quality.
3. Have a stronger push to complete the task.
4 Have a greater division of labour and better co-ordination.
5 Experience fewer difficulties in communication.
6 Show more friendliness in the discussions.
7 Experience greater satisfaction with the group and its products.

Interaction pattern. The other factor that the group itself can control, and the leader can influence, is the interaction pattern, the pattern of communication between members. Is it, for instance, a *wheel*, *circle* or *all-channel*. (See Figure 9.)

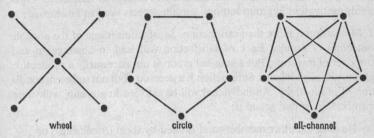

wheel   circle   all-channel

Figure 9

Well-known sets of experiments have been done by numbers of social scientists to demonstrate the relative merits of these communication patterns in small groups. The main conclusions are not unexpected:

1 The wheel is always the quickest to reach a solution or conclusion, the circle is the slowest.
2 In complex open-ended problems the all-channel is the most likely to reach the best solution, the ability of the man at the centre of the wheel determining the outcome of that pattern. The wheel is usually inflexible if the task changes.
3 The level of satisfaction for individuals is lowest in the circle, fairly high in the all-channel, mixed in the wheel with the central figure usually expressing great satisfaction and the outlying figures feeling isolated.

One might suppose, although the research did not test this, that feelings of satisfaction in the all-channel group would depend on the importance of the task. No one wants involvement in a trivial 'Mickey Mouse' assignment. Similarly, not all individuals react positively to being the central figure in the wheel – even in experimental situations people have been known to collapse and withdraw under the overload of communication.

Under pressure of time or competition the all-channel system either restructured itself into a wheel – or disintegrated. In general, then, wheels are good for speedy results where quality is not vital, but morale may be low for all but the leader. Circles are always bad, no co-ordination. All-channel systems are participative and involving and good for quality, but they take time and do not stand up under pressure. These conclusions can be seen at work in numberless committees where often, *pace* Parkinson, the wrong system is used for the wrong task – all-channel for the trivia of the parking lot, wheels for the big merger decision.

Motivation. This topic has been discussed in general in chapter 2. As regards motivation in group settings, certain aspects need to be stressed:

1 Motivation is more than satisfaction. Satisfaction is one of the possible outcomes of groups. Lack of satisfaction will lead to absenteeism and turnover of members. But a satisfied group is not necessarily a productive group, although it helps. Satisfaction is a necessary but not sufficient condition of productivity. An individual will be satisfied in a group, will value membership of that group if:

(a) He likes the other members and is liked by them (friendship); or
(b) He approves of the purpose and work of the group (task); or
(c) He wishes to be associated with the standing of the group in the organization (status).

One or all of these will lead to satisfaction, depending on the psychological contract of the individual with that group and the particular needs subsumed in that contract. You can therefore have a satisfied and productive group in which condition (a) does not apply, in which the members do not particularly like each other.

2 Knowledge of expected results, or standard setting, is crucial if the motivation calculus of individuals is to operate. Hence the importance of realistic standards, of standards accepted by the group, of standards sufficiently high to give them a feeling of achievement when attained. Hence also the importance of knowing the results, of feedback. Both of these items are essential to the motivation of groups. Both are too frequently neglected.

3 Motivation by involvement will only work if the group and the task are important enough to the individual to justify his acceptance of additional responsibility. Otherwise it will be involvement by order – rules and procedures based on coercive or resource power and requiring control and maintenance mechanisms to make it work. One cannot assume that, because someone is nominated to a committee, he will do any more than attend its meetings.

Perhaps, however, the most important aspect of motivation in groups is the establishment of a 'common enemy', discussed in *3.1*. Hopefully, the task assigned to the group will be sufficiently salient and clear to all members that it will automatically become a common enemy. But this cannot be assumed. The leader, particularly, may see the task as much more important than the other members. If the individuals put their own agendas in front of the task the productivity and morale will decline and the whole group will be much more difficult to manage. (See Box 6.5.) The leader therefore needs to do all he can either to:

Re-define the task so that it becomes a common enemy; or
Raise the individual's expectations of the task so that it dwarfs their individual needs.

A solution sometimes adopted, lacking a task of sufficient interest, is to make the building of a group the key task. This is:

(a) Difficult, without an external task;
(b) Counter to organizational interests since a group will be created whose primary goal will be its own satisfaction and survival.

4 Summary and conclusions

4.1 The Summary

The complete model for the analysis of groups now looks like this:

	The group	The task	The environment
	size	nature	norms and expectations
the givens	member characteristics	criteria for effectiveness	leader position
	individual objectives	salience of task	inter-group
	stage of development	clarity of task	relations
which all affect the intervening actors		choice of leadership style	
		processes and procedures	
		motivation	
which determine the outcomes		productivity	
		member satisfaction	

Are there any general conclusions that we can reach; or additional points to make?

4.2 The 'group' ideology

Groups fit well with a democratic culture, with representative systems of government. Participation and involvement go well with assumptions of man as an independent individual. Committees similarly are democratic and representative, but they are extraordinarily difficult things to operate effectively. The model presented in this chapter should help to give an understanding of many of the reasons. In addition, we must remember that:

1 Groups can be used by individuals, and by organizations, to diffuse, and even to lose, responsibility.

2 Committees are often better ways of 'recognizing' problems than 'solving' problems. A 'committee to investigate X' is a recognition of 'X' but that does not necessarily mean that it is the best way to solve 'X'. Committees are often, like Royal Commissions, a way of simultaneously accepting the importance of a problem but deferring its solution.

3 The conforming power of groups was demonstrated in chapter 3. Even strong individuals can be reduced to impotence by a group. But weak individuals can be bolstered – it all depends on the norms of the group and its collective motivation and standards.

The problem is this: if groups or committees are convened or constructed for an inappropriate task, or with impossible constraints; if they are badly led or have ineffective procedures; if they have the wrong people, too many people, too little power or meet too infrequently; if, in short, any one part of the model is badly out of line, frustration will set in and dissonance will be created. The result will either be an activation of *negative power* or a badly-attended non-effective group, wasting people, time and space. The chances of this happening are, in fact, very high. If 50 per cent of managerial time is spent in groups, the cost of wasted time begins to look colossal, let alone the damage done by the use of negative power.

This is why the study of groups, the improvement of the work of groups and committees, merits a deal of attention. It may at least prevent the establishment of another committee to improve the workings of committees! Most attention, by theorists and trainers, has focused on the intervening factors. All the courses on leadership, on supervisory style, on effective membership of groups, on participation as motivation, have been dealing with this part of the model. Undoubtedly much can be done in this area.

But the thrust of this chapter has been to emphasize the more basic ecological conditions – the *givens*. No leadership style, no process, no motivation principle, can work in an impossible situation. More attention needs to be paid to the *givens*. If it were, the conclusion might be that no group was necessary in a particular situation, or at least that it would be bound to be ineffective so let no one waste their energies.

Groups there must be. Individuals must be co-ordinated and their skills and abilities meshed and merged. But let us not be mesmerized. Let us realize that a proper understanding of groups will demonstrate how difficult they are to manage. Let us pay more attention to their creation and be more realistic about their outcomes.

7 On Cultures and Structures

1 Introduction

1.1

The chief delight of Europe is the variety it offers of climate and culture. One of the more pleasurable ways of ending a long English winter is to drive south along the highways of the continent, to watch spring and its blossoms come to meet you up the road, and to linger awhile in the sun, adapting to another culture with different traditions, habits, ways of organizing work and of ordering daily life. Anyone who has spent any time in another country will appreciate how values, beliefs and cherished philosophies affect the way society is organized. He will appreciate too how these values and beliefs are shaped by history and tradition, by the climate, the kinds of work they do, the size of the country and its prosperity.

So too, anyone who has spent time with any variety of organizations, or worked in more than two or three, will have been struck by the differing atmospheres, the differing ways of doing things, the differing levels of energy, of individual freedom, of kinds of personality. For organizations are as different and varied as the nations and societies of the world. They have differing cultures – sets of values and norms and beliefs – reflected in different structures and systems. And the cultures are affected by the events of the past and by the climate of the present, by the technology of the type of work, by their aims and the kind of people that work in them.

Should this variety be so? After decades of management theory should the mix of type and structure be so great? Is there not one optimum span of control, one best way of describing jobs, appraising people, controlling people, of budgeting, forecasting and planning? The contention of this chapter is 'No'; that the cultures of organizations rightly differ, that cultures are affected by a variety of factors, that these diverse cultures are reflected in diverse structures and systems. Indeed it will be argued that many of the ills of organizations stem from imposing an inappropriate structure on a particular culture, or from expecting a particular culture to thrive in an inappropriate climate. Vines don't grow where the sunshine doesn't fall in the right proportions with the rain – nor has anyone yet found a more effective technology for tending the vines than the human hand.

Earlier management theory, in its search for universal formulae or cure-all remedies, did a great disservice in seeking to disseminate a common organizational culture. Fortunately organizations, unhearing or unheeding, were unaffected. More modern theories of organization are increasingly persuaded of the wisdom of the appropriate, of the match of people to systems, to task and environment, of inter-relations between all four, of what has come to be called the *systems* approach to management theory. This is a word sufficiently vague to cover all manner of specific approaches but it tends to connote inter-relationships, feedback mechanisms, and appropriateness of fit. The cultures/structures approach to describing organizations is not really a sub-set of systems theory but it shares with it a concern for linkages and appropriateness. It is, in its interest in the appropriate, akin to those approaches to organizing described generally as *contingency theories*.

1.2

This chapter will first examine four varieties of *organization cultures* which are each reflected in a structure and a set of systems. It will then consider the *influencing factors* on these cultures. Finally it will look at the *implications for organization design*.

2 The cultures

2.1

Roger Harrison, in a stimulating paper referred to in Part Three, has written of 'organization ideologies'. The word 'cultures' is preferred here because it conveys more of the feeling of a pervasive way of life, or set of norms. But the names of the cultures are taken from his ideologies. In organizations there are deep-set beliefs about the way work should be organized, the way authority should be exercised, people rewarded, people controlled. What are the degrees of formalization required? How much planning and how far ahead? What combination of obedience and initiative is looked for in subordinates? Do work hours matter, or dress, or personal eccentricities? What about expense accounts, and secretaries, stock options and incentives? Do committees control, or individuals? Are there rules and procedures or only results? These are all parts of the culture of an organization. This culture often takes visible form in its building, its offices, its shops or branches. The kinds of people it employs, the length and height of their career aspirations, their status in society, degree of mobility, level of education, will all be reflections of the culture. The mammoth teaching hospital has a culture manifestly different from a merchant bank, which is different again from an automobile plant. They look and feel different. They will require different kinds of people, will appeal to different kinds. They have different ways of working. They are different cultures. Even within organizations cultures will differ. The R and D laboratory in the fields of the countryside will have a different atmosphere to the director's floor in the central office. The invoicing department would not be mistaken for the market research department, or the factory for the sales division. What are the possible cultures? There are four: *power, role, task* and *person*.

2.2 *The power culture*

A power culture is frequently found in small entrepreneurial organizations, traditionally in the robber-baron companies of nineteenth-century America, occasionally in today's Trade Unions, and in some property, trading and finance companies. Its structure is best pictured as a *web*:

If this culture had a patron god it would be Zeus, the all-powerful head of the Gods of Ancient Greece who ruled by whim and impulse, by thunder-bolt and shower of gold from Mount Olympus.

This culture depends on a central power source, with rays of power and influence spreading out from that central figure. They are connected by functional or specialist strings but the power rings are the centres of activity and influence.

This organization works on precedent, on anticipating the wishes and decisions of the central power sources. There are few rules and procedures, little bureaucracy. Control is exercised by the centre largely through the selection of key individuals, by occasional forays from the centre or sum-monses to the centre. It is a political organization in that decisions are taken very largely on the outcome of a balance of influence rather than on procedural or purely logical grounds.

These cultures, and organizations based on them, are proud and strong. They have the ability to move quickly and can react well to threat or danger. Whether they do move or whether they move in the right direction will, however, depend on the person or persons in the centre; for the quality of these individuals is of paramount importance in those organizations and the succession issue is the key to their continued success. Individuals employed in them will prosper and be satisfied to the extent that they are power-orientated, politically minded, risk-taking, and rate security as a minor element in their psychological contract. Resource power is the major power base in this culture with some elements of personal power in the centre.

Size is a problem for power cultures. The web can break if it seeks to link too many activities; indeed the only way the web organization can grow and remain a web is by spawning other organizations, other spiders. Organizations which have done this (Slater-Walker and G.E.C. in the U.K.) continue to grow but are careful to give maximum independence to the individual heads of the linked organizations (which incidentally do not have to have a power culture) usually keeping finance as the one string that binds them to the central web.

These cultures put a lot of faith in the individual, little in committees. They judge by results and are tolerant of means. Often seen as tough or abrasive, though successful they may well suffer from low morale and high turnover in the middle layers as individuals fail or opt out of the competitive atmosphere. And it must be remembered that these cultures can be as bad as they can be effective. Many of the family businesses that stagnated and were eventually annexed in Britain after the Second World War were power cultures that had died in the centre. A web without a spider has no strength.

2.3 The role culture

The role culture is often stereotyped as bureaucracy. But bureaucracy has come to acquire a pejorative note in common parlance, so 'role' will be

used here. The accompanying structure to a role culture can be pictured as a *Greek temple*.

Its patron god is Apollo, the god of reason; for this culture works by logic and by rationality. The role organization rests its strength in its pillars, its functions or specialities. These pillars are strong in their own right; the finance department, the purchasing department, the production facility may be internationally renowned for their efficiency. The work of the pillars, and the interaction between the pillars, is controlled by:

Procedures for roles, e.g. job descriptions, authority definitions;
Procedures for communications, e.g. required sets of copies of memoranda;
Rules for settlement of disputes, e.g. appeal to the lowest crossover points.

They are co-ordinated at the top by a narrow band of senior management, the pediment. It is assumed that this should be the only personal co-ordination needed, for if the separate pillars do their job, as laid down by the rules and procedures, the ultimate result will be as planned.

In this culture the role, or job description, is often more important than the individual who fills it. Individuals are selected for satisfactory performance of a role, and the role is usually so described that a range of individuals could fill it. Performance over and above the role prescription is not required, and indeed can be disruptive at times. Position power is the major power source in this culture, personal power is frowned upon and expert power tolerated only in its proper place. Rules and procedures are the major methods of influence. The efficiency of this culture depends on the rationality of the allocation of work and responsibility rather than on the individual personalities.

The role organization will succeed as long as it can operate in a stable environment. When next year is like this year, so that this year's tested rules will work next year, then the outcome will be good. Where the organization can control its environment, by monopoly or oligopoly, where the market is stable or predictable or controllable, or where the product-life is a long one, then rules and procedures and programmed work will be successful. So the civil service (a monopoly in a sense), the automobile and oil industries (long product life-cycles and perhaps some oligopoly situations), life insurance companies and retail banking (long product life-cycles), are usually role cultures and successful ones. Small newcomers to this field, however, may well not have a role culture since their aims will not be stability and predictability, but survival and growth.

But Greek temples are insecure when the ground shakes. Role cultures are slow to perceive the need for change and slow to change even if the need is seen. If the market, the product needs or the competitive environment changes, the role culture is likely to continue to forge straight ahead confident in its ability to shape the future in its own image. Then collapse, or replacement of the pediment by new management, or take-over, is usually necessary. Many large organizations found themselves in this position in the changing conditions of the 1960s.

Role cultures offer security and predictability to the individual. They offer a predictable rate of climb up a pillar. They offer the chance to acquire specialist expertise without risk. They tend to reward the satisficer, the man concerned with doing his job up to a standard. But come disaster – collapse or take-over – and the security of the role culture may be found to be built too much on the organization and too little on the individual's capacities. The role culture is frustrating for the individual who is power-orientated or wants control over his work; who is eagerly ambitious or more interested in results than method. Such a man will only be content in the pediment.

The role organization will be found where economies of scale are more important than flexibility or where technical expertise and depth of specialization are more important than product innovation or product cost. Organizations used to operating in a sellers' market until the mid-1950s, or with the state as their only customer, were quite properly operating in a role culture since there was a high premium on product reliability and few penalties for cost or lack of product innovation.

2.4 The task culture

The task culture is job or project orientated. Its accompanying structure can be best represented as a *net*,

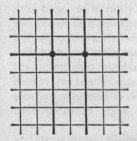

with some of the strands of the net thicker and stronger than the others. Much of the power and influence lies at the interstices of the net, at the knots. The so-called 'matrix organization' is one structural form of the task culture.

The task culture has no totally appropriate presiding deity, perhaps because the Ancients were more interested in style and principle and power than in performance, for the whole emphasis of the task culture is on getting the job done. To this end the culture seeks to bring together the appropriate resources, the right people at the right level of the organization, and to let them get on with it. Influence is based more on expert power than on position or personal power, although these sources have their effect. Influence is also more widely dispersed than in other cultures, and each individual tends to think he has more of it. It is a team culture, where the outcome, the result, the product, of the team's work tends to be the common enemy obliterating individual objectives and most status and style differences. The task culture utilizes the unifying power of the group to improve efficiency and to identify the individual with the objective of the organization.

This culture is extremely adaptable. Groups, project teams, or task forces are formed for a specific purpose and can be reformed, abandoned or continued. The net organization works quickly since each group ideally contains within it all the decision-making powers required. Individuals find in this culture a high degree of control over their work, judgement by results, easy working relationships within the group with mutual respect based upon capacity rather than age or status.

The task culture therefore is appropriate where flexibility and sensitivity to the market or environment are important. You will find the task culture where the market is competitive, where the product life is short, where speed of reaction is important. But the task culture finds it hard to produce economies of scale or great depth of expertise. You cannot organize a large factory as a flexible group; although the technical man in the group may be clever and talented he will, by virtue of having to work on various problems in various groups, be less specialized than his counterpart in a role culture. The task culture therefore thrives where speed of reaction, integration, sensitivity and creativity are more important than depth of specialization. The product groups of marketing departments, the general management consultancies, the merger, take-over and new venture sections of merchant banks, the account executives of advertising agencies – these are all places where the task culture might be expected to flourish.

Control in these organizations is difficult. Essentially control is retained by the top management by means of allocation of projects, people and resources. Vital projects are given to good people with no restrictions on time, space or materials. But little day-to-day control can be exerted over the methods of working or the procedures without violating the norms of the culture. These cultures therefore tend to flourish when the climate is agreeable, when the product is all-important and the customer always right, and when resources are available for all who can justify using them. Top management then feels able to relax day-to-day control and concentrate on resource allocation decisions and the hiring and placing of key people.

However, when resources are not available to all who can justify their needs for them, when money and people have to be rationed, top management begins to feel the need to control methods as well as results. Alternatively team leaders begin to compete, using political influence, for available resources. In either case, morale in the work-groups declines and the job becomes less satisfying in itself, so that individuals begin to change their psychological contract and to reveal their individual objectives. This new state of affairs necessitates rules and procedures or exchange methods of influence, and the use of position or resource power by the managers to get the work done. In short, the task culture tends to change to a role of power culture when resources are limited or the total organization is unsuccessful. It is a difficult culture to control and inherently unstable by itself.

The task culture is the one preferred, as a personal choice to work in, by most managers, certainly at the middle and junior levels. It is the culture which most of the behavioural theories of organizations point towards with its emphasis on groups, expert power, rewards for results, merging individual and group objectives. It is the culture most in tune with current ideologies of change and adaptation, individual freedom and low status differentials. But, as will be seen, it is not always the appropriate culture for the climate and the technology. If organizations do not all embrace this culture it may be that they are not just out-of-date and old-fashioned – but right.

2.5 The person culture

The fourth culture is an unusual one. It will not be found pervading many organizations, yet many individuals will cling to some of its values. In this culture the individual is the central point. If there is a structure or an organization it exists only to serve and assist the individuals within it. If a group of individuals decide that it is in their own interests to band together in order the better to follow their own bents, to do their own thing, and that an office, a space, some equipment or even clerical and secretarial assistance would help, then the resulting organization would have a person culture. It would exist only for the people in it without any super-ordinate objective. Barristers' chambers, architects' partnerships, hippy communes, social groups, families, some small consultancy firms, often have this 'person' orientation. Its structure is as minimal as possible, a *cluster* is the best word for it, or perhaps a galaxy of individual stars:

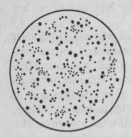

Dionysus is its patron deity, the god of the self-oriented individual, the first existentialist.

Clearly, not many organizations can exist with this sort of culture, since organizations tend to have objectives over and above the collective objectives of those who comprise them. Furthermore control mechanisms, or even management hierarchies, are impossible in these cultures except by mutual consent. The psychological contract states that the organization is subordinate to the individual and depends on the individual for its existence. The individual can leave the organization but the organization seldom has the power to evict the individual. Influence is shared and the power-base, if needed, is usually expert; that is, individuals do what they are good at and are listened to on appropriate topics.

The change in the culture of the modern family from a power or role culture more common in Victorian times with a clear power structure and apportionments of tasks and responsibilities, to a person culture with shared influence and roles apportioned according to expertise, is becoming one of the sociological features of our society. The kibbutz, the commune, the co-operative, are all striving after the person culture in organizational form. On the whole, only their original creators achieve any success. Too soon the organization achieves its own identity and begins to impose on its individuals. It becomes, at best, a task culture, but often a power or a role culture.

But although it would be rare to find an organization where the personal culture predominated, you will often encounter individuals whose personal preference is for this type of culture but who find themselves operating in a more typical organization. The stereotype of the professor is of a person-oriented man operating in a role culture. He does what he has to, teaches when he must, in order to retain his position in that organization. But essentially he regards the organization as a base on which he can build his own career, carry out his own interests, all of which may indirectly add interest to the organization though that would not be the point in doing them. Specialists in organizations – computer people in business organizations, consultants in hospitals, architects in city government – often feel little allegiance to the organization but regard it rather as a place to do their thing with some accruing benefit to the main employer.

Individuals with this orientation are not easy to manage. There is little influence that can be brought to bear on them. Being specialists alternative employment is often easy to obtain, or they have protected themselves by tenure, so that resource power has no potency. Position power not backed up by resource power achieves nothing. Expert power they are unlikely to acknowledge. Coercive power is not usually available, only personal power is left and such individuals are not easily impressed by personality.

3 The influencing factors

3.1

The cultures have been described in impressionistic and imprecise ways. They have not been rigorously defined. A culture cannot be precisely defined, for it is something that is perceived, something felt. However, a self-analysis questionnaire in Box 7.7 will fill out the descriptions in more detail. It will also allow you to identify the prevailing culture in your organization as well as your own personal cultural preference. A fit between the two should lead to a fulfilled psychological contract, to satisfaction at work.

3.2 The factors

The impressionistic descriptions pointed to some of the factors which would influence a choice of culture and structure for an organization. These factors now need to be looked at in rather more detail. The principal ones are:

History and ownership;
Size;
Technology;
Goals and objectives;
The environment;
The people.

3.3 History and ownership

The age of the company, its ownership and its history will affect its culture in the following ways:

Centralized ownership will lead towards a power culture with more control of the resources. Diffused ownership allows diffused influence based on alternative sources of power. Family firms, or founder-dominated organizations, will tend to be power cultures.

New organizations need either to be aggressive and independent (power) or flexible, adaptable and sensitive (task). They are often a combination of the two. Explicit repudiation of role cultures and of the systems, procedures and jargons that accompany role cultures, often emanate from new organizations:

1 Mergers often mean an aggressive organization moving into a static organization – a power culture superimposed on a Greek temple.

2 A new generation of managers often heralds its arrival by a change of

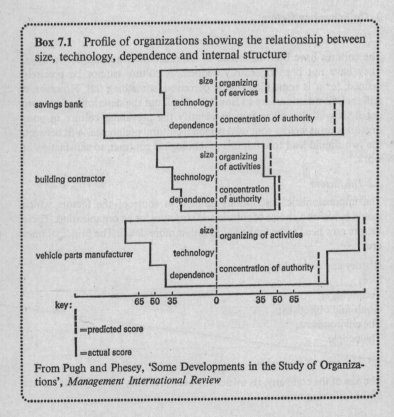

Box 7.1 Profile of organizations showing the relationship between size, technology, dependence and internal structure

key:
=predicted score

=actual score

From Pugh and Phesey, 'Some Developments in the Study of Organizations', *Management International Review*

culture. 'Systems instead of politics' equals 'role replaces power'; 'efficiency not bureaucracy' means 'task instead of role'.

3.4 Size

Size of organization has always proved to be the single most important variable in influencing a choice of structure or of culture. It is clear that, on the whole:

Large organizations are more formalized;
Large organizations tend to develop specialized groups which need systematic co-ordination.

In general, size pushes the organization towards a role culture. Specific actions, spinning-off subsidiaries, or radical decentralization, may allow the core organization to develop a different culture. A web linking a series of temples is quite conceivable. Size, however, does not in itself bring low morale:

Large organizations are seen by their members as offering more potential and being more friendly places;
Large organizations are thought to be more efficient but more authoritarian by their employees.

Box 7.2

(a)

number of levels of authority	system of production		
	unit production	mass production	process production
8 or more		■	■ ■
7		■	■ ■
6		■ ■	■ ■ ■ ●
5		■ ■ ■	■ ■ ■
4	■ ■	■ ■ ■ ■ ■ ■ ■ ●	■ ■
3	■ ■ ■ ■ ■ ■ ■ ●	■	
2	■ ■		

■ 1 firm   ● median

The median is the number of levels in the middle firm in the range — for instance, the sixteenth of the thirty-one mass-production firms

Box 7.2 – *contd*

(b)

system of production

number of persons controlled	unit production	mass production	process production
unclassified	■	■	
81–90		■ ■ ■	
71–80		■	
61–70		■ ■ ■	
51–60	■	■ ■	
41–50	■ ■	■ ■ ■ ■ ■ ■	
31–40	■ ■	■ ■ ■	■
21–30	■ ■ ■ ■	■ ■	■ ■ ■
11–20	■ ■ ■ ■		■ ■ ■ ■ ■ ■
0–10 or less	■		■ ■ ■

■ 1 firm   ● median

(c)

size of firm

system of production	between 400–500 employees	between 850–1000 employees	between 3000–4000 employees
unit			
mass			
process			

Supervisory staff shown in white jackets – other personnel shaded

From Woodward, *Industrial Organization*, 1965

3.5 Technology

Ever since the Tavistock theorists coined the phrase 'socio-technical system' and Joan Woodward in Essex demonstrated that the technology of production was a major determinant in the organization of efficient firms, it has been clear that the kind of technology will have an effect on the culture and the structure.

Trist and Bamforth of the Tavistock Institute in London demonstrated that changing a technology from small group work to three-shift working had a disruptive effect on the relationships of the men during the job, and thus on productivity. The design of the organization must therefore take into account the nature of the work as well as its people.

Joan Woodward classified a range of manufacturing firms in Essex into *unit* (or small batch), *mass* (or large batch), and *process*. She discovered that the length of the line of command, the span of control of the chief executive, the percentage of turnover devoted to wages and salaries, the ratio of managers to others, of graduates to non-graduates and indirect to direct labour, all increased as the technology involved moved along the line from unit to process. However, mass production was more formalized and mechanistic than the other two. She demonstrated that those organizations whose structures were in line with the norm for their technology were the most effective.

Perrow suggested that the continuum in technology was really from routine to non-routine. He is interested in the impact of technology on systems of co-ordination, control, on degree of inter-dependence, on individual influence and power, on goals and motivation. He puts forward a complex scheme for linking these factors to technology.

These studies, and others, in general demonstrated that technology was important. They do not all, however, obviously point towards one or other of the cultures, but:

1 Routine, programmable operations are more suitable to a role culture than any of the others.

2 High cost, expensive technologies, where the cost of breakdown is high, tend to encourage close monitoring and supervision and require depth of expertise. Both are more appropriate in a role culture.

3 Technologies where there are clear economies of scale by mass production of heavy capital investment tend to encourage large size and thence role cultures.

4 Non-continuous discrete operations, the one-off job, unit production, these technologies are suited to power or task cultures.

5 Rapidly changing technologies require a task or power culture to be dealt with effectively.

6 Tasks with a high degree of interdependence call for systematized co-ordination and suggest a role culture. In markets where co-ordination and uniformity are more important than adaptability a role culture will therefore be appropriate.

Technological considerations do not always push in the same way. High cost, rapidly changing technologies will leave the culture ambivalent between role and task. So will a need for swift reaction but high co-ordination. In general, however, the tendency towards increasing automation and high investment in technologies of work is pushing cultures towards a role orientation.

3.6 Goals and objectives

The objectives of an enterprise are seldom as clear-cut as they seem. It is too simple to claim that a business firm pursues profitability. How hard does it pursue it? Over what time-span? With what degree of risk? What constraints does it accept in the way of pressures on people, ethics, level of debt? It is sometimes conceptually simpler to regard profit as a necessary factor in achieving the other corporate objectives such as survival, rate of growth, market share, reputation, increased share value, standard of excellence, good place to work, source of employment, strategic necessity, national prestige. The level of profit required to pursue any combination of these objectives will vary. Strategic necessity, for instance, requires minimal profit generation, whereas increased share value requires a high profit ratio.

The objectives of hospitals, schools and local government are often a mixture of service to a community and maintenance of standards, within the limits however of constrained resources. How do these goals affect the culture and structure?

Quality of product goals are more easily monitored in a role organization; Growth goals are more appropriate to a power or a task culture; Place to work, centre of employment, strategic necessity point towards role cultures; Goals not only influence cultures, they are influenced by them. An organization's goals can change over a period of time as its culture changes. These tendencies are only tendencies. A role culture can achieve growth. A power culture can have strategic necessity as its goal. Goals and objectives are only one of the influencing factors. Too often to be helpful the real goals of an organization are undeclared, even to the top manager himself.

A leading banker once said, 'There are only a handful of people in Britain interested in making money. The rest are interested in making things for money.' He was suggesting that most organizations are wedded to their technology or product or industry, that success is defined for them within those constraints. Role cultures for instance are reliable cultures. They are not cultures in a hurry. They take pride in their product whereas power cultures take pride in their results. The difference in goals may seem semantic but it can be decisive.

3.7 The environment

The environment includes:

The economic environment;
The market;
The competitive scene;
The geographical and societal environment.

The nature of an environment within which an organization works is often taken for granted by those who work within it but it can be crucially important in determining the culture.

Box 7.3 Mechanistic and organismic systems of management

A mechanistic management system is appropriate to stable conditions. It is characterized by:

1 The *specialized differentiation* of functional tasks into which the problems and tasks facing the concern as a whole are broken down.

2 The *abstract nature* of each individual task, which is pursued with techniques and purposes more or less distinct from those of the concern as a whole.

3 The reconciliation, for each level in the hierarchy, of these distinct performances by the *immediate superiors*.

4 The *precise definition* of rights and obligations and technical methods attached to each functional role.

5 The *translation of rights* and obligations and methods into the responsibilities of a functional position.

6 *Hierarchic structure* of control, authority and communication.

7 A reinforcement of the hierarchic structure by the location of *knowledge* of actualities exclusively *at the top* of the hierarchy.

8 A tendency for *vertical interaction* between members of the concern to be, i.e. between superior and subordinate.

9 A tendency for operations and working behaviour to be *governed by superiors*.

Box 7.3 – *contd*

10 *Insistence on loyalty* to the concern and obedience to superiors as a condition of membership.

11 A greater importance and prestige attaching to *internal* (local) than to general (cosmopolitan) knowledge, experience and skill.

The organismic form is appropriate to changing conditions, which give rise constantly to fresh problems and unforeseen requirements for action which cannot be broken down or distributed automatically arising from the functional roles defined within a hierarchic structure. It is characterized by:

1 The *contributive nature* of special knowledge and experience to the common task of the concern.

2 The *realistic* nature of the individual task, which is seen as set by the total situation of the concern.

3 The adjustment and *continual re-definition* of individual tasks through interaction with others.

4 The *shedding of responsibility* as a limited field of rights; obligations and methods. (Problems may not be posted upwards, downwards or sideways.)

5 The *spread of commitment* to the concern beyond any technical definition.

6 A *network structure* of control authority, and communication.

7 Omniscience no longer imputed to the head of the concern; *knowledge* may be located anywhere in the network, this location becoming the centre of authority.

8 A *lateral* rather than a vertical direction of communication through the organization.

9 A content of communication which consists of *information and advice* rather than instructions and decisions.

10 *Commitment* to the concern's tasks and to the 'technological ethos' of material progress and expansion is more highly valued than loyalty.

11 Importance and prestige attach to *affiliations and expertise* valid in the industrial and technical and commercial milieux external to the firm.

From Burns and Stalker, *The Management of Innovation*, 1966.

Some of the major points are:

1 Change in the environment requires a culture that is sensitive, adaptable and quick to respond. A task culture is most suited to coping with changes in the market or the product. Burns and Stalker discovered that firms with what they called an 'organismic' or 'organic' structure responded more effectively to changes in the technology than firms with a mechanistic structure. Organic and mechanistic correspond to the task and role cultures.

2 Diversity in the environment requires a diversified structure. Diversity inclines towards a task culture. Standardization inclines towards a role culture. Thus pure functional organizations with, for instance, one sales department, are usually found in firms with undiversified markets and products with a long life-cycle. They will usually have a role culture.

If the important difference is that between the products, then a product organization is suggested. Only in this way will individual products get differentiated attention. If the important difference is between geographical regions, then a regional organization may be appropriate. If the difference is type of distribution, or customer classification, then that should be your structure. When the difference is a mix of all four, or of two or three, the organization will tend to reflect this. Which structure is subordinate to which may change with time, as for instance regional differences tend to blur and products become more important.

Threat or danger in the environment are best countered by power cultures. Mergers and take-overs, nationalization or economic disaster are examples of threats and dangers. Those organizations which are web-like, with a strong figure at the centre, will be most likely to be successful in

---

Box 7.4 The case of the invisible job

Jim went straight from university into a large and prestigious manufacturing organization. There could, he felt, be no better preparation for a managerial career than an apprenticeship in such a successful and renowned corporation. In his eight years there he did a variety of jobs in a variety of functions and learnt much about the way they ran their business. In particular he schooled himself in methods of investment appraisal, procedures for job evaluation and description, organization design and management development. He was impressed by the budgeting and authority system and by the meticulous standardization of procedures which applied to much of their large business.

Jim was reasonably successful. But circumstances changed and he felt that he would like to move to a smaller but more vigorous organization. One such, a financial organization with funds to invest in new ventures, was looking for a man to analyse new investment opportunities. Jim applied and was quickly accepted. Confident in his mastery of all the proper techniques and procedures, he reported for work.

The office they had provided for him was elegant. His secretary delightful. He was assigned to the management luncheon room and introduced to the directors that he had not already met. Everyone was extremely charming and pleased to see him. At the end of his first day, Jim felt very satisfied

Box 7.4 – *contd*

with his decision to join. The second and third days, however, were less pleasant. Nothing happened. Nothing at all. Jim looked for a formal description of his job but it appeared not to exist. He decided to write one, and by way of preparation asked his boss, a director, for an organization chart. It seemed that there was no such thing. Asked to sketch one, his boss put down a list of all the directors and under them a list of all the other executives. There seemed to be no proper system of departments, no formal allocation of duties. It was unclear, even, who approved investment decisions and whether Jim himself had authority to initiate any investment, or even to spend money on searches and surveys.

Bewildered, at lunch at the end of the week he confessed his mystification to one of the directors and said that he had still been given no work to do and was very unsure of what he was supposed to be doing. 'Why,' said the director, 'you should be out there somewhere, talking to people, getting on aeroplanes, making contacts, getting information. We want ideas, suggestions, projects from you.'

Gradually, Jim grew to understand that there were no rules and procedures, that one had to proceed intuitively, to know by instinct what the directors would approve, what shrink from; that he was trusted completely and expected to do what was necessary, spend what was necessary, to get them into profitable new ventures.

At home, however, he pondered over his collections of procedures, his books of techniques, his manuals and tables. 'Do they know of these things and for some reason have rejected them,' he wondered, 'or should I try to introduce them?'

these circumstances. Successful field generals in time of war tend to be power-orientated. Merger battles are often decided by personalities. For power cultures can move swiftly and decisively, are aggressive rather than adaptive, strong rather than flexible.

3.8 The people

It has already been stressed that different cultures call for differing psychological contracts, that certain types of people will be happy and successful in one culture, not in another. A match between organization, culture and an individual's psychological contract should lead to a satisfied individual. Satisfaction, we know, does not imply productivity but it is a good place to start from. The studies in job satisfaction do not differentiate between cultures or between individual expectation so that the statements above cannot as yet be demonstrated to be true, but they represent a plausible hypothesis. Leading on from there, some further hypotheses can be advanced:

1 Individuals with a low tolerance for ambiguity will prefer the tighter role prescriptions of the role culture.
2 High needs for security will be better met in the role culture.
3 A need to establish one's identity at work will be appropriate in a power or task culture. In a role culture it will be seen as a 'person' orientation and thought disruptive.
4 The impact of individual skills and talents will be more marked in power and task cultures than in role. Hence greater care needs to be paid to the selection and appraisal of individuals in these cultures.
5 Low calibre people resources – in the sense of intelligence or interpersonal skills – would push an organization towards a role culture, where jobs can be defined down to the level of manpower available.

In general, the availability of people with the right orientations will be a significant element in the freedom that an organization has to move towards a particular culture. The individual orientations of the key people in an organization will have a large say in determining what the dominant culture is, irrespective of what it should be. You decide, in large part, on your culture when you decide on your people.

3.9 Conclusion

Any one organization, examining itself in the light of these influencing factors, will find itself pushed towards at least two and perhaps three of the cultures. Often an organization will find that the forces in the environment push it towards a power culture, that its size and technology push it towards role, and the personal inclinations of the middle managers incline it to a task orientation. How is it to decide? Which of the factors should be determining when all influence it but in differing directions?

4 Implications for organization design

4.1

Faced with factors pulling in different ways organizations have to adapt. Most typical is the role culture confronted by a changing environment in which:

The technology is no longer relatively constant;
The rate of change in new products has accelerated;
Overseas imports have disturbed the pricing and distribution mechanisms of the market;

New standards and qualities are required by the client population; Competitive institutions are setting new standards for comparison.

Not only business organizations, but hospitals, schools, government institutions find themselves facing a rapidly changing and often hostile environment. There are three possible ways of adapting. It will become clear that the third is the desirable one:

Adaptation by deliberation;
Adaptation by reproduction;
Adaptation by differentiation.

(It may be, of course, that the organization is powerful enough and large enough to influence and control its environment and needs not to adapt. This is the thesis and the warning of those who predict the continued growth of the large corporation. Organizations undoubtedly attempt this but so far without much long-term success.)

Box 7.5   The range of alternatives

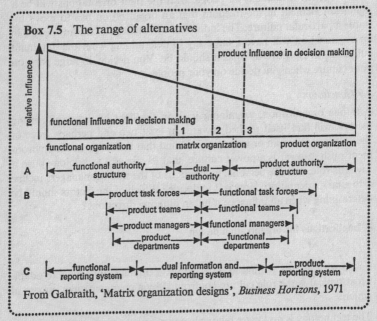

From Galbraith, 'Matrix organization designs', *Business Horizons*, 1971

4.2 Adaptation by deliberation

In this mode the organization seeks to improve the planning and co-ordination of the Greek temple structure by increasing thought, talk and liaison. It seeks to reinforce the formal structure by more formal structures. Corporate planning groups, liason committees, project teams and task forces are created. New, often highly-talented, individuals are recruited. Reports, schemes, committees to monitor, committees to progress, committees to assess, begin to proliferate. Metaphorically, stresses begin to link the pillars of the temple, while nets of planning groups are suspended from the pediment. Structurally, the rudiments of a matrix or project organization appear. Project groupings overlap the functional divisions with product or regional co-ordinators linking the functions. These new groups tend to be small, talented and task-orientated. The quality of their work is often impressive. Alas, too often, it has no impact on the problems of the organization. Deliberation proliferates, often at a high cost and with much frustration, but the organization continues to do too little too late. The new liaison men, the co-ordinators, the planners and thinkers, find that they have little or no resource or expert power to back up their very tenuous position of power; that the previous divisions remain dominant, that they, the deliberators, are but moss on the pillars, or nets suspended from the gutters of the pediment. In order to achieve anything they have to work informally to by-pass the formal structure and rely on personal power and inter-personal skill. Political links develop, supported by underground informal communication channels. It is relatively easy, as the position deteriorates, to amputate the new growths and restore the organization to its original structural purity. There is even a temporary reduction in overheads by so doing since you save the costs of, for instance, the corporate planning department by declaring its members redundant. But the long-term pressing problem will remain.

4.3 Adaptation by reproduction

The second most popular form of adaptation is decentralization or divisionalization. Theoretically, this is diversifying the structure to accord with the differences in the environment. Theoretically, a regional decentralization recognizes that it is the difference between the regions that are vital; similarly with a product group decentralization. Theoretically, the new organizations should be free to adapt their cultures and their structures to their particular set of influencing factors. Theoretically, the mother structure, the Head Office, adapts its form to the new requirements. All this is one form of differentiation, to be discussed in the next section.

Unfortunately decentralization too often becomes a process of reproducing the parent organization in its siblings. Too often the basis for the regroupings is decided by political or personality factors or by administrative convenience. Too often the parent organization remains unchanged, each part of it has merely reproduced itself in half-a-dozen other locations. A Greek temple now presides over a set of Greek temples. Conflicts arise between the temples and between the corresponding pillars in temples. The parent temple can now justify its existence by the need to resolve these conflicts and impose some order. Deviations in cultures or structures are seen as distortions, untidy, inefficient. Work becomes duplicated, responsibility is unclear, reaction time remains slow, initiation drops.

Adaptation by reproduction has at least one advantage. Individual sub-organizations can now be allowed to wither, die or disappear without affecting the health of the whole. This method of adaptation has often proved to be a necessary prelude to the organizational surgery needed for the survival of the whole.

4.4 Adaptation by differentiation

Ideally, of course, organizations should encourage different cultures, different structures, for different situations. Decentralization is one way of achieving this. We have also discussed, briefly, differentiation between products, regions, or classes of client. There is however, another, more general way of looking at the activities of organizations, all organizations – large or small, business or social, manufacturing or service. In each organization there are four different sets of activities:

Steady state;
Innovative/developmental;
Breakdown/crises;
Policy/direction.

Steady state implies all those activities which can be programmed in some way, are routine as opposed to non-routine.

The steady state often accounts for 80 per cent of an organization's personnel. It includes the infrastructure of the organization – the accounting system, the secretarial system, the office services section. It includes, usually, most of the production component of the organization. Most sales activities would come under the steady state category, but not the marketing activity.

Innovative/developmental includes all activities directed to changing the things that the organization does or the way it does it. R and D of course, but also parts of marketing, the development side of production, corporate planning, organization and methods departments, perhaps parts of the finance department.

Breakdown/crises. All organizations have to deal with the unexpected. No one part of the organization will have a monopoly of crises or break-downs, although the part of the organization that interfaces with the environment is more likely to have to cope with the unexpected. Marketing, parts of production, top management are the sectors most exposed.

Policy/direction. The overall guidance and direction of activities must not be neglected. The setting of priorities, the establishment of standards, the direction and allocation of resources, the initiation of action, these are activities which form a category of their own, although there is some degree of overlap with the other sets.

Some parts of the formal structure of the company will fall neatly into one of these categories, e.g. R and D or office services. Others, such as marketing, may have a mixture of categories. Usually each department will find the bulk of its activities in one or other set. That bulk will tend to determine the main focus and culture that is appropriate to it, as shown in Figure 10.

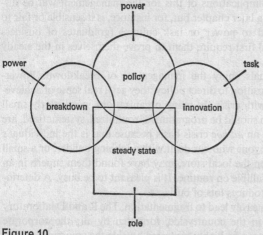

power

power

task

policy

breakdown

innovation

steady state

role

Figure 10

The suggestion is that, if the appropriate culture prevails where that set of activities prevails, then that part of the organization will be more effective. The suggestion is that organizations should differentiate their cultures and structures according to the dominant kind of activity in that department, division or section. R and D, for instance, should be organized differently from the accounting department. The innovative part of marketing can be expected to be more informal, more task-orientated than the assembly-line. The management of crisis should override committees, rules and procedures, and rely on political support for initiative. The management of steady state activities should properly be concerned with rules, procedures, regulations and formal controls. Apply these to the innovation arms of the organization and they will suffocate.

4.5 Implications of differentiation

One culture should not be allowed to swamp the organization. Too often organizations wish to bring everything into the steady state. This may lead to greater security but it may also lead to decay. Similarly a task culture is inappropriate for the bulk of the activities of most organizations.

An individual successful in one culture may not always succeed in another. This is one explanation of the Peter Principle which holds that a man is promoted to his level of incompetence. For instance, individuals successful in the steady-state but promoted out of the pillar into the pediment, find the ambiguity of the power culture too stressful and withdraw into inactivity. The implications of this for the management will be discussed more fully in a later chapter but, for instance, is it sensible or fair to recruit people suited to power or task cultures (graduates of business schools perhaps) and first require them to prove themselves in the steady state?

A lot of individuals enjoy the management of breakdown. Power-oriented, but in no position to direct policy, they get a real sense of achievement from dealing with crisis. In many organizations, particularly small ones, activities which should be programmed, routinized, systematized, are in fact dealt with on an *ad hoc* crisis basis because that is the individual's preferred culture. Anyone who has dealt with a jobbing builder, or a small manufacturer, or even the local store, may have found them superb in an emergency but very fallible on routine. It is pleasant to be busy. A deteriorating steady state produces lots of business.

Differentiation can easily lead to fragmentation. The R and D laboratory can become buried in the countryside, forgotten by all; the corporate planning department can be highly respected outside the company, deliver papers at learned congresses, and be ignored within. The steady state can churn out products not needed by the market, the chief executive sign contracts that no one can fulfil. When representatives of two cultures meet they will find that their priorities, their time scales, their styles of working will all be different. Yet the cultures must work together. For differentiation to be successful there must be integration.

4.6 Integration

The greater the differentiation the greater the potential for conflict. The sales executive, involved in the day-to-day management of breakdown, is going to find the long-term problematical perspectives of the research scientist irritating and irrelevant to his current preoccupations. The production controller will be loath to interrupt his schedules in order to help the crisis of the sales people. These and myriad other potential sources of conflict must be managed if a differentiated environment is not going to tear itself apart or fail to communicate at all. There is a whole range of integrative devices.

Rules and procedures;
Direct managerial contact;
Appeals to the hierarchy;
Temporary cross-functional teams;
Permanent cross-functional teams;
Individual co-ordinators;
Co-ordinating departments.

Every organization needs some integration. A pure role organization will normally use the first three. The greater the degree of differentiation between the cultures the more devices the organization should use.

The role of a co-ordinator is a difficult one. To take it on can easily be a short cut to organizational suicide. To be successful there seem to be four prerequisites:

1 He must have position power and the appropriate status. That is, the job must be seen by all to be important and to be considered so by top management. One way to achieve this is to move into the post a demonstrably successful individual who will carry some of his previous position power with him. He must also have the information appropriate to his position so that he is in fact in a position to take decisions.

2 He must have expert power, and be perceived to have it by all the groups or individuals whom he is co-ordinating. Ideally, he should have experience or expertise on both sides of the fence.

3 He must have the inter-personal skills necessary to resolve conflict situations between individuals in a problem-solving mode. (See chapter 8.)

These are tough requirements. It is easy to understand why so many co-ordinating tasks are not very effectively done. Yet if these requirements are not met there will be ineffective integration and the differentiation will be disruptive rather than productive.

Box 7·6 Differences in 'climate' characteristics in high-performing organizations

Characteristics	Akron (a manufacturing plant)	Stockton (a research laboratory)
1 structural orientation	perceptions of tightly controlled behaviour and a high degree of structure	perceptions of a low degree of structure
2 distribution of influence	perceptions of low total influence, concentrated at upper levels in the organization	perceptions of high total influence, more evenly spread out among all levels
3 character of superior-subordinate relations	low freedom *vis-à-vis* superiors to choose and handle jobs, directive type of supervision	high freedom *vis-à-vis* superiors to choose and handle projects, participatory type of supervision
4 character of colleague relations	perceptions of many similarities among colleagues, high degree of co-ordination of colleague effort	perceptions of many differences among colleagues, relatively low degree of co-ordination of colleague effort
5 time orientation	short-term	long-term
6 goal orientation	manufacturing	scientific
7 top executive's 'managerial style'	more concerned with task than people	more concerned with task than people

From Morse and Lorsch, 'Beyond theory Y', *Harvard Business Review*, 1970

4.7 Does it work?

The sections on differentiation of culture and integration have been very prescriptive. Is there any evidence to support the thesis? There is:

1 A series of studies by Lawrence and Lorsch (referred to in more detail in Part Three) looked at the distinguishing features of high-performing organizations in three environments. The organizations were in the plastics, food and container industries. The industries ranged in the degree of their diversity from plastics (the most diverse and the most dynamic), through food to containers (a relatively stable and homogeneous environment) and sufficient integrative devices to manage that differentiation. Thus, by their measurements, the plastics organization was almost twice as highly differentiated as the container organization, with the whole array of possible integration devices, from rules and procedures through to a coordinating department. By differentiation was meant that individual parts of the organization would have:

(a) Differing time-horizons (long or short);
(b) Differing orientations to the market (customer needs or product quality);
(c) Differing inter-personal styles;
(d) Differing degrees of formality in the structure.

Thus in a differentiated organization the sales director and the research director will be fundamentally concerned with differing problems, over widely differing time horizons – the sales director worrying about specific rebates, the scientist about performance characteristics of a new product. But they would also have differing styles of management and habits of work, different 'cultures'.

2 Morse and Lorsch, in a study similar to the preceding one, looked at the comparison between successful and unsuccessful organizations in two widely different technologies – a manufacturing plant and a research laboratory. They found that the styles of management in the successful laboratory differed markedly from that employed in the less successful laboratory – but it also was the opposite of the style practised in the successful factory. Vice versa, the style of the successful factory approximated to that of the less successful laboratory.

In the more open-ended, long time-horizon environment of the *laboratory* a supportive style worked best, with minimum rules and procedures and a lot of individual and group initiative (a task culture). In the successful *factory*, however, a tight structured approach not only worked best but was appreciated by the employees who, in that situation, wanted to know what they had to do, by when, for whom (a role culture).

3 Joan Woodward showed that the more effective organizations were the ones that had a structure which seemed appropriate to the technology.

4 Anecdotal experience would suggest that different ways of running organizations can be effective. This cannot all be attributed to luck or the genius of the managing director. We also know that if they do not change their culture when the environment changes they will cease to be successful. British industrial history is strewn with firms that grew to success in the days of imperial protection and sellers' markets, pride in their product and a pure role culture. Oftentimes a marketing department did not even exist, sometimes not even a sales division. Confronted by change and threat they seemed fossilized in the past – like the Greek temples at Paestum in Italy, the world passed by and left them isolated in the marshes.

The spate of mergers in the 1960s was often the only way left to rescue the investment of these organizations in the skill, talent, and know-how of their employees from the ossifying effect of their culture and structure. Sir Arnold Weinstock's main task was to destroy the central temples of G.E.C., A.E.C. and English Electric and to replace them at the centre with a small flexible web.

5 Summary

Each organization, each part of an organization, has a culture, and a structure and systems appropriate to that culture. Individuals will each have a preferred culture.

Cultures	*Structures*
power	web
role	temple
task	net
person	cluster

The choice of the appropriate structure will be determined by:

History and ownership;
Size;
Technology;
Goals and objectives;
The environment;
The people.

Box 7.7 What kind of organization?

To be done by individuals (40 minutes) and the scores collated in groups.

1 What kind of organization do you belong to? What set of values, styles of behaviour, characterize it?

2 What kind of organization would you *like* to belong to?

Please complete this questionnaire:

(a) For yourself, your own values and beliefs;

(b) For your own organization.

Rank each statement in order of salience. Put '1' against the statement which best represents the dominant view in your organization, '2' for the next closest. Then go back and do the same for your own beliefs.

At the end, please add up the scores for the first statement under each heading, the scores for the second statement, and so on (e.g. a score of 15 for the first statement would mean that it had ranked top in all categories).

The group should then analyse its combined results.

(a) Ask each individual to note which set of statements had the lowest score for himself; for his organization.

(b) Complete the following matrix for the group

numbers of individuals with lowest score for statements

	number 1	number 2	number 3	number 4
self				
organization				

(c) The four sets of statements describe the four cultures described in the text. If statement number 1 has the lowest total score for any individual that would suggest that culture number 1 is his preferred culture. The numbering of the statements corresponds to the order in which the cultures are listed in the text.

(d) How dominant a cultural preference is in the life of an individual or an organization will be represented by the *difference* between the total scores for the four sets of cultures. A score of 15 would imply that the corresponding culture was totally dominant.

(e) A perfect match between an individual's preferences and his organization's cultures would suggest a perfectly fitting psychological contract. Most people will not have a perfect match. The group may like to explore the reasons for the differences *after* they have read the text.

Box 7.7 – *contd*

Own ranking	Organ- ization's ranking	

1 *A good boss*

.... is strong, decisive and firm but fair. He is protective, generous and indulgent to loyal subordinates.

.... is impersonal and correct, avoiding the exercise of his authority for his own advantage. He demands from subordinates only that which is required by the formal system.

.... is egalitarian and influenceable in matters concerning the task. He uses his authority to obtain the resources needed to get on with the job.

.... is concerned and responsive to the personal needs and values of others. He uses his position to provide satisfying and growth stimulating work opportunities for subordinates.

2 *A good subordinate*

.... is compliant, hard-working and loyal to the interests of his superior.

.... is responsible and reliable, meeting the duties and responsibilities of his job and avoiding actions which surprise or embarrass his superior.

.... is self-motivated to contribute his best to the task and is open with his ideas and suggestions. He is nevertheless willing to give the lead to others when they show greater expertise or ability.

.... is vitally interested in the development of his own potentialities and is open to learning and receiving help. He also respects the needs and values of others and is willing to give help and contribute to their development.

3 *A good member of the organization gives first priority to*

.... the personal demands of the boss.

.... the duties, responsibilities and requirements of his own role, and the customary standards of personal behaviour.

.... the requirements of the task for skill, ability, energy and material resources.

.... the personal needs of the individual involved.

Box 7.7 – *contd*

Own rank.	Org. rank.

4 *People who do well in the organization*

.... are shrewd and competitive with a strong drive for power.

.... are conscientious and responsible with a strong sense of loyalty to the organization.

.... are technically competent and effective, with a strong commitment to getting the job done.

.... are effective and competent in personal relationships, with a strong commitment to the growth and development of people.

5 *The organization treats the individual*

.... as though his time and energy were at the disposal of the persons higher in the hierarchy.

.... as though his time and energy were available through a contract having rights and responsibilities on both sides.

.... as a co-worker who has committed his skills and abilities to the common cause.

.... as an interesting and worth-while person in his own right.

6 *People are controlled and influenced by*

.... the personal exercise of economic and political power (rewards and punishments).

.... impersonal exercise of economic and political power to enforce procedures and standards of performance.

.... communication and discussion of task requirements leading to appropriate action motivated by personal commitment to goal achievement.

.... intrinsic interest and enjoyment in the activities to be done; and/or concern and caring for the needs of the other persons involved.

7 *It is legitimate for one person to control another's activities*

.... if he has more authority and power in the organization.

.... if his role prescribes that he is responsible for directing the other.

.... if he has more knowledge relevant to the task at hand.

.... if the other accepts that the first person's help or instruction can contribute to the other's learning and growth.

Box 7.7 – *contd*

Own rank.	Org. rank.

8 *The basis of task assignment is*

.... the personal needs and judgement of those in authority.

.... the formal divisions of functions and responsibility in the system.

.... the resource and expertise requirements of the job to be done.

.... the personal wishes and needs for learning and growth of the individual organization members.

9 *Work is performed out of*

.... hope of reward, fear of punishment or personal loyalty towards a powerful individual.

.... a respect for contractual obligations backed up by sanctions and personal loyalty towards the organization or system.

.... satisfaction in excellence of work and achievement and/or personal commitment to the task or goal.

.... enjoyment of the activity for its own sake and concern and respect for the needs and values of the other persons involved.

10 *People work together*

.... when they are required to by higher authority or believe they can use each other for personal advantage.

.... when co-ordination and exchange are specified by the formal system.

.... when their joint contribution is needed to progress the task.

.... when the collaboration is personally satisfying, stimulating or challenging.

11 *Competition*

.... is for personal power and advantages.

.... is for high status position in the formal system.

.... is for excellence of contribution to the task.

.... is for attention to one's own personal needs.

12 *Conflict*

.... is controlled by the intervention of higher authority and often fostered by them to maintain their own power.

Box 7.7 – *contd*

Own rank.	Org. rank.	

is suppressed by reference to rules, procedures and
.... definitions of responsibility.

is resolved through full discussion of the merits of the
.... work issues involved.

is resolved by open and deep discussion of personal
.... needs and values involved.

13 *Decisions*

are made by the person with the higher power and
.... authority.

are made by the person whose job description carries
.... the responsibility.

are made by the persons with most knowledge and
.... expertise about the problem.

are made by the persons most personally involved and
.... affected by the outcome.

14 *The appropriate control and communication structure*

Command flows from the top down in a simple pyramid
so that anyone who is higher in the pyramid has
authority over anyone who is lower. Information flows
.... up through the chain of command.

Directives flow from the top down and information
flows upwards within functional pyramids which meet
at the top. The authority and responsibility of a role is
limited to the roles beneath it in its own pyramid. Cross
.... functional exchange is constricted.

Information about task requirements and problems
flows from the centre of task activity upwards and outwards, with those closest to the task determining
resources and support needed from the rest of the
organization. A co-ordinating function may set
priorities and overall resource levels based on
information from all task centres. The structure should
.... shift with the nature and location of the tasks.

Information and influence flow from person to person,
based on relationships which are voluntarily entered
into for purposes of work, learning, mutual support and
enjoyment, and shared values. A co-ordinating function
may establish overall levels of contribution needed for

Box 7.7 – *contd*

Own   Org.
rank.   rank.

| | | maintenance of the organization. These tasks are assigned by mutual agreement. |
| ...... | ...... | |

15 *The environment is responded to as though it were*

		a competitive jungle in which all are against all and those who do not exploit others are themselves exploited.
......	......	
		an orderly and rational system in which competition is limited by law and conflicts yield to negotiation and compromise.
......	......	
		a complex of imperfect forms and systems which are to be re-shaped and improved by the achievements of the organization.
......	......	
		a complex of potential threats and support. It is to be manipulated by the organization to extract nourishment from it, pull its teeth and use it as a play and work space for the enjoyment and growth of members.
......	......	

Questionnaire compiled by Dr Roger Harrison

Within each organization the activities can be divided roughly into four sets:

Steady state;
Innovation;
Breakdown;
Policy.

Each of these sets has its appropriate culture, structure and systems. Organizations that are *differentiated* in their cultures and who control that differentiation by *integration* are likely to be more successful.

The management of differentiated organizations is not easy. Part Two will be mainly concerned with drawing attention to some of the problems. The problem is aggravated by the tendency of many management theorists and writers to remain rooted in their preferred culture. For instance:

1 Classical management theory was talking about role cultures – the management of the steady state.

2 Modern management thinkers concentrate on the task culture and have found their favourite organizations among the project-based companies of

the U.S. aerospace industry and the innovative ends of more traditional organizations.

3 Journalists, historians, and biographers have found the power cultures, centred around a key figure or figures, easier to focus on, more tempting to describe.

4 Sociologists, religious and youth leaders, have been concerned with the clash between the organization and the individual with a 'person' orientation.

It is left to the manager to handle all four cultures, to differentiate and to integrate within his own organization.

8 On Politics and the Management of Differences

1 Introduction

'The gulf between how one should live and how one does live is so wide that a man who neglects what is actually done for what should be done learns the way to self-destruction rather than self-preservation,' said Machiavelli in defence of his treatise on *realpolitik*.

For any book on organization theory to neglect or by-pass the political reality of organizations would be misleading or blind or both, since all organizations of any size are political systems. In all organizations there are individuals and groups competing for influence or resources, there are differences of opinion and of values, conflicts of priorities and of goals. There are pressure groups and lobbies, cliques and cabals, rivalries and contests, clashes of personality and bonds of alliance. Only in the smallest of the 'person' cultures will these differences be absent, and even there for but the briefest of periods. Is this right – or only inevitable? Is man forced into competition – or competitive by nature? Should differences exist – or be ironed out? Is competition helpful, and to be designed into organizations – or a destructive force? Is conflict uncivilized and unbecoming – or the natural outcome of countervailing forces, to be understood and managed but not eradicated?

Whatever the answers to these questions – and we shall suggest some – management, like politics, consists to a large degree in the management of differences. Groups in organizations have different roles, different goals, different skills, so have individuals. The blending of these differences into one coherent whole is the overall task of management. Such a blending will involve giving some groups priority over others, ignoring some preferences and accepting others, curbing some initiatives while provoking others, putting some men down and pulling others up. A car is equipped with accelerator, brake and clutch. Operate them all simultaneously and to their limit, you will generate a lot of noise but no movement. Co-ordinate them and manage their interactions, and you progress.

It is perhaps belabouring the obvious to state it but the resolution of differences or potential differences takes up the largest single chunk of managerial time and energy, and it is not always well done at the end of it all. When asked to describe their biggest problem over the last few weeks, the majority of managers in one study did not list a tricky decision or a technical question but one involving interaction – vertically, laterally or diagonally. In another study:

(a) 87 per cent of middle managers felt that conflicts were very seldom coped with, and that, when they were, the attempts tended to be inadequate;
(b) 65 per cent thought that the most important unsolved problem of the organization was that the top management was unable to help them over-come the inter-group rivalries, lack of co-operation and poor communications;
(c) 53 per cent said that if they could alter one aspect of their superior's behaviour it would be to help him see the dog-eat-dog communication problems that existed in middle management.

Whether man is by nature competitive and aggressive, or rather a creature of innate goodwill turned to aggression by frustration and the lessons of his environment, is a question which has aroused speculation for centuries and will no doubt continue to do so. We shall probably never know the answer for sure. David Hume, in his *Essays*, wrote 'Should a traveller give an account of men who were entirely divested of avarice, ambition and revenge; who knew no pleasure but friendship, generosity and public spirit, we should immediately detect the falsehood and prove him a liar with the same certitude as if he had stuffed his narration with centaurs and dragons.' Freud, however, originally conceived of aggression as the product of frustration (particularly early sexual frustration), then as the death instinct turned outwards. His view of aggression as the product of aggression in the environment was adopted and built on by a whole generation of psychologists and sociologists. Yet Freud, at the end of his life, was to turn round and say 'I take up the standpoint that the tendency to aggression is an innate, independent, instinctual disposition in man'. Once again, heredity or environment? It is hard to believe that the argument will ever be irrevocably unravelled. Fortunately for our purposes in understanding behaviour in organizations it is enough to be able to say that by the age of maturity man has acquired or developed the habits of competition, is a creature used to aggression. The ways of managing that state, of channelling its energies and resolving its problems is the art or the science of politics in organizations.

Enough has probably been said to justify the existence of this chapter. An understanding of the nature of differences, of when they are fruitful and when disruptive, an awareness of the possible sources of conflict and the strategies for handling such conflict, an ability to distinguish between symptoms and diseases, between political tactics and the underlying differences, are all essential to effective management in organizations and even, as Machiavelli suggests, to individual survival. It may well be that such understanding could one day lead to organizations where only fruitful differences exist, but there does seem much to justify the thought that, if organizations have an original sin, it is the inherent seed of conflict that they contain within them.

This chapter will therefore examine in turn *the nature of differences, the seeds of conflict, tactics and symptoms of conflict, managerial strategies, summary and implications.*

2 The nature of differences

2.1

A world without differences is perhaps inconceivable. But of one thing we should be sure: a world without differences of opinion, values, priorities, talents and personalities would be a world without sun and shadows, a bland, dull world. We need to exploit our differences, not deplore them. To do this we must first differentiate between differences! We can, in organizations, usefully distinguish three manifestations of difference:

Argument;
Competition;
Conflict.

Words have overtones, and although one cannot build definitions on overtones we do generally regard argument and competition in themselves as useful things, conflict as not. Argument and competition can become disruptive in which case they degenerate into conflict, or, occasionally, they are bad because they are seen as symptoms or outcrops of conflict. We shall, in this chapter, regard argument and competition as the fruitful aspects of difference, and conflict as the harmful side of it. Conflict, of course, as will become clear, can arise from other sources than argument or competition. In a sense, the managerial dilemma could be seen as how to have argument and competition without conflict, how to prevent them degenerating into conflict, how to turn conflict where it exists into argument and competition. There are, inevitably, the pessimists who believe that all competition will ultimately degenerate into conflict, man being by nature mean, brutish and avaricious. There are the idealists who would banish all competition because it tends to *make* man mean, brutish and avaricious. There are those who shrink from argument, competition and conflict, and those who thrive on it. Most people stand in the middle. Most people believe that argument and competition are valuable as long as they do not degenerate into conflict. The main part of this chapter will be concerned with conflict, but first we need to dwell a little on the characteristics and management of fruitful argument and competition.

(A bit of definition is needed here. By 'fruitful' is meant beneficial for the greater number. Most conflict situations are beneficial for someone – the victor. We are concerned with organizational benefit rather than individual gains.)

Box 8.1

$A = E + h$

The *amity A* . . . which an animal expresses for *others* of its kind will be equal to the sum of the forces of *enmity* (*E*) and *hazard* (*h*) which are *arrayed* against it. By enmity, I refer to those forces of antagonism and hostility originating in members of one's own species. By hazard, I mean those threats which do not originate in one's own species . . .

But it is *E* – enmity, hostility, antagonism, aggression, however you may care to express it – that is the major ingredient in amity's making, for it grows truly on trees. Hazard is fluctuating in supply, unreliable in quantity, temporary in effect. Enmity is the gold of amity's market, the magical fibre in amity's thread. Without enmity, we should be nightingales and no air to tread on, three-spined sticklebacks and no water to fin through, the *larvae* of Capricorn beetles and no tree trunks to bore into . . . for workable amity is one strand of life weaving ineffective bodies and limited brains into a multi-patterned fabric of lasting strength, cohesive in its strength, legitimate in its *grandeurs* . . .

Enmity is the biological condition of cross-purposes. It is the innate response of an organism to any and all members of its own species. Enmity will be suspended, totally or partially, only for such periods of time as two or more individuals are embraced by a single, more powerful purpose which inhibits all or part of their mutual animosities, and channels the inhibited energy into a joint drive to achieve the joint purpose. Since amity persists no longer than mutual purpose, then, when the purpose is either achieved or permanently frustrated, amity will end. Unless a new joint purpose arises to channel joint energies, individuals will return to a normal condition of mutual animosity.

Adapted from Ardrey, *The Territorial Imperative*, 1967

2.2 Argument

John Stuart Mill believed that learning progressed through argument. From the study of groups we know that more heads produce better ideas if they discuss them. Everyday experience confirms that the expression of differing opinions and viewpoints usually helps towards reaching a better solution. Argument, the resolution of differences through discussion, is in principle to be encouraged.

How should it be managed?

(a) From the study of groups have come some prescriptions for groups that are effective in working through differences by discussion – i.e. are effective in argument. As chapter 6 indicated, a lot depends on the context, but most lists put forward include:

Shared leadership;
Confidence and trust in fellow members;
Challenging tasks;
Full use of all member resources.

Box 6.3 gave an example of a fuller list. Much attention has been paid by trainers to developing a group's capacity to handle differences, or argument. Chapter 6 mentions some of the specific approaches used.

(b) Not enough attention is always paid to what might be called the logic of the argument. Many arguments are unproductive, trite though it sounds, because:

People are arguing about different things;
Information is not available to resolve the issue.

In particular, it is necessary for all individuals to be clear and agreed on the real subject of the discussion. Is it concerned with:

Facts;
Goals;
Methods;
Values.

Differing assumptions about goals may confuse the issue. Differing sets of information may lead to differing perceptions of the problem. A discussion apparently about methods may overlay a basic disagreement of values. Inadequate information to resolve a discussion on goals leads to an inappropriate but substitute argument on methods. If the group, or the differing parties, can discern and agree on the proper and/or real cause of the difference the argument is likely to be more fruitful, less frustrating.

(c) Emotions and feelings, if unexpressed, will often become the seeds of conflict. Repressed emotions have to find an outlet somewhere. Denied open expression, they can turn to the more covert mechanisms of the political system. Arguments, discussions or differences, which permit the expression of feelings, which encourage openness, are less likely to degenerate into harmful conflict.

Lawrence and Lorsch, in their analysis of successful integrators in differentiated firms, found that they all encouraged and practised openness in the discussion of differences. They were successful as integrators partly because the differences did not degenerate into political conflict.

However, the expression of feeling in argument is not culturally respectable in the British tradition. Advocates of openness in discussion are often seen as agents of a new group culture. Solitary practitioners of openness can find themselves isolated. For openness requires trust and confidence, and that only comes with a mature and effective group. For this condition of the proper management of argument to apply we shall probably have to await the emergence of new norms in society as a whole.

In conclusion; argument may be the fruitful discussion of differences, it may be the symptom of some underlying conflict. If a symptom, then more effective management of the process of argument will be to no avail. If a genuine difference of opinion or view occurs, then proper management of the process will prevent the argument becoming a new cause of conflict. It is at least always worth-while making the initial assumption that the argument is a genuine difference. It would however be naïve to think that better management of the process of argument is all that is needed to resolve the conflicts in organizations.

2.3 Competition

Competition too can be productive or harmful. Three of its principal positive effects are:

(a) *Competition sets standards.* An economist in one East European government was recently asked why they were building a second petrochemical complex in their relatively small country when economies of scale in that industry would have suggested one larger complex. He replied that they had come to realize that it was often cheaper to suffer the diseconomies of smaller size, in order to arrive at appropriate standards for productivity and effectiveness by comparison with a competitor. Without competition such standards had to be set unilaterally by the central government. In a complex technology with no basis for comparison, this was not possible. By allowing competition, and basing their standards on the best performance, they obtained reliable standards and cut down the central bureaucracy, more than offsetting the lost economies of scale.

One of the most difficult tasks for any manager at any level is to set appropriate standards – for output, cost, effort, efficiency. A basis for comparison is needed. Without competition the only basis often available is last year's figures. Too often, these figures were not good enough in the first place; too often, there are too many reasons to discard them as bases for standards. Competition, even at the cost of distorting the rational structure, may be the economic thing to do.

(b) *Competition stimulates and channels energies.* A look at the story of Bull Dogs and Red Devils recounted in Box 6.1 will demonstrate some of the effects of competition on the competing groups. Within each competing group:

Members identify more closely with the group, forget their individual differences and accept a common objective;

The climate of the group becomes more task-centred with less concern for the individual's psychological needs;

The group becomes more highly structured, more 'organized';

The group demands more loyalty and support from its members, more purposeful activity.

Competition gives a common sense of purpose to a group which helps to channel their energies in a common direction; it may change their psychological contract by raising the salience of the group and the task, thereby releasing more effort and energy in total.

Competition can lend stimulation to both groups and individuals. Sport is more exciting when there is the challenge of competition. Competition can be a way of testing oneself, of discovering new sources of talent or energy. It is often at the heart of change, both social and personal, since it can be the spur to higher levels of activity. Ardrey (see Box 8.1) regards competition and the common enemy of the environment as the very basis for fellowship and goodwill.

(c) *Competition sorts out.* This is perhaps the most obvious feature of competition. Competition distinguishes better from worse, but this is not always its most useful feature. In many organizations, e.g. role cultures, it is more important that everyone is up to a certain standard than that some are better than others. How selective does an organization need to be between groups and individuals? For competition used for this purpose is the one most likely to degenerate into conflict. The consequences of sorting out by competition can be both unpredictable and important. They include:

A sense of relaxation in the victor; or
A feeling of psychological success leading to greater efforts;
A sense of defeatism in the loser; or
A determination to win next time;

Increased competition between the opposing parties often leading to conflict; or

Increased competition leading to new levels of activity.

It is, unfortunately, not easy to predict which outcome will result for either party. To a large degree, whether competition is productive or harmful will depend upon:

(d) Whether it is *closed* or *open*. Closed competition is sometimes called zero-sum competition. One person wins at the expense of the other. There is one contract up for tender, one bidder only can win. There is one cake for shares in which all parties are seeking, but one party can only increase his share at the expense of the others.

Open competition occurs when there is no finite amount, when there is competition but not out of a fixed amount. All parties can increase their gains, get more cake. If one party gets more cake than another it was not at the other's expense. There was enough cake, or even infinite cake, for all parties to garner as much as they were able.

Closed competition leads to bargains or what have been called 'distributive' relationships. Closed competition in organizations, e.g. competition for fixed and finite resources, is more likely to degenerate into conflict than open competition, e.g. when money is available for all new investments that yield a given rate of return.

In most situations, looked at objectively, the competition *could* be open, the game *could* be looked at in such a way that ultimately there *could* be more cake for everyone. In most situations, however, the parties concerned seem determined to regard it as closed competition. Why is this?

Partly because to regard competition as open often requires a long time-horizon, and the assumption of collaborative rather than conflict behaviour from your competitors. In the short term the cake is fixed. To increase the cake means collaborating in the short term. Partly it happens because it is easier to see who has won in closed competition, and, to a lot of people, winning is more important than what is won.

In the end, it matters not whether the game is objectively and in reality, open or closed, infinite or zero-sum. What matters is the perception of the competing parties. This results in a chicken and egg situation. Open competition leads to healthy collaborative competition. But without collaborative attitudes to begin with, open competition is unlikely to occur. (The apparent self-defeating tactics of managements and unions in some labour negotiations can often be understood in this light.)

Open competition, therefore, can be used to channel energies, set standards, and to differentiate. Competition for resources and facilities need not degenerate into conflict. Competition for promotion, recognition or rewards need not become harmful conflict. But for competition to be fully productive, three conditions have to be met:

1 It has to be perceived as genuinely open, i.e. everyone can ultimately win, there is enough cake for all. The performance of competitors is seen as setting a bench-mark rather than pre-empting part of the prize. To be behind at any one stage does not imply defeat but only the need for setting higher standards for the future (e.g. losing a set in a tennis match does not mean losing the match, but only more concentration, more energy).
2 The rules and procedure for arbitration must be seen to be fair and adequate. No one is likely to be collaborative if the umpire is biased or the rules unknown.
3 The major determinants of success in the competition must be under the control of the competitors. They must have only themselves to blame if they fail.

If these conditions are not met, then the competition will be seen as closed, i.e. win-lose, or unfair, or both. In which case a competitor will either:

(a) Resort to the tactics of conflict if the prize is worth winning; or
(b) Withdraw, i.e. competition will not have generated more energy.

Box 8.2

This story is told of the aged but respected Professor of Archaeology whose preferred method of travel was the bicycle. He was found one day, by one of his students, kneeling beside his bicycle which had a puncture in its front tyre. The professor was energetically pumping air into the rear tyre. The student looked puzzled, then eventually tapped the professor on the shoulder and said,

'Excuse me, Professor, but do you realize that you are pumping up your back tyre when it is the front one that has the puncture?'
'Ah, my dear fellow,' said the professor, 'but do they not communicate?'

The assumption that air pushed into any one part of a structure will automatically flow through to all other parts is not confined to the professor.

The benefits of competition will still tend to occur, but they will now carry with them the costs of conflict or of withdrawal. Desirably, the fruits of competition should be gathered without their costs.

Croquet is one gentle English game where supposedly open competition can quickly develop into conflicts. Try amending the rules half-way through, or implementing your own interpretation – let one man know the slope of the lawn but not another, make it clear that if the host doesn't win there's nothing to drink, then stand back and watch the quiet of the English lawn start to smoulder with conflict.

It is reasonably difficult in most organizations to meet the conditions for fruitful competition. Only in a low-technology, diversified 'task' organization under conditions of rapid growth and plentiful resources are they likely to be met in full. In most organizations there are not unlimited resources or opportunities, nor can individual groups have full control over the variables that affect their success. For instance, the technology may dictate that they receive their input from another part of the organization at rates and prices which they cannot influence.

Competition, therefore, is very likely, left to itself, to produce conflict in organizational situations. Hence, the need for the managerial strategies outlined later which will at least contain the potential conflict and limit the costs of the benefits of competition.

2.4 Competition for power and influence

This form of competition merits separate discussion. When 'politics' is referred to in a pejorative sense it is often this form of competition that is in question. Is this form of competition healthy and productive, or is it disruptive, selfishly inspired and harmful? Should it be tolerated, encouraged or banned? The answer to these questions will depend upon the three conditions listed in the previous section, and upon the requirements of the situation.

Is the competition 'open'? Is the pool of power unlimited? This will depend on the type of power in question, and on the organizational situation. Usually, resource and position power are restricted. Only a few people can head up the pyramid, control the resources. Expert and personal power, however, are often available to all. It is open to everyone to increase his personal prestige or professionalism and thereby add to the pool of power in the organization. Only if this deprives others of their power would this situation become win–lose, become a closed competition.

Are the rules unambiguous? In role organizations the rules for achieving position power or even expert power are likely to be less ambiguous than in other cultures. In a power culture they are usually highly ambiguous.

Are the important variables controlled by the participants? Usually they are at the start. The game is to get more variables under one's control. Only in nepotistic versions of the power culture do some people – e.g. the owner's son – have an initial advantage.

Can the difference gap be closed? Competition is only undertaken if there is a possibility of winning. Competition for power and influence only occurs where there is some degree of power equality. Often two bases of power are challenging each other as when the specialist, with expert power, is combating the line departments with position and some resource power. The near equality of power is usually noticed, and usually only important, when role or task boundaries overlap, i.e. there are territorial prerogatives to be resolved. (See sections 3.3 and 3.4 in this chapter.)

Unless the organization is expanding very rapidly, or has a big managerial gap, the pool of power will be restricted. The competition, therefore, will be closed, not open. If, furthermore, the rules of competition are ambiguous, the competition is likely to generate conflict. The organization is now in a position where it will have to review the costs and benefits of the type of conflict.

Power competition is not usually going to be directly helpful to the tasks of the organization. The release of energies and the setting of standards in pursuit of internal power is not a desirable outcome in this case. In fact, it will tend to detract from the organization's business. The only remaining benefit of competition is that of 'sorting-out'. If it is important to the organization to differentiate widely between the performance of individuals or groups in selection or promotion, then it may be worth paying the cost of the tactics of conflict (to be described later). If wide differentiation is not important, if selection or promotion is based on performance to standard rather than going to the best, then cost-benefit analysis would suggest that conflict for power was not in the interests of the organization as a whole.

Politics is, however, a reality. Individuals have their own personal interests, or they have values or goals which they would like to have adopted by the organization. In all cultures there will be pressure groups and blocking groups, groups pursuing their joint interests and groups protecting theirs. Zaleznik has usefully distinguished between coalitions and collusions, collusions being essentially defensive, coalitions more positive. Since individuals will achieve little on their own, coalitions or collusions become essential if one's own viewpoint or interests or preferences are going to be advanced, or, at least, not ignored. The competition for power being essentially 'closed', an increase in the power of one group will mean a decrease in the power of others. Herein lie the seeds of conflict. Coalitions will provoke collusions in retaliation, energies will be devoted to the conflict, to surviving or winning rather than advancing the organization's goals. Since the bulk of power is at the top, it is there that coalitions are the most important. The manager who seeks to rule alone is playing a dangerous role. As Machiavelli pointed out, as many fallen giants of industry would acknowledge, unless supported by a coalition, the man at the top will become increasingly isolated. 'Uneasy lies the head that wears the crown.' Worrying about his own position he will trust no one, destroy dangerous coalitions by transferring key people, keep his possible rivals close to him and divided, become more arbitrary and authoritarian, behave in fact in a way not calculated to do best service to the organization, and may well legitimize the eventual palace revolution. All the tactics of conflict apply to conflict between coalitions. All the managerial strategies apply, plus one – the formation of more powerful coalitions. One may deplore the coalitions and collusions of organizations, but one cannot afford to ignore them. The successful manager, both in personal and organizational terms, is the man best able to reconcile the divergent interests, the differences between individuals and between groups.

Box 8.3

The choosing of ministers is a matter of no little importance for a prince; and their worth depends on the sagacity of the prince himself. The first opinion that is formed of a ruler's intelligence is based on the quality of the men he has around him. When they are competent and loyal he can always be considered wise, because he has been able to recognize their competence and keep them loyal. But when they are otherwise, the prince is always open to adverse criticism; because his first mistake has been in the choice of his ministers . . .

But as for how a prince can assess his minister, here is an infallible guide: when you see a minister thinking more of himself than of you, and seeking his own profit in everything he does, such a one will never be a good minister, you will never be able to trust him. This is because a man entrusted with the task of government should never think of himself but of the prince, and should never concern himself with anything except the prince's affairs. To keep his minister up to the mark the prince, on his side, should be considerate towards him, should pay him honour, enrich him, put him in his debt, share with him both honours and responsibilities. Thus the minister will see how dependent he is on the prince; and then having riches and honour to the point of surfeit he will desire no more; holding so many offices, he cannot but fear changes. When, therefore, relations between princes and their ministers are of this kind, they can have confidence in each other; when they are otherwise, the result is always disastrous for both.

Adapted from Machiavelli, *The Prince*

3 The causes of conflict

3.1 The symptoms of conflict

Before looking at the causes, we must recognize the symptoms.

The symptoms of organizational conflict, the surface manifestations are:

1 Poor communications laterally and vertically. Decisions are taken on the wrong information. Group A is unaware that Group B is working on another part of the same problem. Two levels in the same division are moving in different directions on the same problem.

2 Inter-group hostility and jealousy. This usually comes out in statements beginning:

'Department A is only concerned with keeping their lines straight . . .'
'Division B are totally unaware that . . .'
'If it wasn't for those people in X department . . .'
'They never tell us anything . . .'
'They expect us to know by intuition . . .'
'They seem to have the M.D.'s ear . . .'

3 Inter-personal friction. Relations between individuals, usually in different groups, deteriorates to icy formality or argument. Problems seem to get polarized around people and personalities.

4 Escalation of arbitration. More and more inter-group conflicts are passed up to the cross-over point for arbitration. The cross-over point becomes ever higher in the hierarchy as successive levels of superiors take up the defence of their interested parties. What started as a problem between clerks over a withdrawal of credit becomes a confrontation between the Directors of Finance and Marketing to be resolved by the Managing Director.

5 Proliferation of rules and regulations, norms and myths. It becomes more and more difficult to do anything without riding roughshod over somebody's regulations, somebody's established way of doing things, somebody's private fictions.

6 Low morale of the type expressed in frustration at inefficiency. 'We don't seem to be able to get anything moving . . .' 'It's no use trying to be imaginative around here . . .' 'You would think they didn't want anything to happen . . .'

Most of this frustration, under conditions of conflict, is directed at the higher levels of the organization.

These symptoms will be found at some time in almost every organization. They arise as a direct result of the tactics adopted in conflict. To treat the symptoms will be ineffective if the underlying disease is left untouched. A plaster on a boil will cover it up but if the boil is the result of a deeper ailment, another boil will pop up somewhere else.

Too often, organizations react to poor communications with more communications (meetings, house journals, circulation of documents, etc). If the underlying disease is untouched, the remedy will only complicate the issue and will ultimately be discarded (the graveyard of unwanted house journals was overcrowded long ago. See Box 8.2). If inter-personal frictions is the dominant symptom, banging their heads together, sending them on T-groups, or removing them to other posts, will only have a short-term palliative effect. The underlying conflict will still be there and will show itself in some other way. The strategy for resolving conflict must be related to the disease, not the symptom. Diagnosis, therefore, differentiating between symptoms and cause, is the key to the proper management of conflict.

3.2 The causes of conflict

The causes of conflict have been listed and categorized in a variety of ways. Frustrated argument, escalated competition may be the immediate causes, but they all start from two underlying and fundamental issues:

Objectives and ideologies;
Territory.

3.3 Objectives and ideologies

When two or more groups interact with differing goals, sets of priorities or standards, there is likely to be conflict. The higher the degree of interdependence of the units, the more crucial becomes the relationship of their objectives and ideologies. Ideology is a set of beliefs about the way to behave, about standards and values. Staff groups, for instance, have been shown to be strongly committed to preserving the integrity of control and rule systems, whereas line personnel want more flexibility and the freedom to override rules and regulations. Other ideological differences would be flexibility versus stability, organization goals or societal needs, short run versus long run. People and groups with a power orientation will have different goals and ideologies from those with a role orientation.

This friction, or occasionally clash, between objectives and ideologies leading to conflict can arise when:

1 *Formal objectives overlap*, e.g. the sales/production dilemma. Typically, a sales department measures itself on sales turnover, gross deliveries, total

output or some such index. The production department is primarily concerned with cost, expressed perhaps as variances against budget, or cost per unit sold. Sales are properly concerned with customer satisfaction. Production with optimum schedules. Sales therefore will feel it proper to press for special arrangements to meet a customer's special requirements. This may well involve uneconomic short runs, unscheduled overtime, disruption of work in the factory. In line with their objectives production will resist.

The prisoner's dilemma problem in Box 6.3 is a particular example of this quandary. If objectives are separately defined, situations will arise in which the combination of the individually optimum decisions does not result in the best solution when the situation is looked at as a whole. For the overall optimum to be achieved, there is needed

(a) Agreement on a super-ordinate objective (e.g. profit);
(b) Communication on alternative methods of achieving that objective;
(c) Trust in the other party;
(d) Likelihood of benefit to both parties.

Where these conditions do not exist there is the potential for conflicting objectives. Each party will then be perfectly justified in asserting its priorities. Like the brake and the accelerator working simultaneously, there will be much noise and little progress. (It is worth emphasizing that it is not enough to appeal to a super-ordinate goal – the interests of the organization, profitability, etc. – the goal must be accepted by both parties. There must also be an agreed method of deciding between alternatives and the necessary information to do so.)

2 *Role definitions overlap.* This can lead to conflicting objectives. Advisory functions often regard their function as being to produce new ideas, that being how they justify their existence. Executing functions, busy with day-to-day problems, are more interested in stability and the status quo. Thus it is that line functions acquire a reputation for conservatism while staff functions pride themselves on innovation. Auditing and advisory roles are often of a professional nature, e.g. quality control, accounting and legal positions. They have a professional code or a professional reference group which can provide another set of priorities in addition to the objectives of the organization. The medical department of a pharmaceutical firm hovers uncertainly between its role as the public conscience of the organization and a servicing unit to the marketing department.

3. *The contractual relationship is unclear.* Co-ordination that is imposed will be regarded differently from co-ordination that is requested. Is the inspector helping the supervisor or is he the servant of the factory manager?

Is the credit control section an aid to the sales department or the watch-dog of the Finance Director? If the contract is unclear, it may be differently perceived by each party, leading to conflicting objectives. Diagonal relationships are prone to this type of ambiguity. Does the branch accountant work for the branch manager or the chief accountant? Is he a guest or a policeman or a member of the household? The view that each party takes of their allegiances and their relationships will affect their view of their priorities and their objectives.

4 *Roles are simultaneous.* A department may be both a service department and a co-ordinating department. In the former role they may act on the request of the individual department, in the latter at the behest of the managing director. It may not always be clear to the other actors which role is the current one. One role, moreover, may tend to contain the other. Can he who co-ordinated you yesterday service you today?

5 *There are concealed objectives.* The formal objectives of a unit or a group may conceal some more deeply felt objectives. Usually, these objectives will be for a larger share of resources or for greater influence in decision-making or for increased status. For instance:
(a) As Strauss showed in his interesting study of purchasing agents, professionals who feel they lack proper recognition start to activate their negative power.
(b) If a unit feels that its influence is not in proportion to the demands of the situation, it will start to work for more influence by activating its negative power. Lawrence and Lorsch showed that where the influence of each unit was consistent with competitive factors there was less conflict. Thus, in their more effective container firm where customer delivery and product quality were vital, sales and production were the most influential units. By contrast, in the food industry where market expertise and good science were essential, sales and research were the influential units.
(c) Selby showed that in an organization where research had more prestige than engineering, which in turn ranked above production, there was no conflict if the initiation process followed this ranking. But if a lower status unit, e.g. production, started to make demands on the others, there was conflict.
(d) Dalton and Strauss both demonstrated in separate studies that where a staff group felt asymmetry with a line group – e.g. the staff group had to understand all the problems of the line, get along with and justify their own existence, but not vice-versa – there is resentment and attempts to force the interaction to flow both ways.

The ways of avoiding or controlling the conflicts resulting from *objectives and ideologies* will be discussed later. We are currently concerned with diagnosis, not treatment. Any systematic diagnosis of conflict should start with an analysis of the real objectives and ideologies of both parties in their various roles.

3.4 Territory

Robert Ardrey, in his book *The Territorial Imperative*, has put forward the proposition that a lot of animal behaviour is motivated by territory, the

---

Box 8.4 The territorial imperative

A territory is an area of space, whether of water or earth or air, which an animal or group of animals defends as an exclusive preserve. The word is also used to describe the inward compulsion in animate beings to possess and defend such a space. A territorial species of animals, therefore, is one in which all males, and sometimes females too, bear an inherent drive to gain and defend an exclusive property ...

We may also say that in all territorial species, without exception, possession of a territory lends enhanced energy to the proprietor. Students of animal-behaviour cannot agree as to why this should be, but the challenger is almost invariably defeated, the intruder expelled. In part, there seems some mysterious flow of energy and resolve which invests a proprietor on his home grounds. But likewise, so marked is the inhibition lying on the intruder, so evident his sense of trespass, we may be permitted to wonder if in all territorial species there does not exist more profound than simple learning, some universal recognition of territorial rights ...

Man ... is as much a territorial animal as is a mocking-bird singing in the clear California night ... If we defend that title to our land or the sovereignty of our country, we do it for reasons no different, no less innate, no less ineradicable, than do lower animals. The dog barking at you from behind his master's fence acts from a motive indistinguishable from that of his master when the fence was built. ... Neither are men and dogs and mocking-birds uncommon creatures in the natural world. Ring-tailed lemurs and great-crested grebes, prairie dogs, robins, tigers, musk-rats, meadow warblers and Atlantic salmon, fence lizards, flat lizards, three-spined sticklebacks, nightingales and Norway rats, herring gulls and col-licebus monkeys – all of us will give everything we have for a place of our own. Territory, in the evolving world of animals, is a force perhaps older than sex.

Adapted from Ardrey, *The Territorial Imperative*, 1967

desire to possess, acquire, or preserve territory and territorial rights. In his intriguing and readable book he suggests that the territorial principle applies to societies as well as to animals. (See Box 8.4.) In the Ardrey

---

Box 8.5   The stamping grounds of the Uganda kob

A stamping ground, the breeding arena of a single generation of Kob, looks like nothing so much as a series of putting greens conveniently arranged for the benefit of idle guests behind a luxurious resort hotel ... A stamping ground is not large ... Each little putting green with its close-cropped grass is about fifty feet in diameter and is a territory occupied and defended by a single male. A closely bunched cluster of a dozen or fifteen or eighteen such territories in a main arena may occupy an area no more than two hundred yards across. Here, the champion males out of a population of almost a thousand – a kind of sexual Olympic team – fight, display and jockey for position. Here, needy females come seeking consolation ...

Within the arena ... some properties have greater sexual values than others. In a normal city, real-estate values increase block by block to the city's core; so on the stamping grounds, sexual values increase from the suburban market of the periphery to the flashing excitements of Times Square. Young, ambitious, maturing males fight for a foothold on the periphery, to gain a property even in the suburbs; the peripheral males challenge, fight, wait for an opening to gain better locations in the main arena; and on a few central territories – perhaps only three or four – stand the champions of the moment, challenged by all, envied by all, desired by every female heart.

The female wants her affection but she wants it at a good address ... We need not puzzle over the selective value in the Uganda kob of the female's addiction to high-value property. Since it coincides with the male's sense of value, it results in a scheme of natural selection of a remarkable order. Only a super-kob lasts long on a central territory. If he leaves his property for water and forage he will return to find it occupied and must fight to regain it. On his putting green he will be continually challenged by the ambitious ... In a busy season the proprietor of one of the central territories must somehow sandwich between invasion problems presented by his colleagues perhaps twenty emotional problems presented by his admirers.

The human male, encountering a stamping ground for the first time, cannot fail to identify himself with the contestants before him. And despite his most secret dreams of sex and riot, he will thank a merciful evolutionary destiny that made him a man and not a Uganda kob; it is all just a bit too much trouble.

Adapted from Ardrey, *The Territorial Imperative*, 1967

tradition we shall here extend the principle of territory to the domain of organizations. But in this instance, territory will be interpreted psychologically rather than physically. An individual's psychological territory is his sphere of influence. Territory is only a metaphor, an analogy, but it is a useful one. Consider some further aspects of territory:

(a) Ownership of territory is conferred partly by deeds (organization charts, job descriptions) but partly by precedent, by squatting or staking a claim.

(b) The boundaries of the territory are set out in various ways. Physically, with screens, offices, separate buildings. Procedurally, through committee memberships, circulation lists. Socially, through dining groups, informal groupings, carpets and other status signs. The implications of the metaphor are:

Territory is prized by its inhabitants. They will not willingly relinquish it, nor allow it to get overcrowded;

Some territories are more prized than others (see Box 8.5 for a description of Ardrey's stamping ground);

Trespassing is frowned upon. You enter another's territory by invitation only;

One can seek to increase or improve one's own property even to the detriment of the neighbourhood as a whole.

Let us not push the metaphor too far, but pause to consider how territory can be the source of conflict in organizations.

Territorial violation. If in one's job territory is either taken away or infringed upon by another group, there will be retaliation and conflict. When a head office department queries or overrules one of the branches, the branch is liable to see this as a violation of territory. If a specialist department starts to take decisions previously the prerogative of the line executive, it will be regarded as violation of territory. If one group demands rather than asks for information belonging to another group, this can be seen as uninvited intrusion.

Departments such as Personnel suffer much from accusations of territorial violation. In order to do their job, they require information and seek to influence decisions such as promotion and transfer in the most well-protected territories of a manager – his people. The tactics resorted to in defence of territorial rights are roughly equivalent to putting a fence around the area. They will be discussed in more detail in a subsequent section.

Overcrowding. In a lot of situations there are too many people doing too few jobs. Metaphorically, there are too many animals in one patch of ground. One solution is to enlarge the patch. Within an organization, this can only be done at the expense of other groups. For those groups who interface with the environment, e.g. marketing, it is theoretically possible to capture territory from outside the organization, i.e. to expand the market coverage. This kind of approach must, however, be initiated and supported by the senior man in the group.

A key question to all newly-promoted managers would be: 'Where do you get your personal territory from?' It is all too easy to take it from the current occupants, from one's subordinates. It requires a courageous manager to hand over the existing territory to his subordinates and to regard his job as the enlargement of the whole. The mechanisms for getting hold of territory are simple. The manager can choose from the following: he defines his sphere of interests, nominates particular problems or customers as his personal responsibility, decides that he must represent the group on particular committees, ensures that all incoming mail is seen and screened by him before distributing, re-writes the job definitions of his subordinates.

Overcrowding leads to frustration and energies devoted to protecting one's plot and, if possible, to increasing it. Overcrowding frequently follows structural re-organizations as individuals explore the territory involved in their new positions.

Territorial jealousy. Just as one herd looks covetously at the grazing grounds of another so do groups in organizations look at the territory of other groups or individuals. In particular:

(a) The overt status signs of office size, dining-rooms, cars, secretaries, etc. It is impossible to find a universally acceptable way of allocating these territorial desiderata. Though everyone agrees they are unimportant, they may often be the visible signs of cherished influence or status, and become important because of their symbolic value.

(b) Information jealousy, or the feeling that one would love to know what goes on behind that fence, is another common feature of organizations. All groups believe that they are excluded from information available to the group above them. Often this is true, but seldom to the extent that they believe. A manager coming out of a meeting with his peers, that lasted three hours, may say to his subordinates that nothing of any interest took place. He may well be right, but he will probably not be believed. We long for the fruit in others' gardens until we have tasted it and found it sour.

(c) The in-group phenomenon.

Groups are well-practised in the ways of improving the desirability of their territory. As Festinger, in his work on cognitive dissonance, pointed out, the harder it is to get something, the more we value it when we get it. The highest and most inaccessible mountain peaks are the ones most prized. The smaller and more exclusive the group, the more difficult the admission tests, the tougher the apprenticeship, the more we value membership. Those who get in become more cohesive, identify more with the group, protect its interests and its inviolability more determinedly. Few committees, whose membership is coveted, commit suicide, few groups voluntarily open their doors wider. The effect of all this is to increase competition to enter the territory *per se* – the point and purpose of the territory or groups is almost immaterial. Dining clubs in British universities, fraternities in the U.S.A., the one-time clubs of the British Empire, the Royal Enclosure at Ascot, are all examples of public stamping grounds. In general, if you want to make your group desirable, make it difficult to get into.

'Territory' and 'Roles' are often two metaphors for describing the same phenomenon. Pick whichever is most appealing. Metaphors are merely an aid to diagnosis.

4 The tactics of conflict

4.1

Many of the tactics used by conflicting parties will be identical to the symptoms of conflict listed earlier. Several of the tactics are themselves the seeds of further conflict. In some analyses of conflict these tactics will therefore be found as causes. But they are not the prime cause, since they themselves have their roots in a more fundamental conflict. The principal tactics are listed below.

4.2 Information control

Information gives power. It is hard to argue with apparent facts even if you suspect they are wrong. The manager who keeps some vital data to himself which completely refutes the suggestions of his subordinates, the specialist department that refuses to distribute data before a vital meeting, the filters of 'confidential' and 'restricted', the levels of committees are all possible ways in which information is controlled in order to protect territory or objectives. Since differential information is itself a source of conflict in any discussion, this tactic tends to escalate conflict.

The 'gatekeeper' function of subordinate or specialist groups makes information control a very appealing tactic for increasing influence or enlarging territory. The manager confronted by an apparently open-and-shut proposal, based on details or technicalities with which he cannot be familiar, can often only accept the proposal or express his lack of confidence in the subordinates or specialists. He is in fact deprived of any real influence over that decision unless he asks for an outside opinion, and thereby runs the risk of destroying trust and morale. The use of information control has transferred the major influence on the decision to the 'gatekeeper'.

4.3 Information distortion

This is the misuse of information control. But it is not always deliberate. The perceptual bias that goes with any role can lead to unconscious distortion of information. The specialist, the craftsman, the engineer may be so concerned with quality or standard of performance that information on costs and benefits may be neglected or given only cursory attention. Proposals for new equipment in many organizations are frequently unaccompanied by any assessment of resulting benefits. The decision is therefore taken on cost and quality alone. There has been an unwitting distortion of the total pool of information required.

4.4 Rules and regulations

Groups, particularly specialist groups, who feel their influence neglected will seek to impose rules, regulations and official requirements on other groups. The proliferation of forms from a new division in a central office is often a use of this tactic to draw attention to their existence and their importance. Strauss's study of purchasing agents, already referred to, is a good example of this. Crozier, in his study of French bureaucracies, demonstrates that to circumscribe others with rules whilst leaving yourself free is a recognized route to political ascendancy in organizations.

4.5 Information channels

The answering tactic to rules and regulations is to establish informal contacts, liaison men, the friend in the despatch department who will help one to by-pass formal procedures and give one advance information. At a higher level, the use of a 'friend at court', a protector with influence, is a further example of the use of an informal channel to protect one's interests. A collection of such informal channels may well become an informal clique, necessary in order to get the work done, as the clique sees it, in spite of the organization's rules. These cliques, though often formed from the best motives, can easily develop 'territories' of their own and become very protective of them. Informal alliances of whole departments against a common enemy have also been known.

4.6 Control of rewards

Line people will often retaliate against staff tactics by refusing promotion to a staff expert or rejecting his recommendations. The resources power of the line is usually superior to that of the staff and is brought into play if there is abuse of expert or position power by specialists.

Box 8.6 A defensive collusion

Pettigrew, distinguishing between strategies for power acquisition and those for power maintenance, has described how a group of computer programmers in one organization reacted to the arrival in the organization of the new breed of systems analyst. The programmers used four protective strategies: norms which denied outsiders' competence; protective myths; secrecy norms; protection of their knowledge base through control over training and recruitment policies. (Such strategies are often incorporated in a trade union or professional association – neither of which were available to the computer programmers.)

The Chief Programmer described the first strategy: 'We knew it would not work, people trying to tell programmers what to do – they knew nothing about computers. We objected to suggestions from people who didn't even know what they were talking about. This was particularly so with the Systems Manager who tried to dictate what we did.'

The second strategy, protective myths, implies that a threatened group invents a set of fictions about itself. An example in this case was the fiction that programmers could not operate under time constraints: 'The Chief Programmer has always argued we cannot work under time constraints. This isn't true, it's just his way of giving himself plenty of room for manoeuvre.' (A deputy to the Chief Programmer.)

The third strategy, secrecy, is described by one of the analysts as follows: '... we found there was no record of what had been happening. We found we were becoming terribly reliant on the persons who did the programming... In its worst light it seemed that the programmers were trying openly to manipulate the situation. It looked like their attitude was "I know what's going on, therefore I'm indispensable".'

Finally, the programmers fought hard to retain control of recruitment policies and to prevent the routinization of the core of their expertise.

See further: Pettigrew, 'Occupational specialization as an emergent process', *Sociological Review*, 1973

4.7 Denigration or tale-telling

In conflict situations there will be a strong temptation to point out the flaws in the opposing group. This can go to the extent of duplicating some of the work of the opposition in order to detect its flaws.

4.8

The results of the persistent use of any of these tactics are:

(a) A 'hardening' of the conflict so that it perpetuates itself as each tactic is met with other tactics;
(b) The distortion and control of information, the checks and the barriers all working to promote hostility and suspicion;
(c) Collaboration degenerating into bargaining;
(d) The misapplication of individual and group energies.

5 The managerial strategies

5.1

The purpose of any managerial strategy will be:

(a) To turn the conflict into fruitful competition or purposeful argument;
(b) If this is not possible, to control the conflict.

5.2 Fruitful competition

In order to achieve fruitful competition it is necessary to:

(a) Have agreement on a common goal or objective. This will only happen if that common goal is seen by the participating parties to be a realistic one for them, which in essence means that they will in some sense be rewarded for achieving it. 'Profit' is not a meaningful goal if the participation groups are not in fact judged on profit. Profit, in fact, is more often used as an arbitrating mechanism than as a goal, i.e. to decide between projects or proposals, or between competing claims. Common realistic objectives are usually only possible:

In task cultures;
At the top of role cultures;
At the centre of power cultures.

(b) Have an information system available to the participants, so that they can evaluate progress towards a goal and compare alternative strategies. To establish profit as a goal, and provide information related only to turnover or to costs, is to make a mockery of the goal.

(c) Ensure that the co-ordination mechanisms are appropriate to the degree of differentiation between the departments (see Box 8.7).

Box 8.7 What co-ordination for what differentiation?

Lawrence and Lorsch suggested that the mechanisms for co-ordination should get more complex as the differentiation between the groups to be co-ordinated gets more complex. Diagrammatically their view of the relationship between environment and organization is:

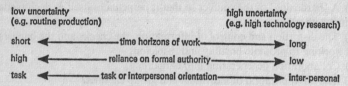

low uncertainty
(e.g. routine production)

high uncertainty
(e.g. high technology research)

short ◄————————time horizons of work————————► long

high ◄——————— reliance on formal authority———————► low

task ◄——————— task or interpersonal orientation———————► inter-personal

Two departments operating in the area of low uncertainty may require only formal rules and occasional formal contact between representatives to maintain co-ordination. At the other extreme, departments such as Production and Research may need permanent co-ordinators and semi-permanent task-forces to manage the differentiation.

See further: Lawrence and Lorsch, *Organization and Environment*, 1967

(d) Ensure that the participating groups have the opportunity to communicate with each other and attain the degree of trust necessary to establish a collaborative relationship.

(e) Ensure that considerations of role and territory do not conflict with the overall goals.

In a sense, this set of managerial strategies could be called 'control by ecology' in that it works by creating the environment for collaborative interaction. These conditions are rarely achieved. But Dutton and Walton (see Box 8.8) studied two similar divisions in one of which these ecological factors were, by fortune or design, properly arranged, resulting in significant difference between the two organizations in the collaborative behaviour of sales and production, and greater effectiveness in the more collaborative organization. In addition to the factors listed in the box, Walton noted that:

'... the status hierarchy was appropriate to the situation in the collaborative combination,' (i.e. the production manager was younger and junior to the sales manager, whereas the bargaining combination had a long-service production manager and a new sales manager).

Box 8.8   Summary of two contrasting approaches to interdepartmental relations

	A bargaining approach	*A collaborative approach*
1 Goals and orientation to decision-making	1 With regard to respective goals and orientation to decision-making, each department emphasized the requirements of its own particular task, rather than the combined task of the plant sales district as a whole.	1 Each department stressed common goals whenever possible and otherwise sought to balance goals. Each party perceived the potentials for inter-departmental conflict in the separate task structures but nevertheless stressed the existence of super-ordinate district goals and the benefits of full collaboration for each party. Each saw the relationship as co-operative.
2 Information handling	2 With respect to the strategic question of information exchange, each department (a) minimized the other's problems or tended to ignore such considerations as it did recognize; and (b) attempted to minimize or distort certain kinds of information communicated.	2 Each department (a) sought to understand the other's problems and to give consideration to problems of immediate concern to the other; and (b) endeavoured to provide the other with full, timely and accurate information relevant to joint decisions.
3 Freedom of movement	3 Several tactics were employed which related to the strategic question of freedom of movement. Each department sought to gain maximum freedom for itself and to limit the degrees of freedom for the other by the use of the following tactics; (a) attempting to circumvent formal procedures when	3 Each department explored ways it could increase its freedom of movement toward its goals with the following behaviour: (a) accepting informal procedures which facilitated the task; (b) blurring the division between production and sales in tasks and positions; (c) refraining

Box 8.8 – *contd.*

A bargaining approach	*A collaborative approach*
advantageous; (b) emphasizing jurisdictional rules; (c) attempting to fix the other's future performance obligations; (d) attempting to restrict interaction patterns; (e) employing pressure tactics – hierarchical appeals and commitment tactics – whenever possible; (f) blaming the other for past failures in performance.	from attempts to fix the other's future performance; (d) structuring relatively open interaction patterns; (e) searching for solutions rather than employing pressure tactics; (f) attempting to diagnose defects in rules for decision-making rather than worrying about placing blame.
Relations were laden with threats, hostility and the desire for retaliation. Inter-departmental interactions were experienced as punishing by both sides. Contacts were limited to a few formal channels, and behaviour within these channels circumscribed by a rigid rule structure. Department officials depended on higher authority. Home-office managers were called upon to resolve opposing views, to suggest solutions, and to support one party against the other.	Relations were characterized by mutual support. Department officials were independent of higher authority. Home office was asked to support initiatives of joint proposals from the plant.

4 Attitudes	4 Each department developed attitudes in support of the above bargaining strategy and tactics.	4 Each department adopted positive inclusive and trusting attitudes regarding the other.

Adapted from Dutton and Walton, 'Interdepartmental conflict and co-operation: two contrasting studies', *Human organization*, 1962

The collaborative combination received more generous resource allocations than the bargaining combination, i.e. competition was more 'open'. The 'hot-spot' job, that of plant scheduler, was handled in a co-operative manner in the collaborative plant, i.e. he was seen as the facilitator of the sales and production teams, and there was a high interaction between him and the two team leaders. In the bargaining combination, the interaction was minimal, and formal rules and regulations were substituted.

The style of the sales manager in the bargaining combination was aggressive and his relationship with his production counterpart antagonistic. In the other combination, the interpersonal style of the sales manager was more co-operative, helped, perhaps, by the support of his higher status.

The collaborative combination was not only more effective for the organization, in terms of productivity, turnover and morale, but also helped the careers of the individuals concerned.

5.3 Control of conflict

It is not, however, always possible to arrange the ecology, to determine roles and relationships in such a way that collaboration can be ensured. Management is therefore forced to strategy (b), the control and regulation of conflict. This strategy is often the best short-term solution. Too often, the longer-term ecological strategy is then neglected or forgotten. Regulation of conflict in a sense recognizes and legitimizes conflict, and therefore perpetuates it. Regulation strategies include:

1 Arbitration. The use of the lowest cross-over point in the organization to resolve conflicts. Only useful when the conflict is apparent and specific. Not very valuable in episodic or continual conflict.

2 Rules and procedures. These are often arrived at by negotiation, e.g. on credit procedure, or scheduling. They can easily become one of the bargaining elements and are seen as not a solution, but another constraint. They are useful when the conflict is recurrent and predictable, but should not be regarded as a permanent solution.

3 Co-ordinating Device ('boxing the problem'). A position is created on the organization chart to resolve the issue in conflict. The position often carries the name of the problem as its title – hence 'boxing the problem' – e.g. sales/production liaison, or 'new product co-ordination'. Box 8.9 describes the productive use of such a device. But Lawrence and Lorsch in their studies of integration showed that where this was overdoing the co-ordination, i.e. where the device resulted from spurious conflict rather than the need for co-ordination endemic in the situation, then this device merely complicated communication and increased conflict. Problem-

Box 8.9 Sales and S. O. L. D.

Andrew Sykes and James Bates give an account of the informal elaboration of goals by groups of clerks in a large British manufacturing company.

The company was big enough to have six sales departments, each responsible for a particular type of product, and eighteen production works, many of which made much the same ranges of products. These, then, were the formally defined sectional or sub-unit goals. They created the predictable friction between production works who wanted to limit the range or products in order to reduce costs, and sales departments who wanted customers' exact specifications complied with so that no business would ever be turned away. But there was much more to it than this.

The sales clerks in each of the six departments were organized in sections which dealt with particular kinds of the product sold by the department. Each clerk had his own list of customers. As personnel turnover was low, each had spent years getting to know these customers' representatives very well; so a network of informal relationship was in existence linking these clerks to people in customer companies.

Inside the company itself, the work-group overlay superimposed on the formal structure included relationships between the sales clerks and the clerks in the works. These relationships were based on acquaintanceships formed when a sales clerk had himself been in the works, as most of them had before moving on (and up) into sales. Naturally enough, a sales clerk did not telephone enquiries to factories in general; he telephoned someone he knew personally, exchanged pleasantries and then got down to business. In this way a sales clerk placed orders with works clerks who would keep an eye on the progress of the orders for him and generally help to get special treatment for his special customers, and in return, works clerks expected further orders if ever they were short. So a system of normative reciprocal obligations existed, being the social norms or expected standards of conduct of these groups of clerks.

The ostensible goals of the whole organization were twofold. Preference should be given to the company's most important customers: and efficient operation achieved by matching sales orders with factory production capacity. Sales clerks were assumed to allocate orders to those works best able to undertake them. But the goals of the groups of sales clerks were to obtain priority for their personal customers, using their personal relationships with works clerks to do so. The groups of sales clerks competed ruthlessly with each other to this end, each believing in its own rightful precedence. It was these group goals which determined the programme of sales and production, rather than the overall company goals. In consequence, an important customer might be kept waiting whilst a works turned out an order for a minor customer because the works clerk knew

Box 8.9 – *contd*

the sales clerk who knew the customer. A sales clerk might give an order to an overloaded busy works because he knew the clerk there, whilst another works which could do the job just as well was running below capacity.

To counter these inefficiencies, which were obvious even if their causes were not, top management set up the Sales Order Liaison Department (S.O.L.D.). Its task was to co-ordinate sales orders and production capacity, with customer priorities in mind. So that this could be done, all communications about orders between sales and works, and works and sales, were to go via S.O.L.D. Direct contact between sales clerks and works clerks was expressly forbidden.

This alteration of the formal structure destroyed the informal reciprocal relationships between sales clerks and works clerks and largely achieved its objective, at the cost of the extra administrative overhead of thirty-five S.O.L.D. personnel, for the hostile attitude which they encountered in both sales and works soon welded them into an in-group whose objective coincided with the formal goal of controlling the pressures from sales and works.

Adapted from Sykes and Bates, 'A study of conflict between formal company policy and the interest of informal groups', *Sociological Review*, 1962

solving groups have a vested interest in maintaining the problem they were set up to resolve. This device, therefore, is not good for episodic or occasional conflict, but it is useful where the conflicting pressures are going to be continual but are not so predictable that they can be handled by rules and regulations.

4 Confrontation. A technique much favoured by those who believe in 'openness' in organizational communications. This strategy will be effective if the issue can be clearly defined and is not a symptom of more underlying differences. It is an approach analogous to arbitration but to be preferred to it in that the solution will be 'owned' and 'internalized' by both groups rather than imposed on them by the arbitrator. Confrontation or Inter-group meetings can do a lot to increase understanding of other people's point of view, but they cannot be a complete substitute for the ecological point of view. An interesting variation on confrontation is an approach known as *role negotiation*, recently developed by Harrison. In role negotiation, the conflicting parties negotiate and trade items of behaviour (e.g. I will stop doing X if you will stop doing Y). It does much to reduce the sores of conflict, particularly between individuals, although it may still leave the underlying disease untouched.

5 Separation. If interaction increases the depth of sentiments, separation

should cool them. This strategy can work if interdependence is not anyway necessary because of the task. If it is, then the interaction will have to be managed somehow, either by a co-ordinating device, or rules and regulations. The strategy of separation works best if two groups are coincidentally interacting and conflicting, i.e. because they happen to be lodged in the same location. It also works if the true cause of the conflict is two incompatible individuals – incompatible in personality, or more often with relative status inappropriate to the situation. To separate the individuals, i.e. by transferring one, may then be a successful strategy. But interpersonal friction is more often the result of conflict than the cause of it. If this be so, then separation of the individuals will merely bring about a temporary lull in the situation, and two more conflicting personalities will soon arise.

6 Neglect. Not a desirable strategy, but one frequently adopted *faute de mieux*. To ignore conflict, often because the apparent cause is trivial, is to

---

Box 8.10 Fending off the specialist

Pettigrew has listed some favoured devices used by the line executive to block the unwanted (by him) report of the specialist:

1 *Straight rejection.* The staff man and his report are dismissed without further consideration. Needs power and self-assurance on the part of the executive.

2 *'Bottom drawer it'.* The report is praised but then left unused. The specialist, grateful for the praise, may not press for utilization.

3 *Mobilizing political support.* The executive calls on support from colleagues with similar interests.

4 *The nitty-gritty tactic.* Minor objections to fact or interpretation are raised to discredit and delay implementation.

5 *The emotional tactic.* 'How can you do this to me' or . . . 'to my chaps'.

6 *But in the future* . . . The report is fine for today's conditions but unlikely to work in the (hypothetical) future.

7 *The invisible man tactic.* The executive is never available for discussion when wanted.

8 *Further investigation is required* . . . The report is sent back for further work on it.

9 *The scapegoat.* Someone else (e.g. Head Office) won't like it.

10 *Deflection.* The executive directs attention to the points where he has sufficient knowledge to contradict the specialist.

See further: Pettigrew, 'The influence process between specialists and executives', *Personnel Review,* 1974

permit it to stabilize if not to perpetuate itself. Like weeds, neglected, it can stifle productive work.

6 Summary and implications

6.1

This chapter started by differentiating differences. *The management of argument* was discussed. *The features of fruitful competition* were analysed as:

Setting standards;
Channelling energies;
Sorting out.

The conditions were described under which these features of competition would obtain without the costs of conflict. The symptoms of conflict were listed. Conflict can arise from argument or competition that has degenerated. But conflict is also inherent in *overlapping objectives and ideologies* which are often caused by problems of role, role interactions and role perceptions, and in *considerations of territory*.

The tactics of conflicting parties are then described. They include information control, information distortion, rules and regulations, informal channels, control of reward, degeneration. The first aim of the management of conflict should be to turn it into a state of collaboration or of fruitful argument or competition. This involves *the control of the ecology* and careful consideration of *roles* and *territory*. In many organizational situations, the structure, or the task, or the technology will, at least in the short term, make it difficult to achieve this optimum. The alternative set of strategies aims at *the regulation of conflict*, by devices such as arbitration, rules and procedure, co-ordinating devices, confrontation, separation, neglect.

6.2 Implications

No one should be frightened of differences. Attempts to create a totally homogeneous, unargumentative, non-disputatious organization or group have usually resulted in low output and ultimately low morale and even the disintegration of the group.

But we must discriminate between productive differences and conflict. This chapter has sought to provide that discrimination, and to suggest that more thought needs to be given in organizations to the management of productive differences, and to creating the environment where differences will be resolved collaboratively. Nevertheless, it would be naïve to think that organizations will exist without conflict. It will probably never, perhaps can never, be totally eliminated. Managers will be able to regulate it more successfully if they understand the reasons for it and appreciate the range and appropriateness of the various regulating instruments.

Some concluding comments and generalizations are worth stating.

We have looked at differences from the point of view of the organization. The individual manager, however, needs to be a 'politician' if he is to be an effective member of the organization; 'politician' in the sense that he has an understanding of, and a sensitivity to, the causes of conflict, the tactics and the strategies. What use he makes of that understanding, whether to promote the goals of the organization, or to further his own particular ambitions – if the two are not compatible – is a question of his principles and priorities. To be 'political' is not, however, necessarily to be purely selfish in one's awareness of the political nature of systems. The belief that organizations can and should be entirely rational is both erroneous and harmful in that it has inhibited much study of the organization as a political process. That omission is now being rectified by many studies. We may expect to understand much more about the reality of organizations as political systems over the next decade.

One of the attractions of the task culture has been that it encourages fruitful differences. Not only its structure, with its emphasis on group goals, but the ideologies of open discussion, the lack of emphasis on status, the reliance on judgement by results rather than by method, all encourage the expression of differences. Ironically, however, this predilection leaves the creators of a task culture politically naïve when they come to deal with role or power cultures. Openness, frankness, genuine disclosure of objectives and of information works well in a pure task culture, but they can put one at a big disadvantage in interactions with the more bargaining approach of a role or power culture. This fact helps to explain why task cultures are often so short-lived, why, too, the advocates of openness, of T-Groups and confrontation meetings, thrive in times of organizational prosperity but are regarded as a luxury when times get hard. Task cultures often fare best when they are headed by a man with a power orientation who understands, instinctively only, maybe, the political nature of his ambassadorial role.

The larger the organization, the greater the potential for conflict. Conflict is a great diverter of energies. It cannot be proven, but one of the reasons why the great organizations only perform moderately well, in spite of their vast resources of money, technology and talent, is that disproportionate amounts of energy are consumed in conflict. Better management of differences could have a significant impact on productivity as well as making organizations more pleasurable places to live and work in.

Part Two
The Concepts in Application

Introduction to Part Two

Part One will have introduced the reader to a bewildering and no doubt sometimes baffling array of concepts, sets of categories, pieces of jargon. The immediate relevance to the problems of his own organization may not have been immediately obvious. God, it has been said, did not see fit to divide up the world to accord with the faculties of universities. Nor did he fashion the problems of organizations to fall neatly under one of the chapter headings of Part One. The purpose of the chapters in Part One was to provide a language. Without a language we are reduced to pointing to particular objects. A child cannot apply experience learnt in one situation to another situation unless the situations are identical or unless he has perceived the linking concept. He may, for instance, have discovered that the electric fire should not be touched. But the lesson will have to be learnt anew for the gas cooker in the kitchen, unless he can comprehend the concept of heat, and thence proceed to the generalization 'all hot things can hurt'. To do this, he needs the ability to think in classes and concepts. He also needs a language that will give some names to the classes and concepts. What the language is may not be material. The Chinese and the American can both appreciate heat although the names for it are different. They will not be able to talk about it across their cultures, but it will be understood within them.

So it is with organizational understanding. Learning by experience, left to itself, can be a painful and a tedious process. It is also inefficient. Unless the present situation matches a past one in all respects the experience of the past may be inappropriate learning for the present. To interpret experience, to learn from others' experience as well as one's own, we need linking concepts and a language. But language to be understood must be used. Jargon is 'someone else's language'. To turn jargon into one's own language we need to use it.

If Part One was the dictionary or the grammar, Part Two is an attempt to show how this language can be used to help with better understanding of the problems that are encountered in all organizations. Problems in organizations come in all shapes and sizes. They are not always clearly labelled. They spring from a telephone call from an irate client or customer, a sudden slump in the output record, a dispute in the factory. The type of problem varies with the level of management, with the nature of the job. But a series of interviews with managers at all levels in two widely different organizations, supplemented by discussions with a wide spread of executives on a management development programme, has suggested a set of four categories into which the majority of the perceived problems of organizations fall.

1 The people in the organization. The compensation mechanics. The attitudes of the organization to individuals and their careers. The methods of appraisal and promotion. The systems of development and of education.
2 The work of the organization. The way the organization is structured. The way jobs are defined and measured. The inter-relationships between different roles. The use of targets and objectives.
3 The systems in the organization. The information and communications systems. The decision-making systems. The control and monitoring procedures. The reward systems.
4 The job of a manager. Knowing what to do and how to do it. His responsibility for, and dependence on, the other three categories. His need to organize and manage change. The dilemmas and role of the man at the top, and the man in the middle. The problems of values and standards.

Part Two therefore is organized under these four headings. Other classifications would have been possible. One could have discussed, separately, mergers or participation. But, on examination, these all-embracing topics are found to be made up of a set of particular problems which fall into one of the four categories listed.

We will not be able to explore in depth all the potential problems in these areas. The intention will be to show how the use of the language of Part One can provide insights, to provide some further check-lists and frameworks, to describe some relevant research findings. If any part of this book resembles a cook-book then this is it. But there is more than one way of cooking eggs and the reader will find, once again, that the choice of the correct recipe, the one appropriate to all the factors in the situation, remains the task of the manager. For if there is one theme running through this book it is that of 'appropriateness'. There is no infallible remedy, only the one that is most appropriate. This puts the onus for decision back on the manager. The researcher or theoretician can only help him in his diagnosis of the situation and his evaluation of alternative remedies.

Organizational success often seems due more to the fortuitous and felicitous combination of circumstances than to any systematic application of theories. The great idea, wrong in one decade, wondrously successful in another. The computer consultants, the Littons and the Rolls Royces, brilliantly successful one year, disastrous the next. Was fortune responsible, or management? Luck, or one good idea, undoubtedly helps. But who knows how many good ideas, how many lucky breaks, have not been exploited because the man in charge did not know how to ride his luck, or did not recognize them for what they were. Successful is he who can identify circumstances as propitious, who knows when to do what and, perhaps as important, when not to do what. There is nothing so practical as a good theory.

But for the theory to become practice someone has to recognize that it is the right theory in the right place. Men prosper, as Machiavelli observed, so long as fortune and their policies are in accord. The manager must woo fortune, but with understanding. For solving problems is easy, it is knowing that it is a problem, it is labelling it and defining it, that are the difficult things. Exploiting opportunities most men can do; if they recognize that it is an opportunity and not an embarrassing vacuum.

Box   Machiavelli on fortune and men's lives

I am not unaware that many have held and hold the opinion that events are controlled by fortune and by God in such a way that the prudence of men cannot modify them, indeed, that men have no influence whatsoever. Because of this, they would conclude that there is no point sweating over things, but that one should submit to the rulings of chance. . . Sometimes, when thinking of this, I have myself inclined to this same opinion. Nonetheless, because free choice cannot be ruled out, I believe that it is probably true that fortune is the arbiter of half the things we do, leaving the other half or so to be controlled by ourselves. . . .

Thus it happens that two men, working in different ways, can achieve the same end, and of two men working in the same way one gets what he wants and the other does not. This also explains why prosperity is ephemeral; because if a man behaves with patience and circumspection and the time and circumstances are such that this method is called for, he will prosper; but if time and circumstances change he will be ruined because he does not change his policy. . .

I conclude, therefore, that as fortune is changeable men are obstinate in their ways, men prosper so long as fortune and policy are in accord, and when there is a clash they fail. I hold strongly to this: that it is better to be impetuous than circumspect; because fortune is a woman and if she is to be submissive it is necessary to beat and coerce her. Experience shows that she is more often subdued by men who do this than by those who act coldly. Always, being a woman, she favours young men, because they are less circumspect and more ardent, and because they command her with greater audacity.

Adapted from Machiavelli, *The Prince*

9 On the People of Organizations and their Development

1 Introduction

It is fashionable to speak of the human assets of organizations. It is also useful, for it reminds us that although people only appear as costs in the formal accounts, they are assets in the sense that they are, or should be, a productive resource; a resource that needs maintenance and proper utilization, that has a finite life, and an output greater than its cost. But it is interesting to reflect on the implications of the ways in which we put human assets into accounts. Salaries and benefits are really regarded as maintenance expenses – something to be kept as low as possible as long as the machine does not break down. There is no capital cost and therefore no need for depreciation. Indeed, the return on investment of most companies would look very strange if their human assets were capitalized at, say, ten times their annual maintenance cost, and depreciated over twenty years. Perhaps, one day, industrial and administrative organizations will start behaving like football clubs and charge realistic transfer fees for their key people assets. It is, in fact, instructive to ponder on the implications of looking at one's employees as players in a football team. For in a football club, the players truthfully are human assets. They have a productive capacity, an earning power, that is potentially far greater than their cost. That cost has both a capital and a maintenance element. Rewards are proportionate to group performance, the asset has a finite life. There is no question of the organization assuming responsibility for the asset beyond the limits of its useful life, nor is there any stigma in the declaration that the asset has grown too old to be worth maintaining. The care and attention and protection given to key assets by leading clubs is of a different order of people maintenance than any known in industry. Training and development become vital, for if you can increase the productive potential of the asset, in a short time, you not only have greater productivity, but an appreciated asset in terms of capital value.

But, of course, in spite of all the fine words, most organizations do not regard their people as assets in anything like the sense that football clubs do. The implications of doing so are a bit threatening. Would anyone buy you for ten times your annual salary? Is your increasing maintenance cost justified by your increased earning power, or only by the fact that you are perhaps a fully depreciated asset? Does one value people assets at cost or at resale value? If the latter, would their value increase *exponentially* like real estate, or in a ⋀-shaped curve like football players? Would the asset belong completely to the organization, or would it have powers of self-determination?

In another sense, however, the application of economic and financial terminology to the management of people has given rise to a whole corpus of methods, systems and procedures for the maintenance, control and utilization planning of these assets. A whole new profession, the management of human resources, has sprung from this conception of the people of organizations as a collection of assets that must be managed in the same way as the other, non-human, assets of the corporation. This conception of the management of people as assets, unattended by the financial or psychological corollaries of that conception, is full of implications for the individual, for the organization and, perhaps, for society. It has given rise to diametrically opposed views on the role of the personnel department; 'the personnel function will assume a more important role in the management of the business' (Frank Fischer) or 'fire the personnel department' (Robert Townsend).

It is all this that justifies a separate chapter on the people of organizations in a book that, in a sense, is all about people and organizations. We shall consider three aspects of the topic, as follows: *the management of human assets*; *the development of the individual*; *the role of the personnel department*; followed by a *summary and discussion*.

2 The management of human assets

2.1

There is a battery of mechanisms in this field, a treasure-house of procedures and forms. Many a large corporation will be proud to talk to you of its manpower planning models, its managerial inventories, its replacement charts and appraisal procedures, its job specifications and training schedules. If some of the terminology occasionally smacks of the world of production, so some of the procedures occasionally, not always, seem to reflect a deep desire that humans might become as predictable and manageable as, perhaps, a very sophisticated machine tool! We shall not attempt to describe all these methods and procedures here. The latest models are well documented in a variety of books and journals, some of which are listed in Part Three.

Every organization, as soon as it gets to any size (perhaps 1,000 people), begins to feel a need to systematize its management of human assets.

Box 9.1   How effectively does your organization manage its human resources?

Can you or anyone else in your company answer the questions listed below?

Number   Question

1   How much money was spent last year to recruit and select people?

2   Was this expenditure worth the cost?

3   Does your organization have data on standard costs of recruitment, selection, and placement which are needed to prepare manpower budgets and to control personnel costs?

4   Was the actual cost incurred last year less than, equal to, or greater than standard personnel acquisition and placement costs?

5   How much money was spent last year to train and develop people?

6   What was the return on your investment in training and development?

7   How does this return compare with alternative investment opportunities?

8   How much human capital was lost last year as a result of turnover?

9   How much does it cost to replace a key man?

10   What is the opportunity cost of losing young, high-potential managers, accountants, engineers, etc.?

11   What is the total value of your company's human assets?

12   Is it appreciating, remaining constant, or being depleted?

13   Does your company really (I mean *really*) reward managers for increasing the value of their subordinates to the firm?

14   Do your compensation and other motivation–reward systems reflect an individual's present value to the firm?

15   Does your organization consider its investment in human resources when evaluating capital budgeting proposals requiring the allocation of people?

16   Does your firm assess the effects of corporate strategies upon its human resources in *quantitative* terms.

Adapted from Flamholtz, 'Should Your Organization Attempt to Value its Human Resources?', *Cost-forme Management Review*, 1971

Perhaps the pay scales have got way out of line with apparently similar level jobs paying very different amounts; perhaps there is a feeling that there are a lot of neglected skills in the organization that other departments could utilize if they were aware that they existed. Perhaps individuals have complained that they don't know where they stand or what their future is; perhaps the unions have requested standardized benefits and procedures.

Whatever the historical origins, some kind of central organization, normally named a personnel department, is formed to put some system into the haphazardry. The systems that they adopt are often modelled on the world of production, because that is the world with the best potential for order and system.

These systems and procedures, often very desirable in themselves, do not always work as well as they should. Often there are unintended consequences. There are three areas of particular difficulty:

Appraisal schemes;
Career planning;
Compensation systems.

We shall examine the problems caused by these three systems, and then seek to draw some general conclusions about the management of human assets.

2.2 Appraisal schemes

These schemes usually have some or all of the following objectives:

(a) To provide a data base for the organization's inventory of people, skills and potential;
(b) To provide a mechanism for the proper assessment of performance by an individual so that he may be appropriately rewarded;
(c) To provide the individual with feedback on his performance and personal strengths and weaknesses;
(d) To help the individual and his subordinate to plan personal and job objectives and ways of achieving them.

All of these are desirable objectives, and forms can be devised which will, on paper, provide for the implementation of all four simultaneously. Unfortunately, as many organizations have discovered the hard way, the four are not psychologically compatible, and some of them, (c) and (d), extremely difficult to do well, even in isolation. Some of the reasons for this are:

1 No individual is going to admit to deficiencies of any significance on a form which will provide data for future job assignment decisions. Yet, unless he genuinely accepts deficiencies, he will have no commitment to dealing with them. (a) is incompatible with (c) and (d). This suggests that any piece of paper dealing with (c) and (d) should not be copied and should remain in the possession of the individual concerned. If anyone else retains the document, this part of the appraisal system will be seen as a control mechanism not a development mechanism.

2 The appraisal interview has little effect on performance improvement. Criticism arouses defensive mechanisms and does not improve performance. In fact, in a famous study in G.E. individuals actually performed worse, twelve weeks later, on those aspects of their job for which they had received most criticism. In that same study the majority of individuals left with a lower estimation of their performance than when they went in. This lowering in self-esteem results in attempts to justify the past, refute the accusations, or reduce the salience of job and superior. Praise is ineffective unless close in time to the behaviour. General commendation is discounted as politeness. (c) does not help towards (d) but will in fact tend to render it useless.

3 Salary is a separate issue. Studies have shown that most individuals in large organizations do not believe that their salary is directly related to performance, but rather to such overall factors as length of service, seniority and qualifications. In the G.E. study, those individuals receiving lower appraisals did not, in fact, receive lower *increments*. But the salary issue does tend to dominate the interview and colour the receptivity of the subordinate. (b) is important but unconnected.

4 The superior's previous relationship with the subordinate will affect the interview. When the subordinate does more of the talking, it was found in the G.E. study that commitment to improvement was higher but this only occurred when this was the style of all their previous interactions. The personal concerns of the superior will colour the interview. Nervousness and tension will tend to make him dominate the session and thus make it unproductive. The interview is difficult, but few managers receive any training in it.

5 An assessment of performance is not necessarily the best basis for deciding on promotions. But it is notoriously hard for a superior to judge the potential of a subordinate for any job higher or different than his own. In fact, in one study, 52 per cent of employees felt that the assessment form had no influence on promotions. In many organizations they are useful only for low-range jobs; for other jobs they are part of the ratifying not the selection procedure. (a) is not very effective.

The traditional appraisal procedure is not, therefore, very effective, in large part, because the superior is expected to be, at the same time, judge and counsellor. This form of role conflict is unacceptable, one has to be one or the other. From studies at G.E. and other spaces, there is now a consensus of recommendations:

1 All the four objectives should be fulfilled by different means, at different times, and often by different people.

2 Criticism only improves performance when:
  (a) it is given with genuine liking for the other person;
  (b) it is related to specific instances;
  (c) the subordinate trusts and respects the superior.
3 Improved performance results when:
  (a) Goal-setting, not criticism, is used. The goals are specific, jointly set and reasonable;
  (b) The manager is regarded as helpful, facilitating, receptive to ideas and able to plan;
  (c) Evaluation of performance is initiated by subordinates, and as a prelude to further goal-setting, not appraisal.

But, as we shall see, even these rather broad conclusions are not the whole answer.

2.3 Career planning

Many organizations have elaborate schemes for planning the career progression of all, or some proportion of, their managerial cadre. This is done with the laudable objectives of (a) providing each individual with a satisfactory career, and (b) ensuring that the organization makes optimum use of its managerial resources. To do this, they rely on either the formal data of assessment forms, or on the informal data of subjective impressions, or on a mixture of both. Many of these schemes do not work as well as in logic they might. For instance:

1 In one organization, after ten years, only 10 per cent of the managers in the scheme were in the positions planned for them ten years before, while 35 per cent had left the organization altogether.
2 Many individuals believe that they have not had the opportunities they wanted and merited – hence they feel frustration. The individual is very dependent on the opinions and influence of his superior.
3 Most systems make it possible for divisional managers to hold good people at the expense of the total organization and of the individual careers.
4 In spite of centralized systems, it is usually possible for the individual manager to promote from within his own department or his own range of acquaintances, possibly neglecting better people, and devaluing the system.
5 Assessment of potential is usually judged only in relation to past performance and present experience. Thus, a chemist is seldom considered for a planning job, or a production man for a sales appointment. The trapped specialist, recruited for his professional skills in his youth and thereby labelled for life, is becoming a more common feature of organizations.

6 Failure can be damaging. Poor performance in any assignment, even a training one, can become a permanent stigma, as it gets written into the record.

7 The individual sees the organization as taking responsibility for his career and his necessary development. He ceases then to develop himself or to think creatively about his future. He becomes dependent on the organization and can well become unsuited for the independent, creative entrepreneurial roles of senior management. To remedy these defects, the following experiments have been tried:

(a) The personnel department initiates all appointments. This strengthens the system but weakens the superior–subordinate bond. Very seldom is the personnel department strong enough to enforce this expedient except at middle and lower levels.

(b) Appraisal forms are destroyed after three years or so, thus obliterating the past and allowing a man a clean slate. Alternatively, assignments of a training nature are evaluated on a different form, recording what he learnt rather than how he performed.

(c) Open, rather than closed, systems of appointment are adopted. Anyone of a certain status can apply for any job and is evaluated and interviewed as if he were an outside applicant. This too often becomes a superficial formality concealing an informal closed system. For it to work, there is needed:

Adequate information to all in the organization about job opportunities and possible career paths;
A counselling service to help individuals evaluate their strengths and weaknesses;
Time spent on proper evaluation of unknown individuals' potential.

(d) Complete open systems are unusual, but variations include:
'Hunting licences' for frustrated individuals to apply for other jobs in other parts of the organization;
A transfer board to which individuals can apply;
Rules prohibiting superiors from blocking the transfer of an individual who wants to leave.

However, in spite of all these corrective devices, it remains true that career planning in many organizations is not a development process so much as a weeding-out process. Career development becomes a human hurdle race, the hurdles being different appointments or different levels of authority. He who clears a hurdle can progress to the next, until there are no more. This sort of system meets the organization's objective, for it ensures the survival of the fittest. Only the strong survive to the end, but the drawbacks are considerable, for the organization as well as for the individual. For example:

1 There are a lot of hurdles. There tend to be many hurdles on the way to the top. Young men cannot get there unless they are allowed to by-pass some hurdles. Rigid hurdle systems tend to have old managements, and high departure rates from younger levels.

2 There is no retrieval mechanism. Many good horses fall at the first hurdle. There is often no remounting mechanism, no way of catching up. Another reason for high departure rates.

3 The intervals are too short. It is in everyone's interest to get over the hurdles as quickly as possible and go on to the next. Indeed, promotion is the favourite form of reward in most organizations. As a result, most successful managers seldom do a job for more than two years until they reach very senior levels. A good rule of thumb in these organizations is 'the faster you move, the more successful'. This practice leads to short time-horizons in each job. Furthermore, it has been demonstrated that in periods up to two years, the most effective form of leadership is highly structuring and authoritarian. As chapter 4 discussed, it is very probable that this style of leadership eventually generates low morale, high turn-over and compliance responses to influence. These long-term costs will not, however, be personally experienced by the fast-moving manager who will carry his structural style to the top with him, effective in the short-term and uncontaminated by its trail of delayed damage. Fast promotion rates can therefore encourage a structuring and potentially damaging style of management throughout the organization.

The need to provide a large number of hurdles, or promotion possibilities (a possible twenty steps for a recruit aged 20?) leads to clutter in the organization. U.S. organizations often have fewer levels of management than their British counterparts, perhaps because they use money as a reward instead of promotion.

As we shall see, there are no neat and tidy overall answers to the problems of career planning. The objectives of the individual and the organization are unlikely to be reconciled in every case by logic and formal systems.

2.4 Compensation systems

Money as a motivator was briefly discussed in chapter 2. Let us briefly review some of those conclusions:

1 Pay is a useful incentive because it is instrumental in satisfying a wide range of needs, although it never appears itself in any need hierarchy.

2 If pay is to be effective in the motivation calculus, the individual must

see that it will satisfy some important needs and also that expenditure of 'E' will lead to more pay.

3 Pay is comparative. The absolute level is unimportant as soon as physiological–economic needs are satisfied. It is the level relative to past or future expectations, to peers or to other opportunities.

4 Pay increases that do not immediately follow on improved performance are not seen as connected with results but rather with such things as seniority, experience and qualifications.

5 Pay does not work as an incentive if it only occurs at the cost of satisfying other needs, e.g. social respect, family life, etc.

Managers who do see their pay as totally dependent on results tend to be the most effective and the most highly motivated, as judged by themselves and by their superiors.

Theoretically, therefore, pay should be a very convenient motivating agent. It is simple. It can be calibrated. It is all-embracing. It does not lead to organizational complexities in the way that promotion does. It leaves the individual with control. It is effective if tied closely to results. It is uncluttered. Why, then, do relatively few organizations deliberately use pay as a motivator? For, with few exceptions, organizations tend to use pay as compensation rather than as incentive. The perceptions of most managers that they are not rewarded for particular results but for seniority and experience is, on the whole, an accurate perception. Seniority is the reward for success and pay follows seniority. They are not treated as two separate forms of reward. Seldom do you find a boss earning less than his subordinate.

The reason seems to be (there is no hard evidence) that if pay is the principal reward and incentive mechanism, there are going to have to be large differentials in levels of pay. If the differentials are not large, pay will not work as an incentive, since pay is comparative. Organizations have to justify these differentials. This is only easy to do when pay is attached rigidly to results which are both unambiguous and attached to one individual. Thus, pay is the principal reward mechanism for insurance salesmen – where, incidentally, it works extremely well. But where success must be judged more subjectively, or where it is hard to isolate an individual's contribution, the organization shrinks from the responsibility of assessing and justifying differentials. Top management of small to medium firms is another instance where results can be measured and can be attributed to a small number of individuals. It is not therefore unusual to find some variety of profit-related pay schemes for the top management of these organizations.

In their worry over differentials, organizations:

(a) Foster secrecy about pay levels. This has proved to be self-defeating. Several studies have shown that lacking firm facts, individuals make estimates of the pay of peers and superiors. These estimates always make the differentials wider than in fact they are. People always suspect that they are more badly paid than they actually are, in comparison to their peers.

(b) Pursue rules for equity. Equity usually means paying a rate for the job, rather than paying the man or paying his results. Under conditions of liquidity, the rate for the job should be assessed as objectively as possible, for equity must be seen to be equity. Jacques' time-span of discretion, job definition and evaluation systems, competitor's rates for similar jobs, job grade levels related to salary grade – these are some of the methods used in the pursuit of equity.

The implications of the pursuit of equity in pay are:

1 The incentive and reward properties of pay are discarded. Pay becomes merely fair compensation, just one part of the psychological contract.

2 Other methods of reward and incentive have to be devised. The usual one is seniority or promotion.

3 Most individuals require some reward or recognition of effort at least every two years, hence the tendency towards frequent job changes and the cluttering effects on organizational structure already remarked on under career planning.

4 Promotion as a reward for performance leads to Dr Peter's principle – people get promoted to the level of their incompetence, since they are promoted on the basis of performance in the job below rather than potential for the job above.

5 If seniority and status are rejected as rewards along with pay, the reward for effort will have to come from some form of job satisfaction. This might appear the cheapest and most desirable form of reward, but studies show that job satisfaction on its own does not last very long as a reward. If not followed by some more tangible or visible symbol of success, only very charismatic tasks will continue to motivate. Praise, as has already been mentioned, is not an adequate reward in itself.

6 Without job satisfaction or any other form of reward mechanism, satisficing behaviour will become the norm. Individuals will perform well enough to get the compensation they are entitled to under whatever rules for equity apply.

7 The pursuit of equity in pay begins to use up much of the energy that should desirably go into the task. It is interesting to observe how many

union arguments in labour negotiations are today based on considerations of equity, whilst managements are still talking of productivity. Yet productivity as a basis for negotiations is essentially results-related pay, something that most managements long ago abhorred.

2.5 The conclusions

Where does this leave us? The three principal mechanisms for the management of human resources have been seen to have many unintended consequences. These consequences all tend to divert energy from the legitimate objectives of the organization. Are the mechanisms then unnecessary? Should they be abandoned and the personnel apparatus reduced to a girl and filing-cabinet as Robert Townsend would have it in *Up the Organization*? Or are they the right mechanisms, but often badly administered?

As a start to answering this question let us recall the diagrammatic representation of the organization in Chapter 7, reproduced in Figure 11.

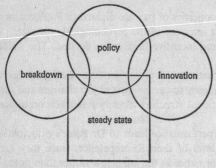

Figure 11

The reader will recall that each of these divisions of activity had its appropriate 'culture', as follows:

Steady-state – role
Innovation – task
Policy and breakdown – power.

It does seem that the management of human assets has to take into account the dominant cultures. The centralized, formalized systems and procedures are appropriate to a role culture – to the steady-state activities of the organization. In this culture, jobs are precisely defined, career progression is up the pillars of the temple, performance in the lower job is the best predictor of performance in the next job in the pillar, performance over and above the job definition is not required, can indeed be injurious to the other procedures and jobs, security of tenure is part of the psychological contract and influence by rules and regulations is the accepted norm. Centrally-managed career plans, formalized appraisals, job-related compensation are all appropriate and fitting to role cultures and steady-state activities.

Obviously the procedures still have to be well administered. Appraisal interviews, for example, need to be well-conducted and cannot achieve the four objectives simultaneously. But the major disadvantages of the normal systems and procedures only show up when they are applied to task or power cultures. In a power culture, individuals are developed in a way that amounts to apprenticeship. The new man is expected to learn from his seniors and to model his behaviour on theirs. Apprentice-masters, the senior managers, choose their own apprentices and their own successors from amongst these apprentices. The relationship between manager and subordinate is crucial, assessment is highly personal and subjective, with promotions depending on personal or political 'fit'. It would be very unusual to find any of the more formal systems of people management being seriously used in power cultures.

In a task culture, results are important, and rewards must be related to results. Status and position power, promotion not being highly valued, is not an adequate reward mechanism. Flexibility and the match of resources to tasks are important, meaning that open systems of career planning are required and are wanted by both individuals and managers. There is big emphasis on goals and objectives; individuals want and expect feedback on performance with pay tied to group results. In a task culture, therefore, there will be systems and procedures, but they will be at the 'open' or 'liberal' end of the scale. They will not be centrally controlled, although there may be a control source of advice and expertise, but will be administered by local managers. Individual differentials will be important within groups but not between groups, where total group differentials will be what matters.

It will be clear, then, that most organizations will need to adopt a differentiated approach to the management of human assets. The formalized, centralized systems will apply to the bulk of the organization, the steady-state. At the top, or in the emergency activities, they are inappropriate, and, in most organizations, are ignored – rightly. In the innovative parts, marketing, R and D, some parts of finance or corporate planning, the individual manager should have much more discretion to override or not use the formal systems of the equity procedures. Unfortunately, most organizations try to reduce everything to the steady-state, instead of looking at the problems of differentiation. Some of the principal problems are:

Can one organization tolerate different methods of compensation, selection and promotion?

How best does one select and develop the integrators or co-ordinators?

How to develop a career planning system which fits a man to a culture, rather than a man to a job?

Should an individual progress through all four divisions of activity, or should he remain in one culture throughout his career?

The answers to these questions are not fully known, partly because the problems have not been looked at in this way before. But they do suggest some practical implications:

1 Separate the innovative areas from the steady-state. In the innovative areas, reward ideas, creativity and inter-personal skills – often the prerogative of the young. Do not require them, necessarily, to move into the steady-state but to remain innovative, progress to policy or to leave. In the steady-state, reward reliability, specialist skill, accuracy, knowledge and experience.

2 Confine life-time careers to the steady-state, but use fixed-term contracts at higher salary rates, for the innovative and policy areas. This way, the organization will reward the role-orientated man with security and financial sufficiency, and the task or power-orientated man with money and independence whilst providing that pressure for results to which he is likely to respond. In this way, the young and creative can be paid more than their counterparts in the steady-state, but the higher pay will be accompanied by a higher risk element.

3 In order to give individuals early experience of the policy or breakdown areas, and to train them in co-ordination skills, it may pay the organization to distort its structure, to create more small relatively decentralized units than strict reason would call for.

3 The development of the individual

3.1

Plato felt that education and learning should continue until the age of 40. Many would now feel that he put too early a date on its closure. Learning and development have become a life-long task.

Individuals do change over time. They acquire new knowledge or technical skills. They become more balanced, or more risk-taking. They find new capacities within themselves, or learn to interact with each other more productively. They learn to cope with stress, or to help others to do so. The problem of managing development within organizations is to

Box 9.2 A re-entry experience

The return to work from a management education programme

I believe that in 1967, and it's probably still true today, it was *fashionable* for companies to send their bright young things off for three months to a business school. It was the thing to do! Statistics were included in chairmen's speeches as to how many executives had attended courses and how *modern* the companies were in their attitude to business training. Fine – it made for some good publicity and for a while the executives selected for this specialized training really *believed* all they heard.

What happened to most of us on our return – eager to put into practice the new techniques and theories we had acquired – was that the company simply didn't want to know! The big build-up fizzled out.

In many cases I believe it was a defence mechanism. Top management didn't know what we were talking about! How *could* they show their own weakness in discussing a proposition which they simply didn't understand? Would you? They simply built up a brick wall for protection and any time a business school technique was even mentioned – it was effectively stifled. Of course, there *is* an easy answer. Don't send middle or junior management off on courses until top management have been educated *too*. But that would mean admitting that top management *need* educating!

Anyway, I soon got out of the habit of mentioning the school at all in discussions with management. When I put up specific reports or proposals, I went to great lengths not to use any jargon or technical terms at all. This worked fairly well, even though I hated to compromise in this way. But at least it meant I was *using* the new methods and ideas I had learned, instead of merely relegating them to the back of my mind – for possible future use. Some of my colleagues, both from my own company and from the programme, found it impossible to do this and simply resigned – to look for greener fields elsewhere.

The backlash, so far as the companies were concerned, was the increasing belief that executives sent to business schools couldn't settle down and left after a few months. The terrible wastage involved brought some companies to the conclusion that business education was bad for *them*. 'Why send people to these schools only to lose them? The old style two- and three-week specialized courses never had this effect – why *give* ourselves problems. Solution – easy – let's stop sending people to business schools.'

So far I haven't got down to specifics but because I believe that my own experiences are not unique and because I believe too that business school education does pay off – even if it's *long* rather than *short* term – let me now be specific.

Box 9.2 – *contd*

Before I came to the school in October 1967, I had been promised all sorts of new and exciting career opportunities by my company – in fairly general terms. That ought to have made me suspicious – but it didn't! I was a group marketing manager and had been with the company for three years – having joined them as a marketing manager. Prior to that I had been with another organization in the industry for five years as a brand manager in both their U.K. and international divisions. I started out as a junior clerical employee in 1949 – before marketing was even invented – and because I was ambitious – my friends called it greedy – I progressed during the ten years I was there. Through the stages of personal assistant, P.R.O., and, eventually, when marketing was new and all the rage, to executive within the newly formed marketing department.

My career then ran out of steam, because the new managing director did not really believe in my capacity. That's really nothing to do with the subject in hand today – but I mention it only to show that when I was promised great new things after attending a course at the school, I *really* believed it. '*At last,*' I thought, 'someone recognizes that my marketing experience has reached a level where I'm ready to branch out into other areas.'

How wrong can you be? When I returned, after my *gruelling* three months, full of enthusiasm and eager for my new responsibilities, I was told that 'due to a slight reorganization whilst I was away, I was to handle a new range of products'. This was the big deal – a new opportunity. When I complained that this was *exactly* the same job that I had left behind, I was informed that the new range of products was in difficulty, and it needed my *new* expertise to bring them up to the required profit level. Quite frankly, my *old* expertise would have done, because basically the job itself had not changed at all.

However, I felt I owed the company something in return for the cost of my course, and anyway I *still* couldn't *really* believe they intended to waste it all. I judged my debt to be equal to a year's service and vowed that if nothing had changed by the end of 1968 or mid-1969 at the latest – I would have totally discharged any obligations and be free to start looking around for something better.

During the first six months, my enthusiasm gradually declined as time after time what I had learned at the school was ignored, misunderstood or simply rejected. I then learnt that the secret was simply not to mention the school or refer to any technique by name or use any of the jargon associated with the course. This wasn't very easy – mainly because I resented having to play that type of political game – and some of you know the frustrations involved. After a while, I discovered something – almost willy-

Box 9.2 – *contd*

nilly I was using the school methods – in an everyday manner. In fact I couldn't help myself.

When the initial impact of the school has worn off, and I suppose I basically mean the eagerness to try *specific* new techniques and ideas – one is left with a *basic* attitude to business and problems which is *different*. The approach to problems and decision making *has* changed. Almost without realizing it, one is doing a *better* job – even if it is the same old one as before!

In time, too, the company gets over the shock created by the returning executive from the school. Given *enough* time, the company even forgets it *sent* the particular employee to the school in the first place. It congratulates itself on having trained the person to the particular degree of effectiveness. This is, on reflection, the break-through point.

understand how one may hasten and channel this process of learning and discovery. There are three major methods of individual learning:

Formal education and training;
Group learning;
Assignment or planned experience.

We shall look at each of these in turn to examine their strengths and their problems.

3.2 Formal education and training

Management education and training is big business. The category includes all formal in-company 'courses', varying from one day to one month. It includes the off-site programmes of consulting firms, independent institutes, business schools and universities. In spite of the proliferation of formal training programmes, there is a fairly common feeling that few of them live up to the high aspirations of their descriptive or promotional literature. What evaluation there has been tends to support the generally disappointing outcome. Why this lack of success? There are three principal reasons:

1 For learning to occur, the individual must want to learn. This, the oldest, most fundamental and most obvious tenet of learning theory is often ignored. If an individual is not interested in the topic, believes that he has no need of it, or has no faith in the ability of the course to teach it him, then it is unlikely that learning will occur 'in spite of himself'. For him to want

to learn, the topic must usually be closely related to a part of his work that he feels important, and the medium for the learning, the teacher or teaching institution, must have expert authority in the would-be student's eyes. A machinist on piece-rate, faced with the installation of a vital new machine tool next week, will clamour to attend a training course put on by the manufacturers. All students should be volunteers, or at least willing accomplices. Assignment by the organization to a programme only tangentially relevant to the individual's existing work – e.g. 'The mysteries of the computer, a background course for the salesman' – will arouse in the individual feelings of compliance. He may attend, but he will not learn. If the course is high-prestige, or expensive, an executive development programme at a foreign business school, he may see his nomination as a sign of high favour by the organization and be delighted to attend. But not to learn, for the implicit message was that he was pretty good already. This has been named the 'accolade effect'.

2 Learning takes place within a context. When we learn something, be it out of a book or from experience, it is put into a frame of reference in our minds. This is a psychological context. There is the more obvious physical context. Things learnt in one country are not always remembered or felt relevant in another. Just as we don't always recognize friends out of context, so ideas or facts out of context are still there, are still lodged in our minds, but they may never get used. So the learning by rote of some financial formulae may be achieved at an off-site course with a high degree of accuracy. But studied and learnt in isolation, they will not readily be used by the individual back in his organization. So much of formal learning takes place in a 'cultural island', unrelated to the particular physical or psychological frames of reference of the individual. Much of that hard-earned learning is not shipped out from the cultural island to the world of work. Thus, evaluation studies have found high scores on content learning at the end of the programme but little evidence of any application.

3 Learning, if it is to last, must be 'owned'. Rote learning, or the memorizing of other people's learning, does not last unless it is immediately and continuously applied. Discovery learning, where the student uncovers the answer or the truth for himself, lasts longer – but again it must be used in the near future, and found useful, 'reinforced'. If learning is not by discovery or is not used and found useful, the individual will not internalize the learning, will not own it. That which is not owned is not maintained and is soon forgotten. The most brilliant lecture on mathematical techniques will make no impact on a group who, though sitting enthralled, will never need to use such techniques. A month later, they will recall the brilliance of the exposition but none of the content. Nichols amongst

others, has shown that on average, only 50 per cent of a lecture can be recalled by the audience at its end, a figure that drops to 25 per cent after two weeks, a statistic not very popular with lecturers!

For formal learning to work as a method of development, the programme must be closely related to the individual's work – in time and in content. He must learn the content in the context of his own world and must apply it as soon as possible. He must want to go on the programme and ideally should clamour for a place. The rotational assignments to regular company training programmes on background topics such as 'communications', 'accounting', 'computers' may keep the training centre full, may give the individual a much needed break, but any development of the individual will be fortuitous and fortunate.

Box 9.3 The success syndrome

In 1968, Hall and Nougiam established the factual existence of the success syndrome, or the truth of the saying that in managerial development nothing succeeds like success. They spell out some of their findings as follows:

1 After their first five years with an organization, those young managers who were more successful felt that their needs for achievement and esteem were met to a significantly greater degree than did their less successful colleagues.

2 Possibly as a result of their greater satisfaction with achievement and esteem, they become more involved with their jobs. By the fifth year their work is significantly more central to them than is the work of their less successful colleagues.

3 With increased job involvement, they are more likely to be successful in future assignments than other managers scoring lower on these dimensions. They are caught in an upward spiral of success.

Moral: If you want a successful older manager, start him in his youth on the spiral of success by giving him an early opportunity, Hall suggests in his first year, to be successful.

See also Hall, 'A theoretical model of career subidentity development in organizational settings', *Organizational Behaviour and Human Performance*, 1968

3.3 Group learning

The realization that an individual's interactions with others were crucial to his effectiveness in an organization led to a concentration on the development of his inter-personal or interactive skills. Conceptual learning or formal knowledge, it was clear, was not going to do very much on its own in this field. A whole corpus of development methods grew up which sought to apply to interactions the three principles of learning outlined in the previous section. The most well-known of these methods is the T-group, which has almost become a generic term for the whole genus of these methods. More structured versions of group learning include Ralph Coverdale's programme and a method for developing interactive skills, pioneered by Rackham, Honey and their colleagues (references to these will be found in Part Three). The methods vary in the degree of structure and in the amount of control exercised by the teacher. But they all have these elements in common:

Learning takes place in a group context, and is applied in that context during the programme;
The individual, early in the programme, receives feedback indicating his learning needs;
Activities and behaviour directly related to working on those needs is organized or occurs;
The individual has an opportunity to try out revised behaviour, or new skills, in the same context in which he learnt them.

There is little doubt that these methods, properly handled, can be very effective in developing skills in group interactions and in building more effective groups (their use for this latter purpose is mentioned in chapter 6). There does, however, seem to be some evidence for thinking that the context is crucial, that is, the learning is anchored to a large extent in the group in which it is learnt. The individual does not carry much of his changed behaviour over to a new group. He has learnt how to be a more effective member of the learning group, but he has not generalized from this experience. To some extent, this is logical behaviour, since each group is a different blend of people, task and environment, with different requirements of its individuals. To be properly effective, therefore, the learning group should be the actual work group, so that the context of learning and application is the same and continuous. This, however, creates new problems:

1 The effectiveness of the group as a context for learning will depend very largely on the previous history of the group. Very authoritarian-structured groups will not easily learn another mode of interaction, no matter how well the training is handled. Not all leaders of groups can accept feedback about their behaviour, not all subordinates can give it. The climate of the work group carries over into the learning group and can contaminate it.

2 Ultimately, the individual will leave that work group, and may leave his learning behind him. To a degree, the longer he practises changed behaviour, the more likely that behaviour is to become part of him, independent and irrespective of the context. But, realistically, group learning is group development more than it is individual development.

The use of groups for learning, group dynamics, has given birth to a host of variations on the original T-group. Groups are used for individual discovery and therapy (encounter groups), to study the development and growth of a group personality, to look at pair relationships (marriage groups), and to provide a shared and often almost psychedelic experience. None of these are necessarily bad or wrong in themselves, but some of them are not as well administered or controlled as they ought to be, nor do they have much place in the planned development of the individual in the organization.

Group learning is not, however, confined to the learning of interactive skills or personal discovery. Fruitful use is beginning to be made of task-orientated learning groups.

Called project groups, or some similar name, they utilize the supportive interactive nature of group work to encourage more specific forms of learning related to problems or skills. Focusing on a particular task or problem, often in their own organization, the individual learns something about group processes and his own inter-personal skills, whilst simultaneously acquiring some particular skill or knowledge, usually set in his own organizational context. These methods, properly designed, can cope with the relevance, contextual and application problems of learning and can help to spread some common philosophies and experiences across the organization. The Reed Group with its cadres, Manchester Business School with their Joint Development Activities are British examples of this form of development. It is too soon to assess the effects, but the overall approach seems likely to work better than many other planned approaches to formal learning.

3.4 Assignment or planned experience

This is the most common form of individual development in organizations and potentially the most effective. But to get personal learning from experience, certain things have to happen:

1 The individual must be able to generalize from particular incidents. He must be able to explain why things worked the way they did. A set of experiences, no matter how successful, does not necessarily give learning unless the lessons are conceptualized. Everyone has encountered the great

manager with a string of success stories who is hard put to it to explain his success. It is easier to learn from failure than from success. Success only means that the total formula worked, but which parts of it were crucial and why, which were universally valid, which particular to the situation, remain unknown until tested.

2 The individual must have some idea of what he needs to learn from each assignment and how it will help him in his development. This assumes a degree of knowledge about ourselves, our strengths and weaknesses, our goals and our ambitions, which is rare in most of us. For the ancient Greeks, 'Know thyself' was one of the key prescriptions for success, inscribed above the temple of Zeus at Delphi.

3 The individual must receive information about his performance, and the standards expected of him, not only in terms of results, but in terms of his particular learning needs, as they relate to knowledge and skills or to behaviour. This kind of feedback is particularly difficult to give and to receive. It requires, as with normal appraisals:

(a) To be given with genuine regard for the individual;
(b) To be related to specific instances and to needs previously listed by the individual;
(c) To have a lot of time spent on it – quarter-hour interviews get nowhere.

As suggested in the section on appraisals, there is good evidence for suggesting that this type of feedback for learning should be separated from performance appraisal, and perhaps given by persons other than the superior – often people in a diagonal or lateral relationship, where the role of judge will not overlay the role of helper.

4 The organization must tolerate mistakes and failures as long as they produce learning and as long as the long-term value of the learning outweighs the costs of the mistakes. One advantage of, and reason for, the continued success of many fast-growing companies has been that mistakes get 'rolled over' by growth. There is greater tolerance for genuine mistakes, more learning and a bigger stock of developed managerial talent to sustain the growth record. In this way, growth breeds growth. A hurdle system of development, where a fallen hurdle means career failure, will not encourage experimentation or the testing of hypotheses about ideas or behaviour. It will breed caution and conservatism, and rule out the entrepreneurial spirit that the organization will say it needs.

5 The organization must make its expectations clear. One study of new graduate recruits has shown that those for whom the organization initially set the highest standards were the most successful after a few years.

We know, from the classroom, that if a teacher thinks his students are clever and able they will become clever and able. Research findings have verified this. If an organization believes that its managers can perform effectively, they will perform effectively if allowed to do so. High expectations, if properly communicated, can create a self-fulfilling prophecy. In chapter 2, this was called the 'halo effect of role perception'.

There are two forms of learning from experience – learning from the situation and learning from the person or modelling. Most planned assignments work on the former basis. An individual is asked to learn from a variety of job or task situations. There is, however, some reason to think that we can learn a lot, all through our lives, by modelling ourselves after chosen individuals, by identification. Apart from some 'personal assistant' schemes, few organizations have tried systematically to develop characteristics and behaviour in an individual by attaching him to suitable models. Fitting people to people might well be a more effective strategy for development than fitting people to tasks. It is easier to learn by modelling than by conceptualizing experience.

3.5 Some conclusions

Once again, development strategies for the individual would seem to depend on the culture. Formal training systems are appropriate to the role cultures and the steady-state parts of organization. The job requirements can be defined fairly accurately in terms of skills, knowledge and abilities. Training requirements for each job at each level can therefore be decided upon and provided in a fairly systematic way. The most effective schemes of formal training are indeed those which grow out of very detailed and specific job definitions.

In power cultures, however, the policy and breakdown parts of organizations, learning will be by experience or modelling and will usually be initiated by the individual. Ryder's use of the personal assistant role in Reed, as a development mechanism, was a good example of an organization-ally-sponsored system of development in what is likely to be a power culture at that part of the organization. Individuals who learn fastest in power cultures are those who have most clearly defined goals and career paths for themselves. Such people are often organizationally mobile, changing their organizations and even industries or occupations in order to develop their knowledge and skills.

In task cultures or the innovative ends of organizations, the group and the interactive skills of individuals are key factors. Although other forms of skill training and personal learning from experience are required, the various types of group learning will flourish most successfully in these cultures. It is no accident that just as the norms, values and practices of a task culture are most in accord with the precepts of the 'liberal' theorists on organization, so group learning is their preferred method of development. Group learning will, however, be rejected by power cultures, along with most formal training schemes, as time-wasting and irrelevant, and by role cultures as threatening and too culturally laden.

4 The role of the personnel department

4.1

Unless your company is too large (in which case, break it up into autonomous parts), have a one-girl people department (not a personnel department). Records can be kept in the payroll section of the accounting department (she answers her own phone and does her own typing) acts as personnel (sorry – people) assistant to anybody who is recruiting. She lines up applicants, checks references and keeps your pay ranges competitive by checking other companies.

Robert Townsend, *Up the Organization.*

Robert Townsend would have us put the personnel function back in its original role as record-keeper and recruitment service. This was where it started. To this role, time has added at least some of the following functions:

Negotiation of industrial agreements;
Administration of industrial agreements;
Relationship with unions;
Determination of wage and salary schemes, promotion and selection mechanisms;
Development of career-planning, succession planning and manpower planning systems;
Administration of training and educational programmes;
Counselling service;
Advisory service on the application of the behavioural sciences;
Development;
Organization structure and design.

To these must be added in some organizations what have been termed the 'rag-bag' functions of personnel, whereby they accumulate tasks and responsibilities that no one else desires, for example:

Office administration;
Canteen services;
Vehicle maintenance;
Secretarial services.

Contemplating this list, it is not surprising to find that the major problems facing personnel departments are:

Role conflict;
Role ambiguity.

4.2 Role conflict and ambiguity

This arises because the personnel function can easily find itself carrying out more than one of the following roles in its interaction with the same department:

Executing (e.g. negotiating, counselling);
Servicing (e.g. canteen, recruitment, training);
Auditing (e.g. appraisal schemes, review of salary grades);
Advising (e.g. on behavioural sciences, training opportunities);
Co-ordinating (e.g. on fringe benefits or career opportunities).

These roles, performed by the same people in the same relationships, are in conflict. The advisor who is also the auditor carries a sting in his relationship which is recognized and can be resented by the other party. When the personnel department 'suggests' a name for a key post, is it advising or executing? When it asks for details of expenditure on secretaries, is it co-ordinating or auditing?

Not only does ambiguity result from the uncertainty as to which role is currently operational in any situation, but the power base of any attempt at influence by the personnel department is often unclear. Desirably, all advisory co-ordinating and auditing relationships should be backed by expert power if they are not to be the source of conflict. Expert power has to be earned, given by the recipient of influence to the department exerting influence. Often this expert power is not given to personnel departments, for it is hard indeed for them to claim it in the absence of generally accepted professional qualifications or proof of the superiority of their advice. If they wish their point of view to prevail, they must rely on position power – but position power that is not backed up is a very weak power base. Control over resources, therefore, becomes key to the success of the department as a whole. Hence, the growth in personnel empires from Townsend's girl to the mammoth departments in some large organizations.

4.3 Some implications

But in most organizations, the jobs listed in 4.1 in this chapter have to be done by someone. Is it not sensible to give them all to one department and let them work out the problems listed above? Before doing this, it is worth pondering the answers to the following questions:

1 Are all the jobs in *4.1* necessary for your organization, or all parts of your organization? What would be lost if they were not done?

It has already been suggested that some of the jobs are more appropriate to some cultures than to others. Some may not be necessary at all. Remember that a department has a vested interest in perpetuating the problems that brought it into existence. Jobs that may not be necessary include:

Uniform pay levels at all levels in all divisions;
Job description and evaluation for jobs in the policy, breakdown and innovative sections of the organization;
Monitoring and checking matters such as medical certificates, minor expense claims, losses (what is the cost of detecting one deliberate mistake?);
Selection procedures, perhaps including psychological tests, over-precise for the nature of the job. If the people specifications are set so that eight out of ten applicants will be suitable, procedures to select the best one out of the eight are unnecessary. All that may be required is to take the first comer, provided he or she meets the criteria.

Box 9.4 The costs of checking

Heinz used to spend £4 a time investigating customer complaints, until someone had the idea of a 25p coupon to be sent automatically.

One organization employed a doctor, nurse and receptionist together with their accommodation. They discovered that 90 per cent of their time was taken with issuing and checking medical certificates for absence from work. They decided to employ an outside doctor on retainer to deal with emergencies, and to accept without question all medical certificates from employees. The cash saving was £13,000 p.a. Absenteeism from sickness fell, while the morale boost from employees' perception of trust, although unmeasured, was considerable.

The discovery of a long history of expense account swindling by one individual led to the institution of an elaborate system of rules and checks for expense accounts submitted by non-managerial personnel. After two years, it was discovered that in spite of the elaborate and costly procedure, the total amount of claims had increased 30 per cent, twice the percentage increase of sales turnover, assumed to be the controlling factor.

---

2 Are the implications of the role complexity understood and accepted? For instance, the controlling functions of the department (auditing, co-ordinating, executing) will tend to dominate the helping functions (advising, servicing). If the personnel department is seen as primarily a monitoring

department, its efforts to help will be liable to misinterpretation and rejection. (See Box 9.4.) Outsiders can invade or be invited into another's territory. Their reception and the work they can do will be largely coloured by the manner of their entry. Once a personnel department assumes any controlling functions, its helping functions will be severely limited.

3 Should the people problems be 'boxed'? Assigning responsibility for overseeing or co-ordinating a set of problems to one division tends to relieve other departments or divisions of responsibility: the problem gets 'boxed', which is not the same thing as solving it. An industrial relations department which assumes responsibility for industrial relations matters will lessen the importance of these issues for the operating department. This may not always be desirable.

The general implication behind each of these questions is that the functions of a personnel department should be differentiated. They should be differentiated according to the requirements of the cultures, according to the roles, and according to the desired locus of responsibility.

One way of making this differentiation operational is to recognize it structurally. One section is given all the monitoring functions, or they can be transferred to another monitoring department, e.g. accounts. The innovatory or advisory element can be separated out, named 'organization development' to distinguish it from personnel, and even made responsible to a separate board member. Industrial relations or management development is often separated out from personnel. Of course, a separate name does not by itself mean a differentiated approach. Too often it is only the reflection of an inter-group conflict for power and influence. But structural changes, if accompanied by appropriate changes in procedures and power sources, can be a way of recognizing the need for differentiation in the personnel function.

5 Summary and discussion

5.1

We have considered the methods involved in *management of human assets*, and in particular *appraisal systems*, *career planning* and *compensation systems*.

We considered the common problems and some remedies, and suggested that a culturally differentiated approach was needed but had not been systematically applied in any organization. We looked at *development of the individual*, and in particular *formal education and training, group learning, assignment and planned experience*, and examined the advantages and drawbacks of each, again suggesting that some methods were more appropriate to some cultures than to others. Finally, we considered *the role of the personnel department* – a role full of complexity, conflict and ambiguity, with perhaps some built-in forces leading to perpetuation of the problems. Again, a differentiated approach was suggested.

5.2

But in looking at the people of organizations there remain some major questions not yet fully covered. These are strategic macro-issues, questions of policy and judgement not easily resolvable by logic or scientific fact. But they need to be raised, even if they cannot be answered.

Should you grow your own timber? Many organizations work on the assumption that they must provide their future manpower needs from their own resources. To continue the agricultural metaphor they create plantations, weed out the weaker growths, transplant and nurture the stronger saplings, plan and plant according to their estimate of future needs. Let us review briefly some of the implications of this philosophy:

(a) It necessitates a manpower plan, including estimates of future manpower needs at all levels, worked back over time to intake requirements for particular years.

(b) It needs progression plans, ineptly called development plans, for bringing forward, and weeding out, the required numbers and calibres for the various levels.

(c) It needs the mechanisms and procedures to implement these plans, the whole battery of appraisal schemes, replacement charts, development plans.

(d) It can easily result in a surplus inventory of potential at the lower levels as the organization overstocks to take care of errors in forecasts, fall-outs, or failure to develop the potential properly. This overstocking at the bottom results in people being overpaid for the work they do, low morale and high rates of departure.

(e) It can result in an overstocking at the older levels of middle management. Organizations feel that they owe continued employment to the individual who has passed his optimum level. Although socially well-motivated, this policy can lead to a cluttered organization, as individuals make work to justify their employment, and to low morale, when individuals feel themselves the recipients of organizational charity. A charity which leads to insecurity and dependency, neither of them very pleasant sensations.

Items (d) and (e) are invisible costs, but when added to the other more measurable items, they amount to a very costly policy. Is it justified? To answer this, one must compare the cost of an alternative policy, e.g. hiring individuals on specific-term contracts, or for specific jobs or ranges of jobs. This would involve:

(a) Higher selection and recruitment costs;
(b) Probably higher salary and wage rates, since the organization, in order to attract people, or renew existing contracts, would have to pay at least the full market rate;
(c) Letting go larger numbers of middle managers, or reducing their salaries in line with reduced jobs;
(d) Inadequate staffing of key jobs, if particular individuals were not available in the market at that time.

Modification of this approach would include drastically curtailing recruitment of men in their early twenties and a lowering of the normal retirement age to fifty.

These philosophies are more appropriate to power and task cultures. Wholesale adoption by organizations would require a radical change in society's attitude to work and career progression. The norms would have to become that:

(a) one could, over a period of time, work for more than one organization;
(b) that earnings do not have to progress monotonically until retirement but can peak in the middle;
(c) that times of work should pay for times of not working.

Interestingly, these norms are currently found at the very top and bottom of the social orders, but not in the spreading middle.

Whether organizations should or should not grow their own timber is a question that only they can answer. But a comparison of the alternative costs would be useful data.

Should you develop the organization or the individual? Attempts by organizations to improve effectiveness by changing individuals have too often resulted in:

(a) Little or no changed behaviour in the individual;
(b) A perception by the individual that the organization is seeking control over his life – resulting in the responses of compliance or rebellion;
(c) The loss of investment when an individual leaves the organization.

A different approach was to improve the effectiveness of the organization by changing some aspects of the organization and the way it did its work.

Box 9.5   The back-firing appraisal scheme

After much research, thought and consultation, the new personnel manager had evolved a comprehensive appraisal and review scheme. The organization had recently got to the size (1,000 employees) where some systematic way of cataloguing their resources in terms of individuals was required, together with a less haphazard way of developing and rewarding people. This was a generally recognized need in an organization where pay differentials, promotion and management development opportunities had hitherto been opportunistic, haphazard and subjectively determined.

The new appraisal scheme was very well thought out. It provided for a proper job definition, a regular performance review initiated by the individual but carried through with his superior, required that the superior's comments be seen and signed as accepted by the subordinate, a space for the identification of development needs, the likely potential of the individual, and even for his suggestions as to the way in which the organization could help him to do his work better. The original of this comprehensive document was kept by the manager, with a copy for the subordinate and for the personnel files.

Indirectly seeking feedback on the reception of his system, three months later, the personnel manager was surprised to hear the following comments reported:

I filled it in as accurately as I could, but imagine my horror when the director in charge of my function – not my line boss, and at least three levels above me, told me three weeks later when discussing a possible new appointment for me, that he fully agreed with my assessment of my weaknesses. And I thought the document was private to me and my boss! Honesty just does not pay!

Just how gullible do they think we are – trying to get our signatures to our shortcomings? Obviously it's a way of preparing the ground for the next redundancy operation. They had a low suit arising out of the last one.

More paper, more forms. I called all my people in together, told them that we had to do this, but that I didn't want to interfere with the normal work of the department. I said that I would fill in my comments on each of their forms, let them take them home overnight, and bring them back signed on the following day. It all seemed to work OK. We had no problems.

I'm sure they mean well, but do they really expect us to put down the truth?

This would have its effect on the individual since the overall approach of Organization Development, as it grew to be called (O.D. for short), was to find ways of integrating the goals and values of the individual with those of the organization. O.D. endeavours to change the culture of the organization so that this integration becomes possible.

The main worth of the O.D. approach lies in its willingness to attack the problems of the organization directly, rather than through the agency of

Box 9.6 A comparison of organization development and management development

Category	Organization development	Management development
reasons for use	need to improve overall organizational effectiveness typical example of tough problems to be solved: inter-unit conflict confusion stemming from recent management change loss of effectiveness due to inefficient organizational structure lack of teamwork	need to improve overall effectiveness of manager managers do not know company policy or philosophy managers are void in certain skills managers seem to be unable to act decisively
typical goals	to increase the effectiveness of the organization by: creating a sense of 'ownership' of organization objectives throughout the work force planning and implementing changes more systematically facilitating more systematic problem-solving on the job to reduce wasted energy and effort by creating conditions where conflict among people is managed openly rather than handled indirectly or unilaterally to improve the quality of decisions by establishing conditions where decisions are made on the basis of competence rather than organizational role or status	to teach company values and philosophy to provide practice in management skills which lead to improved organizational effectiveness to increase ability to plan, co-ordinate, measure, and control efforts of company units to gain a better understanding of how the company functions to accomplish its goals

Box 9.6 – *contd*

Category	Organizational development	Management development
	to integrate the organization's objectives with the individual's goals by developing a reward system which supports achievement of the organization's mission as well as individual efforts toward personal development and achievement	
interventions for producing change	education and problem-solving is on the job; learning while problem-solving and solving problems while learning	sending of manager to some educational programme
		job rotation of managers
	following a diagnosis, utilization of one or more of the following techniques:	specialized training 'packages'
	team building training programmes inter-group confrontations data feedback techno-structural interventions	courses and/or conferences counselling reading of books and articles

	change in organizational
	   structure
	   job enrichment
	   change in physical
	   environment (social
	   architecture)	

time frame	prolonged	short, intense
staff requirements	diagnostician catalyst/facilitator consultant/helper	teacher/trainer programme manager designer of training programmes
	knowledge and skill in the dynamics of planned change experience in the laboratory method of learning	knowledge in the processes of human learning

Box 9.6 – *contd*

values		
	humane and non-exploitative treatment of people or organizations	competition
		belief that 'education is progress'
	theory Y assumptions	belief that managers need challenging periodically
	collaboration	
	sharing of power	manager's right to have time for reflection and renewal
	rationality of behaviour	
	openness/candour/honesty	
	importance of surfacing and utilizing conflict	belief that individual should 'fit' organization's needs
	right of persons and organizations to seek a full realization of their potential	right of person to seek full realization of his potential
	explicitness of values as a value in itself	

Adapted from Burke, 'A Comparison of Management Development and Organization Development'

particular individuals. A combination of appropriate methods of individual development combined with the O.D. approach to the problem areas of the organization would seem to be the happy compromise which meets the needs of the organization and its individuals.

Are the goals and values of the individual compatible with those of the organizations? It has been said that the work of 90 per cent of the people is boring for 90 per cent of the time. The practitioners of O.D. and many of the theorists of the Human Relations school, whilst conceding that this is so, would deny that it need be so. Who is right? Let us at least admit that the 90 per cent figure can be considerably reduced. More people can be given more interesting work with more relevance to their own development and maturity. But let it at the same time be recognized that investment in work, identifying with the organization, can carry its costs.

Involvement consumes energy. Not everybody's psychological contract would put all their 'E' into one bucket. A lot of people prefer what might be called a portfolio approach to life with proportions of 'E' allocated to different activities. Perhaps for the richness and diversity of our society, it is as well that individuals tend to have more than one commitment.

One way of looking at this question is to examine the match between the organizations culture and the cultural preferences of the individuals.

Individuals with a power or task orientation are likely to find role cultures frustrating and inhibiting. Individuals with role orientations will be insecure and threatened in a power or task culture. People with person orientations will tend to shun organization altogether unless they can use their facilities with minimum cost. The organization and the individual could be regarded as integrated if the cultural aspects of psychological contract matched. The organizations usually regarded as integrated in this sense are the successful task individuals. The more successful aero-space firms in the U.S., some consultancy organizations, some Research and Development departments are the examples often cited. But the power cultures of entrepreneurial firms, the financial merchant firms, the pediments of large organizations are also capable of high integration with the individual. So are parts of the civil service, and the steady-states of many organizations where the role culture predominates. For if the truth be told, even though never revealed in questionnaires, 90 per cent of the work force may well be role-orientated, may like to be bored 90 per cent of the time, even if it is not fashionable to say so!

This being so, are organizations justified then in the processes of socialization which they nearly all apply to their new recruits? Socialization is a way of binding them to the organization and at the same time making them more amenable to the preferred ways of influence. In chapter 5 these processes were categorized as *schooling, apprenticeship, co-option, mortification*.

Role cultures tend to use schooling, power cultures co-option and, occasionally, mortification; task cultures favour apprenticeship. The typical larger organization will run induction and training courses for the bulk of its individuals, but the professionally-trained recruit to the innovative groups will be put under care and guidance for his early months. At higher levels, co-option to the clubs of power becomes important and the aspiring individual learns to adapt his attitudes and behaviour to accord with the norms of the club.

Socialization is an effective way of increasing uniformity, and therefore predictability, in an organization. It is also, let it be acknowledged, an effective way of maintaining the *status quo* in terms of the power distribution in the organization. Those who fight to join the club are not going to be amongst those who destroy it. Those who learn the rules and norms the hard way are often the most severe enforcers of them afterwards. Socialization is also comfortable for everyone except those being socialized. It is always pleasant to be on the inside looking out at those seeking to join. Socialization, therefore, is likely to be a feature of organization life for a long time to come.

But it carries its costs. All must have seen, or been part of, or read of, the over-socialized organization where there are norms and customs for everything, where everyone is identical to everyone else, where individuals are but uniform ciphers, where conformity is not only the rule but the delight, and the host of unwritten practices are the delectation of the initiated but a minefield for the newcomer. Such organizations can drown initiative in compliance, innovation in identification. They may be so concerned with perpetuating the customs of the past that they ignore the signs of the future. For it is hard in those organizations for he who thinks differently to gain a hearing. He must identify or leave.

Over-socialization is, therefore, a comfortable but dangerous road for the organization. For the individual acceptance of socialization is in some way, however small, a surrender of his independence. He may of course desire this. The need to belong and to be accepted may make the exchange worth-while. Exclusivity increases the appeal of every group and thereby their influence via the exchange method. But the power of the organization to socialize and to require uniformity from its members results, if unchecked, in the 'organization man', the 'conforming society', the firm as a 'country within a country', the stereotype of 'the man in the grey flannel suit', the 'lonely crowd'. So much of this is alien to all the individualism in our cultures that one would have thought that socialization would have been resisted *en masse* long ago. Perhaps organizations today have replaced the village and the street as the one essential group to which man belongs, perhaps man is secretly proud to be socialized by a firm in the way in

---

Box 9.7 Write your own obituary

Imagine that you have reached the end of your life. Compose your own obituary – a description and analysis of your life that would be published in a newspaper, or read at your funeral, or circulated to friends. Do it as seriously and honestly as you can, for it will then represent an overview of your life as it might turn out to be.

When the obituary is completed study it objectively and answer the following questions:

(a) How many organizations does your life-pattern involve your working for?

(b) To what extent are the life-goals revealed by your obituary compatible with any or all of those organizations?

(c) To what extent would the traditional personnel procedures of the organizations help you to achieve your life-pattern?

which once he was proud to be a Yorkshireman or to belong to Truro. Perhaps organizations today are the main medium for man to acquire his identity, to work towards his ego ideal.

If this be so, and one suspects that it has more than a touch of truth to it, then the responsibilities of organizations to the individuals within them are immeasurably increased. The need for those who run them to understand their organization and their workings becomes imperative and the recognition by organizations that they should be understanding of their members, something devoutly to be wished.

10 On the Work of the Organization – and its Design

1 Introduction

It is not granted to everyone to design an organization. Yet most managers have dabbled with the organizational drawing-board from time to time, whether it be a wistful tampering with the organigram, re-definitions of authorities and responsibilities, the layout of the factory or the office, or the degree of delegation to a group or an individual.

Most organizations are not designed, they grow. Indeed, there are several studies which draw on biological analogies to describe organization phenomena. But not all organizations adapt equally well to the environment within which they grow. Many, like the dinosaur of great size but little brain, remain unchanged in a changing world. Others, 30 per cent in one study in Poughkeepsie, New York, die in the first year of their life. The law of the survival of the fittest is as inexorable for organizations as it is in nature.

For survival, for continual growth and development, in organizations as with individuals, it helps to know what you would like to be before you try to become it. Analysis of the ideal, of what should be, when compared with the reality of what is, may be disillusioning, but it is the proper starting point for improvement and for planned change.

In this chapter we shall examine some of the problems involved in *the design of the structure*, *the management of diversity* and *the design of the job*, followed by *summary and implications*.

In chapter 11 we shall be examining the design of the systems that must accompany the allocation of work and responsibility. In chapter 12 we shall investigate the job of managing the change, the movement from the present reality to a future ideal. In this chapter, we shall consider such fashionable issues as centralization or decentralization, whether you have a product or a functional organization, the problems and possibilities of the matrix organization. We shall examine the topic of job enrichment and the issue of delegation. As with the other chapters in Part Two, it will be the principles involved and the issues raised that will be our concern, not the details of the mechanisms or the structures.

2 The design of the structure

2.1

'Structure' includes the allocation of formal responsibilities, the typical organization chart. It also covers the linking mechanisms between the roles, the co-ordinating structures of the organization, if any are needed. The basic forms make up what might be called the skeleton of the organization. They need to be joined by muscles, nerves and flesh if they are going to work, but the decision on the underlying bone structure is a first priority. How do organizations decide on the appropriate structure – is there a best form, or is there perhaps an inevitable progression as companies get older or larger?

In chapter 7 the view was put forward that the effective organization was that which had an appropriate structure and culture. 'Appropriate' would be determined by a variety of forces, the technology, the market, the size of the organization, its people. The problem now is to make this conceptual doctrine of 'appropriateness' operational in designing an organization's structure.

In pursuing an optimal structure, organizations have normally followed an implicit re-formulation of Ockham's Razor – 'As simple as you can, as complex as you must'. Or, to put it another way, the designer of organizational structures needs to tread a tight-rope stretched between the pressures for uniformity on the one hand and diversity on the other. Let us consider these pressures separately.

2.2 Uniformity

Uniformity implies standardization and common procedures centrally administered. The pressures for *uniformity* can include:

1 The cheapness of standardization. It costs less to produce and to process standard forms. Training for standard procedures is easier and cheaper. There are economies of scale in most standardized operations, e.g. a central computer or legal department *vis-à-vis* separate installations in each unit.

2 The need for interchangeability. Many operations, e.g. airlines, banks, postal services have operations which require that they use common procedures so that interactions within the organization and between organizations can be carried out according to standard procedures.

3 The need for control of process. Some organizations need to monitor the on-going process of their organizations, as opposed to monitoring the

results. Organizations in which one unit is dependent on the output of another, e.g. process industries, vertically integrated organizations, need a uniform system so that fluctuations in the requirements of one unit can be reflected in the operations of another. Any interdependence of operations will result in a pressure for some uniformity of method.

4 The need for a standard product. Many organizations need uniformity of output from a variety of sources. Multiple stores (e.g. Marks and Spencer and Tesco), branch banking or airline offices are some examples of market-induced needs for uniformity. Organizations with more than one production facility for the same product, e.g. British Steel Corporation, or organizations producing wide requirements for industry, e.g. the pharmaceutical industry, have a production-induced need for uniformity.

5 The need for specialization. By pooling all the requirements for maintenance, or for electronics engineers, the organization can build up a competence core in that field and can offer career paths to specialists. But a competence core is only possible if there is some uniformity in the organization. The haphazard employment of specialists becomes too costly, so rules are set for their use.

6 The desire for central control. The requirement of senior management that they 'know what is going on' is a push towards uniformity or control of the process rather than the results.

Standardization permits the centre to be fed with a vast amount of information in a digestible form and in approximately real time. This allows the centre to monitor the daily process of the business, to be the only pool of all relevant information, and to intervene should the occasion demand it. This requirement by senior management for central control can well be a desire rather than a need imposed by the situation.

The stereotype of the French educational system – that at any given hour on any given day, the French Minister of Education could state with complete certainty what every child in any level was doing throughout the country is an example of a system where all the needs for uniformity were felt and fully responded to. Uniformity would clearly reduce the costs of production of teaching materials, would permit the freer interchangeability of children from one location to another, would regulate the flow from one part of the system to another (e.g. into the university system) and would give a guaranteed value to any certificate of education so that employers would know what they were buying. Uniformity is the hallmark of the steady-state. Where the requirements for uniformity are high, a role culture will tend to predominate, carrying with it all the other aspects of that culture in addition to its penchant for rule and procedures.

2.3 Diversity

The other set of pressures in any organization will be for *diversity*. These pressures include:

1 *Regional diversity*. An organization may operate in more than one geographical area. But it may or may not regard these areas as 'different' for its own particular purposes. What is 'Europe' or 'South America' to one organization will be twenty different areas to another. Surrey may differ from Kent for some organizations, but both be defined as Southern England for others.

2 *Market diversity*. Markets can be defined in regional terms (France, or Yorkshire), in socio-economic terms (suburban, middle-class), by end-use (agriculture, industrial), by customer activity (Government, construction industry) or even by their social habits (television viewers, pub-goers). The number of market categories and the degree to which they differ are important aspects of diversity.

3 *Product diversity*. How wide is the mix of outputs, be they soap powders or medical services? Can they all be treated as one, or does each product have its own peculiarities in terms of market, image, need for servicing, quality, etc. A large number of products does not necessarily imply diversity, twenty different sizes of screw can still be regarded, conceptually, as one product. It is the degree of difference between them that is the diversity that matters.

4 *Technological diversity*. Is the organization based on one technology, or a variety of them? If a variety, are the differences between them significant? In high technology organizations, differences are often crucial, as technical knowledge and skills become more hardly acquired and more narrowly focused. Low technologies permit wider ranges of expertise and shorter learning periods. Diversity in high technology therefore is more pressing than in a low technology organization (e.g. insurance, local government, many service industries).

5 *Goal diversity*. Does the organization have one set of goals, to which all divisions and departments subscribe or do the goals vary? How much does the variety matter? For instance, the sales manager's concern with customer service and the problems of today could be far removed from the worries of the research director about the materials required for the 1980s. The personnel department's aims for the welfare of the people may conflict or may be in line with the production department's desire for large-scale automation.

This internal goal diversity is the crux of what Lawrence and Lorsch have called differentiation. They have shown that this internal differentiation is more appropriate, and more common, when the market environment or the technology is changing more rapidly. Plastics is a faster-growing and faster-changing industry than containers, and therefore more internal goal diversity would be expected in a plastics firm than a container firm.

6 *The identity of diversity.* Individuals find it easier to identify with smaller groups than with large organizations. Buried deep in a functional specialization of a large complex, it is hard to feel committed to the aims of the total organization. The goals of the specialization are the important ones, even though they may at times be sub-optimal for the whole. Smaller groupings, in which the specialists are parcelled out, may cost more, but it makes it easier to establish a 'common enemy'; and makes it easier for the individual to identify with a collection of activities, rather than just one. Metaphorically, the individual seeks for a village even in the midst of a town since he needs a territory small enough to feel that he is a significant part of it.

7 *The pull for disaggregated control.* Just as the centre feels a need to hold all the strings in its grasp, so the managers on the periphery feel a need to have more control over the resources that they are required to organize and administer. To be an area manager when in fact all the resources in the area are functionally controlled from head office reduces the role of the manager to that of reporter or public relations representative. Justifiably or not, the groups on the periphery can be expected to strive for a redistribution of control over resource. If power without responsibility be harlotry, responsibility without power is masochism.

Conglomerates are the usual business example of diversity. Untrammelled by uniformity or central control, diversity can be highly exciting – but sometimes ruinous, as several conglomerates have proved. Governments with departments ranging from police and fire brigades to licensing and tax assessments are another example of diversity. The advance of technology in all areas of life, the apparent increase in the rate of change of the environment, the pressures for the agglomeration of activities tend to increase the pressures for diversity. Weinshall has argued that organizations tend to progress from an entrepreneurial structure to a multi-structure as the size or scope of their decision making process (D.M.P.) expands. Scope of D.M.P. appears to be approximately equivalent to diversity. Increasing diversity leads ultimately, then, to a multi-structure organization. Stopford, examining a number of multi-national firms, demonstrated that there was a progression from firms with low product diversification and

Box 10.1(a)

Examples of The Basic Managerial Structures

types of managerial structure	chart	degree of formaliz-ation	degree of centraliz-ation
entrepreneurial	CE (circles connected to central CE node)	informal	centralized
functional	Chief Executive → research and develop, personnel, manufacturing, finance, sales; manufacturing → product A, product B, product C; sales → area X, area Y, area Z	formal	centralized
decentralized — by product line; by geographical area	CE → product A, product B, product C (each → R&D, P, M, F, S); CE → area X, area Y, area Z (each → R&D, P, M, F, S)	formal	decentralized

From Weinshall, 'Application of two conceptual schemes of organizational behaviour in case study and general organizational research', Ashridge Management College, 1971

Box 10.1 (b)

The effect of Size on the Managerial Structure

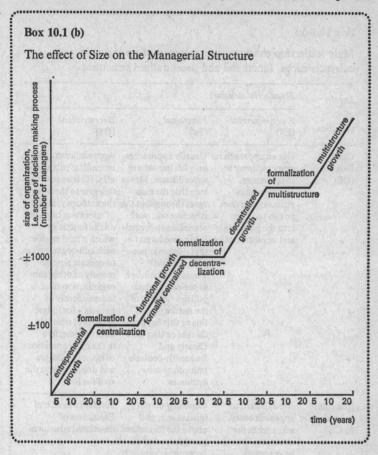

Box 10.1 (c)

Main leadership characteristics required of managers in entrepreneurial, functional and decentralized structures

Level of management	Managerial structure		
	Entrepreneurial (ES)	Functional (FS)	Decentralized (DS)
Chief Executive (CE)	Has an approach to every manager in the structure. Initiates main ventures, but does not go too deep into the planning and implementation	Usually approaches only his immediate subordinates. Makes sure that the managers throughout the structure will work according to formalized procedures, i.e. that whenever possible the DMP would be routinized in pre-established policies (usually of the nature of – 'if this or this happens, do that or that'). Closely and frequently controls immediate subordinates	Approaches only his immediate subordinates. He tries to delegate to them all the authority, in form of allocating to them all the functions which would enable each sub-organization to operate autonomously of other sub-organizations and independently of himself – for longer periods of time. He does not interfere in the daily operations of his subordinates and does not have the staff for it
immediate subordinates to CE	Are expected to approach every manager in the structure. Should have enough initiative for carrying out the main ventures pushed down to them; however, should not have initiative for large ventures, which is the CE's exclusive domain	Generally do not initiate over and above the formalized procedures and usually communicate only with their superiors, peers (the managers reporting to their own superiors) and their immediate subordinates, whom they generally closely control. Formalize as much as possible of the DMP which is left at their discretion	Similar to the Chief Executives of functional structures

Box 10.1 (c) – *contd*

other managers	Very similar to the above (immediate subordinates to CE). However, when the number of managers in the structure grows, they usually feel less free to approach people who are perceived to be in the hierarchy level above the one of their immediate superiors	Similar to 'immediate sub-ordinates to CE'	Similar to 'immediate sub-ordinates to CE' and 'other managers' in functional structure
general		The managers in the FS are usually of either one of two types: *the stabilization type* – put more emphasis on the formalization and less on the growth ('bureaucrats'). *The growth type* – put more emphasis on growth and less on formalization ('functionalist')	

Box 10.1 (d)

The Multi-structure Managerial Structure

(d)

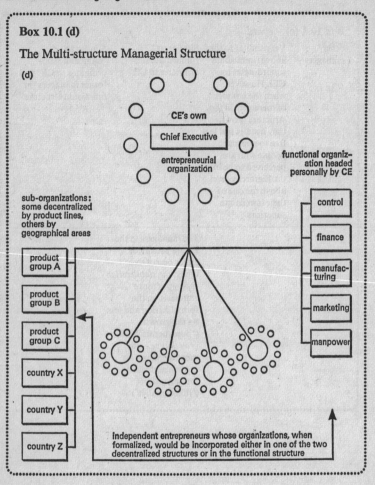

CE's own entrepreneurial organization

Chief Executive

functional organization headed personally by CE

sub-organizations: some decentralized by product lines, others by geographical areas

control

finance

manufacturing

marketing

manpower

product group A

product group B

product group C

country X

country Y

country Z

independent entrepreneurs whose organizations, when formalized, would be incorporated either in one of the two decentralized structures or in the functional structure

low technology, which had a functional structure, to firms with high product diversification, high technology, and high geographical diversification which had what he termed a grid structure. Again, diversity is associated with complexity of structure.

2.4 The implications

There is no organization that does not feel these twin pressures towards diversity and uniformity. Only where the environment is irrelevant, or totally under the control of the organization, can diversity be ignored, uniformity govern and be successful. Totalitarian states, monopolistic state or government organizations, can often afford to ignore the pressures for diversity for a time and still thrive. But even they are eventually threatened by the fate of the dinosaur, to be left behind by a changing environment, huge but decaying.

In practice, in their search for the perfect blend, organizations tend to oscillate from uniformity to diversity, from centralization to decentralization, rather as one adjusts the temperature of a bathroom shower. The process of oscillation is influenced by the prevailing temperature of the water, by the economic and political forces impinging on the environment. When resources are scarce, growth sluggish, the need for central monitoring and uniformity is felt more keenly. Management by results, or remote control, is easier in times of prosperity. The task culture, as chapter 7 pointed out, flourished more easily in the aerospace industry in the days of growth than in the days of retrenchments.

The first two questions that the designer of the organization must ask himself are:

How much diversity?
What kind of diversity?

There is no objective statistical way of answering these questions. Each member of the organization, his view coloured by his role, will have a different answer. But at least a systematic approach would help. To examine each of the pressures for uniformity and diversity, to ask to what extent this pressure must be recognized or can be ignored, to rank order, to put in order of priority the pressures that apply, and to repeat this exercise with the senior members of management would be one way of starting the analysis.

It is unlikely that any organization with more than 1,000 employees, more than one category of product or service, more than one type of client, will not come out of such an analysis with the recognition of some pressures for diversity. The problem remains of recognizing these pressures in the design of both structure and culture.

The matrix organization arose in the aerospace industry out of a need to combine customer needs and priorities within the organizational requirements for economies of scale, long production runs and the development of specialist skills. A product-based organization, with the functions as its servants, would have sacrificed considerations of scale and predictability to meeting customer needs. In the long run this would tend to drive up the product costs. A production-based organization would find it difficult to adapt to the needs of individual markets or customers and would run the danger of losing its outlets, irrespective of the quality of its products. This tendency to place production priorities over customer needs often shows up in a failure to meet completion targets, or at best, necessitates long delivery dates. This need to balance the demands of uniformity and diversity resulted in the creation of product or customer groups, with representatives drawn from each of the functions. The pressures for diversity are channelled through to the functions by their representatives or the product groups.

A decentralized organization, with functional replicas of the central office under regional managers, is a recognition of the importance of the pressure for regional diversity. Regional organization under product organizations recognizes another priority of pressures. Decentralization schemes where the only central department is finance implies that this is the only form of uniformity that is crucial in comparison with the pressures for diversity. In U.S. Corporations, where the home market is relatively homogeneous, distinctions between products are more important and decentralization by product division the common pattern. In Europe, regional differences used to be recognized in the structures of multi-national corporations. Increasingly, as Europe comes to be regarded as one market, the regional organization becomes overlaid by a product organization (e.g. Unilever). Weinshall's 'multi-structure' shows how both forms of decentralization can be, and often should be, contained within one organization along with the entrepreneurial (power culture?) and functional (role culture?) organizations at the centre.

A differentiated organization, in the sense in which Lawrence and Lorsch use the term, an organization in which the goals, time-horizons and working practices of different parts of the organization differ widely, is appropriate to a changing technology or changing market. Combine these pressures with those for diversity of product or region and you should end up with a decentralized differentiated organization. Combine them, however, with pressures for a uniform product and interchangeability and you might find differentiation and centralization. The clearing banks in Britain face strong pressures for standardization, their procedures precisely similar to permit daily monitoring and interchangeability. But they are today facing a changing market, increased competition, pressures to diversify and to utilize new technologies. The answer lies in differentiation without decentralization. The spread of marketing departments, merchant-banking offshoots, development sections, all with personnel, systems and styles different from those traditional to the clearing banks, are signs that the organizations are responding appropriately.

Decentralization is in vogue. The head of one consultancy firm was heard to say 'This firm stands fast on the bedrock principle of decentralization'. Theorists, idealists and practitioners all advocate it. They often rely on the argument that the individual manager is more committed in a decentralized organization with his own command. This, it is held, will release motivational 'E' that will more than offset any diseconomies of scale or loss of central control. This argument is too simplistic. A decentralized organization is often a more satisfying form of environment to work in, it is true. The need to identify with a group, to control the means to one's own destiny are better satisfied with decentralization. But satisfaction does not necessarily lead to productivity and organizations that decentralize for these purposes alone may well be disappointed at the outcome. For decentralization is a response to the pressures for diversity. Only if these pressures are stronger than those for uniformity will it be effective. A sense of identity and control of resources are only two of the pressures that need to be considered. Differentiation is another response to other pressures for diversity. It is a response too often neglected. Decentralization without differentiation may well only lead to uniformity with complications. For a structural allocation in itself solves few problems; the sinews, nerves and muscles must change with the skeleton. Otherwise, role-oriented men, used to rules and regulations, unused to initiative, may find themselves heading up decentralized groups expected to be entrepreneurial after a life of obedience, possessed of expert power without time to acquire it, leaders of groups instead of perusers of papers. It is one thing to prescribe the appropriate diversity, decentralization and differentiation, it is another to manage it.

3 The management of diversity

3.1

Having decided on the right degree and the right form of diversity, the designer of organizations must proceed to staff them and link them with integrating and co-ordinating mechanisms. Excessive diversity in the structure will therefore be unnecessarily costly, cluttering up the organization with un-needed co-ordinating mechanisms. Lawrence and Lorsch, in their oft-quoted study, found that organizations which had more integrating devices than required were less effective and often more frustrating to work in. The most pertinent issues in the management of diversity appear to be *distribution of power, match of culture and structure* and *the integrating mechanisms.*

3.2 Distribution of power

Power, or the capacity to influence, is not something that appears on formal charts, but a consideration of the distribution of power is the key to the effective implementation of the structure. Lawrence and Lorsch found that in their most differentiated industry, plastics, the perceived amount of influence was spread very evenly among the top six levels in the hierarchy. By comparison, in the container industry (an environment more stable and uniform), influence was concentrated to a much greater extent to the top, middle management being represented by their divisional chiefs. In the more diverse environments of plastics and food, the research and sales divisions were perceived to have more influence than production. In our terminology, the task culture was found more appropriate in a changing environment.

Interpreting the findings of Lawrence and Lorsch, increasing diversity should be accompanied by increased influence at middle levels of management. With diversity, top management cannot expect to be in possession of all the relevant information or technical knowledge; decisions must be delegated to those who can take them.

This accords with the norms of a task culture. Power resides where the technical knowledge and the relevant information are to be found. The balance of power swings toward the innovation areas, away from the steady state as the diversity increases, with the promise that the integrative mechanisms, the departments or individuals responsible for linking co-ordination, are seen as retaining at least as much influence as any of the functional, product or regional divisions.

On the other hand, in a more stable, predictable environment where the pressures of uniformity outweigh those of diversity, most situations can be foreseen, and most expertise is channelled into the execution of pre-determined tasks. Unforeseen situations can be resolved at the top of the organization because there alone, in the pediment, will all the information be available. Since, too, the technology is not so fast-changing, the skills available in the pediment will still be relevant to the problems of the

Box 10.2 Distribution of influence in two organizations

Top management has told these fellows, 'We want you to decide what is best for your business, and we want you to run it. We don't want to tell you how to run it.' We assume that nobody in the company knows as much about a business as the men on that team.

Senior manager in a high-performing plastics organization

He (the Chief Executive) does all the scheduling himself, and in essence what you have is a large organization run by one man. This is a refreshing switch from the organization where I had previously worked. I find this very beneficial. If I want something decided, I can go right to him and get a direct decision. You tell him what you want to do, and he will tell you right then and there whether he will let you do it or whether he won't.

Manager in a container organization

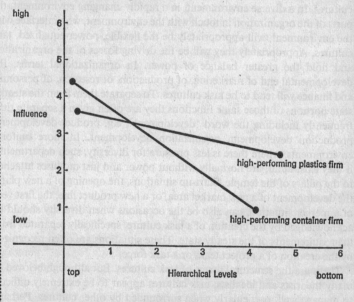

Adapted from Lawrence and Lorsch, *Organization and Environment*, 1967

pillars. Ability to influence at the middle levels will therefore be confined to the specifics of each man's task and will be, in total, considerably less than the influence exerted at the top.

Lawrence and Lorsch found that in one organization in the container industry (relatively uniform), top management had endeavoured to lower the decision-making levels and increase the power of the middle levels of management. This was the low-performing organization and it seemed that the norms, praiseworthy in task culture, were inappropriate and ineffective in the role culture of a steady state.

In Box 10.2 the differences between the spread of perceived power in two effective organizations are described. Both these organizations were effective but one, the plastics firm, in conditions of diversity: the other, the container firm, in conditions of relative uniformity.

3.3 Match of culture and structure

A differentiated organization, it will be recalled from chapter 7, is one in which the tasks of policy, innovations, breakdown and uniformity, or steady-state activities, are carried out by different organizational forms and cultures. In a diverse environment, in a rapidly changing environment, the parts of the organization in touch with the environment, who interface with the environment, will appropriately be the flexible, power-equalized, task cultures. Appropriately they will be the driving forces of the organization and hold the greater balance of power. In organizational terms, the developmental end of marketing, of production, of research, of personnel and finance will tend to be task cultures. To separate them from the steady-state portions of those same functions they are often given a separate title, frequently including the word 'development', e.g. product development, production development, organization development. In more uniform environments, where there is less pressure for diversity, such departments, if they exist at all, are normally without power and just molluscs attached to the pillars of the temple. Start-up situations, the opening of a new plant, the development of a new market area, or a new product line, the first year of a merger situation, can also be the occasions when diversity should be acknowledged by the creation of a task culture, specifically separated from the requirements of the steady state. These situations are often recognized by the creation of a project team or a task force.

These are the structural forms of task cultures. But although beloved of many theorists and idealists, task cultures appear to be extremely difficult to manage well, particularly when surrounded by other cultures. Perhaps it is that organizations have more experience with the management of steady-state activities, perhaps that, when it comes down to hard reality, people are more role-orientated, more fond of the steady state than they are prepared to admit. The project team or task force, set up for a specific job with a finite end, is perhaps the purest example of a task culture. We might therefore expect to find the problems of adjusting culture to struc-

Box 10.3 A Matrix Structure

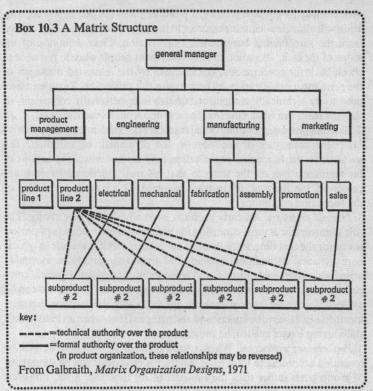

key:

━ ━ ━ ━ =technical authority over the product

━━━━ =formal authority over the product

    (in product organization, these relationships may be reversed)

From Galbraith, *Matrix Organization Designs*, 1971

ture at their height in this sort of organization, particularly if it is super-imposed onto a functional or role-orientated organization. Corning Glass, in a deliberate and systematic application of the findings of Lawrence and Lorsch, set up, in one division, a series of project teams to help manage the pressures of diversity. In the process they experienced 'many problems associated with the clash between values and behaviours of bureaucracy and those of project teams'. Allen Hundert of their Organizational Research and Development department has categorized their conclusions on the management of project teams after two and a half years experience under four headings:

1 *Team formation.* Project teams are a waste of resources when a task can be handled effectively through the existing structure. The task should have a beginning and an obvious end so that members can perceive their progress towards a goal (the 'common enemy'?). If the task has minor impact,

little complexity and low priority, it is unlikely that the permanent organization will allocate adequate resources to it. The new team must be protected from the surrounding bureaucratic organization. Clear definition of the scope of the task, allocation of fully competent people who do not need to check back for confirmation, commitment by the interested managers of the permanent organization, all help to give this protection. Team members need to be technically competent but also inter-personally competent, so that the team can work effectively as a group from its earliest days.

2 *External problems.* The individual members can encounter problems with his peers, colleagues or superiors in the permanent organization. The manager in the functional organization may try to control the actions of his representatives on the team so that his own functional interests are preserved, but the goals of the team distorted. This is really a violation of the formation conditions.

3 *Internal problems.* An early problem is usually that of role clarity. The role of integrator is most confusing for people who are members of project teams for the first time, since that has never been a legitimate role in typical bureaucracies. In addition, problems of trust and confidence inevitably arise. Long-engrained attitudes and behaviours of inter-departmental competition must be dealt with openly so that these barriers to progress can be avoided. One other internal problem has to do with the need for changing membership. It has to be understood and accepted that, when an individual's skills are no longer needed, he should leave.

4 *Performance evaluation.* When a team member knows that he will be measured according to total team results, his behaviour will be supportive of group goals rather than the sub-goal of his function. A lot, however, depends on how the team defines its task. If a team decides its goal is fruitless, then to admit that, on adequate evidence, must be considered success. Too often, only successful implementation of a possible idea is recognized as achievement, with the result that a lot of effort goes into what all those concerned know to be unlikely to achieve success.

In the matrix organization, the project team is permanently cemented into the structural skeleton in the form of a product, or regional grouping composed of representatives from the mainstream structure (Box 10.3 shows how it might be represented). The cultural clash in a matrix organization will be similar to that experienced by project teams.

To some extent, these kinds of problems will be encountered by any task culture operating in a large organization where the steady state is likely to be traditionally dominant, and the more permanent feature of the organization. We must also remember, however, that even in the best organization, there are crises, and the need for the management of breakdown. Here we have seen that a power culture, with norms as distinct from the role culture as those of any project group, will appropriately dominate. Those at the top, too, concerned with policy and the future, with the overall design and climate of the organization, are likely to operate in a different culture. The structural recognition of the policy sector is normally an executive or management committee of some form.

Less often is there any structural recognition of the breakdown activities. Sometimes, when the crisis is extreme, an emergency task force is created, e.g. to deal with a threatened strike. More often, breakdown is part of the everyday life of most line managers. Herein lies the rub, for the manager finds that in one role he has to combine two or more activities, perhaps steady state with breakdown – a frequent combination for a works manager. The cultural norms of role and power appropriate to these two activities are incompatible. We shall consider the problems of the manager in dealing with this cultural role incompatibility in chapter 12. Here we are concerned with the organizational mechanisms for handling a mix of different cultures, the integrating mechanisms.

3.4 The integrating mechanisms

The array of integrating mechanisms is:

Use of the cross-over point in the hierarchy;
Rules and procedures;
Direct managerial contact;
Co-ordinators (individuals);
Co-ordinating departments – temporary or permanent.

They were discussed in principle in chapter 7. Here we need to add some considerations of practical implementation. It was argued earlier that the first three were appropriate mechanisms for the steady state, and indeed Lawrence and Lorsch found that these three mechanisms were used in all the organizations they studied. But in the effective container organization (the more uniform environment) they were the only mechanisms used. In fact, when in one of the container firms, a co-ordinating department was instituted, it was discovered to be ineffective, and merely an irritant. As the department in question described it:

The traditional method of resolving conflict in this company is by taking it upstairs. This often cuts the legs off our own work. It spoils the effort we are making to create an impartial image as a referee. We are not the final authority. Either party can take the matter up further. We don't have the authority to solve these problems at the lower levels.

The first question, therefore, for the designer of organizations, is the familiar 'Is your mechanism really necessary?'. An integrating mechanism without power to integrate becomes a way of boxing the problem. (See chapter 8.) Role cultures are inclined to create liaison groups – which end up by perpetuating the problem they were set up to solve, largely because they did not fulfil the conditions of team formation outlined in the last section.

A co-ordinating individual or group is often genuinely needed in conditions of diversity or differentiation, because it will often happen that:

(a) Decisions need to be taken where the information is not referred up the line;
(b) Paper systems are too inflexible in conditions of diversity and ambiguity;
(c) The individual managers are too prone to let face-to-face contact degenerate into conflict if left to themselves.

When these more elaborate mechanisms are introduced, the following points need to be borne in mind:

1 Tested expert power, allowing influence by persuasion with some degree of magnetism, is the preferred power base for co-ordinators. This expert power must be granted by both groups and will grow as it is tested and proved effective. Lawrence and Lorsch quote a description of an effective co-ordinating group:

That group, their influence goes far beyond the description in the organization chart. [The manager] by nature is a hell of a good marketing man and very experienced in the food business. Consequently, the influence of him and his group extends way beyond the normal boundary.

Inexperienced youth, no matter how clever, is unlikely to provide the right background for the kind of expert power described by this statement. What is needed is a man, or men, with proven and recognized experience in both areas.

2 When conflicts do occur, it is desirable that they be dealt with in a collaborative, problem-solving way, by argument rather than conflict. As chapter 8 demonstrated, this will depend largely on the underlying relationships between the conflicting parties. The ecology has to be right. But it will also depend on the ability of the co-ordinator to manage the difference, to control the argument so that it remains productive. He requires, therefore, a degree of expertise in working with groups and in interactive skills. Lawrence and Lorsch again quoted from a high-performing organization:

I'm an easy-going sort of fellow, but I get mad sometimes. When we get something to fight about, we just say it, face the problem, and it is over. We get the issue out on the table and solve it. It has to be done that way. The production vice-president does it that way. We all follow his lead.

3 The rank and position of the co-ordinators must be high enough in the organization to allow them access to the necessary information and sufficient position power to implement the decisions arrived at. Be it noted, however, that whilst position power is necessary for the collation of data and for the implementation of decisions, it is not an effective power base, on its own, for co-ordination. Co-ordination based on position power alone will turn into influence through rule and procedures, not persuasion, and will then become administration rather than co-ordination.

In many instances, the co-ordinator will in effect be the head of the task culture, the development group, the project team, the start-up cohort. In other words, there will be no officially appointed linking mechanism, but if the task culture group is to be effective the requirements for co-ordination will have to be met by the leader of the group himself. If that be so, then his ambassadorial role, inherent anyway in the leadership of the group, will be broadened or enriched (depending on how you look at it) by the foregoing role requirements of the co-ordinator.

It should be apparent from all this, that the role of co-ordinator is not an easy one, particularly if it be combined with the role of group leader. Organizations in future need to pay much more careful attention to the selection and development of these key individuals. The individual will need, for instance:

To be expert in more than one field of the organization's work;
To be able to handle role ambiguity, incompatibility and conflict without letting the role pressure turn into strain;
To have good inter-personal skills;
To be highly committed to the organization, since he will have little energy left for other activities.

No structure, however well related to the diversity of the environment, will work effectively without a culture appropriate to the structure and people appropriate to the culture, and links between the cultures. The designer of the organization forgets this at his peril.

4 The design of the job

4.1

Even if the design of the total organization is beyond his grasp, every manager or supervisor has some responsibility for the design of the jobs under his control. The scope of the job, the degree of responsibility or control kept by the individual, his participation in discussions and decisions, the methods of supervision and control, are all issues that he needs to consider. The issues usually come to the surface under the headings of *job enlargement*, *participation* and *delegation*. Each of these merits some discussion, to highlight some of the dilemmas and to lead to a better understanding of when and where they are appropriate.

Box 10.4 Motivation and the design of jobs

A group of inmates from a mental institution were given jobs on a butter-wrapping assembly line. Not only were they able to learn their jobs within the first few hours they were employed, they proved to be among the best workers the company had ever employed. Their productivity was much higher than that of other employees and they seemed to be able to work long hours without ever being bored or needing breaks. Their job satisfaction was very high and they had excellent attendance records.

An observer at an automobile assembly plant recently reported that he saw the following episode take place. One of the workers on the line waited until the foreman was not looking, and then slipped his wrench into the belt that drove the assembly line. The result was that the line literally came to a crunching halt. How did the other workers react to all of this? They cheered loudly when the line stopped.

A pigeon has been trained to do the job of an inspector in a drug factory. Previously, inspectors were assigned the job of watching thousands of pills pass by on a conveyor belt and discarding the defective ones. People working on this job tended to have high absenteeism and turnover rates and to be only able to work for short periods of time. But not the pigeons. They proved to be better inspectors from both an error point of view and an hours-worked point of view. Reported by Lawler in 'Motivation and the Design of Jobs'

ASTME-VECTORS, 1971

4.2 Job enlargement

The theories and practices of job enlargement are in large part a reaction against what has been called the micro-division of labour, or the industrial engineering approach to work. They are also examples of deliberate attempts to implement some assumptions about the motivation to work. Let us first examine the rationale that underlies the micro-division of labour approaches:

1 If jobs are broken down into their smallest elements, unskilled people can do them with little training. Workers are therefore less indispensable as individuals and cannot dictate to management.

2 If jobs are broken down, and training times are low, the work-force is more interchangeable. If a worker is sick, gets fired or just does not show up, production will still continue.

3 The personnel department of one U.S. automobile plant explained that a 70 per cent turnover on their assembly line did not bother them because they had so defined the jobs that anyone off the street could be taught a job in one and a half hours.

4 A high degree of mechanization means that the worker will not get physically tired, and can therefore work long shifts.

5 Standardization of jobs would seem to ensure better control of quality, particularly when allied to mechanical pacing, as on an assembly line. If a man is only doing one operation he is likely to become more expert in it, and do it better, than if he is required to carry out a variety of tasks.

6 If jobs are closely defined and machine-paced, production will be more predictable and more easily controlled by management. The supervisor is better able to control a number of simple and well-defined operations than a smaller number of complex tasks where the worker might be more knowledgeable than the supervisor.

On the other side of the coin, it has been argued and often demonstrated, that:

1 The micro-division of labour induces fatigue, boredom, distraction, accidents and anxieties. The indirect costs of these things are reflected in spoilage, absenteeism and turnover.

2 The true costs of monotony come in very high wages for low skill levels, high incidence of strikes and wastage.

3 Moderately complicated tasks resist interruption and generate psychological impulses towards their own completion.

4 Men, unlike most machines, work more efficiently at a variable than at a constant rate.

5 When work is minutely subdivided the individual feels that the simplification of the work is some reflection on himself.

6 Minute sub-division inhibits the worker from identifying his contribu-

tion with the end product. He will not therefore take any autonomous action to correct obvious deficiencies.

7 Excessive specialization reduces the opportunity for social contact or team-work. Long periods of unrelieved social isolation are hard for most individuals to tolerate.

Examples of job simplification and its effects are provided in Box 10.4.

When variety is lacking, employees will often find ways of providing it. In automobile assembly-lines, the game of making anagrams out of the letters of the model name is well-established. In mass-production activities, individuals will break up the assignment into manageable segments (e.g. I will do 500 boxes and then have a break). Social groups, trivial games or rituals are used to break up the monotony. Spanners in the lines, wildcat strikes, unpredictable absenteeism, are often means of providing a necessary variety. A frequent problem for designers in mass-production industries is to make products assembly-line proof. In addition, it is claimed that a well-designed job should:

1 Allow the individual some scope for setting his own standards regarding quantity and quality.
2 Allow the individual to have some control over the ancillary and preparatory stages so that he does not have to suffer from others' mistakes.
3 Allow for interlocking tasks and job rotation where there is a necessary interdependence between jobs, or a high degree of personal stress, as with danger or noise or isolation.
4 Allow for scope for comments and recommendations by the worker on any re-design.
5 Provide for feedback on performance to the individual.

Based on these assumptions, company-wide schemes of job-enrichment have been instituted, and well documented, in a wide variety of organizations, including I.B.M., Texas Instruments, I.C.L., Shell, to mention only the most well-known. Advantages claimed for these and other instances include in one analysis:

Increase in job satisfaction (22%);
Decrease in costs (22%);
Increase in quality of work (17%);
Increase in quantity of output (15%);
Decrease in monotony (14%);
Other (4%);
Not ascertained (8%).

Several organizations have experimented with the abandonment or partial abandonment of the assembly line, substituting for it assembly stations, where one employee, or a group of employees, assembles a whole or a substantial part of the product. An electronics firm, for instance, that manufactured measuring instruments on an assembly line turned over to unit production. Each worker was given a whole instrument to assemble. In many cases this represented a week's work for one employee. When he finished the assembly work, the employee tested the instrument, signed it and sent it to the customer. The employee was also personally responsible for correcting any problems that might cause the instrument to be sent back to the factory. It took about six months for the workers to learn the skills necessary to assemble the instruments. In the long term, production went up very slightly, but, more important from their point of view, quality was very high without the need for inspection and quality control experts, absenteeism and turnover went down to low levels, production flexibility was greatly increased and the job satisfaction of the employees was higher.

This is a rather dramatic instance of job enrichment, although it has been repeated, with similar results, in at least a score of other reported cases. Job enrichment does not have to be such a *volte-face* in working arrangements to achieve some of the results listed above.

What can we conclude about all this? Is job enrichment *de rigueur* for the modern company? There are some general conclusions, but also some caveats and distinctions, to be drawn:

1 Micro-division of labour can easily create a self-fulfilling prophecy. Monotony can lead to boredom, apathy and frustration so that the tight control and prescribed operations become necessary even if they were not so at the outset.

2 Organizations would, therefore, be well-advised to take the monotony out of jobs, for monotony is costly. To reduce men to extensions of machines cannot ultimately be right or profitable. A large proportion of the work-force will do much the same job for the whole of their working life. Even if they do not seek for self-actualization at work, they may at least expect variety.

3 Even those who want their jobs enriched will expect to be rewarded with more than job satisfaction. Job enrichment is not a cheap way to greater productivity. Its pay-off will come in the less visible costs of morale, climate and working relationships.

4 Bavelas and Strauss told of a treatment in which girls were given control of their own conveyor belt, resulting in a phenomenal production

increase, and no loss of quality. This unique programme disintegrated, however, because the experimental group began to make much more money than the others. To avoid embarrassment management cancelled the 'learning bonus'. The assembly line reverted to its previous speed and within a month six of the eight girls had left.

Box 10.5 Individual differences

In 1965 Turner and Lawrence attempted a comprehensive study of the attitudinal and behavioural responses of workers to different aspects of their jobs. The original hypotheses were that workers responded favourably (high satisfaction and low absence rates) to jobs which are more complex, have more responsibility, more authority, more variety, etc. In short, 'desirable' responses would accompany higher level jobs.

The hypothesis concerning attendance was confirmed for a sample of 470 workers from eleven industries working on forty-seven different jobs. The hypothesized positive relationship between job level and satisfaction was not confirmed. This finding, plus the presence of a number of curvilinear relationships, led Turner and Lawrence to the conclusion that the workers in the sample had been drawn from two separate and distinct populations whose members responded in different ways to similar job characteristics. The investigators, by splitting their group of workers on a succession of variables and analysing further the relationship between task attributes and job satisfaction, were able to determine that workers from factories located in small towns responded dramatically differently from workers who came from more urban settings. The workers from small-town settings tended to respond to task attributes in the manner predicted by Turner and Lawrence. Workers from cities indicated no relationship between task attributes and attendance and responded with *low* job satisfaction to supposedly desirable attributes and with high satisfaction to such 'undesirable' attributes as repetitiveness. Turner and Lawrence suggested an explanation, based on a notion of alienation or 'anomie'. They argued that workers in large cities would fail to develop strong group or subcultural norms and values due to the extreme size and heterogeneity of the city population. They would be normless, or 'anomic', and would fail to respond positively to the white-collar-orientated attitudes attached to the larger, more autonomous, more skill-demanding jobs. Turner and Lawrence were able to show that the differences in the satisfaction measures were not due to chance but to the particular backgrounds of the workers involved, backgrounds which stemmed from the location of their work.

Adapted from Turner and Lawrence, *Industrial Jobs and the Worker*, 1965

5 Not everyone is capable of doing an enlarged job. Selection systems based on minimum criteria for the unenlarged job may severely restrict the possibility of schemes for job enrichment. Under job enrichment, selection and placement generally come to assume more importance.

6 To increase responsibility, without decreasing the monotony, is an undesirable form of job enlargement. Automation has thrown up a number of jobs which essentially consist in watching a dial but with high consequences if deviations are not acted upon. The burden of responsibility linked to the strain of monotony can be stressful.

Job enlargement is not a once-for-all process. It needs constant self-renewal. We humans are often stimulated by variety. We seek to reduce it to order and system; having done so, we get bored by the routine. Children having mastered a new game are bored with it. Airline pilots make demands for more precise regulations, only to find that systematization takes the fun out of the job.

In general, however, although there are pitfalls in any programme for job enrichment, the pressures are inexorable in the long term. The work role forms such a key part of the physical and psychological world of the average individual that he continually seeks for more opportunities to realize part of his identity in his work. Rising levels of education can only hasten this trend. These inexorable pressures are beginning to have their effect on technology and may ultimately spell the end to the assembly line and mass production. For it has been suggested (Lawler) that in a continuum from unit, through mass, to process production or automation, the trends will be to move to one end or the other, as set out in Figure 12.

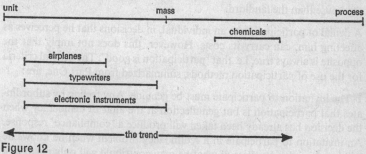

Figure 12

4.3 Participation

Participation is sometimes regarded as a form of job enlargement. At other times it is a way of gaining commitment by workers to some proposal on the grounds that, if you have been involved in discussing it, you will be more interested in its success. In part, it is the outcome of almost cultural belief in the norms of democratic leadership. It is one of those 'good' words with which it is hard to disagree. Box 10.6 describes the work of an extremely participative group, an 'autonomous work group' as it has been labelled. Much of the discussion on leadership and the workings of groups in Part One has been to do with participation, participation in the job, that is, not participation in its broader sense of 'industrial democracy'.

As with many of the precepts of management, it is worth considering the consequences of doing the opposite, in this case of 'no participation'.

It is, for instance, psychologically true that people like to have some say in their own destiny, some control over the facts that affect them. To use the territorial metaphor, an individual likes to be master in his own house. If this wish is denied, if the landlord exercises his legal right to paint the wall some obnoxious colour, the tenant may be forced to accept the situation, but he will be less likely to protect those walls, to guard them from damage. In psychological terms, he will respond with compliance rather than identification of internalization.

The compliance mode of response, it will be recalled, requires continual maintenance and will usually elicit only satisficing behaviour, behaviour sufficient to fulfil the minimum requirements of the contract. 'No participation', therefore, in issues that concern an individual's psychological territory will lead to compliance at best, often, if the action is perceived as territorial violation, to non-compliance or covert rebellion. Nor must one forget the very practical point that the ideas and knowledge of the man directly involved may be very valuable – the tenant can know more about the house than the landlord.

A denial of participation to an individual, in decisions that he perceives as affecting him, can carry its costs. However, this does not imply that the opposite is always true, i.e. that 'participation is good'. The general criteria for the use of participation methods, summarized from Part One, are:

1 The invitation to participate must be genuine. Any feeling by subordinates that participation is but genuflection at the altar of democracy when the decision has already been taken will produce a 'compliance' response. An invitation to participate in a redundancy problem when he knows he will lose his job regardless of what he may contribute will only result in a credibility gap.
2 The problem must be worth the time and the effort in the eyes of all concerned. Participation takes time and consumes energies. If the issue or the task is trivial, or foreclosed, and everyone realizes it, participative

Box 10.6 The effects of participation

Bavelas worked with a group of women performing a sewing operation on a group incentive basis. He selected one group whose production averaged 74 units hourly. He asked them to set their own production goal. After considerable discussion, they agreed unanimously on a goal of 84 units hourly, which they exceeded within five days. A goal of 95, set at a later meeting, could not be met. The goal was then reduced to the relatively permanent level of 90 units. During the next several months, the groups output averaged about 87 units.[1]

At the Harwood Manufacturing Company, Virginia, in the 1940s, producing men's pyjamas, shorts and children's blouses, a controlled experiment on the introduction of changed working methods was conducted by Coch and French. Three types of group were formed – (i) a 'no-participation' group of eighteen hand-pressers, (ii) a 'participation through representation' group of thirteen pyjama folders, and (iii) a 'total participation' group of fifteen pyjama examiners. In each case the planning of the job-process change was handled in the manner indicated. The findings showed that 'total participation' groups re-learned their jobs most quickly; 'participation through representation' re-learned more slowly; and 'no-participation' groups generally failed to achieve their previous production standards.[2]

The Scanlon Plan is a formal attempt at worker-participation. Workers participate in this system by making suggestions and sequentially meeting to discuss and evaluate the ideas which could yield higher production. Departmental committees may put those ideas into action, as may lower-level supervisors. Higher level committees are instituted to evaluate plant-wide improvements. Savings are shared by all unit members where a change is made.[3]

Although there are exceptions, particularly with very large organizations, most evaluations have attested to the significant technical and economic advantages of Scanlon type schemes.

1 Quoted by Norman Marci in H. Miffin, *Psychology in Industry*, 1946
2 Described by Coch and French 'Overcoming resistance to change', *Human Relations*, 1948
3 The Scanlon Plan is described by Lesieur in *The Scanlon Plan*, 1958

methods will boomerang. Issues that do not affect the individuals concerned will not, on the whole, engage their interest. Similarly, if a work group does not have effective control of the factors determining its output, e.g. the speed of the line is pre-set, or a prior shift sets up the machine, then participation within such reduced limits will seem meaningless.

3 The 'contract' must be clear. If the 'group' is asked for a decision then

that decision must be accepted. If advice only is required then this should be stated.

4 The individuals concerned must have the skills and the information to enable them to participate effectively.

5 Lastly, and perhaps most important, the manager must want participation and not indulge in it because he feels he ought to.

Given these conditions, participation will tend to result in increased commitment from the individuals – a feeling of 'ownership' in the process. That which one 'owns' one cares for, and invests in. Those studies of particular applications of participation (some of them summarized in Box 10.6) that met the conditions produced increased contributions. Studies on participation as a general style of management have been inconclusive – because, it is argued, the conditions listed would only apply spasmodically, the style was not always the 'best fit'. Although participation in particular situations may always be appropriate, as a general approach to management it is best suited to 'task cultures'.

4.4 Delegation

Delegation is another of those 'good' words; one cannot, it is generally felt, have enough of it; managers, when questioned, feel they ought to do more of it and wish they got more of it from their superiors. What are the problems? Is there any better understanding that we can gain of this important part of job design?

The essence of the delegation problem lies in the trust–control dilemma. The dilemma is that in any one managerial situation, the sum of trust + control is always constant. The trust is the trust that the subordinate feels that the manager has in him. The control is the control that the manager has over the work of the subordinate. The implications of this constant sum are that:

(a) Any increase in the control exercised by the manager decreases the amount of trust perceived by the subordinate ($control + X = trust - X$);

(b) Any wish by the manager to increase his trust in his subordinate, i.e. to give him more responsibility, must be accompanied by a release of some control if it is to be believed ($trust + X = control - X$).

The dilemma is illustrated by the little story in Box 10.7. Control costs money, but trust is risky. This is another aspect of the dilemma. To monitor, check or control the work of the subordinate requires the time of the supervisor, along with the time and energy of those who compile figures and records for use in the control procedures. Furthermore, where a

Box 10.7 The delegated letters

Jim, newly fired with enthusiasm for job enlargement, felt that he must practise it on his only subordinate – his secretary. By the nature of his work, Jim, a consultant, was usually in his office only in the morning of every second day. During this period, he planned his activities, dictated letters and signed those that had been typed during the previous two days. It occurred to him that if he asked his secretary to sign the letters in his place, (a) the letters would not have to wait two days for signature, or up to five days if an alteration was required, (b) he would not have to spend a considerable amount of time in the morning re-reading his own dictation.

He therefore approached his secretary, Rosemary, with the suggestion that once he had dictated the letters, she should type them, sign them and send them off without any further reference to him. At first, Rosemary was a little reluctant – the thought of the increased responsibility, no check on her mistakes, worried her. However, after thinking about it, she argued that it would add a more interesting element to her work and would undoubtedly be more efficient.

The next day, Tuesday, Jim dictated his letters as usual. On Thursday morning he was in the office again. This time the normal folder of letters to be signed was not there awaiting him, and he felt an initial surge of irritation at Rosemary's inefficiency until he remembered their agreement. He dictated Thursday's letters as usual, Rosemary made no comment about the new system and Jim decided to leave things alone for a bit. But all that day, he felt strangely naked. Did Tuesday's letters get done, he wondered, did they get typed accurately – one of them was really rather important.

Late that evening, after the office had shut, he crept into Rosemary's office, opened the files and checked the copies of the letters he had dictated and she had signed.

control mechanism exists, the tendency is for the subordinate to rely on it – i.e. to push things to the limit in the expectation that if he pushes them too far he will be pulled back. (For example, if there are limits on promotional expenses to be paid to sales agents, a salesman will be tempted to spend up to the limit rather than exercise his judgement on each case; a secretary will rely on her boss to do the final proof-reading of her letters; the subordinate will check his proposed course of action with his superior.) This tendency to rely on the control mechanism will help to perpetuate it as the superior finds that he has to use it, unaware that a self-fulfilling prophecy has been at work.

Trust, on the other hand, is cheap. Trust leaves the superior free to do other things; trust, if given and accepted, breeds responsibility and obviates the need for controls, as the controls become, in a sense, self-administered (the secretary refers the letters she is worried about to her boss, the salesman consults his manager in doubtful cases). But trust is risky, for the superior is held accountable for things that others did, even if they did them in ways he would not himself have chosen. Trust can be misplaced, trust can be abused. And since trust means the absence of superior-administered controls, trust can leave the superior feeling naked and a little lonely ('What are they all up to, I wonder'), like an anxious mother when the children are mysteriously quiet.

True delegation, effective delegation, is delegation with trust and with only the necessary minimum of controls. But trust is hard to give, for:

1 To give trust, the superior has to have confidence in the subordinate to do the job. This is easier if he has prior experience of his work and capacity, or if he has selected him himself – it is difficult with new or unknown subordinates.

2 Like a leap into the dark, trust must be given if it is to be received. This is not as trite as it may sound. If a superior wishes to get the benefits from trust, he must initiate the process, give trust and release control and then sit back and wait. If proved wrong, he can withdraw the trust and replace the controls. It is hard for the subordinate to initiate the process, although long acquaintance is often the basis for trust.

3 Trust is a fragile commodity. Like glass, once shattered, it is never the same again. The subordinate must always live up to the trust invested in him if that trust is to continue. The superior cannot withdraw the trust except by explicit agreement in specific circumstances.

4 Trust must be reciprocal. It is no good the superior trusting his subordinates if they do not trust him.

The proper amount of delegation, the proper blend of trust and control, will depend on the situation – the degree of risk, the skill and experience of the subordinates, the self-confidence of the superior, the pressures he feels from above. But delegation is made easier if:

1 The superior is allowed to select or at least approve his key subordinates, and they have some say in his appointment. (Sometimes found in task and power cultures, seldom in role cultures.)

2 The territory of trust is clearly defined for each individual, and is not violated. The individual must have full control within those limits. (Unclear territorial boundaries lead to misapprehensions, e.g. 'I thought I had discretion to . . .'.)

3 There is control of ends, not means. Control of results, i.e. after the

event, is not a violation of trust; control of means, i.e. during the event, can be. This implies that results can be determined and are known to the subordinate as well as to his superior.

In the light of this discussion of trust and control, it is possible to see why it is that management by objectives *should* work well but so often fails. Management by objectives at its best is:

(a) An agreed definition of the territory of trust;
(b) An agreed specification of desired results;
(c) A programme for action initiated by the subordinate.

Add to the considerations of trust and control what we know about the motivation calculus and the connection between objectives and performance, namely that:

1 The higher the objectives, the stronger the pull, provided that the individual feels they are attainable.
2 The more the individual is involved in setting the objectives, the more likely is he to feel they are his and to be committed to them.
3 If rewards are tied to performance against objectives, the individual will set the grade low in order to be sure of attaining the rewards.
4 In order to check that his calculus was right, he needs knowledge of results, i.e. feedback.

If any M.B.O. scheme meets all these desiderata it becomes a useful mechanism for delegation and improving performance. If, however, it is used either:

(a) as a way of imposing targets on people;
(b) of controlling means rather than ends (e.g. hours at work, relationships with staff, method of organizing work);
(c) to award merit increments,

then the scheme will tend to be perceived as a control mechanism and as indicating low levels of trust. It may well result in *reduced* performance or at least in lower than optimum performance.

4.5 Autonomous work groups

Autonomous work groups are a practical application to a whole group of a blend of participation and delegation. The conditions of both will apply. When the conditions are met, the results can be dramatic, as in the Durham Coal Mining Studies (Box 10.8). There is, however, some doubt as to how long the effects will last. The results obtained at Hawthorne, for instance,

Box 10.8 The Durham studies

Eric Trist and his colleagues were able, in the Durham coal mines, to study the results of two different forms of work design in the same place and with the same technology over a period of two years. The first system was the conventional Longwall organization, a semi-mechanized system involving automatic coal-cutters and a conveyor-belt for loading the coal. A single face of up to 200 yards could be worked in place of the many short faces under the old hand-got system with groups of two or three men per shift. There were forty men divided over three shifts in the Longwall system. The men were assigned to a specific task group with liaison between the groups carried out by supervisors. Delays on one group or shift would then affect other groups and subsequent shifts. Each group was paid separately.

The second system, which Trist called the 'Composite system', in-corporated many features of the old small-group hand-got methods. The men were multi-skilled and moved from role to role. The group accepted responsibility for the deployment of its members. There was also rotation over shifts, so that no man was pinned to a particular shift or task. Payment was on an overall output basis for the whole group of forty and divided up by them, usually in equal amounts.

The different outcomes were as follows:

	Conventional system	Composite system
productive achievement (% of coal face potential)	78·00	95·00
ancillary work at face (percentage hours per shift)	1·32	0·03
percentage of shifts with cycle lag	69·00	5·00
absenteeism (% of possible shifts)		
no reason given	4·3	0·4
sickness or other	8·9	4·6
accident	6·8	3·2
total	20·00	8·2

Reported in Trist, Murray, Pollock, *Organizational Choice*, 1963

were not maintained. In another study, at Ahmadabad, there was a major change in managerial strategy after four years. It could be that the sense of experiencing a new way of working, of being the focus of managerial and research attention, may generate much of the improvement in morale

Box 10.9   The autonomous group

The example I wish to quote is from a study of a quite ordinary group of craftsmen working in a factory. These craftsmen, twelve in number, were engaged in complex metal work requiring a high degree of skill and they worked in a small shop by themselves in the midst of a large factory. I was assisting the management to organize the various departments of the factory and after considerable economies in six departments, I came to this particular craft shop. To my surprise and righteous horror (*sic*) I found this group was allowed to:

(a) Supply estimates for material and labour costs for inclusion in sales quotation.

(b) Say what particular methods should be adopted in the doing of any particular job, and

(c) Suggest what times and money rates should be allowed for each job.

The foreman of this shop was also the foreman of a larger shop and, in fact, he was not a skilled craftsman. When a new job was to be quoted, the job description was sent to the shop and the men got together and worked out methods, times and prices; the result went back via the foreman to the sales department in order that a quotation could be sent. I was, as said above, surprised and horrified at this unplanned, non-specialized and dishonesty-provoking procedure and set about to improve organization and method. As I went deeper into the study of department economies, I found:

(a) The group's estimates were intelligent.

(b) The estimates were honest and enabled the men, working consistently at a good speed, to earn a figure *less than that common to similar shops on organized piecework*.

(c) The overhead costs were lower than they would have been if the shop had been run on modern lines.

(d) There was no group leader in the dominating sense of leadership. One skilled person received the job data and undertook to collect and co-ordinate the data supplied by members of the group, i.e. the leader was a secretary leader rather than dominant in group thinking and activity.

(e) Leadership shifted from one person to another as the situation required.

(f) The group psychic texture I would describe as a mild W.E. one.

(g) Inquiry among the group members showed no evidence of the group having or exhibiting aggressive feelings about other groups in the large factory. Some pity for the other groups engaged on the less skilled varieties of work organized on modern lines was expressed.

(h) The foreman who was nominally in charge of this group dubbed it the best group in the factory and the least greedy.

> **Box 10.9** – *contd*
>
> (i) The manager of this and many other groups took this group's honesty for granted. 'They never trouble me, they do good work, costs are low and profits good, why should I worry?' summed up his expressed attitude.
>
> Reported by Argyris in *Personality and Organization*, 1957

and output (the Hawthorne effect). More likely, some of the conditions will cease to be met over time. For instance:

1 The ways of working and the standard outputs may become so standardized that participation in deciding on them is no longer sensible or the task is no longer complex enough to merit the investment of so much 'E'. Complexity is resolved by systematization and we then lose interest. (Participation, condition 2.)

2 The group leaders may not have the required skills to be representatives and co-ordinators rather than commanders. (Participation condition 4.)

3 The contract is changed without explicit recognition of the fact, e.g. new constraints are placed on their work as the quality of raw material is changed, or customer requirements are tightened, or time limits and quality tolerances are raised without the group being consulted or involved. (Participation conditions 3 and 5.)

4 The membership of the group may change and the newcomers have no wish to participate. (Participation condition 5.)

5 The management may change and the new management have no real trust in the group's ability to set its own standards, and will in consequence start to check its procedures. (Delegation condition 1.)

6 The group has one conspicuous failure. (Delegation condition 3.)

7 Results are not made known to the group, or the task is re-defined so that clear measures of the group's performance are no longer possible. (Delegation condition 7.)

The overall risk with autonomous work groups is that they will come to set norms and objectives that do not match those of the organization. The power of the group to determine the behaviour and attitudes of its individual members has already been seen, and although the reported studies always describe groups where there is a synchronization of group and organization goals, there is clearly a possibility that the groups might misappropriate the trust and the relaxation of control. The 'leap in the dark' element of delegation, the willingness to give away control and rely on trust, is much more difficult where groups rather than individuals are concerned.

The stimulus of the initial complexity can wear off all too quickly and the participation become a chore rather than a challenge. Management then begins to introduce controls, trust is correspondingly withdrawn, and the experiment with autonomy breaks down.

Box 10.10 The full job

Paul Hill has set down the psychological requirements of a full job for the individual.

1 The need for the content of the work to be reasonably demanding of the individual in terms other than those of sheer endurance, and for it to provide some variety.
2 The need for an individual to know what his job is and how he is performing it.
3 The need to be able to learn on the job and go on learning.
4 The need for some area of decision-making where the individual can exercise his discretion.
5 The need for some degree of social support and recognition within the organization.
6 The need for an individual to be able to relate what he does and what he produces to the objectives of the company and to his life in the community.
7 The need to feel that the job leads to some sort of desirable future which does not necessarily imply promotion.

From Hill, *Towards a New Philosophy of Management*, 1971

---

5 Summary and implications

5.1

We have examined the *design of the structure* and recognized the need to achieve a balance between the pressures for uniformity of standardization, and those of diversity. As in chapter 7, the general conclusion was that a structurally differentiated organization, sometimes but not always decentralized, would normally be required. The problems of the *management of diversity* were discussed, the need to fit culture to structure, to decide on the balance and location of power, and to provide for appropriate integrating mechanisms. Within the scope of the individual manager was the *design of the job* and, in particular, the possibilities and problems of job enrichment, participation and delegation.

5.2 Implications

Most of the particular implications have been spelt out in the individaul sections. A couple of general reflections remain:

1 As organizations grow in size, as multi-nationals proliferate, the problems of integration multiply along with its costs, and so apparently do the felt pressures for uniformity. There is no clear evidence that bigness is best, although in some capital-intensive industries, bigness may be necessary. Most of the giants in size are well down in the profitability table. One wonders whether the pressures for uniformity are really there, whether diversity and differentiation might not be given a freer hand. Management sophistication can be too highly valued, as organizations take as much pride in their systems as in their results. Perversely, organization theory would suggest that more trust and less control, more diversity and less uniformity, more differentiation and less systematization might be the ways that organizations should move.

2 The long lists of conditions that attend success in the enlargement of jobs, in delegation, in the general area of making work more challenging and exciting, may well be enough to put off even the most determined idealist. This would be a pity. Although not all men will seek to achieve their full self-concept through the medium of their work, yet most men spend most of their conscious lives at work. If this work can be made more exciting, if the organization can simultaneously benefit in terms of reduced absenteeism and turnover, if the individual can earn more for increased productivity and the organization requires fewer people for more output, all must in the longer term benefit.

But, too often, the ideas of participation, job enrichment, delegation and autonomy, raise false hopes in men and manager. Disillusionment can breed cynics on both sides. It is right that the difficulties, that the conditions for success, be understood. We must remember that we are pulled by the alternating desires for complexity and simplicity so that enriched jobs become reduced to simplicity and so become monotonous once more. There is no standing still, only a constant need to take two steps forward in case we have to take one back. But let he who finds this daunting at least concentrate on removing the negative aspects of work. The monotony, the stress, the unnecessary ambiguity, double-checking and concern with the means can be reduced to some extent in all activities. With them will go the costs of low morale, high turnover and absenteeism. Herzberg, in pursuit of optimum motivation, might call this working on the hygiene rather than the motivating factors. But many an organization needs to reflect that, even if they can't turn all their horses into champions, they can at least clean the stables out.

11 On the Systems of Organizations

1 Introduction

The great advantage of the 'systems' approach to organization theory is that it embraces in its folds the contributions of a wide number of disciplines ranging from those of the cybernetician and the engineer, to biology and the natural sciences. For to all of these 'system' is a meaningful concept. The solar system, a cuckoo clock and the United Nations are all included in the word. As a result, perhaps, the approach of systems theory has lost some of its bite in that it is now too all-embracing. Anyone using it has to be clear which set of metaphors or analogies he is drawing on. We will here pursue our biological or anatomical metaphor and continue to regard the organization as a caricature of the human body. If the structure is its skeleton, the jobs, perhaps, its muscles, the people its blood and guts and its physical perspectives its flesh, then there still remain the nervous system, the respiratory system, the circulation system, the digestive system, etc. As with a body, the systems of an organization overlap and interlink the parts, the structure and the members. They are of a different logical order from the structure or the component pieces, for they are defined by their purpose, and are concerned with flows or processes *through* the structure. They are in fact 'systems' – it remains the best, if the vaguest, word, meaning at its broadest only an interdependent set of elements.

The systems of organizations can be looked at in many ways. One can, with Brown, distinguish the legislative, executive and representative systems. One can regard organizations as systems for decision-making, as socio-technical systems, as open systems, searching for homeostasis, or, with Stafford Beer, one can see organizations as sets of activity systems interacting with the environment but linked at various levels by co-ordinating systems. Most usefully, however, for the purpose of understanding the role of systems in activating the parts of the organization, we can follow the traditional systems theorists and examine the

Adaptive systems: those systems which are concerned with fitting the organization into its environment, with shaping its future, dealing with divergencies and deciding its policies.

Operating systems: those systems which are concerned with the daily existence of the organization, the intake, processing and export of its materials or orders or cases, the basic essential logistics of the process of work; they include the operation systems of sales and finance as well as those of production.

Maintenance systems: those systems which work to keep the organization in a healthy and effective condition, the reward and control systems for people, the linking mechanisms between sections of the organization and differing types of systems.

Information systems: the nerves of the organization, without which none of the systems would function; serves the three above, running through them and around them.

Anyone studying the effectiveness of an organization would do well to find out what form these first three systems take in any organization, how well they work and how well they are served by the fourth. He may find, as I have on occasion, that there *are* no adaptive mechanisms that could be classified as systems, or that, despite all the best methods and philosophies of job design, delegation and participation, the productive systems are so ill-conceived that, with the best will in the world, the organization is in a perpetual state of breakdown.

We have already examined the maintenance systems, without calling them by that name, when we looked at the management of human assets in chapter 9 and the management of diversity in chapter 10. The adaptive systems will be discussed in chapter 12 when we consider the management of change. Here we will be concerned with the underlying principles of the information systems, and with some particular aspects of the operating systems, namely *budgets, computers, communication systems*. These systems are essentially to do with the management of the steady state. But our preoccupation with the difficult problems of the operating systems must not blind us, as it has so many managements, to the existence of the other types of system. We shall, therefore, be continually interested in the implications of using methods and technologies appropriate to one set of systems in the service of another. The parable of the spindle, quoted in Box 11.1, is one example of what can happen to even a comparatively simple operation like a restaurant when the operating systems are either haphazard or non-existent.

In explaining his parable, Porter points out that the spindle

1 Acts as a memory device for the cook;

Box 11.1   The parable of the spindle

The head of a great and prestigious restaurant chain was troubled. In spite of good wages, fine conditions, and a genuine interest in the welfare of the people, the human relations problems, the turnover of staff and the general state of morale in his business were all disgraceful. Baffled, he turned to the social sciences for help. A psychologist, a sociologist and an anthropologist were asked for their assistance.

This was the mission which the scientists were assigned: find out why the waitresses break down in tears; find out why the cooks walk off the job; find out why the managers get so upset that they summarily fire employees on the spot. Find out the cause of the problems, and find out what to do about them.

Later, in one of the plush conference rooms, the scientists sat down to plan their attack. It soon became clear that they might just as well be three blind men, and the problem might just as well be the proverbial elephant. Their training and experience had taught them to look at events in different ways. And so they decided that inasmuch as they couldn't speak each other's languages, they might as well pursue their tasks separately. Each went to a different city and began his observations in his own way.

The sociologist. First to return was the sociologist. In his report to top management he said:

I think I have discovered something that is pretty fundamental. In one sense, it is so obvious that it has probably been completely overlooked before. It is during the *rush hours* that your human relations problems arise, that is when the waitresses break out in tears. That is when the cooks grow temperamental and walk off the job. That is when your managers lose their tempers and dismiss employees summarily.

After elaborating on this theme and showing several charts with sloping lines and bar graphs to back up his assertions, he came to his diagnosis of the situation. 'In brief, gentlemen,' he stated, 'you have a sociological problem on your hands.' He walked to the blackboard and began to write. As he wrote, he spoke:

You have a stress pattern during the rush hours. There is stress between the customer and the waitress ... There is stress between the waitress and the cook ... And up here is the manager; there is stress between the waitress and the manager ... and between the manager and the cook ... and the manager is buffeted by complaints from the customer. We can see one thing which, sociologically speaking, doesn't seem right. The manager has the highest status in the restaurant. The cook has the next highest status. The waitresses, however, are always 'local hire' and have the lowest status. Of course, they have higher status than bus boys and dish washers, but certainly lower status than the cook, and yet they give orders to the cook.

It doesn't seem right for a lower status person to give orders to a higher status

Box 11.1 – *contd*

person. We've got to find a way to break up the face-to-face relationship between the waitresses and the cook. We've got to fix it so they don't have to talk to one another. Now my idea is to put a 'spindle' on the order counter. The 'spindle', as I choose to call it, is a wheel on a shaft. The wheel has clips on it so the girls can simply put their orders on the wheel rather than calling out orders to the cook.

When the sociologist left the meeting, the president and his staff talked of what had been said. It made some sense. However, they decided to wait to hear from the other scientists before taking any action.

The psychologist. Next to return from his studies was the psychologist. He reported to top management:

I think I have discovered something that is pretty fundamental. In one sense, it is so obvious that it has probably been completely overlooked before. It is during the *rush hours* that your human relations problems arise. That is when the waitresses break out in tears. That is when the cooks grow temperamental and walk off the job. That is when your managers lose their tempers and dismiss employees summarily.

Then the psychologist sketched on the blackboard the identical pattern of stress between customer, waitress, cook and management. But his interpretation was somewhat different:

Psychologically speaking, we can see that the manager is the father figure, the cook is the son, and the waitress is the daughter. Now we know that in our culture you don't have daughters giving orders to the sons. It louses up their ego structure.

What we've got to do is to find a way to break up the face-to-face relationship between them. Now one idea I've thought up is to put what I call a 'spindle' on the order counter ... It's a kind of wheel on a shaft with little clips on it so that the waitress can put their orders on it rather than calling out orders to the cook.

What the psychologist said made sense, too, in a way. Some of the staff favoured the status-conflict interpretation while others thought the sex-conflict interpretation to be the right one; the president kept his own counsel.

The anthropologist. The next scientist to report was the anthropologist. He reported to top management:

I think I have discovered something that is pretty fundamental. In one sense, it is so obvious that it has probably been completely overlooked before. It is during the *rush hours* that the waitresses break out in tears. That is when the cooks grow temperamental and walk off the job. That is when your managers lose their tempers and dismiss employees summarily.

Box 11.1 – *contd*

After elaborating for a few moments, he came to his diagnosis of the situation. 'In brief, gentlemen,' he stated, 'you have an anthropological problem on your hands.' He walked to the blackboard and began to sketch. Once again there appeared the stress pattern between customer, waitress, cook and management:

We anthropologists know that man behaves according to his value systems. Now, the manager holds as a central value the continued growth and development of the restaurant organization. The cooks tend to share this central value system, for, as the organization prospers, so do they. But the waitresses are a different story. The only reason most of them are working is to help supplement the family income. They couldn't care less whether the organization thrives or not as long as it's a decent place to work. Now, you don't have a non-central value system giving orders to a central value system.

What we've got to do is to find some way of breaking up the face-to-face contact between the waitresses and the cook. One way that has occurred to me is to place on the order counter an adaptation of the old-fashioned spindle. By having a wheel at the top of the shaft and putting clips every few inches apart, the waitresses can put their orders on the wheel and not have to call out orders to the cook. Here is a model of what I mean.

Triumph of the spindle. When the anthropologist had left, there was much discussion of which scientist was right. The president finally spoke. 'Gentlemen, it is clear that these men don't agree on the reason for conflict, but all have come up with the same basic idea about the spindle. Let's take a chance and try it out.'

And it came to pass that the spindle was introduced throughout the chain of restaurants. It did more to reduce the human relations problems in the restaurant industry than any other innovation of which the restaurant people knew. Soon it was copied. Like wildfire, the spindle spread from coast to coast and from border to border.

Adapted from Porter, 'The parable of the spindle', *Harvard Business Review*, 1968

2 Acts as a buffering device. The cook no longer has to adjust his output to the input flow of orders. The waitresses can place their orders when they like, the cook takes them off when *he* is ready for them;

3 Acts as a queuing device: the orders, not the waitresses, wait in line;

4 Acts as a visual sorting device: the cook can see if there are several orders of the same type that he can prepare together;

5 Acts as a record of what went wrong when a mistake occurs so that corrections can be made and blame, if necessary, correctly apportioned.

328 Understanding Organizations

Without these procedural aids, these operating systems, the organization was 'sick'. No amount of incentive schemes, hygiene improvements, T Groups or Conflict Laboratories would have helped.

It probably did not need the parable of the spindle or the analogy of nerves to remind the reader that the systems of an organization, or the lack of them, can have marked effects on the attitudes and behaviour of the people in the organization. Historically, however, the design of the various forms of operating systems, being based on systems of information and, until recently, largely financial information, has been usually entrusted to the financial arm of the organization, or these days, to the people who tend the computer. Accountants and computer experts, however, had little in their early training or experience to do with psychology, or group behaviour or organization theory. For them, reality is essentially numerical. We cannot therefore be surprised that the systems they designed did not always take account of some of the complexities of human nature. The world is changing fast, and these accusations are no longer so true of the present generation of accountants and/or of computer experts. But many will still be found who agree with the Traditional Management Accounting Model of the Firm outlined by Caplan in Box 11.2.

This book has tried to say that organizations, even simple rudimentary business organizations, are much more complex and less clear-cut than Caplan's model would suggest. Goals are not only those of profit maximization, nor are they necessarily additive. Organizations are more realistically regarded as coalitions of groups responding to a variety of pressures. Individuals are not all always lazy and economically motivated. Authority is not the only basis for influence nor is economic resource power the only kind of power that matters. Things are not so rational nor so objective as economic management theories would have them be – not even the apparently 'hard' data of the accounts. We must, therefore, expect to find that the apparently logical system will not always work out so well in practice, that budgets may be ignored, or abused, that information may become a weapon in the hands of some of its possessors, that systems can be used to invade territory and be resented for this reason. I carry in my own memory too many instances of systems that I devised which strangely failed to produce the results I had envisaged not to sympathize with the frustrations of those whose exquisitely designed sheafs of figures, ratios and indices are misapplied or misunderstood by those whom they were intended to help.

Box 11.2   Traditional management accounting model of the firm

1 *Assumptions about organization goals*

(a) The principal objective of business activity is profit maximization (economic theory).

(b) This principal objective can be segmented into sub-goals to be distributed throughout the organization (principles of management).

(c) Goals are additive – what is good for the parts of the business is also good for the whole (principles of management).

2 *Assumptions about the behaviour of participants*

(a) Organization participants are motivated primarily by economic forces (economic theory).

(b) Work is essentially an unpleasant task which people will avoid whenever possible (economic theory).

(c) Human beings are ordinarily inefficient and wasteful (scientific management).

3 *Assumptions about the behaviour of management*

(a) The role of the business manager is to maximize the profits of the firm (economic theory).

(b) In order to perform this role, management must control the tendencies of employees to be lazy, wasteful, and inefficient (scientific management).

(c) The essence of management control is authority. The ultimate authority of management stems from its ability to affect the economic reward structure (scientific management).

(d) There must be a balance between the authority a person has and his responsibility for performance (principles of management).

4 *Assumptions about the role of management accounting*

(a) The primary function of management accounting is to aid management in the process of profit maximization (scientific management).

(b) The accounting system is a goal-allocation device which permits management to select its operating objectives and to divide and distribute them throughout the firm, i.e. assign responsibilities for performance. This is commonly referred to as 'planning' (principles of management).

(c) The accounting system is a control device which permits management to identify and correct undesirable performance (scientific management).

(d) There is sufficient certainty, rationality and knowledge within the system to permit an accurate comparison of responsibility for performance and the ultimate benefits and costs of that performance (principles of management).

(e) The accounting system is neutral in its evaluations – personal bias is eliminated by the objectivity of the system (principles of management).

Adapted from Caplan, *Management Accounting and Behavioural Science*, 1971

2 Management information systems

2.1

We have stressed that information systems are essentially servicing other systems. They are not always so regarded in organizations. The concept of an integrated management information system occasionally seems to imply that all other systems are subsumed within one total complex of information. This can be a dangerous and misleading attitude, for it may lead to forgetting that information systems, as with everything else in organizational design, need to be appropriately differentiated. We shall approach the problem of differentiation in information systems from two angles, differentiation by purpose and differentiation by work-flow.

2.2 *The purposes of a system*

There are several ways of classifying the systems of an organization, by, for instance, the topic dealt with, e.g. credit control inventory management, or by departmental affiliation, e.g. personnel or production systems. Not often, however, does one find systems classified according to their purposes in organizations. If one attempts to do this there appear to be four main possible purposes that a system could serve:

1 Planning – the bringing together of information to prepare the strategic, tactical or immediate programmes for action, e.g. a weekly production schedule or a two-year investment programme.
2 Logistic – the flow of information necessary to link parts of the organization, to allow certain specific actions to happen or to stop others occurring. Inventory management, payroll administration, the quarterly accounts, are all examples of information flows that have to happen in some way to keep the organization functioning normally.
3 Control – information that is required to monitor the work of the organization, to point out requirements for corrective action or opportunities for improvement. Variance analysis or monthly sales reports are examples of this category. Control is used here in the sense of 'monitoring', not in its wider sense of 'managing'.
4 Motivation – information used to give individuals or groups more involvement and motivation. Targets and objectives, general information on the organization are the items in this category.

This list of purposes may sound self-evident. In a way, if the purposes were not immediately recognizable there would be something wrong with the list. Yet the purpose of an information system will determine the kind of information that is required, the frequency with which it is gathered, the urgency, degree of accuracy and the use to which it is put.

Consider, firstly, the type of data:

1 Sales data for long-term planning purposes should perhaps be broken down into probability bands or into a set of contingency figures ('if the economy expands at 4 per cent per annum . . .'). Sales data for inventory scheduling purposes should be expressed, however, as one figure, no matter how much doubt really surrounded it.

2 Estimates for financial planning purposes should perhaps take a pessimistic view ('if the worst happens . . .'), whilst those for facilities-planning should adopt the expansionist possibility.

3 For day-to-day control, speed may be more important than accuracy. Yesterday's results are often needed today, even if there is the likelihood of a 5 per cent error. But data for the audited accounts must be more accurate, in which case it will be delayed.

4 Data expressed in financial terms may be necessary for financial control purposes and for the management of cash and credit. But many of the operational activities of the company do not easily lend themselves to financial expression. The most obvious example is the productive function, where another form of data is required.

Consider, secondly, the behavioural impact of the purpose, or the assumed purpose:

1 If sales data are used as a basis for control, for review of performance, individuals will set forecasts in the lower band, yet we know that the higher the target the better the performance as long as the target remains feasible.

2 If sales data are to be used as the basis for the allocation of resources, estimates will be in the higher bands. Similarly, prudent sales people have been known to build some of what Cyert and March once called 'organizational slack' into the forecasts on which the inventory is based. Stock-outs cost them personally more than an inflated stock position.

3 Data to be useful in planning or control or motivation is comparative. Performance or expected results are measured against something (target, last year, competition). The choice and emphasis given to the basis for comparison by the reporter will depend on his assumptions about the purpose. If the data is for control he will be concerned with justification and the lowest set of comparative data; if for planning, then data on the competition may be more relevant.

4 Data provided for motivational purposes, e.g. to allow the individual manager to assess the profitability of his part of the organization, can be

inappropriate as a way of arriving at the right transfer price or the viability to the organization as a whole of a new investment (see Box 11.3).

Box 11.3 The dangers of R.O.I.

1 In a highly profitable division of a multi-divisional company, the purchasing agent requested permission to increase the inventory in order to take quantity discounts; the return on investments would have been 25 per cent on the inventory increase. His request was refused because the division was already earning 35 per cent on its book investment. Therefore, a 25 per cent investment would have averaged down the 35 per cent. Incidentally, the company as a whole was earning less than 10 per cent.

2 A division manager can optimize his profits by spending money for advertising and sales promotion as long as more than $1·00 in contribution (revenue minus the out-of-pocket costs) is earned for each $1·00 spent. If his selling price is $1·00 and his internal transfer price plus variable added costs is $0·90, this will mean that each added sale will contribute $0·10. Consequently, he will advertise only as long as $1·00 of advertising produces at least $10·00 in sales (assuming, of course, that he knows these figures and wants to maximize profits). From the corporation's point of view, however, this may be all wrong; the profit centre approach may be making him too conservative. The corporation may be able to earn $1·00 for each 50 cents of out-of-pocket or marginal costs. From its standpoint, it would be better if the division manager keeps increasing advertising as long as $1·00 in advertising produces at least $2·00 in sales.

3 An analysis of a proposed investment for a division showed that it would return 15 per cent after taxes. In the next two years, however, the rate of return would be negative to the division because (a) declining balance depreciation reduced the accounted profits, and (b) the net book value of the investment was near the gross book value. Consequently, the division manager did not submit the investment proposal because he did not want to affect his R.O.I. adversely in the next two years. However, the company's cost of capital was 10 per cent, and from its standpoint the investment was sound.

4 In order to increase his rate of return, a division manager reduced his research costs by eliminating all projects that did not have an expected payout within two years. He believed that if he did not improve his rate of return, he would be replaced.

5 A division manager scrapped some machinery that he was not currently using in order to reduce his investment. Later, when the machinery was needed, he purchased new equipment.

Quoted by Henderson and Dearden in 'New systems for divisional control', *Harvard Business Review*, 1966

But data are data, it may be argued, facts are facts. Not so. Very often, as indeed we all know but too often forget, numbers are but the quantified expression of an opinion. This is necessarily so for data about the future. But it is often true of data about the present or the past. The valuation of assets, the allocation of costs, the definition of a 'sale' or a 'delivery' are all merely conventions, arbitrary agreements. And a convention suitable for one purpose may be fallacious for another. The lowest legal valuation of assets may boost the apparent profitability of the firm and aid its capital-raising activities. It may also and simultaneously cloud its eyes to its true worth. The fables of those who grew rich by putting their own numbers to other people's assets are too well known to need enumerating. What is junk to one man is antique to another. Shops are not only shops, they are also real estate to be re-developed. Even numbers of things and objects that can be physically counted are not necessarily factual data. Do you count those that are faulty, that never get paid for? Do you count them in the factory, or on the lorry? The 'facts' depend on arbitrary definitions and the definition that suits one purpose will not suit another. In one organization a 'delivery' was only counted when it was loaded on to a lorry consigned to a customer. The export manager occasionally found at the end of the month that he had, in the warehouse, goods consigned to overseas customers awaiting the docking of a suitable vessel. He was then accustomed to order them to be loaded on to a lorry overnight until the first of the following month when they would be booked back into stock. By this means he boosted his monthly 'deliveries'.

Different purposes will, and should, elicit different numbers from the same base. There is nothing amiss in this. The trouble arises when numbers are *assumed* to be facts, when data provided for one purpose are used for another. If data supplied for inventory control purposes with appropriate organizational slack built into it are then used as the justification for an expensive new machine, the organization may find itself with an over-equipped factory. If those same figures are unexpectedly used as a basis for assessing the sales department's performance, they may find themselves with a de-motivated sales force. Budgets, as we shall see, are notorious examples of using data for, often, all purposes simultaneously.

The belief that numbers are facts leads, as we shall see in the section on computers, to the concept of data banks from which numbers can be reshuffled into a wide variety of forms for each of the four purposes. The existence of this one bank of 'facts' has an effect, often unconscious, on the individual's assessment or definition of the facts under his control. In producing the numbers, or supervising their production, he will tend to be primarily interested in one of the four purposes. It is not, unfortunately, easy even for him to know which purpose is dominant. Research, for instance, has indicated that people are stimulated to maximum effort by moderately difficult targets. What is 'moderately difficult' varies from person to person, but for individuals with high needs for achievement, it can be targets which they have a one-in-four chance of achieving. Many managers, therefore, quite sensibly set high targets for themselves and their groups. But operational plans built on these targets will have a 75 per cent chance of being too lavish, and performance evaluations or control based on them will unreasonably downgrade the individual three times out of four. More often, the individual is affected by the possible use of the numbers for control purposes. He therefore plays safe: the organization plans on the basis of the numbers and a self-fulfilling prophecy develops whereby the organization achieves its low targets, congratulating itself on the accuracy of its planning.

Rather should he ask himself two very obvious but key questions:

What is the information for?
Who is the information for?

These questions will lead him to a consideration of some of the following points:

1 Degrees of accuracy, detail and urgency will vary with the purpose. One multi-national organization is proud of and famed for its comprehensive information system which contains, at one count, 12,000 figures in each monthly set that goes to the divisional manager. Most of the production and sales managers have found, however, that it tells them too much too late. They have each, therefore, surreptitiously, devised their own inaccurate but approximately real-time and very simple systems. The official system was devised in the centre and is useful in the centre for overall monitoring purposes – it is of no use to the operational divisions. Another company, part of another famed multi-national group, found that it had to employ a whole new section to complete the forms required by the centre when it was taken over. Two years later the general manager claimed that they did not understand 25 per cent of the forms, 50 per cent were useless to them since they were in units of currency or measurement of another country, leaving only 25 per cent of any local value.

2 He who controls the information will in effect control the operation. If the information is for control purposes, data on an individual's territory should be his possession, at least in the first instance. In one factory variance analysis data goes first to the supervisor concerned, for him to act on it. Only if no corrective action is taken, or explanation offered, within a defined time limit is the information then automatically passed to his

superior. The sales manager, who produces the first proof of the sales record from behind his back at the monthly meeting of his regional managers, undoubtedly has increased his control, but he has deprived them of some independence and possibly, thereby, of some commitment, initiative and incentive.

3 How should the numbers be collected? Particularly for maintenance purposes, and often for control, it should be possible so to define the data required that it can be collected automatically and routinely. Individual bias or error can be avoided by making the data independent of individuals. Individuals need only be involved in the definition of the data and the design of the system. Payroll operations, invoicing procedures, control measures which essentially point out deviations from the norm, inventory control and re-order procedures, are all examples of systems suitable for automated collection of data. It is, however, important to consider who should have the right to override or tamper with the systems against frauds and error. Wasserman covers the security aspect well in an article in the *Harvard Business Review*.

But often the individual bias is exactly what is required, particularly in the area of planning and motivation. Here, ownership of the data will encourage commitment, automated data collection will seem threatening and alien, data from other sources will be suspect. It is psychologically unlikely that anyone will feel commitment to the plans emanating from a separate planning department except for the members of that department, and, perhaps, their functional chief. Many good ideas are still-born in such departments because of what Americans call the N.I.H. syndrome (Not Invented Here). The data and the ideas are alien to those who would have to carry them out, and are therefore rejected. Ownership is not transferred.

2.3 Implications of the work-flow

It seems likely that the nature of the work-flow will determine to some extent the type of co-ordinating mechanism required. A system of data collection and processing which is inappropriate will tend to throw up inefficiencies or subsidiary systems. There are two principal ways of looking at the work-flow.

Joan Woodward and a research team at Imperial College, London, have produced a schematic description of the types of control system based on a study of a number of organizations in different technologies. They distinguish between *unitary* systems which are single-systems, and *fragmented* systems which are multi-system and many-centred. They also distinguish between methods of control which are *personal*, i.e. depend on personal intervention, and those which are *mechanical* or automated. They plan these two dimensions across each other to produce a figure with four quadrants (see Figure 13 below).

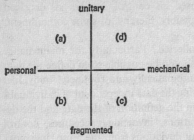

Figure 13

They then suggest that there is a progression through the quadrants as the technology advances. A small entrepreneurial organization engaged in unit production would tend to have unitary and personal (a) forms of co-ordination – that is, the manager of each operation would control it directly, and the top manager would intervene directly to co-ordinate his subordinates. As the firm grew and the tasks got more specialized, the co-ordination would remain personal, but would become more fragmented, i.e. would move to quadrant (b). Subsequently, production engineering and operations research techniques, administration rules and procedures would appear along with impersonal control mechanisms of both an administrative and a mechanical kind. Initially, these developments would be fragmented and integrated, the firm using different methods in different parts, i.e. in quadrant (c) on the diagram. Finally, an integrated co-ordinated system would emerge if the work-flow was itself an integrated one, i.e. the system would move to (d).

When the team compared the technologies of the firms they studied, with their place on this control system 'progression', they came up with the following results:

Production method	System (%)			
	(a)	(b)	(c)	(d)
unit and small batch	75	25	—	—
large batch and mass produced	15	35	40	10
process	—	—	5	95
total firms	28	21	18	33

Thus, in general, it would seem that, rightly or wrongly, for this was a descriptive not a prescriptive study, unit production firms and process firms have a centralized control system. But, whereas in unit production firms it is personal, in process production it is automated. Large batch and mass production technologies tend to have fragmented systems – hovering between personal and automated procedures.

Another way of looking at the work flow is to ask whether activities of the operation in question are *Facsimile*, *Sequential* or *Independent*:

Facsimile operations are those where each part of the organization is a mirror image – reduced or enlarged, perhaps – of another. Marks & Spencer outlets, branches of clearing banks, booking offices of airlines, post offices, Mothercare outlets, food chain stores, hotel chains, etc. are good examples of facsimile operations. Here, the control is by standardization. The pressures for uniformity are high and the individual store or branch manager is independent within well-defined limits. The manager of a Mothercare outlet has to conform to prescribed prices, display methods, stock patterns, and the store manager even has to maintain a Catalogue Desk to take orders for the mail-order side of the business – in direct competition with the stores. Standardization is implemented by *rules and procedures*, forms and methods of data presentation.

Sequential operations are integrated ones, quintessentially the process industries of oil and petro-chemicals. But the sequential description would apply also to organizations which are vertically integrated or which so arrange their work that goods or outputs from one part of the organization become inputs to another. The control and co-ordination of sequential activities is ensured by *Planning* or *Scheduling*. The scheduling can, of course, be routinized, taking the form of regular meetings or prescribed data inputs to a central source or set of sources, but such routines are standardization in a form different from that of facsimile operations unless the organization consists, as some multi-national giants do, of facsimile sets of sequential operations.

Independent. If the work-flow consists of a series of independent operations which happen to co-exist under the same roof or the same organizational umbrella, but have no necessary inter-relation, except to share common facilities and services, then the operations can equally be called independent. True conglomerates, small businesses who have acquired, by the chance of history, two or three separate activities, are examples of independent operations. Control and co-ordination here is less important. Use of facilities, including cash, is, perhaps, the key area involved. What co-ordination is involved is personal, i.e. is achieved by *direct personal interaction* between individuals.

Organizations seldom fit wholly and squarely into one or other of these categories. Even conglomerates prefer the cash operations of their affiliates to be handled in a facsimile manner so that each can be managed centrally through decentralized subsidiaries. Even in a small firm the flow of work through purchasing, production, sales and distribution is sequential, requiring planning and scheduling, whilst the operations of their two geographically separated plants may be required to be facsimile rather than independent and necessitate standard operating procedures in order to ensure identical outputs.

In other words, as always with organizations, there is a method of co-ordination appropriate to the flow of work and to the technology. At one extreme, an international oil company, consisting of facsimile sets of sequential operations, themselves arranged sequentially (i.e. a vast sequential oil production in Venezuela, or Kuwait, or Nigeria, which produces inputs for vast sequential sales operations in Germany, Australia or Japan), will have layers of planning and scheduling alternating with standardized procedures and forms. At another extreme, the mini-conglomerate, those small independent factories in different parts of the country that happen to be owned by one family, will need to co-ordinate only in a crisis or an emergency, when it will be done by individual interaction.

The trick, of course, is to fit the method of co-ordination to the type of operation. For co-ordination costs money, and unnecessary standardization of basically independent operations can be very expensive as well as frustrating. Planning is often a euphemism for breakdown management of unscheduled facsimile operations – the outputs from two different factories do not match, the union is exploiting discrepancies in fringe benefits between two sites, the national customer is complaining of differential treatment of credit by two branches. Standardization is inappropriate where scheduling is required. Standardized inventory formulae may not take account of sales drives or sudden uplifts in demand, but may make planning between sales and production a matter of crisis rather than routine.

2.4 Implications

The designer of information systems, therefore, has a complex set of considerations to bear in mind and to try to combine. The purpose of the information, the person for whom it is intended, the nature of the technology and the type of operation, are all important. Last, but not least, he will find that the culture of any particular part of the organization will be an intervening variable. Control by standardization is unpopular in power and task cultures, since it appears to limit independence, but is appropriate to role cultures. Personal methods fit with power cultures, personal and scheduling with task cultures. A decentralized organization treated as a facsimile operation will not display the entrepreneurial energies that some people imagine come automatically from decentralization. Sequential operations, where the scheduling is centrally managed, will impair the independence of separate outfits. As the next section will demonstrate, it is hard for sequential or integrated organizations to devise sets of data that allow each manager to operate independently, to do arm's-length trading with another part of the complex, and still to protect the overall interests of the organization. Sequential operations inevitably mean that some units will have to yield to others, that individual unit optima will lead to total sub-optimization. The information system will be the clear expression of the dilemma. The nerves follow the skeleton; only by changing the structure into independent units will the same data serve both unit and organizational ends.

3 Budgets

3.1

A recent accounting text (Black), defined the steps in the 'budgetary control' process as follows:

1 Preparation of a plan consistent with the goals of the business.
2 Review, discussion and adjustment of the plan as needed to facilitate its accomplishment.
3 Communication of sub-sections of the plan to responsibility centres within the organization.
4 Comparison of actual performance with planned results.
5 Analysis and explanation of variances from the plan.
6 Corrective action when significant unfavourable variances occur between planned and actual performance.

This list, which many at first sight would think unexceptionable, nicely epitomizes the budget dilemma. For here, the same set of figures is expected to

Form the basis of a Plan (1, 2);
Act as operational data (3);
Be a basis for control and analysis of performance (4, 5);
Act as a stimulant for change (6).

The discussion earlier in this chapter would lead one to suppose that one or more of these goals or purposes may be achieved, but at the cost of the others. In particular, the control and analysis of performance is likely to predominate, particularly if the control is exercised by someone other than the individual performer. Twenty years ago, Argyris investigated the impact of budgets on people in some U.S. organizations. Some of his results are reported in Box 11.4. It would not be unusual to meet

---

Box 11.4   Budget battles

Present at the meeting were the supervisors of the two departments, two budget people, the supervisor of the department that supplies the material, and the top executive, whom we shall call the Leader.

LEADER: I've called you fellows down to get some ideas about this waste. I can't see why we're having so much waste. I just can't see it. Now (*turns to one of the supervisors*), I've called in these two budget men to get some ideas about this waste. Maybe they can give us an idea of how much some of the arguments you're going to give are worth.

COST MAN I (to LEADER) (*Slightly red – seems to realize he is putting the supervisors 'on the spot'*): Well, er . . . we might be wrong . . . but I can't see how. There's an entire 1 per cent difference and that's a lot.

SUPERVISOR A to SUPERVISOR B (*Trying to see if he can place the blame on* SUPERVISOR B): Well, maybe . . . maybe . . . some of you boys are throwing away the extra material I sent back to your department.

SUPERVISOR B (*Becomes red, answers quickly and curtly*): No, no, we're re-working the extra material and getting it ready to use over again.

SUPERVISOR A (*Realizing that the argument wasn't going to hold much water*): Well, you know, I've been thinking; maybe it's those new trainees we've had in the plant. Maybe they're the cause of all the waste.

LEADER: I can't understand that. Look here – look at their budget; their (trainees') waste is low.

The meeting continued for another twenty minutes. It was primarily concerned with the efforts of Supervisor A and B to fix the blame on someone other than themselves. The leader terminated the meeting as follows:

LEADER: All right, look here, let's get busy on this, all of you, all of us, let's do something about it.

Supervisor B left the meeting, flushed, tense and obviously unhappy. As he passed through the door, he muttered to himself, 'Those g—— d—— budgets!'. (Note that the budgets are immediately blamed for the unhappiness.) Supervisor B hurried down to his area of the plant. He rushed into

Box 11.4 – *contd*

his office and called his own subordinates abruptly. 'Joe – get over here – I want to speak to you – something's up'.

The subordinates came in, all wondering what had occurred. As soon as they had all assembled, the supervisor started:

SUPERVISOR B: 'Look, we've just got to get at this waste. It makes me look like a ———. Now let's put our heads together and get on the ball.'

The supervisor set to work to locate the cause for the waste. Their methods were interesting. Each one of them first checked to see, as one of them put it 'that the other guys (departments) aren't cheating us'. A confidential statement finally arrived in Supervisor B's hands from one of the subordinates to the effect that he had located the cause of the waste in another department. Supervisor B became elated, but at the same time was angry at the fact that he had been made to look 'sick' at the meeting with the leader.

SUPERVISOR B: I'm going to find out why they are making the waste. I don't mind taking a little – as long as it's me that's doing the trouble.

Supervisor B roared out of his office and headed straight for the office of Supervisor A, where the confidential source had located the waste. Supervisor A saw him coming, and braced himself for the onslaught.

SUPERVISOR B: ———, I found out that it's you boys causing the waste. ———, I want to know why. . . .

SUPERVISOR A (*cuts off Supervisor B, spits out some tobacco and says*): Now, just hold onto your water. Don't get your blood up. I'll tell you. . . .

Quoted by Argyris in 'The impact of budgets on people', *Controllership Foundation*, 1952

with those same quotations today. Argyris was concerned with determining the effects of the manufacturing budgets on line supervisors. He found that the budget staff regarded themselves as watchdogs whose principal function was to be constantly looking for deviations from the budget and reporting these deviations to top management. The accountants believed that budgets were a legitimate way of applying pressure to line executives and were at a loss to explain why the latter did not see the budget as a challenge and a stimulus. The line executives complained that the reports contained only results and not reasons for the results, that the budgets were inflexible, that they were continually getting tougher and more unrealistic. Furthermore, they felt that using the budgets to apply pressure implied that they were idle, uncommitted and unable to manage their own operations. The results were:

Constant conflict between line managers and staff;
Much energy expended on the explanation of variances and the apportionment of blame;
Rejection of budgets by the line as a realistic mechanism for planning or motivation or liaison;
Accountants were placed in a position where success involved finding failures in others;
Collusive groups were formed for mutual protection. 'Meeting the budget' became the priority goal of the executives.

3.2 Participative budgeting

In an attempt to rectify some of these ills, many organizations moved to some variety of participative budgeting, where the responsible operator or executive was invited or encouraged to participate in, or even initiate, the budgeting process. Participation, as we have seen in the previous chapter, is normally to be encouraged as a way of giving an individual some control over his territory and some feelings of ownership. However, participative budgeting did not always work out as well for organizations as they expected. As Becker and Green pointed out some years ago, participation *can* lead to decreased performance.

The reason should by now be clear. If rewards are tied to performance against target, the temptations will be to set that target low. If failure to meet a budget is punished, organizational slack will be built into the budget to give more leeway. If a budget means 'availability of resources', the more that is budgeted for, the more slack or freedom is available. In short, many applications of participative budgeting may have been good for the individual but they failed to produce optimum results for the organization. The reason lies in an inadequate understanding of human behaviour, and of the connection between control and motivation.

A more sophisticated approach, tried by at least one organization, is to pay two sorts of rewards, one for increasing the target, and one for meeting the target. Thus, the risk of failing to meet a higher target is offset by the reward for setting it that high in the first place. Sales organizations sometimes separate out the salesmen's targets and the figures used for planning, i.e. a sum of all the individual targets would exceed the figure used for operational planning on the assumption that not all targets would be met. These kinds of schemes are not always feasible in all situations, but they are attempts to recognize that budgets cannot serve three or four purposes at once. Stedry's studies (reported in Box 11.5) throw some further light

Box 11.5 The Stedry studies

Stedry's empirical investigation was in the form of a laboratory experiment intended to measure the relationship between performance, aspiration levels and externally-imposed budgets. It is of interest both because of its findings and because it represents one of the earliest – and still one of the few – attempts to apply the methodology of laboratory experimentation to research in accounting. The experiment involved approximately 100 university students performing problem-solving tasks. These students were divided into four groups based on the nature of the budget that they were given – 'low budget', 'medium budget', 'high budget', and 'implicit budget'. Stedry found that the budget variable appeared to influence performance – i.e. no specific budget standard was given to them – followed by the medium, high and low budget groups, in that order of performance.

Each of the four major groups was further divided into three sub-groups. In one sub-group, the subjects were given the budget and then asked to indicate what they hoped to accomplish – in effect, to set their aspiration levels. In another sub-group, the students were requested to indicate their aspiration levels before they were given the budget. The third sub-group was not asked to establish aspiration levels at all. The results suggest that a significant inter-relationship exists between budget levels, aspiration levels and performance. For example, the best performance was in the high budget group which set its aspiration levels *after* receiving the budget. However, the high budget group which set its aspiration levels *before* receiving the budget showed the poorest performance of all the groups. One possible interpretation of these findings is that when the subjects established their aspiration levels after they had received their budgets, the aspiration levels tended to reflect the performance objective contained in the budget. In a sense, the budget goals became internalized. On the other hand, when the aspiration levels were set first, the budget goals represented a separate and conflicting level which the subjects were unwilling to accept. Several specific points are worth noting. First, low budgets were usually associated with very low performance. Second, implicit budgets in general were associated with good performance. Third, the influence of aspiration levels on performance varied depending on the budget level and on whether the aspiration levels were established before or after the budget was received. Although the outcome of a single experiment of this type can hardly be viewed as conclusive, Stedry does provide a wealth of interesting insights into the relationship between motivations theory and budgeting.

Stedry, 'Budget control and cost behaviour' as quoted by Caplan in *Management Accounting and Behavioural Science*, 1971 on participative budgeting, although it is hard to know how much one can generalize from rather artificial experimental studies in this field to organizational reality. They do, firstly, suggest that low budgets can create a self-fulfilling prophecy condition and, secondly, that asking people to set their own targets after indicating expected levels is the most effective way to proceed – i.e. subordinates should *not* initiate the budgeting process, but should have the final say. This is in line with Argyris's recommendations, but it would be dangerous to regard it as the only important variable. The significance and importance of the originator of the budget as a setter of expectations in the eyes of the subordinate will affect the weighting he puts on the expectations. The degree of risk he, as an individual, is prepared to accept in setting targets for himself is another element, coloured in turn by the degree to which rewards and punishment are related to the achievement of those targets.

In general, we can tentatively conclude that in individual budgets:

1 An individual needs knowledge of goals and of results achieved if his motivation calculus is going to activate any more 'E'.
2 Most individuals can be encouraged to set their targets higher by demonstrations that others have high expectations of them (the Halo Effect).
3 Different levels of targets will be effective for different individuals, depending on their psychological contracts, sets of needs and perceptions of the motivation calculus.
4 Targets for aspiration should be separated from budgets for planning.
5 Budgets for planning cannot always be used in the ongoing operations of the firm, since the degree of accuracy and risk permitted or required will vary with the purpose of the budget.
6 Performance figures used as feedback against targets should be separated from figures for control. Budgets for control are only useful if they lead to corrective action. They should, therefore, be the instruments, in the first instance, of the responsible executive.

Considering this list of desiderata, it is clear that the same sets of figures can be employed in quite different ways. Performance results can be used as feedback or as control. Targets can be weapons or incentives. There is no foolproof system design, for all ultimately depends on the manner of its application. A better understanding of the complexity of the process may help to better use of budgets or at least to more realistic expectations of them. Budgets, of course, do not apply just to individuals. The trend towards decentralization, the creation by large organizations of semi-autonomous divisions, the rise of the so-called ''profit centre' faces these large organizations with a problem:

Box 11.6 How people use budgets

1 *A factory manager:*

The job of budgets is to see to it that we never forget we've got a job to do. Sure, we apply pressure with budgets. I guess budgets aren't worth very much unless they have a lick in them.

I go to the office and check that budget every day. I can then see how we're meeting the budget. If it's OK, I don't say anything. But if it's no good, then I come back here (*smiles*) and give the boys a little . . . Well, you know. I needle them a bit. I give them the old . . . hum . . . well . . . you know what . . . the old needle.

2 *A supervisor:*

Budgets should be realistic. They should reflect the true picture. Take the error budget for example. There is something, the error figure is way too low. I know it. The people know it, and so do the financial people know it. So I suggested to the financial people that they should increase it. They refused. They feel that if they increase the budget to a realistic level and the people meet it, they'll have no reason to cut down errors.

We, on the other hand, feel differently. Our people see the figure, and they know it is ridiculously low. So they say, 'Oh, these financial guys do that so they can have the opportunity to wear the flag'.

3 *A foreman:*

You can't use budgets with the people. Just can't do anything like that. People have to be handled carefully and, in our plant, carefully doesn't mean budgets. Besides, I don't think *my* people are lazy.

No, sir, I can't use budgets to increase production. I don't go up and say to a man, 'My budget is up $5,000 this year, John'. He'll look at me in scorn. No sir, anything like that is using a whip. And the men don't like it.

4 *A supervisor:*

Let's say the budget tells me where I was off. I didn't make it. That's of interest. But it doesn't tell me the important thing of why I didn't make it or how I am going to make it next time. Oh some, they might say all I need to do is increase production and cut out waste. Well, I know that. The question is how to do it.

Quoted by Argyris in 'The impact of budgets on people', *Controllership Foundation*, 1952

1 How to provide information to all managers at each point where a decision should be made.
2 How to motivate each manager in such a way as to optimize total company performance.
3 How to find a thesis for evaluating divisional performance.

Often with a whoop of joy, companies alighted on the concept of return on investment (R.O.I.) as a common measure which would make profit the guide and king throughout the organization. Henderson and Dearden (Box 11.3) have described some of the outcomes of this attempt to find one common measure. R.O.I. for independent work-flows can work well; but for the sequential operations of integrated organizations it will be both cumbersome and fallacious. Henderson and Dearden, writing on Financial Analysis, Planning and Control, recommend three separate budgets:

1 A contribution budget (revenues less variable costs).
2 A fixed-and-managed cost budget.
3 A capital budget.

In our terms, they are recommending separate data systems for separate purposes. Furthermore, although they do not stress this point, the manager will be judged differently on each system. The capital budget should reflect his capacity to foresee and provide for the future; the fixed cost budget, largely items outside his short-term ability to influence, will not impinge on the performance that he can influence which will be the contribution budget of variable costs and revenues. R.O.I., as they point out, can be affected by changes in sales volume, product mix, pricing, costs or assets used. In a sequential operation, many of these items may be outside the control of the manager of a particular unit. The measure of performance becomes, therefore, very loose and ambiguous. We know from behavioural research that the more precise the objectives the more effective they are in influencing behaviour. We might expect in total, therefore, to find R.O.I. ineffective as a motivating mechanism, inaccurate as a medium of planning or operational decision-taking, unfair as a method of evaluating, not very helpful in pointing to areas for corrective action. Looked at another way, R.O.I. as a standardized measure applied to a sequential operation is unlikely to be very appropriate.

4 The computer

4.1

No chapter on the systems of organizations can ignore the computer. Indeed, with an expenditure in 1968 of close on $4 billion on computer hardware in the U.S. alone, with estimates that investment in Britain in computers will soon be approaching 10 per cent of all manufacturing investment, no company or government can afford to ignore them either. Considering the magnitude of the investment it is indeed, as McRae says, 'a remarkable tribute to the marketing skill of the computer manufacturers' that there is so little demonstrable evidence of the pay-off of the investment. Most companies, perhaps circumspectly, have no records to demonstrate the financial benefits of their investment. They tend to rely on statements like 'the present complexity and scope of our business could not be handled without the computer', or 'the computer has allowed us to do so much in the way of data handling and analysis that would have been inconceivable before'. McKinsey & Co. in 1963 found nine out of twenty-seven installations that were 'unmistakably successful' and eighteen that were 'marginal at best'. In 1968 they were able to state, in the second McKinsey Report, that 'as a super-clerk, the computer has more than paid its way. For most large organizations, going back to punch cards and keyboard machines, would be as unthinkable as giving up the typewriter for the quill pen.' But they go on to say 'Yet in these same companies ... mounting computer expenditures are no longer matched by rising economic returns ... Faster, costlier, more sophisticated hardware; larger and increasingly costly computer staffs; increasingly complex and ingenious applications; these are in evidence everywhere. Less and less in evidence, as these new applications proliferate, are profitable results.' The savings that come from computerizing routine clerical and accounting operations do not seem to be repeated in the more complex applications. What has gone wrong? There seems to be two major problem areas which might be broadly labelled 'The Seduction of Technology' and the 'Master–Servant Issue'.

4.2 The seduction of technology

Everyone loves toys, especially if they are expensive. The thought of a television set on your desk which can instantly portray the effects of a 10 per cent increase in advertising has distinct allure for many a marketing executive. The notion of a mathematical model of the market which will simulate the outcomes of a wide variety of policies is ingenious and appealing. It fits well, too, with the desire of any professional to work on the frontiers of his technology, to press forward his skill and knowledge. Thus it is that computers have thrown up many a device which has given pleasure to both the user and the deviser. But the financial feasibility of such technological seductions is not always apparent. McKinsey, in their 1968 report, note that proposals were submitted to one company chief in 1967 which would have consumed 80 per cent of computer staff time available for development, but no indication was given of potential savings or benefits. When the irritated chief executive asked for such indications, none were forthcoming. One of the proposals was, 'Design a computer-based "strategic management information system".' This was candidly described by its sponsor, the manager of the systems and procedures department, as 'a basic research project', as indeed it would have been. Management's information needs had not been determined; the cost of making information available was uncertain; and the proposed techniques for putting the manager (assuming he was interested) in a position to manipulate the information (if it could be provided) had never really been tried out.

In another instance, the president of a German chemical company was asked to examine and approve a proposal for an exciting new management information system. Featuring the latest desk-side cathode-ray tube inquiry terminal that would display on demand any data in the computer files, the system would enable the president to compare current production figures, by product and/or by plant, against plan. It would break down current sales figures in half a dozen different ways; it would display inventory levels, current labour costs and trends, material costs – in short, just about any kind of operating data he might care to request. The president turned the proposal down. As he explained his decision to a McKinsey interviewer, 'I care more about what will happen five years from now than what happened yesterday. Anyway, I get all the routine data I can handle. What would I do with more?'

Dearden has analysed what he calls 'The Myth of Real-Time Management Information' and can see justification for real-time facilities only in production control systems. Nowhere else is the immediate availability of the information necessary, nor indeed are the human minds at the receiving end always capable of the absorption of immediate or instantaneous information. To watch a group of executives confronted on a screen by immediate numerical projections of their suggestions or ideas is to realize how inhibiting to reflection or deep discussion this immediate feedback can be. For many people it is so threatening that it induces mental inertia – a sort of figure-induced hypnosis.

The technological allure of the integrated information system with its central data bank and endless possible combinations and computations of numbers has led, on occasion, to:

1 The concept of numbers as facts, referred to earlier.
2 Information overload, as executives find that they are required to assimilate, understand and interpret vast accumulations of data.
3 Data so far removed from its source, by translation into ratios or indices, that it is no longer reality-based for those who use it.

In general, technically feasible activities should only be indulged in if they (a) are also operationally feasible and (b) have some sort of financial justification.

The seduction of technology can easily lead to proposals which are technically feasible, but not understood or wanted by those who have to use them, or which, even if understood or wanted, are unlikely to produce benefits in proportion to their costs. Two factors in particular lend impetus to the lure of technology.

1 The dominating expert power of the computer experts. Carrying with them the glamour of a new and seldom understood technology and the image of modernity and professionalism, a rejection of their ideas can seem to connote conservatism, traditionalism and reluctance to change. The mathematical model of the firm can become the status symbol of the decade.

2 The sunk costs of the original investment in the hardware and the programming staff makes it easy to justify new developments by short-term marginal costing. As Box 11.7 shows, new programmes account for only 20 per cent of all costs. The translation of the marginal development costs into the more noticeable new maintenance and fixed costs if the programme is adopted, can often be ignored at the time of the new proposal.

4.3 The master–servant issue

This issue, in one form or another, lies at the heart of the question of operational feasibility. The computer, with its store of information, its capacity for analysis of inter-relationships and trends, its ability to issue orders and make up schedules, to bill customers or change suppliers, to route vessels or turn on pipe-lines, can seem to many an executive to be a competitor that he cannot fight, a master with whom he cannot talk. Put this feeling up against the desire of the computer professionals to advance their technology and to have their ideas and procedures adopted by the organization, and the seeds of conflict are already sown. For instance:

1 'The computer centre proposed that they design a model of the corporate distribution system, to be used in both long-range planning and the daily management of operations. Cost data on the present distribution system were scanty and out of date. Moreover, responsibility for distribution lay with the marketing vice-president, a man who had made no major changes in distribution policy or practice for fifteen years, and had a well-earned reputation for being hostile to innovation. Perhaps understandably, he had not been consulted on the proposal. Yet, his support would obviously be indispensable to its success.' (McKinsey Report)

2 The purchasing department of one manufacturing company found that the computer-operated purchasing schedule was inhibiting their negotiat-

Box 11.7 The cost of a computer

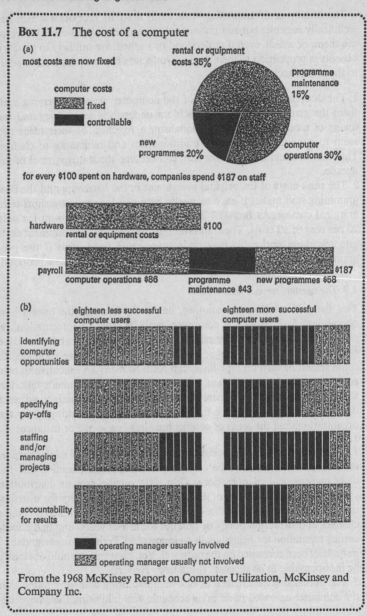

(a)
most costs are now fixed

computer costs
▨ fixed
■ controllable

rental or equipment costs 35%

programme maintenance 15%

computer operations 30%

new programmes 20%

for every $100 spent on hardware, companies spend $187 on staff

hardware — rental or equipment costs — $100

payroll — $187
computer operations $86   programme maintenance $43   new programmes $58

(b)

eighteen less successful computer users

eighteen more successful computer users

identifying computer opportunities

specifying pay-offs

staffing and/or managing projects

accountability for results

■ operating manager usually involved
▨ operating manager usually not involved

From the 1968 McKinsey Report on Computer Utilization, McKinsey and Company Inc.

ing tactics with major suppliers through a rather inflexible system for arriving at optimum quantities. Their requests for a revised programme were turned down on the grounds that it would be too expensive to re-write the programme at a time of financial stringency in the organization. Rebuffed, they decided to ignore the computer schedules and re-introduce their own hand-operated routines.

3 The information manager in one company, a highly intelligent youngish man imported from a competitor to set up the computer system, was aghast at the inefficiency and lack of intelligence of the production division. Seeking to rationalize their operations he has set up computer routines for a large proportion of their operations, but in the process has so antagon-ized the production executives that no communications now take place apart from the most formal of memoranda between the production and computer divisions. As one result, a kind of work-to-rule developed in the production division when all computer schedules would be religiously ad-hered to, even when it was apparent that the situation called for them to be overridden.

4 In one company, the question 'Who is responsible for stock control?' produced an embarrassed silence from the assembled managers until some-one replied 'I suppose it is really Tom' (the computer manager).

5 McKinsey's investigations demonstrate that when the operating manager is involved in all aspects of any proposed computer applications, there is a much higher likelihood of its success.

In general, computers are a very tempting method for territorial invasion, or, to extend the metaphor, for surveillance by satellite. As we saw in chapter 8, territorial invasion is a frequent source of conflict and arouses a variety of defensive tactics. The computer should be the servant, or at least the ally, of the operational manager if full and effective use is going to be made of it. The implications of this principle include the following:

1 Methods such as project teams, headed by operational not computer managers, should be adopted to investigate and implement major new proposals.

2 Better education of the operational managers to break down the mystique that still surrounds so much of computer activity.

3 Central computing centres with information managers reporting to chief executives are far more threatening to operational managers than subordinate computer people under their command. Several small com-puter facilities, though initially more expensive, may ultimately be more useful and more used than one major facility. Technologically, it has long been feasible to operate individual units in conjunction with one central

processing facility. The organization structure *now* needs to keep pace with technological possibility.

4 More care needs to be taken to prevent the public use of private information. Although this is a major concern for society, the words are here used in an organization setting. Information that is private to a manager (i.e. affects the details of his operation) must be protected from circulation to other parties without his knowledge or will. Publication, or the possibility of publication, will be seen as a reduction in independence. Again, the technical aids are available; it is organizational willingness that is lacking.

4.4 In conclusion

The achievements of computers in a variety of fields are well established, even if their financial justification remains obscure. The Boadicea booking system for British Airways, the seismic analysis of oil companies, the cheque-handling system of the clearing banks, the control centres of railroads, the hotel reservation schemes, the stock replenishment schemes of retail chains, apart from the myriad payroll and basic accounting systems, are but some of these applications. McKinsey lists four types of application:

Administrative and accounting uses;
Operations control systems;
Product innovation and improved customer service;
Information systems and simulation models.

It is in the first two of these that computers have made most impact, particularly the first. Clearly, the potential is there for the others, but hitherto it has largely been unrealized.

One way of looking at this is to suggest that computer applications are most likely to be successful either in steady-state parts of the organization, or where the work-flow is facsimile in type. Using the categories of organization activities and work-flows as the axes, a matrix could be constructed to demonstrate this point.

	facsimile	sequential	independent
policy/breakdown	1 low	2 very low	3 very low
steady-state	4 very high	5 very high	6 high
innovation	7 moderate	8 low	9 very low

Figure 14

Where the pressures for uniformity are high (facsimile operations and steady-state activities) and the rate of change slow (steady-state), it will be possible to set up systems that can be automated and will work as effectively on the data of tomorrow or next year as on the data of today. Furthermore, in facsimile or sequential operations, the high need for co-ordination will produce obvious pay-offs.

Where, however, the rate of change is more rapid (innovative activities) or the need for action so urgent (breakdown and sometimes policy), the slow adjustment cycles, not of the computer hardware but of the software, make it too cumbersome a tool for any non-repetitive task. Operational feasibility is good in steady-state independent operations, but with a low need for co-ordination the pay-off will be small.

Thus it is that the core of the steady-state, the accounting and clerical routines, have been the most obvious successes, and market management by mathematical model, though tantalizing in its technological challenge, has been so unsuccessful. Computerized information systems applied to the steady-state are useful and productive; applied to policy and innovative areas they are often discarded by the users as unrealistic, too cumbersome, or too costly in terms of the results they generate.

5 Communications systems

Clearly, if the systems or organizations are to work well, the information must not only be well-developed, but it must be well-communicated. If there is one general law of communication it is that we never communicate as effectively as we think we do. Consider for instance the following very typical findings:

1 Burns, in 1954, studied the production department of a British firm. He found that although the department manager recorded himself as having given 'instruction or decisions in 165 of the 237 episodes', his deputies recorded receiving instruction on only eighty-four of those occasions.
2 Jones at Columbia University discovered that the retention of content matter at the end of a lecture was only 50 per cent – a figure that dropped to 25 per cent after two weeks.
3 A study of communications in 100 firms by Pigeon Savage Lewis Inc, an advertising and communications firm, discovered that, of information disseminated by the President, the first level down recalled receiving only 63 per cent, the third level only 40 per cent and the fifth level only 20 per cent.
4 Floyd Mann (in Box 11.8), shows how inaccurate are the hierarchical communications in one, not atypical, company. Poor communications, as

was stressed in an earlier chapter, are a reliable symptom of some under-lying disorder in the organization or in the relationship between the people concerned. For instance:

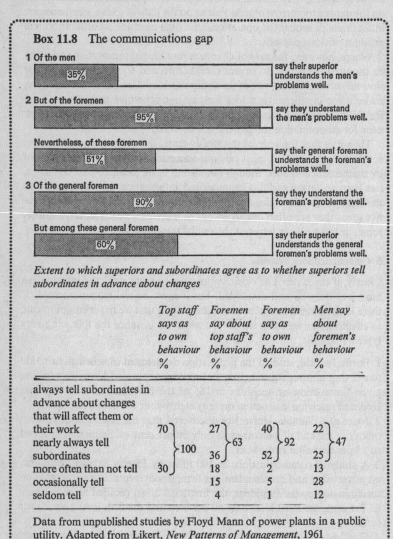

Box 11.8 The communications gap

1 Of the men — 35% — say their superior understands the men's problems well.

2 But of the foremen — 95% — say they understand the men's problems well.

Nevertheless, of these foremen — 51% — say their general foreman understands the foreman's problems well.

3 Of the general foreman — 90% — say they understand the foreman's problems well.

But among these general foremen — 60% — say their superior understands the general foremen's problems well.

Extent to which superiors and subordinates agree as to whether superiors tell subordinates in advance about changes

	Top staff says as to own behaviour %	Foremen say about top staff's behaviour %	Foremen say as to own behaviour %	Men say about foremen's behaviour %
always tell subordinates in advance about changes that will affect them or their work	70 ⎱	27 ⎱	40 ⎱	22 ⎱
nearly always tell subordinates	⎰ 100	36 ⎰ 63	52 ⎰ 92	25 ⎰ 47
more often than not tell	30 ⎰	18	2	13
occasionally tell		15	5	28
seldom tell		4	1	12

Data from unpublished studies by Floyd Mann of power plants in a public utility. Adapted from Likert, *New Patterns of Management*, 1961

(a) *Perceptual bias by the receiver*. We only hear or perceive what we are ready to hear or receive. Unwelcome news can get filtered out or distorted (see chapter 3).

(b) *Omission or distortion by the sender*. For various reasons, the sender will contaminate or leave out items in the message. Read found that individuals with career ambitions systematically withheld information potentially threatening to their position. Less ambitious people contaminated significantly less.

(c) *Lack of trust*. If we do not trust someone, we are careful to screen the information. Mellinger, in a study of 330 scientists, found that when an individual lacks trust in the recipient, he tends to conceal his own attitude, the result being evasive, compliant or aggressive communications.

(d) *Non-verbal obliterates the verbal*. The emotional overtones of a communication may distort the reception of the data (see chapter 3).

(e) *Overload*. Too much information in a channel faces the recipient with a screening query, or stereotyping problem. After experimental studies of overloading, Shelly and Gilchrist concluded that overload results 'in more or less self-perpetuating conditions of communication confusion'.

(f) *Information secretion*. The use of position power to garner and secrete information instead of sharing it (see chapter 5). Davis, in his study of the 'Jason Company', investigated two incidents. 'Individuals who told the news to more than one other person amounted to less than 10 per cent of the sixty-seven executives in each case.'

(g) *Distance*. The further away one is, the less one communicates. Barnlund and Harland summarized a variety of studies by concluding 'an inverse relationship has been found between the physical distance separating persons and the likelihood of communication between them'.

(h) *Relative status*. Individuals with low perceived status have difficulty in initiating communications in groups or with those of superior status. Just as he who talks more in a group has more influence, he who has more influence *can* talk more.

(i) *Immediacy*. The more immediate communication drives out the less. Thus, telephone calls can interrupt discussions which in turn displace written communications. It is apocryphally related that when Maynard Keynes had an audience with President Roosevelt there were so many telephone interruptions that he eventually excused himself, went outside and dialled a surprised President, explaining 'this seems the only way I can communicate with you!'.

(j) *Tactic of conflict*. Information withholding or distortion is a common tactic in organizational conflict (see chapter 8). Conflict often leads to the literal break in communications.

(k) *Lack of clarity*. Last but not least. What is obvious to the sender is obscure to the recipient. Sensible compression to one is jargon to the other. Circumlocution, woolly sentence construction, imprecise definitions, can all so easily lead to misunderstandings.

Given this incomplete list it is perhaps worth admiring the fact that any sensible communication takes place at all. There are, however, some positive steps that can be taken *in addition* to removing any causes of blockage:

1 Use more than one communications net. There are various 'nets' – hierarchical, expert group, status group, friendship group. Most formal communications go through one or other of the first two. Use of the informal nets to prepare the ground or underline the formal, substantially improved retention levels. In one study, Habbe found that 60 per cent of employees got their information from 'reading things', 40 per cent from 'talking with people'. Burns found that informal channels successfully and usefully pre-warned executives of forthcoming crises or policy changes. If you know whom you are going to meet at a party before you go, you remember the formal introduction very much better.

2 Encourage two-way rather than one-way communication. In two-way communication, the recipient is encouraged to intervene in the message to get clarification or to ask questions. Experiments show that two-way communication takes much longer but substantially improves comprehension and retention, particularly if occasions are created to check the degree of understanding.

3 Keep the linkages in the communication chain as few as possible. The more people in the chain the more possibilities of distortion. If the list of positive steps is much shorter than the list of possible causes of breakdown, this is because the most effective way to improve communication systems is to *remove* the negative factors. Communications are symptoms. Good communications imply a well-designed healthy organization.

6 Summary and conclusion

6.1

The systems of organizations were initially classified under *adaptive systems*, *operative systems*, *maintenance systems*, served by *information systems* which in turn are served by *communication systems*.

Information systems need to be differentiated according to *purpose* and *technology*.

Two important mechanisms used in organization systems are *budgets* which typically try to fulfil too many purposes and may well fail in them all. (Devices to rectify this include participative budgeting and computers.) Suggestions were put forward to explain the gap between the technical potential of the computer and its practical realization.

Finally, the problems of communication systems were listed.

6.2 Conclusion

The failure to differentiate between organizational cultures and workflows, between types of system and the purposes of information, between steady-state and policy or innovation, has led in many instances to frustration and disappointed hopes, to vast expenditures on unused computer facilities, to sophisticated but unwanted information analysis.

The discussion in this chapter was aimed at demonstrating that the formal management of information by budget, computer or hierarchical dissemination is appropriate in the main to the steady-state and to the operating systems. The power culture and the task culture are not well-suited to routines. Change and speed of reaction are crucial to their existence. This is not to say that they do not require information or targets or objectives. Of course they do. But the manner of their presentation, and the method of their collection will tend to be less routinized, less programmed and less formal.

12 On Being a Manager

1 Introduction

It has never been easy to define what a manager is, or what he does. It is a useful concept, 'management', the missing 'x' which makes resources equal output. But the 'x', the exact qualities that are important, this tends to shift from equation to equation. Definitions of the manager, or the manager's role, tend therefore to be so broad that they are meaningless, or so stereotyped that they become part of the background. 'Yes, of course', we say, and take no further notice.

At an opening session of a series of management seminars in one company I asked if there was any agreement on the essential part of a manager's job. With few dissentients they said that 'making decisions' was for them the vital part of the managerial function. We agreed, therefore, that for our next meeting in a week's time each of them would prepare a description of the most critical decision that he, as a manager, had taken that week. We would then analyse the way he had gone about it. The assumption here would be that if we could improve his decision-making capability we would improve his capacity as a manager. The next week a group of embarrassed managers faced each other. 'It was a strange week, last week, somehow I didn't seem to have any decisions to take', said one. The others looked relieved. All said that they had found the same thing. Another managerial stereotype bites the dust! A manager, of course, does not just, or even mainly, 'take decisions'.

This chapter will not attempt to give a pre-emptive answer to that question 'What is a manager?'. We shall consider, however, some aspects of the job of being a manager that are especially pertinent to the understanding of organizations. Times change and times, we are constantly being reminded, change increasingly faster. The work organization, and particularly the manager, seems often to be the lynch-pin in the whole change process of society. A crucial role, if that is any consolation to its occupants! Perhaps, however, a little understanding will help to relieve the stress.

The chapter will consider in turn *the manager as G.P.*, *the managerial dilemmas* and *the manager as a person*.

2 The manager as G.P.

2.1

The analogy of General Practitioner has been hauled in from the medical world to help to characterize one role of the manager. The notion of G.P. is not intended to suggest that in other roles the manager may not be a specialist, or consultant or what-have-you. But be he a so-called general manager, a manager of specialists, or departmental supervisor, he must remember that in his G.P.'s role he is the first recipient of problems. He it is who must:

Identify the symptoms in any situation;
Diagnose the disease or cause of the trouble;
Decide how it might be dealt with – a strategy for health;
Start the treatment.

It is true that he may wish for expert help, or a second opinion, at any of these stages. Indeed, the good manager is often he who recognizes that he needs specialist help and is not averse to asking for it. But the *responsibility* for each of these stages lies with the local manager.

Like much that is true in life, this statement seems too obvious to be meaningful. Too many times, however:

1 The symptoms are treated instead of the disease – low morale is met by exhortation or a Christmas party, poor communications by briefing meetings or a house journal.
2 The prescription is the same whatever the disease – the equivalent of 'give him antibiotics' is often 're-structure the division' or 'send him on a course'. It is as true in management as it is said to be in medicine that when you select a consultant you select a treatment. That is not necessarily bad, as long as the correct diagnosis has already been made. *That* is the job of the manager on the spot.

2.2 The symptoms

What are these *symptoms*? In a managerial situation they will appear as problems. They may be such general things as low morale, inter-group bickering, inter-personal hostility. They may be particular instances such as stock-out, a disastrous tender price, a faulty shipment. Managerial judgement is involved in deciding whether the problem is a one-off instance or a symptom of a deeper malaise. If, however, the instinctive managerial reaction to a problem is not 'Whose fault is it?' but 'What is wrong here?' it will be a reaction that errs on the right side. Organizations find it very easy to grow accustomed to their blemishes. Remarks like 'that is a characteristic of this industry' often mean 'we've had this squint for so long that it has become part of our identity'. The usefulness of outsiders in organizations, as consultants, directors or advisers, often consists mainly in pointing out that one does not necessarily have to have a squint. Similarly, managers in all parts of the organization do not *have* to treat their problems as endemic. If they regard them as symptoms and look for the underlying cause they may find it is something very responsive to treatment.

Box 12.1   Squints are not always necessary

Scene: Far Eastern Headquarters of an old-established agency business.

The young trainee was assigned to the despatch department. He was puzzled by the requirement that orders to the warehouse to load goods on board outgoing ships should have to be made out on a shipping advice and also on what was called a loading note. Furthermore this loading note was made out with fourteen copies. When he commented on this and queried it they said:

The warehouse was on an island, not the mainland;
They had been doing things this way for the last twenty years;
Did he really think that such a famous, successful and well-established company did not have a good reason for what it did?

The trainee said no more.

Six months later an efficiency expert from London discovered as part of a large investigation that the loading note had originated as an emergency handwritten device in the chaotic days after the war when telephone communication had broken down between the mainland and the island where the warehouse was. Orders to the warehouse had been scribbled on a piece of paper and sent across by motor launch to be followed later by the formal shipping advice. In time the scribbled notes acquired a name, 'loading notes', were typed, got filed, got counterfiled, were run off on a duplicating machine, became a printed form, were sent to the London office for record and audit purposes, until in due course, and twenty years later, fourteen copies were filed in various sites, and never subsequently looked at by anyone. The telephone link between mainland and island, had, incidentally, been restored after two months.

The loading note was discontinued and the efficiency expert calculated that he had saved his year's salary by that one action.

2.3 Diagnosis and strategy

If symptoms are problems, what corresponds to diagnosis and strategy?

Diagnosis is essentially the theme of this whole book. The first eight chapters outline the kinds of diagnostic interpretations that can be used to explain or understand an organizational situation. Diagnosis implies understanding and understanding implies that you can explain a particular instance by placing it in a general category. The first part of this book can be viewed as a list of categories. If the manager can see that a breakdown in procedures is an instance of an inappropriate culture in one part of the organization, then he has placed the particular instance in a general category. He has identified the cause of the symptom through his understanding of the general organization.

This stage of diagnosis is often instinctive. But instinct can be fallacious.

Box 12.2 Is there time for treatment?

The British subsidiary of the multinational giant was very performance-oriented. There were monthly targets, quarterly performance reviews, annual budgets, two-year plans and five-year forecasts. The visitor was impressed, both by the systems and by the performance. The systems had been instituted by the managing director when he arrived from the headquarters some eighteen months before. Indeed, most of the management team dated from his arrival and were very eager to make their mark. It was, they all felt, a very busy but very stimulating environment. Only one thing puzzled the visitor. What was going to be underneath those upward-sloping lines in the five-year forecast? 'Oh, they're projections,' said the marketing director, 'we don't have much time to worry about them. The future around here ends in eighteen months' time when the boss returns to H.Q.'

Three years later the visitor was passing by once more. The activity was still impressive. The M.D. was new, so were most of the management team. The forecasts still pointed upward but it seemed to the visitor, from his memory of his last visit, that they did not start where the others left off. The earlier forecasts had been thrown away however, 'unrealistic', 'drawn up by the previous management'. Only the personnel manager was left of the previous team. He was very busy. 'Lots of activity at the moment,' he said, 'new faces and new structures. The M.D. believes in action – and returns. He wants a two-year pay-off on any expenditure. We've got a much more streamlined organization now but the middle management turnover is a bit worrying.'

The visitor passed on, wondering whom he would meet there on his next visit.

It is useful to subject it at times to some discipline. To use the chapters of a book such as this as a diagnostic check-list – 'do any of these ideas explain the current situation?' – may not be so time-wasting or academic as it seems at first sight. For to leap from sight of symptom to application of treatment looks efficient but may be just habit.

Strategy for health is another matter. There will be times when no cure is possible. There will be more times when any strategy for health involves remedies too costly or too painful to contemplate in the present.

When considering a strategy for health, a manager should reflect upon the variables that he can influence in the organization. These have already been described in the three preceding chapters (9–11). They are:

The people;
The work and structure of the organization;
The systems and procedures.

Favourite strategies under these headings include:

People
    Hiring and firing;
    Re-assignment;
    Training and education;
    Selective pay increases;
    Counselling or admonition;
i.e. changing people, either literally or figuratively.
The work and the structure
    Re-organization of reporting relationships;
    Re-definition of the tasks;
    Job enrichment;
    Re-definition of roles.
The systems and procedures
    Communication systems (e.g. committee structure);
    Reward systems (payment methods, salary grades);
    Information systems and reporting mechanisms;
    Budgets;
    Decision-making systems (e.g. stock control, debt control).

But in taking his pick from one of these strategies, loosely gathered under the three variables of people, work and systems, the strategic-thinking manager needs to ponder three complicating factors:

1 The variables interact. Changes in one will produce changes in another. If you alter the structure you will affect the people in it. This is called by

some the systemic effect of change. It can be represented diagrammatically by placing the three variables in a triangle so that each is linked to the other. If you think of the sides of the triangle as perhaps one being a steel bar, a second a piece of string, and the third a rubber band then visually one can imagine how moving one corner of the triangle will produce shifts of different dimensions to the two other corners.

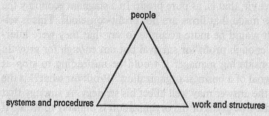

Figure 15

2 All the three variables, linked together, happen within a context, within an environment. The environment can be the organization as a whole. If the manager is the chief executive then the environment he looks at will include the industry, the market, the country as a whole. There are many aspects to the environment but the three that are usually most crucial to any organizational situation are:

The goals;
The culture;
The technology.

3 Whilst it may be possible in the longer term to affect the context in which one operates, in the short and medium term the context is given. The manager as strategist must, however, be *clear* about the context in which he operates, since this will limit and influence the variable that he can control. Diagrammatically the first triangle sits inside another:

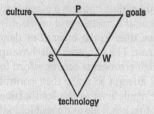

Figure 16

For instance:

(a) *Goals*. It is often too simple to regard profit as a goal; too simple in that it will conceal the real purposes of the organization. Profit is often more truly an intervening variable, the means by which the organization seeks to achieve something else such as growth, survival, diversification, respectability. It would not usually be regarded as sensible merely to put it in the bank, to treat it, that is, as pure profit. In a stagnant economy the charge is sometimes made that firms are not profit-conscious. This is seldom strictly true. It would be more accurate to say that they were interested in generating enough profit for survival but not enough for growth. For the strategy-considering manager it would be misleading to stop at 'profit' as the true goal of a business organization. 'Profit for what?' is the key question. And the answer may well affect his strategy. A strategy that is out of line with the true goals of the organization is unlikely to work. If

---

Box 12.3 Money or ...?

A young millionaire, noted for his take-over activities, once attributed his success to the simple fact that he was interested in making money. Most of the people that he competed against in take-over situations were interested in making or doing things *for* money. The difference had a crucial effect on valuations. To take the simplest example – the latter would see a factory as a building for manufacturing toys and would value it, both psychologically and financially, in terms of its suitability for that purpose. He, however, would instinctively see it merely as a site. To call him an asset-stripper, he maintained, was only another way of saying that his aims were different from theirs.

'security and a quiet life' is the true objective of the organization, strategies for job enrichment may well seem an unnecessary encumbrance.

(b) *Technology*. Technology sets limits to freedom. Consider for instance the maximum cost of a mistake by a low-paid employee. In the textile industry one might ruin a bale of cloth, in the airline business a plane-load of people. The systems needed to ensure against a mistake will necessarily be more complex and tight in one instance than in the other. But tight controls can easily be felt to imply lack of trust. The symptom will show up a lowered morale, but technologies with high error-costs cannot afford to rely on trust alone. Such technologies will attempt to make their control procedures automatic, or to use industry regulations as the legitimizing device (as in many airline procedures), but this is not always possible.

Technology too, and very obviously, affects the size and autonomy of work groups. Whilst it is conceivable to think of abandoning the assembly line in the manufacture of car engines and substituting small work-groups, it is hard to envisage the same degree of self-programming in a continuous process industry.

To an increasing extent technology will become the servant of the manager but to many a middle manager it is today a constraining force. As such it must be considered in any strategy formulation.

(c) *Cultures.* Chapter 7 explored the notion of culture and how this linked with goals and technologies as well as other determining factors. In the short term it is hard to kick against the prevailing culture and many an attempt to change organizations has failed for this reason.

2.4 The implementation

The manager, therefore, has a choice of six strategic variables. In the short or medium term he will be confined to the inner triangle but the longer-term factors must not be ignored, particularly by the more senior men in an organization. But in considering his strategy the manager will also reflect upon its feasibility, *the implementation or treatment.*

He will realize that whereas he may see it as a cure for a malaise, most others will regard it as change. He will know from past experience that change is to managers what motherhood is to a teenage girl 'something to be approved of but postponed for a while'. He will understand instinctively that many of the strategies he has considered are not feasible, because the point of initiation is one that he cannot influence, that the parts of the organization that he can influence are perhaps politically ineffective, that change which is imposed will not be change that will be self-maintaining. If he has read chapter 5 of this book he will understand that the implementation of change is largely a matter of sources of power and methods of influence, that organizations react psychologically rather than logically and that persuasion or rational argument is only a possible method of influence when he is regarded as the appropriate expert. Having realized all this he may well begin to feel that the ends are not worth the very troublesome means. But having recovered from his initial depression he will see that the appropriate psychological progression would be:

1 Create an awareness of the need for change (preferably not by argument or rationale but by exposure to objective fact).
2 Select an appropriate initiating person or group ('appropriate' in this context refers to sources of power as perceived by the recipients of the strategy).
3 Be prepared to allow the recipients to adapt the final strategy. (That

which one adapts one can more easily call one's own. Ownership equals internalization, i.e. is self-maintaining.)

4 Accept the fact that, like the good psycho-analyst, the successful doctor gets no credit but must let the patient boast of his sound condition.

5 Be prepared to accept a less than optimum strategy in the interests of achieving something rather than nothing.

(Effectiveness = strategy × likelihood of success.)

Change is not to be advocated for its own sake. But the organization that can adapt to changing situations and requirements is the organization that survives. The assumption that a given organizational form which works to-day will still be right in five years' time is too often a misplaced assumption. The adaptive manager is he who knows when change is needed, what change is needed and how to bring it about without disruption. The wise manager will not sit in his consulting room awaiting the onset of an epidemic, he will invest in a degree of preventive medicine.

3 The managerial dilemmas

3.1

There is usually some crude justice somewhere in the divisions of society. Managers are paid more than workers but in return they find themselves faced with a set of constant dilemmas. These dilemmas can be described in a book, but they can only be resolved by the man in the middle of them, the manager. The principal managerial dilemmas are:

The dilemma of the cultures;
The dilemma of time-horizons;
The trust-control dilemma;
The commando leader's dilemma.

Each of these needs a few words of explanation and description.

3.2 The dilemma of the cultures

In chapter 7, the organization was described as being made up of a set of cultures. The role culture was suggested as appropriate for steady-state activities, the task culture for developmental work, the power culture for emergencies, crises and breakdowns. The manager, as he climbs the seniority ladder, will find that his job embraces all three of these cultures. There is a management style and a set of behaviours, or procedures and attitudes appropriate to each. A failure to behave in a culturally appropriate manner will result in a breach of the psychological contract, in lack of trust, in ineffective management. The manager must, therefore, be flexible in his style and behaviour, he must cover all three cultures. Worse still, he must, if he wishes to preserve his own identity and to claim that 'he' makes a personal difference, retain some elements of the person culture. Without some elements of this Dionysian set of beliefs he will have little personal power and will add little 'character' to his organization. In short, the effective manager must be culturally diverse and culturally flexible. But he must at the same time avoid the sin of unpredictability. He must be flexible but consistent, culturally diverse but recognizably an individual with his own identity. Therein lies the dilemma. Those who fail to resolve it, who relapse into one culturally predominant style, will find themselves rightly restricted to that part of the organization where their culture prevails. Middle layers of organizations are often overcrowded with culturally rigid managers who have failed to deal with this cultural dilemma.

3.3 The dilemma of time-horizons

The manager is, above all, responsible for the future. For most of the time the present, for good or ill, is under way. There is often very little he, as manager, can do about it. He can, with greater ease, influence the future. Much of his time should be given to anticipating the future, making assessments of contingencies, and adjusting his plans and his resources accordingly, setting the culture and the climate, picking and developing his people. In general, the higher a man rises in an organization, the longer needs to be his time-horizon and the more of his time he should spend thinking about it.

But this management of the future has to go hand in hand with the responsibility for the present. Whilst it may be true that he can do little to change the present and can only comment on the past, he must nevertheless preside over both, must be interested in today as well as tomorrow, must inspire and control, know enough of what is happening to be able to judge whether an intervention might after all be profitable.

It is not easy to live in two or more time dimensions at once. It is hard to plan creatively for five years hence with a redundancy interview scheduled for one hour's time. Just as routine drives out non-routine, so the present can easily obliterate the future. By concentrating on the problems of the present the future becomes in its turn a series of present problems or crises, intervention by the manager in a power role becomes legitimate, even essential, there is still less time available for the future, the manager feels indispensable and legitimized by crisis. The cycle has become self-fulfilling. Unless the manager is able to live successfully in two time dimensions he will make the present more difficult than it need be and will unsuccessfully manage the future.

3.4 The trust–control dilemma

In chapter 10 the issue of delegation was explored. The trust–control relationship was seen to be complementary. If control is increased, trust is decreased. An increase in trust is only believed and therefore only effective if accompanied by a decrease in control. Trust, it was pointed out, is a much cheaper way of running things as well as being more fitting to the dignity and rights of humankind.

The managerial dilemma is always how to balance trust and control. The dilemma is particularly acute for the manager in the middle, most crucially so for the supervisor or first level manager. Trust implies giving someone the right to make mistakes. The mistakes that you might tolerate in your subordinate may not, however, be tolerated by your superior. In other words, the degree of control is often dictated not by the manager but by the manager's manager. Ultimately the chain stops at the top. As in so many other ways the example of top management is crucial to the trust–control issue. It is noticeable, for instance, that in successful organizations there tends to be more trust and less control, junior managers perceive they have more influence over their work. This is usually interpreted as meaning that more shared influence (more trust, in our terminology) leads to more success. The sequence, however, is perhaps more likely to work the other way round. When things go well it is easier to relinquish controls. Trust flourishes with success. Maybe the trust in turn contributes to further success but one suspects that in many cases the cycle starts with success not with trust. The practical message for any middle manager must often be – 'First get your trust record, then you'll be given freedom which amounts to trust.'

One of the pre-conditions of trust, it was noted in chapter 10, was a knowledge of, a confidence in, one's subordinates. This most easily happened when the manager could select his own men. Usually this luxury is denied to the middle manager. Given a group of men he has to learn to know them and they him. He has to experiment with trust. Too much control is expensive, time-consuming and self-defeating in motivational terms. Trust, however, can often survive only one mistake. Therein lies this dilemma. A manager will often find himself being more controlling than he would like to be.

3.5 The commando leader's dilemma

The commando leader likes to be given a clear objective (e.g. capture that bridge) but allowed great freedom as to how he does it. A commando group is a collection of expert resources; there is a high degree of group loyalty. Commandos often develop cults, special group norms, badges, uniforms or languages. There is a great amount of camaraderie, of mutual trust and shared objectives. It is in fact the epitome of a project organization or task culture. Many a manager, and almost all young managers, have a personal preference for a task culture. To lead a project group in an organization can well be an exhilarating and inspiring task, reviving all one's faith in the purposeful challenge of work. And organizations *need* commando groups, particularly in the developmental area. But few organizations, if any, can be made up totally of such groups. Organizations, like armies, have to have a steady-state; and commando leaders, though valuable, are often perceived as a nuisance. It is not unknown for the G.O.C. to heave a silent sigh of relief when he hears that the commando leader was taken prisoner in the final assault.

The lure of the task culture, of the project group, can often prove dangerous to the career structure of the younger manager. His dilemma lies in finding how to keep a proper balance between the demands of his group and the demands of the total organization.

Box 12.4 'Thank you, John, but . . .'

John was a highly competent, resourceful young manager. Early in his career with the multi-national corporation he was identified as a man who could be trusted with an independent command at an early age. Soon he was manager of his own subsidiary company in one of those isolated but interesting corners of the old empire. Admired and respected by his local staff he was highly successful. Soon he was moved to a larger but equally interesting outpost. Again success was quick and impressive. He was beginning to acquire a reputation for unorthodox but successful trading methods. A striking figure, he dressed a trifle bizarrely and drove strange cars. He inspired almost a devotion among his staff. He was known to be a hard man to succeed in any post.

The years passed, and so did a succession of outpost jobs. Always glowing reports. He was 38 now, married with growing children and anxious to return to London. Head office, however, had no vacancies for him. 'Sorry, John,' they said, 'but we don't think you would fit in here. Not enough of a bureaucrat, are you? Perhaps you ought to take six months' pay and find yourself a niche back in the Indian Ocean where you've done so splendidly for us.'

3.6 Dealing with dilemmas

There is no universal panacea for these dilemmas. They are present with most managers most of the time. The following points are more in the nature of reminders than remedies.

(a) *Stress heightens the dilemmas*. Stress shortens time-horizons, polarizes issues, exaggerates the importance of the present, makes difficulties into crises and inhibits creativity. Stress in fact is the one thing a man, and especially a senior manager, should be without. And yet, for many a manager stress is almost a battle honour. To succumb to it is weakness, to be without it is dishonourable. In a way, a heartless way perhaps, it is not the physical and medical outcomes of managerial stress that are the worries. If a man has a heart attack, develops an ulcer, has a nervous breakdown, he is himself a victim but he is also incapacitated as a manager, prevented from causing hurt to others. It is the less respectable symptoms of stress, the general impairment of judgement and the tendencies listed at the beginning of this paragraph, which can really foul up organizations and the lives of others. Managers, as a social duty, must manage stress, not court it.

Stress, as chapter 3 demonstrated, is largely inherent in the managerial role. The managerial dilemmas are not only heightened by stress, they can also add to the stress. The factors that cause managerial stress cannot all, should not all, be avoided or eliminated. But the stress that they cause can be managed, can be mitigated. Some of the ways for achieving this are noted below.

(b) *Create stability zones*. Alvin Toffler in his stimulating book *Future Shock* notes how those men who live the most mobile and stressful lives do have what he calls 'stability zones' in their lives (see Box 12.5).

Decisions use up energy. New situations imply new decision rules. If one is to manage stress it is important to conserve energy, to reserve energy for the important problems and the strategic decisions. A 'stability zone' can be a place or time for rebuilding energy reserves. Holidays, week-ends, days off – these are important stability zones. Not enough managers pay enough attention to them. Holidays are seen as self-indulgence. Conferences, overseas visits, courses – these are more respectable forms of 'getting away'. But they are less effective than a straightforward holiday as buffers to stress and considerably more expensive. Managerial holidays need to be clothed in a new respectability.

The family is for many a stability zone. Perhaps a demeaning role for

Box 12.5 'Stability zones'

One man I know has run through a series of love affairs, a divorce and re-marriage – all within a very short span of time. He thrives on change, enjoys travel, new foods, new ideas, new movies, plays and books. He has a high intellect and a low 'boring point', is impatient with tradition and restlessly eager for novelty. Ostensibly, he is a walking exemplar of change.

When we look more closely, however, we find that he has stayed in the same job for ten years. He drives a battered, seven-year-old automobile. His clothes are several years out of style. His closest friends are long-time professional associates and even a few old college buddies.

Another case involves a man who has changed jobs at a mind-staggering rate, has moved his family thirteen times in eighteen years, travels extensively, rents cars, uses throw-away products, prides himself on leading the neighbourhood in trying out new gadgets, and generally lives in a restless whirl of transience, newness and diversity. Once more, however, a second look reveals significant stability zones in his life: a good, tightly woven relationship with his wife of nineteen years; continuing ties with his parents; old college friends interspersed with the new acquaintances.

A different form of stability zone is the habit pattern that goes with the person wherever he travels, no matter what other changes alter his life. A professor who has moved seven times in ten years, who travels constantly in the United States, South America, Europe and Africa, who has changed jobs repeatedly, pursues the same daily regimen wherever he is. He reads between eight and nine in the morning, takes forty-five minutes for exercise at lunchtime, and then catches a half-hour cat-nap before plunging into work that keeps him busy until 10 p.m.

From Alvin Toffler, *Future Shock*, 1971

the wife – to be manager of a stability zone – but a very important one for her husband and his colleagues and subordinates.

An important way of creating stability zones is through the creation of routines. Routines are a way of coping with stress. Carried to extremes or applied inappropriately they inhibit creativity and change. But just because they are a way of coping with stress, they are useful in moderation as buffers. Many decisions can be taken by habit. What time do you get up in the morning? What train do you catch? What do you do for the first hour at the office? When do you have those meetings? To make each of these decisions afresh every day is energy-consuming, and will tend, just a little, to make you more prone to stress. Take them by routine or habit and that energy is conserved for more useful things. Does this make you a creature of habit, a predictable unexciting individual? In little things, perhaps, and much to the benefit of your colleagues. 'A creature of habit' is often a creature of wisdom.

(c) *Over-stimulation* or information overload adds enormously to stress. Ways of handling this include:

Specialization – only allowing some information to penetrate;
Simplification – the use of mottoes, rules of thumb, heuristics, e.g. 'do what we did last time';
Isolation – blocking the access of information.

If abused, as they frequently are, these techniques lead to inefficiency. In moderation they are sensible attempts to handle the problem of over-stimulation once it has occurred.

(d) *Use catalysts.* Our vantage point will colour what we see. The blind man and the elephant, the wood unnoticed because of its trees, the Eskimo who thought a tree was a god; the folklore of the world is full of stories of how our past experience and present involvement affects and distorts our image of reality. The present undoubtedly can impair our vision of the future.

Outsiders can be valuable in restoring perspective. They can ask pertinent questions even if they do not know the answers. The self-confident manager will find it a stimulus to expose his thinking on his management of the future to interested outsiders. To the insecure the stranger is a threat, to the confident he is a catalyst. Consultants are the ritual form of outsider. To ask them for answers as well as questions is often to require, and pay for, more than you really need. It is their role as catalyst and stimulus that is often the most useful. It is no accident that many consultants' solutions lie gathering dust on book-shelves, whilst the organization evolves its own solutions to the problems the outsiders raised.

Non-executive directors on boards of companies are another institutional form of the outsider as catalyst. They perform other custodial duties as well sometimes, but their role as catalyst and stimulus can be the most rewarding. 'Boards', someone said, 'are usually long, narrow and wooden!' Often, but not necessarily so. The outside director is becoming more common in the U.K. although he is still regarded more as a bearer of status than of stimulus. A pity, for a proper perspective on the future must be one of the major tasks of the board of any company. If outsiders are valuable anywhere they are valuable at this level.

The 'outsider' role does not, however, have to be so formally institutionalized. The requirement that a manager reveal his thinking on the management of the future to anyone not immediately involved in his operation, is a most useful discipline. The need to explain something to others will force you to understand it yourself. The best way to learn is to teach. Teaching others about one's job has been found by many to be more illuminating to the speaker than to the listener. We need, in organizations, to do more to encourage and promote the role of official listener. We need to institutionalize the inside outsider, the man from one section of the organization sitting as non-executive director on the 'boards' of the other sections. This is done under the guise of training and development by some organizations. Union Carbide in the U.S. experimented with the idea at a higher level by requiring executives from one division to act as members of planning groups in other divisions. More perhaps could be done with divisional boards in large companies, usually composed of the senior divisional managers and head office representatives. The concept of departmental boards has not, to my knowledge, been developed in any business organization.

(e) *Compartmentalize*. Just because it is difficult to work in two time-dimensions at once, so one should seek to arrange it so that one does not have to. One way is, of course, to deal only with one of the dimensions, usually the present. The more desirable method is to organize the work so that it is sorted by time-dimension rather than by topic. Most meetings in organizations are topic-centred, e.g. overseas marketing, competition, salary review. Few are time-centred. As a result, the agendas of most organization meetings cover a variety of time-horizons.

A study of a number of senior managers' diaries has revealed that problems are juxtaposed, randomly, in terms of the time-dimensions which apply to them. An incident from the past is followed by a problem in the present, when the five-year forecast is required by that evening.

Ask any individual manager for his major continuing problem and he will normally reply 'time'. Time to think, time to plan, time to talk with my people. Yet the same man finds time for food and for sleep, for Sundays and holidays. But these are institutionalized priorities – time for the future is not. The organization of work in organizations is usually haphazard. Diaries get filled up on a first-come first-served basis. Meeting agendas look like a cafeteria menu.

Some organizations make some attempt to compartmentalize. Long-term planning meetings are held away from the office. Certain days are regularly annotated for review or for planning. Some individuals attempt to compartmentalize their days into immediate and long-term divisions. Some have two offices – different territories for different kinds of problems. On the whole, however, there is too much adherence to the maxim that a manager has his door ever open, that a manager's place is at his desk or in a committee room, that a manager should be available at all times. This is a recipe for stress, for putting the present in place of the future, for letting problems drive out plans. Why not, instead, compartmentalize your work? Stay at home occasionally if that aids your thinking. Use what academics call office-hours for seeing subordinates. Remember that if a manager is thought only to be working when he is seen to be working, then he is unlikely to be doing as much long-term thinking as he should.

Organizations can help by institutionalizing thinking. A library as a place for reflection, recognition that days at home are not 'slacking', the bi-annual sabbatical in addition to a holiday. This kind of measure will help individuals to compartmentalize the future into the present.

Box 12.6   A senior manager's diary

One senior divisional manager sat down to separate out what he regarded as the major responsibilities of his job. He listed six key areas for himself:

A Relationships with head office;
B Long-term and strategic planning;
C Operational responsibilities for particular ongoing activities;
D Co-ordinating function;
E Standard setting, performance, morale, priorities;
F External relations.

He then analysed his diary for the previous three months and came up with the following approximate proportion of time spent on each of the key areas.

A 20%   D 25%
B 10%   E 5%
C 35%   F 5%

Should he have been worried?

---

4 The manager as a person

4.1

The last quarter-century has seen the emergence of 'the manager' as a recognized occupational role in society. Management has become at least a semi-profession. It is not a profession in the sense of medicine, for instance, with formal admission procedures, a recognized body of relevant knowledge, codified and enforced standards of practice. Nor is it a profession in the sense that a member of it is entitled to ask a set scale of fees for his services from the public. It is, however, a recognized occupational role, and one that now embraces something like 10 per cent of the total work force of the U.K.

The emergence of a new kind of middle class, dependent not on property, nor on the earnings from the practice of their own trade or profession, but on the salary paid to them by another, has begun to create real dilemmas for society, some of which are only beginning to emerge. It is not the purpose of this book to analyse the emerging society, but there are some questions that are beginning to be matters of urgent importance to organizations which arise from the existence of the managerial middle class. For instance:

(a) Does an organization owe an individual a career, or only skill-related earnings? Before management became a semi-profession, organizations seemed to view themselves as latter-day villages with many of the accompanying responsibilities of squirearchy towards their tenants. If they admitted someone to their patronage they were thenceforth responsible for that someone unless that someone renounced the patronage. The emergence of managers as would-be professionals has meant that individuals now believe in transferable skills, wish to be rewarded for these skills and resent patronage or paternalism. The obverse of this, of course, is that the organization has no obligation to hire the professional when his services are no longer required. Earnings will increasingly be related to marketable skills, redundant skills will be cut from pay-rolls, organizations will feel less obligations towards their managers and managers less commitment towards an organization. Since skills become redundant there will be a tendency to try to gather a lifetime's earnings during the extant life of the skill. In short, salaries will tend to increase but more people will retire early. Alternatively, deferred salaries, i.e. pensions, will increase, thus permitting early retirement.

(b) Does society have any responsibility towards the redundant semi-professionals? If the trends continue there will be a growing body of ex-managers, in middle age but with redundant skills. They can be looked upon as a problem or a resource. It would be nice to think that society will find ways to utilize these people who will normally be financially underwritten by their previous earnings and whose skills, although no longer competitive in industry or commerce, might well, at lower prices, be in demand in other sectors of society.

(c) Will the erosion of the organization as the alternative village have an effect on society?

Yes, assuredly. The semi-professional manager must become an independent, self-oriented individual if he is to survive in a world based on skill-related earnings. When he and his type represent 10 per cent of the total working force and perhaps 40 per cent of the middle class, these values will tend to predominate in middle-class society. The new manager is mobile, used to temporary systems, small and possibly changing families. He is rootless, has few loyalties beyond his immediate family, is moving fast but not always in any clear direction. The society he heralds is not for all of us a pleasant one to contemplate – selfish, clannish, competitive with values related to means rather than ends. It will be a society full of stress and devoid of loyalties, rent by internal schisms and mediated by money or by force.

It is probably unfair to ascribe this pessimistic view of the future to the growing professionalism of managers, but this will make its contribution.

4.2 The implications

The changing role of the manager has its implications for the manager. He must become pro-active in the management of his career. In a world of skill-related earnings it is of little use relying on the village elders to nurture and guide your upbringing. Increasingly it will come to be seen as the individual's responsibility to maintain, alter or boost his skills, to find the right market for his skills and to sell them to the appropriate buyer. Traditional management development looked upon its managers as resources in whom it made sense to invest. The initial responsibility lay with the organization. The individual could rest assured that if he did that which was asked of him development and subsequent advancement was guaranteed. He was encouraged to be reactive, to respond to organizational initiatives. This concept of management development is fast being eroded. The societal *responsibility* of the organization is to offer opportunity and perhaps facilities for the individual to improve his skills, to re-qualify or re-align himself professionally. It is in the *interest* of the organization to see that it has first call on the individuals and skills it wishes to retain. It will retain them by, to some extent, paying for the future in the present. The rewards, in terms of higher salaries, stock options, deferred bonuses, pension schemes, will be intended to provide for an individual's future as well as his present. There will then be no obligation to continue to employ the individual when the benefits of his skills begin to be less than their costs. Managerial talent will thus become much more expensive, organizations will become more discriminating, management complements will be fined down, the average age of top and middle management will decrease. Managers of all levels of ability may expect to find themselves and their skills unwanted at their current rates of pay by their early fifties. They will *all* be 'redundant', although society will doubtless find a kinder word. The only difference between the more and the less successful will be that the former will have their future financially protected by their past earnings.

The individual must, therefore, look to himself. Are his current skills likely to be in demand in ten years' time? If not can he acquire new ones; if so what, and how? Going back to school is one alternative. But so many of the managerial skills, whilst they may be taught in the classroom, can only be tried and tempered by experience. Mobility, within or without the same organization, will be the major method of skill acquirement. Since organizations are unlikely, under the new conditions, to want to move individuals much before the expiry date of their current skill, it will be left to individual initiative to prompt and negotiate the transfers.

Self-development is not as easy to practise as it sounds. It implies:

A clear idea of ultimate priorities and directions;
A knowledge of one's own strengths and weaknesses;
A willingness to regard the present as an investment for the future.

1 *Priorities* may well change over time. Travel and variety may be important to the young man, finance to the married man with growing children, self-realization to the older man. The career line will no longer have to progress steadily upwards in terms simultaneously of income, status and interest. Individuals may consciously start to plan for a second career. The portfolio approach to life may become more common, when an individual gains his income from one set of activities, his main interest and purpose from another.

2 *Self-knowledge* is uncomfortable at first. As chapter 3 indicated, we are at pains to protect our self-concept, not to explore it. Yet we may have so many talents and abilities which the zig-zag of our experience has not yet uncovered. What is called a defect in one environment (e.g. meticulousness) may be an asset in another. To make the most of ourselves we must expose ourselves to a range of opportunities and experiences, yet to do so may mean facing up to realities which we had hoped to ignore.

3 *Investment*. Culturally we are conditioned to a personal investment period that finished by the early twenties at the latest. In the new managerial world our stock of learning and conditioning will need continual replenishment. The formal classroom will be the least important of the sources, although it will have its place. The pro-active individual needs to see every experience as a learning opportunity, he needs to be able to learn from success as well as failure, to enrich his stock of concepts and skills as he works. How is this achieved? To learn from experience one must:

(a) Conceptualize the particular incident so that it becomes part of a general rule rather than an isolated anecdote. A collection of anecdotes is no more than a basis for some stories unless they can be linked by concepts. (b) Apply the scientific method to life. Hypothesize, test, hypothesize again. In every significant event one should train oneself to make some predictions about the interplay of variables and the expected outcome. This procedure is the obverse of the first since here one is applying general rules or concepts to particular events. If the prediction is correct the hypothesis is confirmed, the general concept has had another concrete application. If the prediction is incorrect, do not leave it there. Some variable or mix of variables has been left out of account. Some explanatory concept is missing.

Box 12.7 Selfishness or . . .?

I was a young trainee in the giant corporation. After three years of assorted experience I was back in the head offices, sitting in the waiting room of the personnel department, waiting to hear how they proposed to dispose of the next three years of my life. As I was sitting, expectant yet unsure, an old Scotsman on the point of retirement came by, saw me and paused:

'What are you waiting for, laddie?'
'To hear what they've got in store for me,' I replied.
'Ah, invest in yourself, my boy, invest in yourself. If you don't no one else will.'

---

5 In conclusion

5.1

This chapter has looked at:

The manager as G.P.:
The recognition of symptoms;
The meaning of diagnosis;
The types of strategy;
The implementation or treatment.
The managerial dilemmas:
The dilemma of the cultures;
The dilemma of time-horizons;
The trust–control dilemma;
The commando leader's dilemma;
Some ways of handling the dilemmas.
The manager as a person:

Management as a semi-profession;
The need for self-development.

5.2

This chapter has been very much a personal anthology culled from many years of dealing with managers and of being a manager. Other men's anthologies are of interest but are seldom taken to heart. The wise reader will now write his own chapter 12. He will now set down in some more permanent form his own conclusions about the work and management of organizations, his own sets of precepts and heuristics. It is pointless to re-invent the wheel but some chiselling and hammering may help to make it your particular wheel. What we own we value, and are that much more likely to use.

Indeed, the book as a whole is an anthology of other men's findings and thoughts, cast into my words, analogies and metaphors. It has been immeasurably more valuable to me to write it than it can ever be to anyone to read it. If some bits of it cast light on the world as you see it, gather those bits, add them to valued insights from other sources, then burn the rest. There should perhaps be a ritual bonfire every year of the bits of books that no one wants.

Those who manage, or help to manage, organizations seem to me today to have an immensely important role as the rivets of our society. To understand the organizations in which they work must be helpful to them, help them perhaps to make those organizations in their turn more understanding of their people. I would like to think that this book may contribute a little to making the managerial rivets more comfortable and more effective.

But in the end, the best advice one can give anyone who would wish to understand organizations is – try working in them, then go write a book!

13 On the Future of Organizations

1 Introduction

This chapter has been added four years later. The second part of the book will need additions and changes for as long as it is read, because the ways in which we apply our understanding of people, roles and systems need continuous modification and improvement. There is no perfect organization. The first part of the book, on the other hand, should stand up better to time's inspections. I could today add more and, in some cases, better examples. Occasionally some new research has produced a small refinement to our understanding. Some things, too, could be better said and some infelicities removed but the underlying truths about people in relation to people should remain valid in the future.

Fashions change, not people, and Part Two is really about organization fashion or the ways in which we currently see fit to deck out the truths about people in organizational dress. Some fashions are fleeting, others enduring, because some fit our underlying needs and the circumstances of the times better than others. Different times emphasize different priorities which in turn underline some of the truths and ignore others. Wars have always been great disturbers of priorities, and therefore of fashion, but a creeping change in a society's age profile or a major piece of social reform may be just as pervasive. The speed of universal suffrage and the progressive emancipation of women have probably had more to do with changing the ways we run organizations than any refinement of the basic truths or any research into effectiveness. Who would care to predict the impact on organizations when the babies of the post-war boom, which flowered in 1968, reach middle-age in 1988? Organizations have to be the mirrors of our societies however much we may regret that fact and yearn for other times and other places.

This chapter, therefore, is an attempt to be a guide to future fashion. It will look at some fashions on their way out and try to discern some on the way in and to show what this will do to the way we run our organizations. It will then examine some of the problems and possibilities that these changes will present to the manager and to society as a whole. The Chinese ideogram for crisis combines the signs for danger and for opportunity. We need to see both signs clearly when we look into the future lest we be carried away by enthusiasm into extravagant experiment or by dismay into dogged reaction. Two things at least we can be sure of: organizations of some shape and size will still be needed, and people will still be people however we present them.

2 The changing assumptions

2.1

The late Dr Fritz Schumacher was a great believer in curvilinear logic. He argued that many graphs flatten out after a time; they may even turn back on themselves. Every graph is based on a relationship between two factors. The more you have of one the more (or less) you will have of the other. Curvilinear logic does not say that the relationship ceases, it only claims that you can no longer rely on more of one factor producing more of the other; it may only produce the same or even less. Fertilizer improves crops – up to a point. Too much fertilizer will damage not improve. The basic proposition (that fertilizer improves crops) is not contradicted by the obvious fact that you can have too much of a good thing. We automatically apply curvilinear logic to domestic life – to sleep, food, even work. We believe Herzberg when he uses it to create his hygiene factors in motivation. We are less good at seeing the logic *before* it begins to work, in the unfamiliar. It is not to be wondered at. When one of our basic assumptions runs out of steam there is no longer any confident basis for predicting the future. We then enter a condition which has been variously called Discontinuous Change, a Paradigm Shift or even the realm of Catastrophe Theory. It is an uncomfortable situation until some new assumptions have emerged.

I want now to argue that some key assumptions in organizational thinking have reached the end of their useful life. They were only true up to a point, or for a time. We can no longer rely on them for the future. We need a new fashion, maybe a new paradigm.

There are four common assumptions which now need reconsideration. Each of them has heavily influenced the way we have run organizations in the past. They are all now open to question. The first two, however, are still valid, but only up to a point, and in many cases they have reached that point. The second two may need to be abandoned altogether. These assumptions are:

That concentration plus specialization = efficiency;
That hierarchy is natural;
That labour is a cost;
That an organization is a form of property.

We shall consider each in turn.

2.2 Concentration plus specialization = efficiency (the first assumption)

This formula has been at the heart of industrial organizations for at least two hundred years and from there it has spread into other forms of organization where, arguably, it has had less validity. Concentrate your activities, then specialize. That way came the economies of scale which pulled down costs, made yesterday's luxuries today's commonplaces and

---

Box 13.1 Paradigms

The word paradigm was given a new dynamism by T. B. Kuhn in his book *The Structure of Scientific Revolutions*. A paradigm is a conceptual framework, a way of looking at the world, a set of assumed categories into which we pile the facts. When Copernicus suggested that the earth was not at the centre of the universe he was, though he knew it not, a paradigm revolutionary. But it was the minds of men that changed, not the motions of the planets, and the way in which they now viewed that same universe had a profound effect on their beliefs, values and behaviour.

Economic surplus is another example. Today, and for many centuries, it has been assumed that surplus is good. Called 'profit' or 'wealth' it is every man's and every community's legitimate goal. It was not always thus, however. When distribution was difficult, in the early Middle Ages, and markets did not exist for the great majority of products, then surplus meant waste. There was no point in producing more than you and your family and friends needed because you could not dispose of it. Work in those days was necessary, not good. You did as little as you could because more than enough was of no benefit. But with better distribution methods and proper markets things began to change. Luther and Calvin made the notion of surplus respectable, the modern industrial age was born and the Protestant work ethic created.

Social paradigms seem to change when a new technology coincides with a shift in values or priorities. The new paradigm then needs its articulate exponent to spell out and legitimize the new assumptions on which we can begin to build a new era of continuous change. Capitalism, and the concept of money, not land, as the key form of prosperity, needed the two technologies of mass-production and limited liability to make it work. It needed Adam Smith to make it understood and respectable. The result was the rise of the merchant and managerial classes and all the values and social changes which that gave rise to, including exponential economic growth.

Could it be that a new technology of micro-electronics will combine with a new value system to give us a new paradigm, a paradigm only awaiting its prophet?

turned production into the servant of the consumer society. Management became in effect the art or science of co-ordinating the right specializations with the appropriate concentrations. It should be noted that both components had to be present. Concentrations without proper specialization only increased the overheads (as many mergers have demonstrated), while specialization without the necessary size only produced high unit costs.

There are, however, two flaws in the formula, which impose their own limits on the equation. Specialization demands specialists and breeds them. Today's society is a society of specialists whether they have degrees to prove it or a union card. 'Respectable' specialists belong to professions and have associations. Less 'respectable' ones have closed shops and belong to unions. The difference is often only semantic. Now this desirable combination of concentration and specialization has produced those tightly designed organizations which are the joy of the organizational draughtsman in which every cog in the machine has a valid part to play. This is excellent until one of those cogs seizes up, in which case the whole machine grinds to a halt. We see the effect of the tightly designed organization often enough today, for various groups of specialists have come to see that if they can co-ordinate themselves they have the means to hijack the organization. The principle of concentration therefore yields ripe plums to any greedy group of specialists, for in the short term it nearly always pays to buy off the hijackers provided they are not too selfish or avaricious.

The preferred method for dealing with selfish specialists is to appeal to their commitment to the total enterprise, but here the principle of concentration works against us. Humans find it hard to identify with groups in which (a) they do not know everyone at least by sight, or (b) they have no power, formal or informal, to influence events. Concentration too often requires unit sizes and methods of co-ordination making both of these conditions impossible. Only in times of crisis will the individual identify his needs with those of the organization and even then the tale of crisis may not be believed. Imaginative leadership and skilful communications can do something to help out but they are fighting against heavy odds. *In the end* the formula 'concentration plus specialization = efficiency' will self-destruct unless productivity increases always exceed inflation (i.e. the benefits of the formula exceed its cost), which has *never* happened in any industrialized country in recent history. When the costs of the formula exceed its benefits the organization must either become bankrupt or pass on these costs in the form of increased prices. We have seen enough of both these results to realize that this 'organizational assumption' has limits and is subject to curvilinear logic.

Box 13.2   Productivity and wages – some selected statistics

1 *The pressure to reduce labour*[1]
Increases in hourly earnings vs increases in productivity

		1964–73	1975–7
(Average Annual Percentage Increase)			
U.S.	hourly earnings	5·5	8·3
	productivity	1·8	1·4
Japan	hourly earnings	14·5	11·8
	productivity	8·8	4·2
U.K.	hourly earnings	8·9	17·6
	productivity	3·2	0·7
Germany	hourly earnings	8·9	7·4
	productivity	4·6	3·7

2 *The results*[2]

Germany	loss of jobs 1962–75, due to:	
	changes in productivity	6,531,100
	import substitution	1,684,400

1 O.E.C.D., *Economic Outlook*, July 1977
2 World Bank, *Prospects for Developing Countries*, Nov. 1977

The other flaw in the argument has already been outlined in chapter 10 (section 4.2). Another phase for specialization is 'the micro-division of labour', and the psychological costs of this have been well established. Specialization, after all, does mean limitation. This can be marvellous if you are a medical consultant, a professor or an R and D expert when there are unplumbed depths to explore within the small plot you have been given or have chosen. Every day can be new even if your focus remains unchanged. Try, however, digging a plot when there is concrete all around and one foot down. It does get boring – even alienating. Yet specialization has to be defined and confined if the benefits are going to be achieved.

The results are predictable. Work becomes instrumental and is done only for its extrinsic rewards. Therefore, the incentive to exploit any hijack opportunities is much greater. Alternatively, give work a miss. The levels of absenteeism and sick leave are now running at a fairly uniform rate in Northern Europe, twenty-four days annually per worker. This exceptionally large figure must be an index of alienation. To the organizations it is another straight ten per cent on the labour bill.

2.3 Hierarchy is natural (the second assumption)

Organizations have long assumed that one man had to be placed above another to make things happen. It is possible, however, that they were confusing the logic of organizational design with the messages of history. It is true that any organizational work has to be arranged in a logical sequence which roughly corresponds with the order of decisions. The nature of the task must be decided before it is actually embarked upon, the raw materials must be ordered before they are treated. But there is no *logic* which says that this horizontal decision sequence needs to be turned into a vertical ladder so that those who take the necessary earlier decisions are higher in the hierarchy than those who implement them. That is where history comes in, for those who got there first obviously set things up that way. Elliott Jaques, in work referred to in chapter 9 (section 2.4), has demonstrated that those whose jobs involve a 'longer time-span of discretion' do in fact receive more pay. In other words, those positioned earlier in the decision process are in fact higher in the pay league and usually in the authority league. Jaques has gone further; he has turned this into a principle, arguing that those with the larger decisions *should have* proportionately more money.

So far he has had the instinctive support of nearly everyone but as organizations have got larger the worm has begun to turn. Individuals are less prepared to accept *impersonal* authority, less prepared to accept that people they have never met or known and over whom they have no control, should have the right to take decisions which affect their own working lives. When the decision sequence is clear, when the decision-makers are known, when there is some way of influencing those decision-makers if need be, then there is acceptance that greater responsibility should have greater rewards and that the hierarchy of command is necessary and appropriate. No one, however, likes to be at the receiving end of a bureaucracy, particularly when those at the other end appear to be disproportionately better off. Time was when the disaffected could do little about it, but the advent of hijack power has meant that those at the receiving end have negative power at least equal to the positive power of those at the other end.

To call all this 'industrial democracy' is to risk losing the point in a label. The point is that authority increasingly has to be earned – it cannot be assumed. The idea that one's role gave one sufficient position power to do one's job is becoming less and less true. This means:

1 That the game of organizational chess which top managers like to play with positions and people is no longer so straightforward, when it is only

expert or personal power that is effective, for these forms of power (see chapter 6) have to be earned.

2 That the number of levels in a given hierarchy is restricted to the number which can be self-justifying, so that the man at the 'top' can be known and, one hopes, respected by those at the bottom. This is vastly different from the current situation in operating groups.

3 That any decision must increasingly be taken with the consent of those who will have to implement it. This does *not* mean that they have to participate in it (for that would be to ask for more responsibility than is in their psychological contract) but it does mean that they must *know what* is happening and have the chance to comment.

When these principles are followed there is effective industrial democracy. When they are not, the diminishing returns of the old assumption that hierarchy is natural are soon apparent. The assumption is not false but it has its limits and these limits have been exceeded in too many instances.

Box 13.3 Bertrand Russell on work

Work is of two kinds: first, altering the position of matter at or near the earth's surface relative to other such matter; second, telling other people to do so. The first kind is unpleasant and ill-paid; the second is pleasant and highly paid. The second kind is capable of indefinite extension: there are not only those who give orders, but those who give advice as to what orders should be given.

From *In Praise of Idleness*, Unwin Paperbacks, 1976

2.4 Labour is a cost (the third assumption)

Management have long been accustomed to representing their labour as a cost and recording it as such on their profit and loss account. This is another historical situation which is hard to justify logically, but which has had an unquantifiable impact on the way organizations are managed. Costs, after all, are something you minimize and would ideally like to dispense with. Substitute the word 'people' for costs and it is very easy to see how labour can be alienated once it becomes figures not individuals.

Traditionally labour was a variable cost and people could be laid off without notice. Today it is a fixed cost and some organizations even find it profitable to pay an attendance bonus. Gradually, however, some people have begun to query the different ways in which property or capital is handled compared with labour. In 1978 Dunlop proposed to close their tyre factory at Speke in Liverpool. The workers found it natural to argue 'if tyres don't sell that well any more it is management's responsibility to find something which we can make which will sell'. The Dunlop management took the argument seriously enough to set up a joint task force to look for projects. They failed to find any but a point of principle had been established. Excess assets are not returned to the market until management has fully explored all possible alternative uses for them, and even then there are reasonably efficient markets both for money and for property. Labour, on the other hand, has traditionally been dumped on an inefficient market as soon as it is surplus to immediate requirements.

There are those who would argue that if only the labour market were truly efficient we could return to the concept of labour as a variable cost which would undoubtedly make things much easier for management. We must suspect, however, that this assumption (that labour is a cost) is not one of those assumptions which has reached its limit but one of those which has been reversed. It is hard to see how it will ever be turned back again. Labour may remain on the profit and loss account, not the balance sheet (as with the football clubs mentioned in the introduction to chapter 9), but it must henceforth be treated as an asset to be disposed of only after proper thought has been given to its alternative uses.

Many would see this development as right and proper but it significantly affects the way organizations go about their business. For instance:
1 Recruitment and selection become key activities at all levels if you have to keep what you take. It would be logical to expect those jobs to become more important and more highly rewarded.
2 The variables which management can play with in their planning must become the products, not labour or even plant. It is equivalent to saying that you cannot easily change your family, only the things it does. To a management who regards the ending of a product line (with its associated labour) as a purely economic decision, this change in thinking will be hard.
3 Since the labour force is less easily replaceable (because you cannot get rid of it) it will in future make more economic sense to invest time and money in building up the skills and commitment of the individuals even though the pay-off is long-term. In the past you could buy in skills, now you will have to develop them.

2.5 Organizations as property (the fourth assumption)

The Marxist complaint has always been that organizations have been viewed by society as the equivalent of land. Those who provide the money are the owners and can dispose of it as they please. They are, in company law, very privileged owners since they can ruin the property without ruining themselves. The limited liability of companies may have been a most imaginative device to encourage the entrepreneurial use of capital but it has always seemed to some to be an unearned privilege.

Ownership has traditionally entailed both rights and responsibilities. Historically the rights have been better protected by the law, leaving the responsibilities to be taken care of by conscience. In particular, the owners have always had the right to all the residual profits and the right to make decisions on new expenditure and the choice of staff – the critical decisions.

Progressively, the responsibilities of ownership have become enshrined in law. Conscience was in many cases demonstrably not enough. Employment and financial legislation, product liability and consumer protection laws, environmental requirements and disclosure provisions have all proliferated in the last two decades until owners feel more like puppets than free men.

Recently, however, the whole concept of ownership has come into question. Does it really make sense to regard the shareholders as owners when these shareholders are principally institutions representing thousands of anonymous individuals who have no way of knowing what part of what company they own, nor any way of representing their views? Is it not more sensible, it is argued, to regard shareholders only as the providers of finance, with financial privileges proportionate to the risk they run, rather than owners? Who then are the owners? Or does ownership no longer have any real meaning? Is stakeholding the new concept, implying that there are a number of interested parties each with rights and duties appropriate to their interest? In most countries company law is still behind leading practice but more and more an organization is coming to be thought of as a *community* rather than a *property*. The difference is more than semantic. A community belongs to no one, instead one belongs to a community. People have different interests in regard to the community and play different roles within it but no one is owned by anyone else. The fruits of success belong in a sense to all the interested groups. The consumer is entitled to some surplus profit invested in a better or cheaper product, the employees (which now include all the managers) to some bonus, the financiers to a return proportionate to the risk, the state to a higher amount of tax, etc.

Organizations have readily recognized the legitimate constraints placed upon them by the stakeholder concept but they have been less ready to recognize that the old patriarchal ideas of property are dying, if not dead, and will be replaced by the notion of community.

Box 13.4   When stakeholding means something

The Watts, Blake, Bearne group of companies produces ball clay for pottery and china clay for ceramics in Devon, England, where it first started over 250 years ago. It is also, through its international subsidiaries, the largest producer of high-grade plastic clays in the western world.

In the U.K. W.B.B. employ 770 people (plus 142 overseas). They are a profitable (22·7 per cent on capital employed) and growing organization (8 per cent p.a. in real terms).

W.B.B. have worked out an operational definition of stakeholding which has involved some basic rethinking as to what is due to whom. Each year they produce a statement of the distribution of wealth created. In 1978 it looked as follows in percentage terms:

Total remuneration of employees	60%
Company taxes	21%
Shareholders (dividends)	7%
Company (retained for development)	12%
	100%

It is not the statement itself, however, which is so unusual but the fact that they promised *in advance* to give the employees 60 per cent of the value added if this turned out to be in excess of their annual remuneration (which in 1978 came to 58·15 per cent of value added). They are, in other words, stating publicly that a major proportion of the residual surplus, with due provision made for the future of the company, belongs to the employees.

No one can say unequivocally that the continued growth in the sales and profitability of W.B.B. and their excellent industrial relations record is due to this practical and responsible application of the stakeholder concept, but as the outward and visible sign of a managerial philosophy it must have helped.

2.6

Paradigm shifts are uncomfortable. It is not easy when the assumptions with which one grew up turn out to be less true or less certain in maturity. It is understandable that those in the centre of things resist any changes in their assumptions for as long as possible. It is only realistic to expect that any new assumptions will come from the young, outsiders and the newer organizations and will be resisted as rash experiments, dreams or unrealistic philosophies for as long as possible. Some, of course, will be just that but assumptions do change when new technologies and new values arise. Military history is full of the lessons of those who fought the next war with the strategies of the last. The stubborn insistence of the French in the Middle Ages that warfare was essentially a combat of knights blinded them to the potential of the longbow as a weapon of war and set them up as easy prey to the English for a hundred years. The reluctance of the generals in the First World War to acknowledge that the machine gun had altered for ever the tactics of war wiped out a generation of Europe's manhood. Let us hope that today's organizations will not persist too long in fighting the challenges of tomorrow with the methods of yesterday.

3 Clues to the future

3.1

So much for the bad news. Is there any good news? What assumptions will emerge to take the place of the outworn ones? What new paradigms are in the offing? No one sensibly sets himself up as a seer. The future is yet to be created and any sketch plans are bound to be modified by events. However, there do seem to be various clues to some new influences on organizations. Some of these clues may turn out to be false (others have obviously been overlooked) but taken together they do contribute a hazy outline of a new kind of organizational thinking. The clues are:

The communications revolution;
Fees not wages;
Tools not machines;
The economics of quality.

We shall examine each in turn before trying to sketch out what they imply for organizations.

3.2 The communications revolution (the first clue)

The principle of concentration maintained that you pulled everything into the centre and pushed it out again. Rationalization used to mean closing depots and any outlying facilities. This procedure looks like going into reverse. The costs of physical transport will almost certainly go on rising faster than others, mainly because there is at present no practical general alternative to fossil fuel and this is bound to get more expensive as supplies run down, even if each new price rise brings in additional resources, but also because the realistic limits of size and specialization have already been reached in most forms of physical transport.

On the other hand electronic communications systems are getting cheaper in real terms every year, as well as becoming more adaptable and more relevant to our actual needs. Just when it is getting more expensive to move people and things around it is getting cheaper to move information around. It used to be just the opposite; to control operations you needed to have them under your eye. There is some sort of revolution of assumptions going on.

There may soon be very strong *economic* arguments for separating physical manufacture from distribution but linking it electronically to central design and control facilities. Sub-assembly would then become much more common, with the prime manufacturer selling very sophisticated kits to regional agents or even to the actual point-of-sale. Mobile factories or community workshops could proliferate, bringing the manufacturing to the locality in its simplest form.

It will certainly be sensible for organizations to think again about siting new manufacturing facilities as close as possible to the region they will serve. The design and control functions can still be kept in the centre, where the economies of scale and co-ordination can still apply. Many technical operations can now be scaled down without greatly affecting the economics, certainly when the economics of manufacturing are set against the new economics of distribution. New manufacturers entering the U.K. are setting up networks of small plants in the different regions believing that any extra cost in the replication of some facilities will be more than compensated for by the lowered distribution costs and the greater ease of running small plants from a human point of view.

3.3 Fees not wages (the second clue)

This is a shorthand way of saying that the contract between man and organization may be due for a change. At present most people receive a wage or salary. Wages are money paid for time spent and most people effectively sell their *time* as employees. The employer decides, ultimately, how that time should be spent. Fees, on the other hand, are money paid for work done. Professionals and craftsmen charge fees. The calculation of the fee may be based on the time spent but as far as the customer or client is concerned he is paying money for a finished job. When the surgeon has taken out your appendix and presented a bill you are not interested in how much time he took but in whether the job was properly done.

As the costs and the bureaucracy of employment continue to escalate (as they will), more and more organizations are discerning that much of their work can be contracted out to individuals, specialist groups and other organizations. There are three advantages to this:

1 The organization avoids the overheads and the responsibilities of employment (see the argument in the preceding section that labour must now be treated as an asset).

2 The organization can concentrate its control function on quality and price and does not have to worry about all the hygiene factors of management.

3 The relationship between organization and individual becomes much more one of adult-to-adult than parent-to-child. If a piece of work is unsatisfactory the organization refuses to accept it. This is felt to be a more acceptable statement than the criticism of a superior or senior manager that one's work is not up to standard.

There are, of course, some costs. The organization must devote more attention to planning, scheduling and contract setting. Their skills at costing and inspection will be crucial. It is managerially simpler to have all the work under one's direct control; theoretically this permits greater flexibility. In fact it also lays one open to hijack power as well as all the overheads involved. Subcontracting takes many forms:

1 There is franchising. Marks and Spencer in England franchise their production although they do much of the designing and can provide much of the finance. Hamburger chains franchise their product. Other organizations franchise their sales. Some organizations franchise both production and sales keeping only research and design as the critical functions. Publishing is a long established example of total franchising although publishers might not call it that.

2 There is specialist subcontracting. The construction industry has long realized that it does not make sense for any one organization to attempt to provide all the skills needed in a major construction job. The boards outside any major building project provide a vivid example of the contractual organization. On a smaller scale, new businesses frequently contract out accounting and pay-rolls, their market analysis, their delivery. The advertising world is built on a monopoly of subcontracting and is itself beginning to realize that many of its own skills can be subcontracted in turn, leaving the agency very much in the position of a privileged broker.

3 There is group subcontracting. The organization contracts with a group of actual or potential 'employees' to do certain work for a certain price. The 'lump' in the building industry used to be an example of this form of subcontracting until it was outlawed by the trade unions. A shipbuilding firm in the north-east of England has an interesting variation. It negotiates a rate per hour wage for its labour force. It then contracts with a group to do a certain job (e.g. welding the stern of a ship) for a given number of hours to be paid for at the agreed rate. The currency in the contract has become hours not money but the principle is the same.

When contracting with its own employees the organization is in fact treating the wage as a retainer and paying a contract fee in addition. In this way it gets the motivational benefits but still retains all the costs and problems of employment. It is really an extension of the old piece-work system and can easily inherit all the same problems and difficulties.

In the era of the big organization, self-sufficient in all its aspects, we have forgotten that most businesses have always been based on the principle of contracting. Even today most manufacturing companies are in fact assembly operators with often over 1,000 suppliers of parts or pieces. The contractual organization has always been with us. We need now to recognize the principles and practices involved and extend these to individuals and small groups as well as to other organizations. Many of an organization's specialist skills and services could be placed on a contractual basis, using the same people to the mutual benefit of both parties.

3.4 Tools not machines (the third clue)

This distinction was emphasized by Schumacher in his book *Small is Beautiful*. A tool is something which extends the capacities of the individual. A machine is another thing again, greater than a man, needing men to service it but essentially independent of them. The industrial revolution substituted machines for tools, introducing mass-production and the microdivision of labour. The next stage in the industrial revolution, founded on the silicon chip, is likely to be a return from machines to tools. Today one can purchase for £200 an automated sewing machine which effectively puts the textile factory of a hundred years ago into a suburban bedroom. Machines can now, in many cases, be reduced in scale until they are the equivalent of a very sophisticated tool, to be used as an extension of a man. The robots of the modern factory are, in effect, the tools of modern man.

The impact of this switch back from machines to tools has yet to be appreciated by organizations and society. Within organizations it allows the whole process of splitting up the work into its component parts to be reversed. A man or a small group can once again be responsible for a complete piece of work. True, the tool will do most of it, but tools are ultimately the servants of man, while machines have been his masters. The robot will weld the car body, but man will have trained the robot and can retrain it.

The advent of these sophisticated tools, however, permits yet more adventurous ideas. The work need no longer be done under the same roof. While men had to come to machines, tools go with men. There could be a return to a sophisticated network pattern, with organizations providing the tools and the raw materials and the individual using them at home, at a communal workshop or at the old factory if he so chooses. Such a concept of out-work fits well with the other pressure, to substitute fees (for work done) for wages (for time spent).

It could go farther still. J. Gershuny has argued that we are heading for a self-service society in which the manufacturing sector increasingly produces capital goods for use in the home. Just as the automatic washing-machine displaced the laundry, so other forms of domestic capital equipment will allow us to do for ourselves things that others at present do for us. The average household now contains more capital equipment per head than the average factory at the turn of the century.

This last phenomenon will have a big impact on the product strategy of business organizations. There may be an increasing market for sub-assemblies, leaving the customer to do the final work for himself. Many service occupations (e.g. automobile servicing) may return to the customer to do himself with new tools. A form of domestic import substitution may actually reduce the total number of transactions while increasing output. It is a technologically sophisticated route to self-sufficiency.

Combine this new self-sufficiency with a capacity for more out-work and more subcontracted service work and you end up with the notion of *flexi-lives*, with individuals able to make more independent choices as to how, where and when they work. This new-found choice may mean great freedom for those who take it. It may not be so great for those who find flexi-life thrust upon them as conventional employment is reduced. It will not make the management task any simpler but it will certainly make it different and, with care, more efficient.

Box 13.5 The household economy?

[A] third stategy is . . . to start to consider the redesign of the household. Consider: if more time were available there would be no need to make the use of household capital so unrewarding. Take cooking for example: it is potentially the ultimate in non-alienating production. A pleasurable task in itself, it uses one's own capital and one's own labour for one's own consumption. So why stop at cooking? The level of investment in a middle-class kitchen could easily provide an adequate basic carpenter's or metal-working shop, or a pottery lathe and kiln. A very wide range of needs could be provided for in this manner, and a small commune or co-operative could provide an ever wider range . . . As production in the money economy gets more efficient and simpler capital goods get cheaper, the facilities for me to do this get ever more readily available.

From Gershuny, *After Industrial Society: The Emerging Self-Service Economy?*, Macmillan, 1978

> **Box 13.6   The unions and the new society**
>
> The role of the unions becomes interesting as fees start to replace wages. At present they are essentially pay brokers in the wage economy. As this diminishes their role will shrink, unless they change it. At first, therefore, they may be expected to resist any trend towards the contractual organization (a strike by oil-company drivers in the U.K. in December 1979 was about this very issue) but ultimately the economic and social pressures are likely to prove too strong for them. There is, however, another role waiting to be taken up, that of certificating the growing number of independent workers. How will one know that plumbers, fitters, maintenancemen or carpenters are competent unless there is some certificating body? It is a role that the professional associations perform for the professions. It is a role that the old guilds used to perform. It is already badly needed in the growing 'informal economy'where a variety of trades, unpoliced and unregulated, are practised. Will the unions become certificating bodies?

3.5 The economics of quality (the fourth clue)

Economics is the study of value added. Traditionally this added value has been measured by the transaction price of the finished goods or services – what people will pay for them. A society's economic wealth is measured by the sum of all those transactions. It follows that the more of these there are the richer society is judged to be. As far as economics is concerned it makes no difference whether these transactions are in good commodities or bad, whether they involve building schools, nuclear power plants or guns. It is all wealth. The same concept was generally thought to apply to individuals. Individual wealth is conventionally measured by one's expenditure or one's capacity for expenditure. More wealth is good, for individuals and for societies. It has only been the distribution of that wealth within society which has seriously concerned politicians, and it has been assumed that all individuals, or at any rate most individuals at work, would like more personal wealth even if it did then bring difficult choices as to how to spend it. As a result, assumptions built on the rationality of Economic Man have been heavily embedded in our societies and organizations for generations, even though everyone would acknowledge that Economic Man is only part of our complex psychological calculus (see chapter 2).

There are signs, however, that the premises which underlie the economics of quantity may no longer be as valid as they once seemed. Let us look at some of the reasons.

(a) *Hirsch's theory of positional goods*. Professor Hirsch, in a book published shortly before his death in 1978, argues that after a certain stage in material growth societies achieve a state of prosperity in which most people have all that they need on which to live relatively comfortably. Of course, *relative* poverty will always exist and pockets of *absolute* poverty may still be found due to mismanagement or inefficient policies, but the bulk of the population is well provided for. For what, then, do people work? When you have one good washing-machine you do not really need two. Hirsch suggests that at this stage people work for the things that set them apart from their neighbours. At first these might be material things (a bigger car or better stereo system) but ultimately they want things that have a built-in exclusivity, such as a house with an uninterrupted view; privileged educational facilities or membership of an elite club. Because the value of these things lies in their exclusivity it follows that you cannot, by definition, have too many of them because they would then lose their appeal. Too many unusual houses and the house no longer has its uninterrupted view. This, says Hirsch, is the real limit to material growth. There is a built-in social limit to man's ambitions. Only the few, and not the many, can be satisfied by positional goods. What then do the others do? They may envy. They may even seek to disrupt a society that reserves its top rewards for a few. Many, certainly, will increasingly re-adjust their motivation calculus realizing that if the real rewards are unattainable, they must be content with what is available.

Quantity, Hirsch implies, is not eventually enough. This suggestion strikes at the heart of conventional economics.

(b) *A shift in values*. Another interpretation of the satiation of material ambition would give a new priority to non-materialistic goals. If people have all the money they actually need, if not want, and if they also see that more money does not actually bring the desired happiness, they may prefer to trade money for other things; for discretionary time, for instance, for better conditions at work including more freedom or autonomy as well as better lighting or better food.

Under this interpretation we may increasingly expect union agreements to feature shorter working weeks and provision for more autonomy at work. At present most people in Northern Europe, America and Australia still work the 'three forty-eights' (forty-eight hours per week, for forty-eight weeks a year, for forty-eight years of their life). We may well see this dropping to three thirty-fives as individuals increasingly trade money for time.

If this interpretation is correct one would expect the non-materialistic values to show up more markedly in the new generations who have grown

Box 13.7 Changing values

Ronald Inglehart has made a major study of what he terms the post-materialistic (*P. Mats.*) values in Europe and the U.S.A. A slice of his results is given below.

Some selected statistics[1]

Values by age, controlling for education in seven nations

Respondent's education

	Primary			Secondary			University		
Ages	P. Mats.	Mats.	No.	P. Mats.	Mats.	No.	P. Mats.	Mats.	No.
16–24	31%	13%	(1,139)	23%	22%	(1,995)	13%	39%	(492)
25–34	38	8	(1,839)	30	15	(1,635)	16	37	(362)
35–44	44	7	(2,169)	33	13	(1,352)	19	31	(259)
45–54	44	6	(2,119)	34	14	(1,015)	25	20	(165)
55–64	49	6	(2,175)	37	9	(693)	36	12	(122)
65+	52	4	(2,221)	51	4	(535)	34	12	(123)

Spread between youngest and oldest cohorts

+21	−9		+28	−18		+11	−27	

Based on combined results of the 1970 and 1971 European surveys, plus the American survey of May, 1972

1. Ronald Inglehart, *The Silent Revolution*

up in affluence, particularly those who have been best prepared, through education, to take advantage of the materialistic society. Box 13.7 suggests that this is in fact happening. If the future leaders of our society have begun to turn from the economics of quantity to the economics of quality then the premises of economics must indeed be rewritten.

(c) *The personal economy and Micawber wealth.* Economics have always been principally concerned with the formal transactions of people, where goods or services are traded for money in one way or another, but a large slice of life has always taken place in the more informal economies of the household, the voluntary agencies and free recreation. Because nothing is officially traded, those activities, which add value of one sort or another, have never been counted. Indeed a slice of apparent economic growth has always been due to some of these informal, personal activities getting formalized and therefore counted. When you buy potatoes instead of growing them the formal, visible economy grows but the number of potatoes grown and consumed remains the same. Similarly if activities pass back from the formal economy to the household the economy may appear to shrink even though the same activities are still performed. There are at present signs that the personal economy may be growing in all the industrialized countries now that more people have further discretionary time, better education and more tools and equipment to do things for themselves.

This trend will not only conceal the true state of affairs from formal economics in government or elsewhere, it will introduce more people to a new concept of wealth. Those who live principally in the personal economy do not measure wealth by the capacity for expenditure. They instinctively look upon it much as Mr Micawber did in Dickens's picture of him. Mr Micawber was fond of saying that happiness was an income of twenty pounds when expenditure was nineteen pounds nineteen shillings and six-pence, which turned to misery if the expenditure was twenty pounds and sixpence. Wealth to Mr Micawber was not the capacity to spend but the difference between what you had and what you needed to spend. The difference is subtle but crucial. Under the Micawber definition you can increase your wealth either by increasing your income or by reducing your expenditure needs. In the personal economy the latter is often the most favoured as people, instead of buying something, learn how to make it or do it themselves.

If economic activity moves back to the household we may well see a big switch from the economics of quantity to the economics of quality.

For organizations the consequences are clear. They will no longer be able to rely on the wage packet to be the panacea in issues of motivation, relationships or authority and control. Pay will still matter, of course, but so will other things. When people only have to work a little to satisfy their material needs you will need to rely on the other parts of your calculus to get them to work more than a little.

4 Possibilities and problems

4.1

The changeover in fashions and assumptions opens up a mixed bag of possibilities and problems. We will look briefly at three of them:

The federal organization;
Spliced careers;
New patterns of planning.

4.2 The federal organization

Federalism is the way to combine the autonomy of individual parts with the economics of co-ordination. Many of the pressures described in the previous sections will push organizations towards a smaller size of spending unit. Opinions vary about what that optimum may be. It depends partly on the technology and the way the work has to be organized, but most people put the upper limit at around 500 people. These individual units, however, can still be co-ordinated centrally provided that the right information is available at the right time. Information, however, is one of the few things that we seem to be certain to have in more abundance and in greater variety than ever before. It is just as well because one of the few consistent findings of the research on organization structures has been that more decentralization is always accompanied by more information.

Federalism, however, is subtly different from decentralization. The subtleties are not always well understood, particularly in those countries which do not have a tradition of federalism in their political life. The British, for instance, have always seen federalism as a way of weakening one's past enemies or, at least, as a form of compromise when a central government was unrealizable. In fact, the supposed compromise usually turned out to be a strength (in Australia, West Germany, even Canada for a long time).

Decentralization implies a delegation of power from an all-powerful centre. Federalism implies that the power really resides with the constituent parts (e.g. the states) who cede part of that power to the centre for the benefits of all. Thus, in federal states, the capital is seldom the most important city – it is there only for the co-ordination of government and is usually not a centre of economic or artistic activity.

Federal organizations, similarly, will rely on a small nerve centre co-ordinating a range of small, nearly autonomous operations which can be widely dispersed geographically. The concept of a holding company which has been a financial and legal reality will begin to mean more in strict organizational terms and will be as common in the integrated manufacturing company as it is in the financial world.

Unlike the traditional holding company, however, the federal centre may not always own the autonomous parts. In order to give proper expression to the ideas of stakeholders and community the ownership of those autonomous parts may well be more widely distributed (amongst employees and stakeholders) than is currently fashionable. The power of ownership will not therefore reside in the centre but in the parts. It is this shift in power which will make federalism a reality, making the centre truly the servant of the whole, not the master of it.

Dovetailing into the federal organization is the concept of the contractual organization. The contractual organization is built on the notion of fees rather than wages and on the principle of subcontracting. One way to keep the staff of the main-stream operations under 500 is to hive off as much of the operation as you can to outside individuals, groups or organizations.

Carefully worked out and carefully monitored, a subcontracting programme can provide the flexibility which will defeat the power of the hijacker, and the means to ride the interacting life cycles of one's product range without disrupting too much of the core of the organization. It remains true, however, that the management of a contractual organization, even with all the information you need on-line, is different from, and probably more difficult than, the management of a more conventional organization.

Federal, contractual organizations pose problems as well as possibilities.

4.3 Spliced careers

In 1980 it is still true that 90 per cent of those who work do so in an organization. Most of those will assume that they will continue working in that

---

Box 13.8 Federal organizations

It is interesting to speculate on some of the more successful federal organizations and states.

The International Postal Federation is an impressive organization. In spite of the increasing inefficiency of most national postal services it is still taken for granted that the letter you mail in Paris to Santiago in Chile will reach there in a reasonable time, safely and still comparatively cheaply. As a model of co-ordination and efficient operation it ranks high and yet who knows where its head office is or who might be its chief executive?

Switzerland, similarly, is a very efficient country. Whether one shares the values of the Swiss or not, no one denies that it is a country that works well, in spite of four different languages, some of the most difficult terrain in the world, and a record of independence in the cantons for many centuries. Yet who could tell you the name of the first minister in the Swiss government? How many are even sure of the name of the capital city?

I.T.T. is a famous conglomerate, a household name even when it has not sought such fame. It has a very intricate but deliberate federal structure in its European operations. At a recent conference attended by senior managers of many of the I.T.T. companies in Europe the speaker opened one session by asking all those who worked for I.T.T. to raise their hands. Only two hands went up although all twenty-two managers present were theoretically I.T.T. employees. Those two were people who worked in the federal headquarters in Brussels. The others all identified with their own national companies (which did not include I.T.T. in their title) *not with the parent organization.*

organization, or one very like it, until they retire at some age around sixty. This will soon be an uncommon assumption. The 'three forty-eights', as we have already noticed, are probably on the way out.

In years to come people may look forward (with mixed delight and apprehension) to a more varied work career. For some it will still be true that they will work for an organization for forty years. For more, however, it will be a mix of employment and self-employment. This mix could happen in various ways:

(a) *End-to-end*. Employment will give way to self-employment as people in their forties or early fifties begin to see the advantages of more flexible contract work outside the firm. For many people such self-employment may happen involuntarily as firms begin to retire employees even earlier, perhaps substituting a capital sum for a pension. In case this seems odd or inhuman it is wise to remember that the Armed Services in Britain have been pursuing such a policy for many years. Of course, most of those leaving the forces have opted for more employment, but this option may not be so readily available in the future. We may see it becoming increasingly common for 'responsible' employers to prepare their people for exit by ensuring that they have the necessary skills to stand on their own before they leave employment. In-company courses geared to exit may become more frequent.

(b) *Alternating*. The more professionally skilled may choose to alternate periods of employment with periods of self-employment, rather as some married women do today, opting in and out of the full-time work force to suit their domestic circumstances. For some the idea of a sabbatical, or re-training, will be an increasingly necessary and attractive possibility and the development of continuing education, paid for by either the state, the firm or the individual, must be one of the growth areas of the future, along with new certificating bodies.

(c) *Complementary*. There will almost certainly be a growth in part-time employment. When organizations need extra labour or skills they will be increasingly tempted to look for part-time employees who will not require the same kind of organizational guarantees that apply to full-time workers. Many people will make up the balance of the work they require with self-employment. Because it is marginal, both to society and to the individual, much of this work will take place in the so-called informal economy. Rather than disparage this economy, society may well find that it provides a useful alternative to unemployment and is indeed a preparation for eventual full-time legitimate self-employment. A shorter working week will give everyone the opportunity for some part-time self-employment. This will not necessarily be undesirable.

The 'spliced careers' of the future will bring fundamental changes to the personnel functions in organizations. The counselling side of their work is bound to increase as the options for the individual multiply. The variety of employment and contract arrangements, although they will increase flexibility, must also bring administrative headaches. The question of training (for the individual and for the organization) will be a major issue with smaller organizations undoubtedly seeking to ride on the backs of the bigger ones by poaching their people in mid life. The whole question of pensions and individual rights will become more complicated and some major rethinking will be necessary if we are to avoid the situation where a small number of present-day employees are supporting three or four times their number of past employees in an inflationary age, unthought of when the schemes were originally funded. As *self-employment* of various sorts becomes more common the notion of *unemployment* may be of decreasing relevance and importance – the world does not have to be divided between employed and unemployed when there are so many variations on the theme of work.

4.4 Patterns of planning

Discontinuous change makes planning difficult. When change is in a continuous pattern it is possible to project the trends and to make some reasonable assumptions as to the actions and reactions required. But when the trends run off the graph paper, or reverse themselves, the process no longer works. What does one do when the facts run out? Many people do nothing or, rather, they do the same only more so. If aggressive advertising has always helped in the past it seems reasonable to do even more aggressive advertising when the situation seems even more dismaying, but if the problem has changed there can be no guarantee that yesterday's solutions will work tomorrow.

Under conditions of discontinuity change comes in from outside and new ways can overtake you before you are aware of what is happening. You are by-passed unless you change your approach to the future.

Organizations have traditionally approached the future by attempting to reduce uncertainty. Whole theories of management have been based on reduction of uncertainty. Such an approach works out well when you can control, or at least predict, your environment. It is potentially self-destructive when change is discontinuous and the environment unpredictable. In such situations organizations have no alternative but to adopt the experimental approach. This approach is akin to systematic gambling. Different openings and possibilities are explored. Initial success is re-inforced and failures are discarded. Expensive bids are laid off through alliances and security is sought in variety rather than certainty. Oil companies bidding for exploration contracts in the English North Sea understood the concept.

The experimental approach puts planning back into the boardroom for it is a matter of sequential decisions rather than scenario paintings. Estimates, scenarios and careful monitoring are all necessary but on a walk into a fog a light is not much use, you have to stop and feel your way. Loose-linked organizations help to contain the risk and to provide the flexibility for experiment. The federal contractual organization which may be thrust upon us for other reasons may be well suited for discontinuous change but the managers in them may not adapt so readily.

5 In conclusion

We have argued that fashion is as important to organization design as any underlying theory of behaviour. Changing values in the environment linked

---

Box 13.9 The vanishing laboratories

I was meeting with the board of a firm which ran a number of photographic laboratories, processing camera films for various chemists and photographic dealers who collected and returned these films to the private customer.

The discussion that morning concerned the new technologies which were beginning to affect the industry. There was general agreement that the day was not far off (five to seven years) when a large box could effectively replace the laboratory. This box could be placed in a corner of a shop and would process any film dropped into it, making the laboratories and the collection/delivery system obsolete.

After a break for coffee the board started to discuss the next item on the agenda – the long-term plan. This was discussed without any apparent reference to the previous topic except that they agreed that increased emphasis on efficiency was desirable in the light of probable 'new competition'. In other words, no real action was taken to deal with the discontinuous change which they all foresaw. Within ten years, though, such a box will have been developed by some newcomer to the industry and all the traditional structure of that industry will be outmoded and by-passed. Yet that board was not in the box-inventing game. They ran laboratories and all they knew was how to run them better. Was it their fault if discontinuous change made their laboratories irrelevant? Can you plan for discontinuous change?

to a changing technology will affect current assumptions of what makes organizational sense. What has appeared to be true for ever may turn out to be only partially true. When that happens change is discontinuous and disconcerting. You can then no longer run tomorrow's organizations on yesterday's assumptions.

The assumptions which appear to be losing their value are:

That concentration plus specialization = efficiency;
That hierarchy is natural;
That labour is a cost;
That an organization is a property.

Four clues to the future are:

The communications revolution;
Fees in place of wages;
Tools in place of machines;
The economics of quality.

These will produce new challenges to organizations, including:

The idea of federalism;
Spliced careers;
New patterns of planning.

It will, one hopes, be an evolution not a revolution. Technologies, products, ideas – they all have life cycles. They flourish then wane. So it is with organizations and the assumptions on which they have been built. The trick is to manage the switch from the end of one life cycle to the start of another. Firms which can do this with their products remain in business. Organizations which can allow old ways to die and new ways to grow will survive and have the chance to prosper. The acceptance of death as the prelude to new life is an age-old recipe for the survival of nature, society and the human race. It also applies to organizations.

Part Three
A Guide to Further Study

Introduction to Part Three

The many writers on aspects of Organization Theory are particularly prolix. It is a full-time occupation to keep abreast of all the outpouring of research, theory and speculation in even one of the subdivisions of the field. Anyone who, like myself, is interested and involved over the whole range of topics, must settle for selectivity in his reading and further study.

This part of the book is a signpost to one brand of selectivity. Others could list several totally different selections; they might all be equally good. I have tried to keep my lists of references short and yet to include in each list some overview of the field, some of the classic works, as well as references to any of the really crucial research studies. But I have above all sought to share with the reader my perceptions of the most interesting and thought-provoking works.

Those already knowledgeable in the literature of the field will no doubt be amazed at my omissions and puzzled by some of the inclusions. Whilst I feel that no apology need be made for a personal anthology, anyone following the trail I have laid should always remember that it is indeed very personal and makes no claim to be all-encompassing.

In addition to providing lists of references this part of the book also contains some short discussions of a few of the underlying assumptions in the area. I have not always found myself satisfied with the premises on which some of the research and theory is founded and have thought it proper to share with any reader my doubts and preconceptions since these undoubtedly colour the interpretation taken in the main text.

The comments, and the references, are listed by section and chapter.

Chapter 1

Chapter 1 in Part One made some assumptions but did not attempt to delve into either of two distinctly murky areas:

The philosophical base of the social sciences as opposed to the physical sciences;
The nature, meaning and origins of 'organization theory'.

1 The philosophical base of the social sciences

This question must lie at the heart of any book or piece of research in this area. Any inquirer into this topic would do well to start with John Stuart Mill and Book 6 of his *System of Logic*. Mill's position, though perhaps rather simplistically stated, underlines the attitudes of a large number of contemporary social scientists. Mill believed that the 'moral sciences' were 'a blot on the face of science'. The way to remove this was to generalize the methods used in those subjects 'on which the results obtained have finally received the unanimous assent of all who have attended the proof'. The social sciences should in fact be just a branch of science in general. The problems, he believed, lay in the complexity of human situations. Therefore we can only make statistical generalizations about the probable outcome of human situations. 'The agencies which determine human character are so numerous and diversified . . . that in the aggregate they are never in two cases exactly similar.'

Weber's viewpoint is also important. He says:

Every interpretation aims at self-evidence or immediate plausibility. But an interpretation which makes the meaning of a piece of behaviour as self-evidently obvious as you like cannot claim just on that account to be the causally valid interpretation as well. In itself it is nothing more than a particularly plausible hypothesis.

He goes on to say that the appropriate way to verify such an hypothesis is to establish statistical laws based on observation of what happens. In this way he arrives at the conception of a sociological law as a 'statistical regularity which corresponds to an intelligible intended meaning'.
There are two major issues involved here.

1 Is 'understanding' improved by supplementing it by a different method altogether, e.g. statistics? Or is it akin to historical understanding – the unravelling of an inter-relationship between events in their context, which cannot necessarily be tested statistically? Is Mill right and is it merely a problem of complexity, or is the problem not one of degree but of kind? Is 'understanding' in the social sciences of a different logical order than in the physical sciences?

A good discussion of these issues, but difficult for non-philosophers, is provided by Winch in *The Idea of a Social Science*. He mentions a pleasing analogy:

The difference is precisely analogous to that between being able to formulate statistical laws about the likely occurrences of words in a language and being able to understand what was being said by someone who spoke the language. The latter can never be reduced to the former; a man who understands Chinese is not a man who has a firm grasp of the statistical probabilities for the occurrence of the various words in the Chinese language.

One could add that the latter facility has some obvious utilities, which can be practised by someone who has no understanding of the language at all.

2 Can human decisions be 'predicted' in the sense that Mill meant? Can the laws of causality in their simple form (whenever A, then B) apply to a human decision? Or does the use of the very word 'decide' imply our conviction that a human being has the power and the right to override the influencing forces? Should we therefore follow Popper and talk of 'trends' rather than of laws in social science generally as in history? This does not mean that we cannot often anticipate decisions, only that we cannot, logically as well as statistically, expect to be able to predict them with total certainty.

Bertrand Russell, towards the end of his life, gave an interesting lecture on the philosophy of history, published in *Portraits from Memory*. He makes the following points:

1 History is both a science and an art. When it is described as scientific two things are meant:

(a) The ascertaining of facts in a scientific manner;
(b) The search for the discovery of causal laws.

Although (b), as well as (a), is entirely laudable it is not what gives most value to historical studies. In history we are interested in the particular fact as well as the causal sequences.

Even when causal sequences are established as regards the past, there is not much reason to expect that they will hold in the future, because the relevant facts are so complex that unforeseeable changes may falsify our prediction. . . For these reasons I think that scientific laws in history are neither so important nor so discoverable as is sometimes maintained.

2 If history is to be of value to any besides historians it must be interesting. This means that it must be well presented and presented with feeling. The historian writing for non-historians is encouraged to have views. His examination of the facts should be impartial but his interpretation is allowed, indeed encouraged, to be personal.

Russell is not advocating intellectual idleness. He sees a division of labour in the study of history. There are those whose time is spent in the unearthing and definition of basic facts and observations. But just as Einstein did not himself make the observations on which his doctrines were based, just as Kepler's laws were based on the observations of Tycho Brahe, so there is a need for the interpreter, the man who can hold a multiplicity of facts within the unity of a single temperament.

Russell was talking of history. We are concerned with organization theory. I would hold that his remarks are just as pertinent to the latter. Scientific observations and the scientific unearthing of the facts of organizational behaviour are most important; so is the establishment of any causal sequences that can be traced. But we should not expect such causal sequences to be endlessly repeatable, to hold good for all time, nor should we look to them for a total understanding of organizations and what happens within them.

The distinction between those who work for other theorists and those who interpret the basic findings is also important. Those who seek to do both will tend towards a perceptual bias. They will inevitably seek to interpret the world in the light of their particular discoveries. Interestingly, as with historians, the organizational interpreters are assessed by society not so much on the scientific validity of their work but on whether leading practitioners find it interesting and meaningful.

I have stressed the arguments against scientism in organizational theory, partly because I think they need to be made, but partly because this book is clearly an interpretative approach and must be judged as such. For those who wish to explore further into the scientific side of the field and its methodology I would recommend Kaplan, the first few chapters of Cummings and Scott and the section on Methodologies in March, which has a wealth of further references.

2 Organization theory

This field of study has in the past been bedevilled by the fact that for many years the leading theorists grew up in one or other of the supporting disciplines of anthropology, sociology, psychology or social psychology. Inevitably their theoretical perspectives and their research training coloured their approach to this area of problems. Thus the sociologist tended to regard individual differences as deviations from a norm of zero, whilst the psychologist tended to relegate all the organizational determinants of behaviour to the category of 'the environment', something that should be held constant as long as possible in order to permit the study of individuals. The advent of 'systems theory' at least meant that a wide variety of disciplines appeared to be talking in approximately the same language about similar problems. However, an inter-disciplinary approach, respectable in its own right, is beginning to emerge. Pugh's paper 'Modern organization theory', to be found in numerous anthologies as well as under the original citation, is a very good overall view of this problem although it is, in my view, slightly coloured by the Weberian philosophy on the social sciences.

Pugh distinguishes between the following categories.

Management theorists;
Structural theorists;
Group theorists;
Individual theorists;
Technology theorists;
Economic theorists.

Other reviews of the field take either an historical perspective (a good concise one is to be found in the first half of Baker). Others focus more on the individual theorists. The Penguin book of readings on organization theory, edited by Pugh, is a useful way of tasting the original writings of the leading theorists, and contains references to further readings. Perrow takes a critical look at the various approaches to organization theories before coming up with a neo-Weberian approach. The book is a readable and knowledgeable review from a sociologist.

This book does not attempt such an overview, partly because it is available elsewhere, but also because this quasi-biographical approach to organization theory, though an interesting way of following the trends of thought, does not always seem to be particularly helpful. The viewpoints of these leading theorists will always be discussed where relevant, but anyone looking for a complete and systematic overview of the literature in this field should consult March.

I have not found any definition of a political system among the political theorists that exactly fits mine, but Easton's discussion of the political system is perhaps the most relevant. There is an increasing interest by sociologists in the political aspects of organizations. Burns and Stalker, in their introduction, examine some of the origins and consequences of political behaviour in organizations. Crozier in France and Dalton in the U.S.A. have contributed valuable field studies, although their conception of 'political' is more restricted than mine. The growing body of work by Pettigrew has been particularly helpful to my thinking.

References

BAKER, R. J. S. (1972), *Administrative Theory and Public Administration*, Hutchinson.

BURNS, T., and STALKER, G. M. (1966), *The Management of Innovation*, Tavistock.

CROZIER, M. (1964), *The Bureaucratic Phenomenon*, Tavistock.

CUMMINGS, L. L., and SCOTT, W. E. (eds.) (1969), *Readings in Organizational Behaviour and Human Performance*, Irwin.

DALTON, M. (1959), *Men Who Manage*, Wiley.

EASTON, D. (1953), *The Political System*, Knopf.

KAPLAN, A. (1964), *The Conduct of Inquiry*, Chandler.

MARCH, J. G. (ed.) (1965), *Handbook of Organizations*, Rand McNally.

MILL, J. S. (1843), *System of Logic*, Longman. (This edition published 1971).

PERROW, C. (1972), *Complex Organizations*, Scott, Foreman & Co., New York.

PETTIGREW, A. M. (1973), *The Politics of Organizational Decision-Making*, Tavistock.

POPPER, K. (1959), *The Poverty of Historicism*, Routledge & Kegan Paul.

PUGH, D. S. (1966), 'Modern organization theory', *Psychol. Bull.*, vol. 66, pp. 235–51.

PUGH, D. S. (ed.) (1971), *Organization Theory, Selected Readings*, Penguin.

RUSSELL, B. (1958), *Portraits from Memory*, Allen & Unwin.

WEBER, M. (1956), *Wirtschaft und Gesellschaft*, J. C. B. Mohr.

WINCH, R. (1958), *The Idea of a Social Science*, Routledge & Kegan Paul.

Chapter 2

1

The field of motivation theory is enormous, and the studies range widely. In Part One I have not attempted to list any of the studies or to give a systematic review of the literature but rather to pull some of the theories together into a reasonably coherent model. In doing so I found the book edited by Vroom and Deci to be an invaluable, concise collection of the principal source material.

2

Vroom, in his introduction, gives an overview of motivation theory which I have followed in part. Schein cites the principal research studies. Vroom's earlier book is a systematic and detailed review of the theories up to 1964. For studies prior to 1955 the Brayfield and Crockett review (in Vroom and Deci), on the relationship of attitudes to performance, is useful. All of these works, in their turn, list the primary sources.

Porter and Lawler's work gives a good overview of satisfaction theories, and suggests, amongst other things, that satisfaction is the result rather than the cause of productivity.

The essence of Maslow's approach is contained in an extract in Vroom and Deci's book of readings. McGregor and Likert are also represented in that collection, but since their principal works will tend to be referred to on several occasions in this book, I have listed them among the references.

Schein usefully discusses assumptions about man. Levinson's views are concisely presented in his 1972 article.

The motivation calculus model traces its ancestry back to three parents:

1 The Path–Goal approach originally suggested by Georgopoulous, Mahoney and Jones in 1957 and reproduced in Vroom and Deci.
2 Vroom's emphasis on valence, instrumentality and force in his 1964 book.

3 Porter and Lawler's expectancy model in 1968 which was built on the two preceding sources and tested by their own research.

All of these theorists were concerned to develop specific testable hypotheses arising out of their models. Desirable though this is, it did limit them to looking at fairly specific decision situations, usually where the individual was in effect choosing between two activities or two levels of activities. I have been concerned to extend the implications of their models and to link them with other concepts such as psychological maturity, the psychological contract, dissonance reduction, in order to give them wider, but less exact, predictability.

Porter and Lawler's work is most fully described in their 1968 book, but their 1968 article is a shorter description of their views and findings.

Herzberg's work is best described in his 1966 book. A lot of controversy has centred around Herzberg's work. Most of it has concentrated on his methodology and the fact that, given the way he asks his questions, you are likely to find the dissatisfying elements located in the conditions of work and the satisfying ones in the employees' contribution. Anyone interested in pursuing this controversy should read House and Wigdor. For my own part I find that his basic argument has a lot of face validity, given that motivation is essentially a subjective phenomenon, i.e. as the individual concerned sees it.

An interesting repeat of Herzberg's study in Texas Instruments is described by Scott Myers.

McClelland's views are to be found in his 1961 book and are aptly summarized and commented upon in Kolb *et al*. Whyte has another approach called Sentiments and Symbols which it was not possible to summarize in Part 1 but is worth studying.

A motivation model based on McClelland's concepts is put forward by Atkinson and well described by Litwin and Stringer (1968). It is very similar to the motivation calculus.

Personality theory is a fascinating area which has not been linked closely enough to motivation theory. Argyris's discussion of the fusion of the formal organization and the individual is one such link. His book (1960) will direct the reader to the most relevant personality theorists such as Erikson, Kelly, Sullivan, Fromm and Horney. In this work Argyris also discusses the question of psychological growth.

The importance of goal-setting will recur as a topic later in this book. A most interesting review of the research is contained in Dunbar.

4

It was probably Levinson who originally used the term 'psychological contract' but the principle of reciprocity has been around in sociology for some time. I have followed Schein's application of the concept.

The discussion on the type of contract has been much influenced by Etzioni's classification of organizations based on the predominant type of power and the type of investment of the members. He does not himself talk of a psychological contract and I have used the device of the contract to blur his distinction between the type of power used and the type of involvement, mainly because I have not found the distinction very helpful, nor all his words to describe them very illuminating. Nonetheless, his categorizations, though very broad, I have found a very helpful starting point in the analysis of the underlying type of contract in any organization.

5

Many of the discussions of motivation assume that the style of leadership or the manner of the working of groups have a significant effect on motivation. They certainly have a significant effect on performances and this will be discussed in the relevant chapters. I prefer to regard the motivational assumptions as one of the factors to be considered when deciding on an optimum organization of work or style of leadership. To me it makes more sense to argue that a group-centred style of leadership is appropriate under a co-operative psychological contract rather than to maintain that a group-centred style is more 'motivating' in general terms. For this reason the studies and theories bearing on leadership style, group processes, productivity and morale, will be reviewed and analysed in chapters 4 and 5 rather than under the heading of motivation.

Dissonance theory (mentioned in implication 4) is a most interesting set of concepts. Devised by Festinger in 1956 the theory states that when an individual finds himself in a situation when the cues he receives from reality do not accord with his prevailing image of what that reality should be, he will experience dissonance. He will either have to tolerate the dissonance, reduce it by altering either his image of reality or the reality, or finding a way of explaining or rationalizing, the discrepancy.

For those who wish to explore the subject further, the best source is Brehm and Cohen's analysis and extension of Festinger's original work in this field.

A good, and reasonably concise, review of the literature on money and pay is provided by Opsahl and Dunnette. Their conclusion that nothing much is known about money is not, I think, justified by all the work that they review, although much of the work tends to be negative in the sense that it disproves some of the conventional myths.

There is a rich and varied literature on the concept of the 'self'. For those who wish to delve into it I have found that Mead's original work back in 1934 provided an excellent starting point. Many of the studies in this area, however, have been concerned with the problems arising out of the self-concept and resulting in various forms of neurosis. Horney's 1951 book is a good example of this approach.

7

The concept of psychological success and a competent self-identity has been elaborated principally by Argyris, and by White. Hall used the concept to postulate certain hypotheses about career development.

References

ARDREY, R. (1967), *The Territorial Imperative*, Collins.

ARGYRIS, C. (1960), *Understanding Organizational Behaviour*, Dorsey.

ARGYRIS, C. (1964), *Integrating the Individual and the Organization*, Wiley.

BREHM, J. W., and COHEN, A. R. (1962), *Explorations in Cognitive Dissonance*, Wiley.

DUNBAR, R. L. M. (1971), 'Budgeting for control', *Admin. Sci. Q.*, March.

ETZIONI, A. (1971), *A Comparative Analysis of Complex Organizations*, Free Press.

HALL, D. T. (1971), 'A theoretical model of career subidentity. Development in organizational settings', *Organizational Behav. Hum. Performance*, January.

HERZBERG, F. (1966), *Work and the Nature of Man*, World Publishing Co.

HORNEY, K. (1951), *Neurosis and Human Growth*, Routledge & Kegan Paul.

HOUSE, R. J., and WIGDOR, L. A. (1967), 'Herzberg's dual factor theory', *Personn. Psychol.*, Winter.

KOLB, D. A., RUBIN, I. M., and MCINTYRE, J. M. (1971), *Organizational Psychology*, Prentice-Hall.

LEAVITT, H. J., and MUELLER, R. A. H. (1951), 'Some effects of feedback on communication', *Hum. Rel.*

LEVINSON, H. (1972), 'An effort towards understanding man at work', *European Bus.*, Spring.

LIKERT, R. (1961), *New Patterns of Management*, McGraw-Hill.

LITWIN, G. H., and STRINGER, R. A. (1968), *Motivation and Organizational Climate*, Harvard University Press.

McClelland, D. C. (1961), *The Achieving Society*, Van Nostrand.

McGregor, D. (1960), *The Human Side of Enterprise*, McGraw Hill.

Maslow, A. (1954), *Motivation and Personality*, Harper & Row.

Mead, G. H. (1934), *Mind, Self and Society*, University of Chicago Press.

Myers, M. Scott (1966), 'Conditions for manager motivation', *Harvard Business Review*, January-February.

Niles, F. S. (unpublished), *The Influence of Parents and Friends on Adolescent Girls*, M. Ed. thesis, University of Manchester.

Opsahl, R. S., and Dunnette, M. D. (1969), 'The role of financial compensation', in L. L. Cummings and W. E. Scott (eds.), *Readings in Organizational Performance and Human Behaviour*, Irwin.

Porter, L. W., and Lawler, E. E. (1968), *Managerial Attitudes and Performance*, Dorsey.

Porter, L. W., and Lawler, E. E. (1968), 'What job attitudes tell about motivation', *Harvard Bus. Rev.*, January-February.

Schein, E. H. (1965), *Organizational Psychology*, Prentice-Hall.

Vroom, V. H. (1964), *Work and Motivation*, Wiley.

Vroom, V. H., and Deci, E. L. (eds.) (1970), *Management and Motivation*, Penguin.

White, R. (1959), 'Motivation re-considered: the concept of competence', *Psychol. Rev.*, vol. 66.

Whyte, W. F. (1969), *Organizational Behaviour*, Irwin.

Chapter 3

Role theory was introduced to the social sciences by Linton in 1936 but it was not until 1966 that Katz and Kahn were able to propose role concepts as 'the major means for linking the individual and organizational levels of research and theory'.

1

Role theory was a seductive but oft-discarded conceptual system in organization theory – discarded partly because there is very little agreement about the definition of the concept of role. Neiman and Hughes, after reviewing the treatment of the term by more than eighty writers, decided that the concept was 'vague, nebulous and non-definitive'. However there does seem to be some central core of meaning.

Roles are associated with positions in organizations;
Roles are involved in interactions.

I have avoided a precise definition of 'role' in the main text. A precise definition involves defining it in terms of behaviour, or expected behaviour, or relationships, when the dilemma truly is that role is all three. In 'role' the social scientist is using a language from the world of real organizations. Like many words in common use it has a variety of meanings, a variety that mirrors the complexity of the concept. To define away that variety is to avoid both the guts of the problem and the richness of the concept.

Another reason for its dismissal as a useful concept is what is called its lack of predictive power. By this, I think, is meant that statistical predictions of e.g. morale or tension cannot easily be made from situations of role problems. This is partly because the situations are hard to contrive experimentally, where many of the other variables could be controlled, and because in field studies too many other variables, particularly personality variances, intervene. Nevertheless it has generally been accepted as a very good explanatory concept and I have found it a good predictor of trends even if not of the magnitude of the trends. Thus one can predict that an individual will experience role ambiguity in a certain situation. The way in which he will respond to that piece of role stress will depend very largely on his personality and on his motivation calculus at the time. The outcome is not precisely predictable to an outsider – but knowledge of the existence of the role problem will certainly be helpful in any organization diagnosis.

The most useful of the sources in this area, and one to which I am greatly indebted, is Kahn *et al*. My language is not always the same as theirs but much of the thinking is. The authors, in this book, have gone a long way towards making role theory operational and advancing it as an analytical tool. In Katz and Kahn's book on organizational theory Role Set is made the core of their way of thinking about organizations and describing them. There is also a useful discussion of role theory in Krech, Crutchfield and Ballachey's basic text on social psychology. Similarly Hunt provides a useful and recent review of role theory. All these authors trace some of the ancestry of role theory back to the founding fathers – Linton, Newcombe and Menton. Pettigrew's writings on role and stress have also been of great help and stimulus to my thinking. Not all have yet been published but the short article in *Management Today* is well worth reading.

McGrath's collection of readings provides a useful overview of the whole area of stress. Levinson's book is also worth reading and very practical. The area of executive stress is giving use to a whole anthology of short articles in the popular journals. DuBrin's recent textbook provides a good summary.

5

The whole topic of people perception and interactions deserves much fuller treatment than I have been able to give it here. I found Hargreaves' analysis of the topic theory useful. As presented in his 1972 book it is applied to the educational world, but he does provide a good overall summary of the variety of approaches. Goffman's 1959 book is readable and exciting as is his later book which deals more specifically with role problems. There is another major approach to interactions not mentioned here, namely exchange theory, of which Homans is perhaps the leading opponent. This will be discussed briefly in chapter 5 on power and influence. For other approaches, congruency theory and the so-called psycho-dynamic theories, see Zaleznik's chapter in March.

6

Eric Berne's original idea of the three ego states and roles of Parent, Adult, Child has since been built into the approach to inter-personal behaviour christened 'Transactional Analysis'. Transactional analysis is not discussed in this book in any detail, but Berne's original book is worth reading and Harris' later work.

Wallen uses the idea of individual roles in a group to form the basis for a whole theory of leadership.

References

BAGLEY, J. (1957), 'A cross-cultural study of perceptual predominance in binocular rivalry', as reported in H. Cantril, 'Perception and interpersonal relations', *Amer. J. Psychiat.*, vol. 2.

BERNE, E. (1964), *Games People Play*, André Deutsch.

DEARBORN, D. C., and SIMON, H. A. (1958), *Selective Perception: a Note on the Departmental Identifications of Executive Sociometry.*

DUBRIN, A. J. (1974), *Fundamentals of Organizational Behaviour*, Pergamon.

GOFFMAN, E. (1959), *The Presentation of Self in Everyday Life*, Doubleday.

GOFFMAN, E. (1962), *Encounters*, Penguin.

HARGREAVES, D. (1972), *Interpersonal Relations and Education*, Routledge & Kegan Paul.

HARRIS, T. A. (1969), *I'm O.K. – You're O.K.*, Harper & Row.

HUNT, R. G. (1967), 'Role and role conflict', in E. P. Hollander and R. G. Hunt (eds.), *Current Perspectives in Social Psychology*, Oxford.

KAHN, R. L., et al. (1964), *Organizational Stress: Studies in Role Conflict and Ambiguity*, Wiley.

KATZ, D., and KAHN, R. L. (1966), *The Social Psychology of Organizations*, Wiley.

KRECH, D., CRUTCHFIELD, R. S., and BALLACHEY, E. L. (1962), *Individual in Society*, McGraw-Hill.

LEVINSON, H., (1970), *Executive Stress*, Harper & Row.

MCGRATH, J. E. (ed.) (1970), *Social and Psychological Factors in Stress*, Holt, Rinehart & Winston.

MARCH, J. G. (1965), *Handbook of Organizations*, Rand McNally.

PETTIGREW, A. (1972), 'Managing under stress', *Manag. Today*, April.

WALLEN, R. (1963), 'Three types of executive personality', *Dun's Rev.*, December.

Chapter 4

1

There is a wealth of literature on leadership. Much of it is inextricably entangled with either motivation or with group process studies. A lot of the studies are concerned with small component parts of the leadership process. There are few coherent attempts to draw it all together.

Cummings and Scott state, in their introduction to the section on leadership styles:

These broadly-defined classes of variables exert significant and reasonably predictable influences on the effectiveness of a leader's behaviour; namely, the characteristics of the subordinates with whom he is interacting, the nature of the leader's own characteristics and predispositions, and the nature of the situation within which the leader attempts to exert influence.

However, none of the readings which they then reproduce attempts to connect up these three classes of variables in any consistent way, although Fiedler's much quoted description of his views goes some way toward it. This discrepancy between the admitted complexity and interactive nature of the problem and the simplicity of the studies is typical of this field. It is obviously difficult to design any research to deal adequately with the interactive nature of the problem, but the piecemeal approach has (a) resulted in a lot of inconclusive work, and (b) allowed devotees of particular approaches to flourish without too much foundation for their views.

A collection of some of the most recent studies appears in the March 1971 edition of the *Administrative Science Quarterly* edited by Hollander. Hollander uses the terms 'style', 'structure' and 'setting' to describe the leadership variables, but once again the studies reported do not deal with the interaction between these variables.

2

The 'trait' approach has two kinds of advocates. The prescriptive theorists and the descriptive. Of the prescriptive, Barnard is perhaps the most noteworthy. Of the descriptive the studies by Ghiselli and by Wald and

Doty are the ones that are most worth studying. Both are to be found in Huneryager and Heckmann's book of readings for managers.

3

Style theorists are best studied in their original works, e.g. Likert, Mc-Gregor, Blake and Mouton. A good review of a lot of the studies in this field is provided by Argyle *et al.*, in Vroom and Deci's book of readings. Kalman, in Cummings and Scott, has a good review of the Ohio State Work on consideration and initiating structures.

Although many of the style theorists pay lip service to the importance of the task and situational variables they tend to be advocates or prophets of the participative culture. There is too little critical evaluation of when it works and when it does not – most of the studies are primarily concerned to establish that it is correlated overall with satisfaction or with productivity and are insensitive to explanatory conditions.

The influence of some of these 'prophets' has been great but can, I think, be better explained on a cultural basis than on an efficiency criterion. They represented a more democratic humanistic approach to the use of man in organizations and came at a time of reaction against scientific management.

4

There is not space here for a detailed review of Fiedler's work. It is briefly described in his 1965 article, but that article does not describe the measures he uses to arrive at his conclusions. There is some doubt as to whether his measure of LPC really does measure what he says it does or whether it really is co-terminous with a structuring authoritarian style.

For a more detailed study of his work it is necessary to study his book and Mitchell's evaluation of his methodology. Fiedler has recently suggested that leaders who differentiate highly between co-workers have a differentiated approach to style; under stress they show consideration, under favourable conditions they show high initiation of structure. If this were so then Fiedler's measure of LPC is beginning to look like a trait of a 'good' or differentiating leader. Evans and Dermer (unpublished) have provided a good review and an experimental study on this whole question of the meaning of Fiedler's LPC measure.

It is beginning to look as if differentiation could indeed be the beginning of a new approach to trait theory. Fiedler's other variables would then fit in well as determinants of the leader's freedom to differentiate in behaviour as well as cognitively. This is the sort of approach suggested in 5.4, although there is no research evidence to back it at this stage.

Vroom and Yetton have carried the contingency theories of leadership even further. They have looked at two aspects of a decision, its quality and the likelihood of its implementation, in terms of the nature of the task, the quality of the subordinates and their relationship to the leader. They have then produced a formal decision tree which minimizes the time taken for a decision after consideration of these other factors. By making the full contingency idea operational they have made it testable and teachable. So far they have found a lot of pragmatic evidence to validate it although it is perhaps too mechanistic and limited in that it deals only with formal decision-making acts of the leader. The whole procedure is well described in their recent book.

5

The Best Fit Approach is an attempt to make operational the interactive nature of the three variables that have been postulated by many writers. In particular, Tannenbaum and Schmidt in a well-known article in 1958 list most of the factors and items. But they stop short at listing them and do not go on to suggest how the leader should attempt to rate them or what factors in the environment might help or hinder him. Rackham, Honey and Colbert describe how effective leadership behaviour was perceived quite differently in two different companies, B.O.A.C. and I.C.L. and even within divisions of B.O.A.C.

A recent article by George and Von der Embse takes into account some of the cultural and organizational factors and recounts a study which attempts to quantify their effect. Their approach seems reconcilable with that of the 'Best Fit'.

The implications and applications of the Best Fit approach are, as yet, a matter of conjecture. There is some good anecdotal evidence to suggest that this is in fact the way that leaders behave in organization settings and that the roles of ambassador and model are important. Guest's study of managerial succession, mentioned in the text, is one case which could be interpreted in the light of this general model, which is the reason for its inclusion in Part 3 in encapsulated form.

Leadership theory is only one way of looking at the ways for getting things done in organizations. Chapter 5 discusses some of the more general aspects of power and influence. The two chapters need to be read closely together. Leadership theories were discussed first, primarily in order to deal with the popular stereotypes of trait and style. Similarly leadership is closely tied in with the working of groups. The material covered in chapter 6 is therefore equally relevant.

References

BARNARD, C. I. (1938), *The Functions of the Executive*, Harvard University Press.

BLAKE, R., and MOTOUN, J. (1964), *The Managerial Grid*, Gulf.

CUMMINGS, L. L., and SCOTT, W. E. (1969), *Readings in Organizational Theory and Human Performance*, Irwin & Dorsey.

EVANS, M. G., and DERMER, J. D. (unpublished). *What Does the LPC Scale Really Measure?*

FIEDLER, F. E. (1965), 'Engineer the job to fit the manager', *Harvard Business Review*, vol. 43.

FIEDLER, F. E. (1967), *A Theory of Leadership Effectiveness*, McGraw-Hill.

GEORGE, N. and VON DER EMBSE, T. T. (1971), 'Six Propositions for Managerial Leadership', *Business Horizons*.

GHISELLI, E. E. (1963), 'Managerial Talent', *Amer. Psychol.*, October.

GUEST, R. A. (1962), *Organizational Change: The Effect of Successful Leadership*, Urwin & Dorsey.

HOLLANDER, E P. (1964), *Leaders, Groups and Influence*, Oxford.

HUNERYAGER, S. G. and HECKMANN, I. L. (eds.) (1967), *Human Relations in Management*, Arnold.

LIKERT, R. (1961), *New Patterns of Management*, McGraw-Hill.

McGREGOR, D. V. (1960), *The Human Side of Enterprise*, McGraw-Hill.

MITCHELL, T. R., *et al.* (1970), 'The contingency model', *Academy of Management Journal*, 13.

RACKHAM, N., HONEY, P., and COLBERT, M. (1971), *Developing Interactive Skills*, Wellens Publishing.

TANNENBAUM, R., and SCHMIDT, W. (1958), 'How to Choose a Leadership Pattern', *Harvard Business Review*, March-April.

VROOM, V. H., and DECI, E. L. (eds.) (1970), *Management and Motivation*, Penguin.

VROOM, V. H., and YETTON, P. (1973), *Leadership and Decision-Making*, University of Pittsburg.

WALD, R. M., and DOTY, R. A. (1954), 'The Top Executive – A First Hand Profile', *Harvard Business Review*, vol. 32, no. 4.

Chapter 5

1

The literature on power and influence is a growing one but not easy for the general reader to absorb. It has either had its roots in political theory and been concerned with the power bases of élites, or with evolutionary movements, with the changing nature of the power structures of whole societies, or the justifications for representative government. Alternatively, when it has delved into the *minutiae* of organizations it has done so in a piecemeal manner. No wonder that Dahl was able to describe it as 'a bottomless swamp'.

Weber, Urwick, Simon, Bennis and Presthus are five writers who have talked of 'authority'; by which is meant either the narrower sense of the power inherent in office, or the wider sense to include other bases of power. They all list position authority, expert or physical and competence authority, and personal or charismatic authority. For most of them position authority would, I think, include resource power. Simon, for instance, lists (a) power to hire and fire, (b) power to promote and demote, and (c) incentive rewards as 'the most important sanctions of managers over workers in the industrial organizations'. There is also considerable discussion of the issue of power given to the leader by the group. For Simon this is where authority gains its greatest force. I regard this as expert power backing up position power. Simon also distinguishes techniques of persuasion for personal power. I find it more sensible to separate altogether methods of influence from sources of power.

Peabody's article, in Cummings and Scott's book of readings, presents a review of these writers, as well as an interesting study of perceived bases of authority. Tannenbaum in the same collection, looks at levels of perceived influence as affecting behaviour and motivation, and reviews the principal research in this area.

The best overall review of all the literature relevant to power in organizations is that by Cartwright in March's *Handbook of Organizations*. He reviews a wide range of theories and studies and suggests some of the lines of approval that I have used. Likewise his earlier book, *Studies in Social Power*, is a useful compendium. Katz and Kahn in the *Social Psychology of Organizations* have much to say about the range and domain of various types of influence. Pettigrew has a growing body of work in this field, and the recent book of readings edited by Thomas and Bennis provides a useful overview.

2

Ecology as a method of influence has something in common with Skinner's ideas on human conditioning. He, however, sees it as much more powerful in its potential than I do.

Examples of ecology would be Herzberg's 'job enrichment' approach or Trist's work on the modification of work-flow patterns. Steele's recent writing on the importance of the physical environment is interesting and provocative.

Not everyone would distinguish power and influence in the way that I have done, but French and Raven's article in Cartwright's study has a discussion of power bases that is useful. Their terms are slightly different from mine and do not completely overlap, but there is a lot of convergent thinking. Homans too, the leading exchange theorist, merits study, particularly his 1961 book. His view of interactions as exchanges of rewards and costs I find almost too all-embracing to be useful but his description of it is certainly stimulating.

3

In dealing with responses to influence I am heavily indebted to Kelman's discussion of attitude change in his article. I have in several fields found this a most helpful categorization. The thoughts on the results of identification are, however, my own conclusions from personal experience.

The role of 'gatekeeper' in organizations, particularly in regard to information flows, is discussed by Pettigrew who describes an interesting case-history of the use of this role to influence a major investment decision. Allen has also described the role of technological gatekeepers in R and D establishments. Both of these writers are more interested in the positive aspects of their role than in the potential it gives them for negative power.

March and Simon's book *Organizations* is lucidly summarized from the perspective of 'vocabulary' by Perrow in *Complex Organizations*.

4

A good discussion of the socialization process is provided by Caplow. He describes rather more methods of socialization than are listed here but they can be concentrated into the four varieties in this chapter. He provides short examples of socialization, one of which is represented in Box 5. He also refers to other writings on this topic.

Hargreaves, in his social-psychological treatment of education, gives a good discussion of the various approaches to attitude change – a subject that has produced more literature and research than almost any other part of social psychology. I have used dissonance theory as a way of explaining most of the work in this field. I do not find that dissonance theory explains anything that cannot equally well be explained by concepts of power and influence, group process or the motivation calculus, but it is a good way of joining these together and seems to have some appeal to the newcomer to social psychology. Festinger's original 1957 book is the prime source, but Brehm and Cohen's later collection of all the research is perhaps more useful.

References

ALLEN, J., and COHEN, S. I. (1969), 'Information flow in research and development laboratories'; *Admin. Science Quarterly*, 14(1).

BREHM, J. W., and COHEN, A. R. (1962), *Exploitations in Cognitive Dissonance*, Wiley.

CAPLOW, T. (1964), *Principles of Organization*, Harcourt, Brace & World.

CARTWRIGHT, D. (ed.) (1959), *Studies in Social Power*, Univ. of Michigan, esp. French and Raven's article.

FESTINGER, L. (1957), *A Theory of Cognitive Dissonance*, Stanford.

HARGREAVES, D. (1972), *Interpersonal Relations and Education*, Routledge & Kegan Paul.

HERZBERG, F. (1968), 'One more time: how do you motivate employers', *Harvard Business Review*, 46.

HOMANS, G. C. (1961), *Social Behaviour: Its Elementary Forms*, Routledge & Kegan Paul.

KATZ, D. (1960), 'The functional approach to the study of attitude change', *Public Opinion Quarterly*.

KATZ, D. and KAHN, R. L. (1966), *The Social Psychology of Organizations*, Wiley.

KELMAN, H. C. (1958), 'Compliance, internalization and identification: three processes of attitude change', *Journal of Conflict Resolution*.

MARCH, J. G. (1965), *Handbook of Organizations*, Rand McNally.

PEABODY, R. L. (1969), 'Perception of organizational authority' in Cummings and Scott (eds.), *Readings in Organizational Behaviour and Human Performance*, Unwin.

PERROW, C. (1972), *Complex Organizations*, Scott and Foreman, Glenview.

PETTIGREW, A. M. (1972), 'Information control as a power resource', *Sociology*, May.

PETTIGREW, A. M. (1972), 'Some notes on power and political processes in organizations', paper presented to the British Psychological Society, London, 22 April 1972.

PETTIGREW, A. M. (1973), 'The influence process between specialists and executives', *Personnel Review*, winter.

SIMON, H. A. (1947), *Administrative Behavior*, New York.

SKINNER, B. F. (1973), *Beyond Freedom and Dignity*, Penguin.

STEELE, F. I. (1971), 'Organization development and sticks and stones' in H. A. Hornstein *et al.*, *Social Interventions: a Behavioral Science Approach*, Free Press.

TANNENBAUM, A. S. (1969), 'Control in organizations,' in Cummings and Scott (eds.), *Readings in Org. Behaviour and Human Performance*, Unwin.

THOMAS, J. M., and BENNIS, W. G. (1972), *Management of Change and Conflict*, Penguin.

TRIST, E. L. (1960), *Socio-Technical Systems*, Tavistock.

WEBER, M. (1947), *The Theory of Social and Economic Organization*, Free Press.

Chapter 6

1

Much of the literature on groups is closely limited with that on leadership and motivation. For instance, a lot of the work on participation is really work on the effectiveness and motivation of groups under differing leadership styles. Most of the work on groups focuses on what, in the chapter, I have called the 'intervening factors'. Few studies look at the more comprehensive model studied here. One of the few that does is the chapter on 'The effective group' in Krech, *et al.*, *Individual in Society*, their introductory text to social psychology. Schein also takes a more comprehensive approach. The basic sources for the study of groups are:

1 The study of group processes – in particular Bales with his extensive way of recording group interactions, and the Leavitt-type studies of communication links.
2 The group-dynamics school, derived from the concepts of Kurt Lewin, and resulting in a whole range of training and group development methods. Schein and Bennis' book on group methods is a good overall description.
3 Field studies of group relations and the informal organization. In particular Mayo, Roethlisberger and Dickson, followed by Whyte and Homans particularly. Whyte has detailed some most revealing studies of groups in a wide variety of settings. They are described and interpreted in his book on organizational behaviour. Homans' *The Human Group* is a classic in the field, although I have not found his conceptualizations as interpretatively helpful as I expected.

Although I have tried to draw together the more useful of the research studies, I have found in my experience that the things that determine how groups operate are often more simple and more fundamental than many of the studies suppose. Much of the chapter therefore represents a conceptualization of my experience as well as an interpretation of the available research.

2

The early group studies, e.g. the Hawthorne studies and Trist's coalminers, were the foundation for a whole approach to organizations in which a man's needs were assumed to be very largely satisfied and determined by the norms of his work group. Mayo, in particular, was so impressed by the Hawthorne studies and subsequent interviews that he concluded:

1 Man is basically motivated by social needs.
2 As a result of the rationalization of work, meaning has gone out of work and must be sought in the social relationships on the job.
3 The focus of the work group will do more to influence behaviour than the incentives and controls of managers.
4 A supervisor will only be effective to the extent that he can satisfy his subordinates' social needs.

This approach had a big impact on management theory and practice, especially because it was so contrary to the presumptions of scientific management. The impact was so big that the cult of the group began to dominate managerial thinking. The importance of the group definitely needed to be re-organized but, like many of these approaches, it suffered from over-generalization and has now fallen back into its proper perspective.

For a long time it was thought that groups aided creative thinking through brain-storming. It was fifteen years before anyone thought to test it, and then it was only found to be true in certain respects. The results are reported in detail in the article by Taylor *et al*.

The 'risky shift' phenomenon in group decision-making is interesting, partly because it was discovered in an experimental setting and has never been validated in the field. An enormous literature has grown up around this subject. The effect is so predictable that it has become a classroom exercise and most research now concentrates on trying to explain it. The most recent comprehensive review is Clark's article in *Psychological Bulletin*.

3

'Competence Motivation' is a term coined by Morse and Lorsch in an interesting article comparing motivation in high-performing and low-performing organizations.

The findings on group size are fairly predictable and very constant. For a good review of the studies see Lewenstein's article. The studies on homogeneity and heterogeneity are interesting, but seldom explore the dimensions of heterogeneity far enough until Schutz's studies in compatibility. Schutz's measures are complex and his research design intricate – sometimes so intricate that it is hard to draw any obvious conclusions from it. But he did try to assess the various elements of compatibility and he did draw attention to its relatively greater importance in tasks of complexity. His work is reported in his book. Heterogeneity of influence is discussed by Leavitt in his provocative article.

The prisoner's dilemma exercise has many imitators. Morton Deutsch did some research with one of them with predictable results; only 13 per cent of the pairs reached the optimum solution. He publishes his results in the *Journal of Conflict Resolution*.

The concepts of forming, norming, storming and performing are taken from an interesting article by B. W. Tuckman, which reviews a whole range of group process studies.

The T-group approach to developing group processes has already been referred to in these notes. For those who want to discover more about the current possibilities, The National Training Laboratories in Washington or The Group Relations Training Association in Great Britain are the best sources of information. Details of the Coverdale approach can be read in their 1961 booklet.

Very little research work has been done that is specifically related to the influence of the task on group design or performance. A pity because anecdotal experience suggests that it is a very important factor.

Fiedler's work on leader power and position has already been mentioned (chapter 4). So has Festinger's work on cognitive dissonance (chapter 5).

Festinger is also the co-author of a study of social pressures in a housing group which produced some conclusions about interactive patterns. The interaction thesis is supported by Homans. I have some worries about it, since any such research is likely to be self-fulfilling, i.e. increased interactions that did not lead to friendship would have ceased and would not therefore be known to the researchers. Festinger's study is more longitudinal and therefore more reassuring on this count.

A good discussion of group processes and procedures and ways to improve them is included in Schein's excellent description of his personal consulting methods in organizations. This book also contains a short review of the history of group theory.

Deutsch looked at the productivity of co-operative well-maintained groups back in the early days of group studies. His conclusions are summarized in the text and reported in his 1949 article on human relations.

The interactions and communication patterns of groups have stimulated a vast amount of research. The comments in the text represent an amalgam and an attempted integration of the more important results. Unfortunately, not all the experiences used the same networks. Leavitt, in particular, who did much of the earlier work on this, did not look at the all-channel net, being perhaps more interested in the communication distortion that results from links in a chain. The distortion effect was not mentioned in the text since it is not usually a feature of groups working together, but it is a well-established and well-known phenomenon. I have also used Guetzhow's work, following on Leavitt, on communicative patterns.

References

BALES, R. F. (1950), *Interaction Process Analysis*, Addison-Wesley.

CLARK, R. D. (1971), 'Group-induced shifts toward risk', *Psychological Bulletin*.

COVERDALE, R. (1967), *Training for Development*, Training Partnerships.

DEUTSCH, M. (1949), 'An experimental study of the effects of cooperation and competition upon group process', *Human Relations*.

DEUTSCH, M. (1958), 'Trust and suspicion', *Journal of Conflict Resolution*.

FESTINGER, L., *et al.* (1950), *Social Pressures in Informal Groups: A Study of a Housing Project*, Harper.

GUETZHOW, H., and SIMON, H. A. (1955), 'The impact of certain communication nets upon organization and performance', *Management Science*.

HOMANS, G. C. (1950), *The Human Group*, Harcourt Brace & World.

KRECH, D., CRUTCHFIELD, R. S., and BALLACHEY, E. L. (1962), *The Individual in Society*, McGraw-Hill.

LEAVITT, H. J. (1951), 'Some effects of certain communicative patterns on group performance', *J. Abnorm. Psych.*

LEAVITT, H. J. (1962), 'Unhuman organizations', *Harvard Business Review*.

LEWENSTEIN, E. R. (1971), 'Group size and decision-making committees', *Applied Soc-Studies*.

MAYO, E. (1945), *The Social Problems of an Industrial Civilization*, Harvard.

MORSE, J. J., and LORSCH, J. W. (1970), 'Beyond theory Y', *Harvard Business Review*, May.

SCHEIN, E. H. (1969), *Process Consultation*, Addison-Wesley.

SCHEIN, E. H., and BENNIS, W. G. (1965), *Personal–Organizational Change Through Group Methods*, Wiley.

SCHUTZ, W. C. (1958), *FIRO: a three dimensional theory of interpersonal behaviour*, Rinehart.

TAYLOR, D. W., BERRY, P. C., and BLOCK, C. H. (1958), 'Does group participation facilitate or inhibit creative thinking?', *Admin. Sci. Quarterly*.

TRIST, E. L., *et al.* (1963), *Organizational Choice*, Tavistock.

TUCKMAN, B. W. (1965), 'Developmental sequence in small groups', *Psych. Bulletin*.

WHYTE, W. F. (1969), *Organizational Behaviour*, Irwin.

Chapter 7

1

This chapter is really suggesting a way of describing organizations, of classifying them. It has long been realized that one had to distinguish between various types of organization. The problem has essentially been to decide on the categories. I have found cultures and structures, although a low-definition set of types, to be the most fruitful approach. But there are a number of other conceptualizations which the reader ought to be aware of. I have found that they either focus too exclusively on one aspect of an organization – its technology, its market, etc. – or else that they are purely descriptive and give no guidance as to the implications.

The most important conceptualizations are, firstly, those already mentioned briefly in the text.

1 Roger Harrison's categorization of four ideologies. His identification of four separate ideologies I have found most helpful. He does not go into the implications of mixed ideologies in one organization nor the rights or wrongs of such a mix. It is a largely descriptive approach.

2 Lawrence and Lorsch in a now famous book, *Organization and Environment* first put forward the concept of a differentiated organization and tested it in the field. In a most perceptive and realistic book they emphasize four types of differences; orientations towards the market, orientations towards time, orientations towards people, and degree of formality in the structure. It focuses perhaps too much on the diversity of the market as the influencing factor, but has been the single most influential prod to my own thinking on organizations.

3 Burns and Stalker were in a way the forerunners of Lawrence and Lorsch in that they identified the need for a different structure when the technology of the market was changing. They did not, however, in distinguishing between mechanistic and organismic (later organic) structures, discuss the problems of the mix, although they talked of it as a continuum.

4 Other forerunners of Lawrence and Lorsch, 'contingency theorists' as they term them, are Fouraker, Chandler and Udy. These are discussed in Chapter VIII of Lawrence and Lorsch's work. Joan Woodward's was the forerunner of several 'technology' approaches. Her study of Essex firms set

out to test whether traditional management principles in fact led to success. Her differentiated conclusions resulted. Attempts to replicate her findings have not always been successful, probably because technology is only one of the influencing factors and cannot be looked at in isolation. The replicating studies did not take into account the other possible factors.

5 Perrow has suggested that the essence of the technology question is whether the individual tasks are routine or non-routine. From this essential distinction flow the methods of control and co-ordination, the degrees of individual discretion and power, the type of social structure and motivation, the goals and the climate of risk. It is a complicated model which seems to suffer from the need to fill up, under each heading, all four cells of an assumed matrix. However, its general conclusions would fit well with the less closely defined cultural approach. In particular, his two most important cells fit closely with task and the role cultures.

Other approaches are:

6 Blau has recently published a systematic theory relating organizational size and structural differentiation. Katzell first demonstrated the cause of possible influencing factors and the need to find genotypic dimensions.

7 Homans wrote of the effect of the external system (physical, cultural and technological environments) on the internal system (activities, interactions and sentiments) and postulated that they are all interdependent.

8 Katz and Kahn in their discussion of open systems stress the linkages between the organization and its environment. They speak of the combination in an open system of a steady state and dynamic homeostasis and of a tendency towards differentiation. They are descriptive rather than prescriptive.

9 Miller and Rice of the Tavistock Institute have also advocated an open system model in which the activity system, the task group and the sentient group interact, and have presented a variety of organizational models evaluated on this basis. One of their suggestions is that task and sentient groups will coincide fully only when the task is short-term, i.e. project groups make for high involvement.

10 Pugh and his colleagues have sought to measure more precisely some of the independent and dependent variables such as size, technology, dependence, formalization, centralization and their inter-relationships. They have shown that size is a major explanatory variable and, interestingly, that formalization does not have to accompany centralization.

For a good review of these and many other approaches to the description and categorization of organizations see Lichtman and Hunt's paper.

2

The cultures have not been rigorously defined in the text since a rigorous definition might destroy the 'flavour'. The questionnaire in Box 7.7 is an attempt to contribute a little more rigour and can be used as a set of definitions if need be. Self-completed questionnaires are, however, subject to cultural bias. Few people will accept a power orientation or a person orientation although to an outside observer that might be clearly their preferred culture. I have found the questionnaire more useful as a guide to my external rating of the organization after living with it for a time.

The task and role cultures appear frequently in the literature under other names, e.g. organic and mechanistic. The power and person cultures seem unrecognized by most theorists but to me seem significant realities. Similarly, the fit between a preferred personal culture and the dominant organization culture is one way of approaching the tricky question of establishing the psychological contract, but one which is not made explicit by many theorists. Etzioni's classification of organizations, mentioned in chapter 2, is an approach along these lines, but his 'calculative' category can embrace all the cultures.

3

The work by Pugh *et al* on measuring some of the influencing factors and their effects has already been mentioned. Leading on from that, Payne and Mansfield have recently investigated the effects of size and content on the perceived climate of the organization.

Trist and Bamforth's study of the changes from a task to a role technology (in my words) gave rise to the concept of the socio-technical system, the inter-relations of the technology and the social structure of the organization. A review of most of the studies of the impact of technology is contained in Mohn's paper.

Cyert and March in their *Behavioural Theory of the Firm* regard goals as the outcome of bargaining among potential members of a coalition about five classes of goals – production, inventory, sales, market and profit.

The impact of the environment on the organization, the link between the organization system and its content, has been the focus for most of the studies in this area. The important ones are those cited at the beginning of this set of notes.

4

Burns and Stalker have given a graphic description of some of the ways in which mechanistic organizations try to adapt to a changing technology. Galbraith's hypothetical account of how a matrix organization should evolve is interesting to set beside Burns and Stalker.

The concept of steady state is found in Katz and Kahn's text on social psychology. The thought of breakdown as a separate set comes from John Morris who has used it as part of a more similar approach to management development and not in the context of culture. Leavitt and Whistler in an interesting article suggest that organizations of the future may look like a football on top of a bell – the football having characteristics similar to my power culture.

The discussion of integration is largely dependent on the study by Lawrence and Lorsch who talk of the integrator rather than the co-ordinator. The role stress associated with such a position is discussed in chapter 3.

The studies by Lawrence and Lorsch and by Woodward have already been cited. The study by Morse and Lorsch is more concerned with motivation but is a good instance of the 'best fit' leadership approach.

The description of the development of G.E.C. – English Electric in Graham Turner's *Business in Britain* is both illuminating and readable. Indeed, his colourful descriptions of most of Britain's larger concerns, when read in the light of 'cultures', are very interesting and revealing.

References

BLAU, P. (1970), 'A formal theory of differentiation in organizations', *Amer. Soc. Review*.

BURNS, T., and STALKER, G. H. (1966), *The Management of Innovation*, Tavistock.

CYERT, R. M., and MARCH, J. G. (1963), *A Behavioural Theory of the Firm*, Prentice-Hall.

GALBRAITH, J. R. (1971), 'Matrix organization designs', *Business Horizons*, Feb.

HARRISON, R. (1972), *How to Describe Your Organization*, *Harvard Business Review*, Sept.-Oct. 1972.

HOMANS, G. C. (1950), *The Human Group*, Harcourt, Brace and World.

KATZ, D., and KAHN, R. L. (1966), *The Social Psychology of Organizations*, Wiley.

KATZELL, R. A. (1962), *Contrasting Systems of Work Organizations*, *American Psychologist*, vol. 17.

LAWRENCE, P. R. and LORSCH, J. W. (1967), *Organization and Environment*, Harvard.

LEAVITT, H. T., and WHISTLER, T. A. (1964), 'Management in the 1980s', in Leavitt and Pugh, *Readings in Managerial Psychology*, University of Chicago Press.

LICHTMAN, C. M., and HUNT, R. G. (1971), 'Personality and organization theory', *Psych. Bulletin*, vol. 76.

MILLER, E. J. and RICE, A. K. (1967), *Systems of Organization*, Tavistock.

MOHN, L. B. (1962), 'Organizational technology and organizations', *American Psychologist*.

MORRIS, J. F. (1971), 'Developing managers structure and development management', *Admin. Sci. Quarterly* (2); *Personnel Review*, December.

MORSE, J. J., and LORSCH, J. W. (1970), 'Beyond theory Y', *Harvard Business Review*, May–June.

PAYNE, R. L., and MANSFIELD, R. (1972), 'Effects of organizational structure, organizational content and hierarchical position on perception of organizational climate', Working Paper, London Business School.

PERROW, C. (1970), *Organizational Analysis*, Tavistock.

PUGH, D. S., HICKSON, D. J., HININGS, C. R., and TURNER, C. (1968), 'Dimensions of organization structure', *Admin. Science Quarterly*.

TRIST, E. L., *et al.* (1963), *Organizational Choice*, Tavistock.

TURNER, G. (1971), *Business in Britain*, Penguin.

WOODWARD, JOAN (1965), *Industrial Organization*, Oxford.

Chapter 8

One of the very few discussions of the political aspect of organizations which explicitly uses the words *power* or *politics* is Zaleznik's article 'Power and politics in organization life', which examines the competition for individual power in organizations. As he states in his opening paragraph, 'A sense of disbelief occurs when managers purport to make decisions in rationalistic terms while most observers and participants know that personalities and politics play a significant if not an overriding role. . . Somehow, power and politics are dirty words. . .' The same comment applies to the literature on organizational politics. It is meagre, compared with that on leadership, or motivation. It talks about lateral relations, or conflict, or the management of differences – seldom explicitly about politics or power.

'The management of differences' is the title of the last chapter in McGregor's *Professional Manager*, and provides a brief introduction to the whole topic. According to the editor, this subject was beginning to dominate McGregor's thinking when he died. A well-known paper by Schmidt and Tannenbaum explores the management of individual differences or disputes. Much of what they say is also applicable to groups. Lateral relations are fully discussed by Sayles in his book on managerial behaviour. He identifies several more sets of roles than I do in this chapter, but many of them seem to overlap. A good analysis of organizational conflict is provided by Dutton and Walton's article which also provides a review of the available literature. Dalton's *Men Who Manage* is a blow-by-blow account of the conflicts and differences in two organizations. His descriptive material is more abundant and more valuable than the conceptual analysis. Cyert and March's famous *A Behavioural Theory of the Firm* is relevant to this topic, although this treatment regards organizations and their constituent parts too rationally for my liking. Caplow, in his book on organizations, has a long chapter on conflict which has some useful concepts, although the examples are drawn more from international and national affairs than those of organizations. Thomas and Bennis's book of readings on change and conflict is a useful compendium. Ardrey's book *The Territorial Imperative*, and Machiavelli's *The Prince* are of a different order. They both provide fascinating analogies and parallels from different worlds. One cannot look to them for precise and proven theorems in the field of organizations, but if we are concerned with insight as much as with scientific evidence, then these two authors should not be missed.

The exchange theory of power, which I personally find useful as far as it goes but ultimately inadequate, is well set out by Peter M. Blau. The work of Andrew Pettigrew, focusing on the political relationship between specialists and line executives is stimulating and reality-based. Crozier's *Bureaucratic Phenomenon* is one of the best field studies of power relationships in organizations. Most of the other interesting studies have concerned themselves with such places as hospitals and prisons where the political problems are perhaps more obvious. Of these perhaps the most insightful is Anselm Strauss's study of relations between the various groups in the mental health world.

1

Rackham *et al.* in their book (1971) cite their investigation of key problem incidents as perceived by a range of British managers to explain the importance of interactive skills. The percentages on perception of conflict are taken from one of Argyris's studies, quoted and commented on by him most recently in his *Intervention Theory and Method*.

3

Much of the discussion in this section is based on Schmidt and Tannenbaum's *Management of Difference* which deals essentially with the resolution of particular disputes between individuals, is insightful and practical.

The topic of competition *within* an organization has not been extensively discussed. Zaleznik's article is one of the few to deal with it. He distinguishes between coalitions and collusions and cites several supportive instances, but otherwise, the possible beneficial effects of competition are usually summed up in one paragraph as an introduction to the problem of conflict. I feel this does the topic less than justice, particularly since competition *between* organizations is one fundamental tenet of capitalism.

There is of course a wealth of literature on aggression, and whether it is innate or induced. Ardrey provides a readable but polemical introduction to this field. As I state in the chapter, I feel the need for the student of organizations is to recognize that man does have this tendency towards aggression, however acquired.

4

Dutton and Walton identify nine antecedents of conflict – mutual dependence, asymmetries, rewards, organizational differentiation, role dissatisfaction, ambiguities, common resources, communication obstacles. These are often the results rather than the cause of conflict. But they provide a good integration of the various studies on conflict.

Strauss's detailed analysis of the role of the purchasing agent is a useful example of many of the causes and symptoms of conflict, as are Seiler's study of relative status rankings and the oft-cited Lawrence and Lorsch's comparison of effective firms in these industries.

Some examples of Ardrey's thinking is given in the boxes. Anthony Jay and Robert Heller, amongst others, have recently picked up the idea of using the concepts of the popular anthropologists and zoologists in organizational contests (e.g. The Naked Manager). But a systematic application of Ardrey's concepts to organizations has not, to my knowledge, been attempted. I have found the metaphor of territory, and the assumptions underlying it, to provide many insights in organizational analysis.

5

Pettigrew's paper gives a detailed account of the use of information control to bring about a particular solution to an investment decision in an organization. The implication is not that this decision was right or wrong, but that information was used as a power resource to obtain it.

6

Dutton and Walton's study of conflict and collaboration in two contrasting divisions is most illuminating. It is nicely observed, and interesting conclusions are drawn from it, most of which are reflected in the chapter.

Schein, in his discussion of process consultation, gives a good description of what is involved in group confrontation. A whole set of intervention methods have grown out of this particular strategy. Argyris, in his book *Intervention Theory and Method*, goes into considerable depth on the conceptual underpinnings and practical applications of this method. Although sound in principle, the strategy is often applied too indiscriminately. If the cause of the conflict is rooted in the objectives or the allocation of territory – then better understanding and better communications between conflicting groups may help to remove stereotypes each of the other, but will really only paper over the deeper cracks.

Harrison's approach of role negotiation is a practical and viable way of getting rid of some of the unnecessary irritations of conflict and making it manageable. Particularly useful for individuals in small groups, it has been used in intergroup situations. He has described it in a paper for *European Business*.

Organization development, whose primary focus has traditionally been on improving the process of group and intergroup interactions, has sometimes proceeded as if unaware of the political reality of organizations, and in dealing with the symptoms of conflict rather than its causes, has earned itself, on occasion, the label of ineffective.

References

ARDREY, R. (1967), *The Territorial Imperative*, Collins.

ARGYRIS, C. (1970), *Intervention Theory and Method*, Addison-Wesley.

BLAU, P. M. (1964), *Exchange and Power in Social Life*, Wiley.

CAPLOW, T. (1964), *Principles of Organization*, Harcourt, Brace.

CROZIER, M. (1964), *The Bureaucratic Phenomenon*, Tavistock.

CYERT, R. M. and MARCH, J. G. (1963), *A Behavioural Theory of the Firm*, Prentice-Hall.

DALTON, M. (1959), *Men Who Manage*, Wiley.

DEUTSCH, M. (1969), 'Conflicts: productive and destructive', *Journal of Social Issues*.

DUTTON, J. M. and WALTON, R. E. (1962), 'Interdepartmental conflict and co-operation: two contrasting studies', *Human Organizations* 20.

DUTTON, J. M. and WALTON, R. E. (1969), 'The management of inter-departmental conflict', *Admin. Sci. Quarterly*, March.

HARRISON, R. (1972), 'When power conflicts trigger team spirit', *European Business*, Spring.

LAWRENCE, P. R. and LORSCH, J. W. (1967), *Organization and Environment*, Harvard University Press.

McGREGOR, D. (1967), *The Professional Manager* (ed. W. E. Bennet and C. McGregor), McGraw-Hill.

MACHIAVELLI, N. (1967), *The Prince* (trans. G. Bull), Penguin.

PETTIGREW, A. M. (1972), 'Information control as a power resource', *Sociology*, May.

PETTIGREW, A. M. (1973), *The Politics of Organizational Decision-Making*, Tavistock.

RACKHAM, N., HONEY, P. and COLBERT, M. (1971), *Developing Interactive Skills*, Wellens Publishing.

SAYLES, L. (1964), *Managerial Behaviour*, McGraw-Hill.

SCHEIN, E. H. (1969), *Process Consultation*, Addison-Wesley.

SCHMIDT, W. and TANNENBAUM, R. (1960), 'The management of differences', *Harvard Business Review*, November–December.

SEILER, J. A. (1963), 'Diagnosing inter-departmental conflict', *Harvard Business Review*, September–October.

STRAUSS, A. *et al.* (1964), *Psychiatric Ideologies and Institutions, Glencoe, Ill.*, Free Press.

STRAUSS, C. (1962), 'Tactics of lateral relationship: the purchasing agent', *Admin. Sci. Quarterly*, vol. 7.

THOMAS, J. M. and BENNIS, W. G. (1972), *Management of Change and Conflict*, Penguin.

ZALEZNIK, A. (1970), 'Power and politics in organizational life', *Harvard Business Review*, May–June.

Chapter 9

Personnel administration as a subject has generated a very mixed bag of literature, ranging from the 'How I did it', through cook-book type prescriptive formulations, to detailed studies of particular phenomena or particular situations. There are good and bad examples of each variety; the problem often is to get past the allure of the title to the meat within.

In this chapter it is not possible, nor intended, to review all the systems of personnel management, but rather to look at some of their problems and implications in the light of the conceptual frameworks introduced earlier in the book. Much of the time, it is not the details of the system or the strategy that matters, but the intent behind it, the way it is introduced, the way it is handled, that is crucial. This is more the focus of this chapter.

Readings on Personnel Management, edited by McFarland, is one overview of the literature in the field, which focuses quite heavily on the prescriptive end of the scale. The book on managerial behaviour by Campbell *et al.* is a compendium and detailed review of all the research in this general area. Examples of 'How I did it' approaches are Robert Townsend's *Up the Organization*, and Carl Dueu's account of his career as a company doctor. A combination of these four very different books is perhaps an appropriate start on this vast and overlapping topic. Another overview is provided by the collection of reprints issued by the *Harvard Business Review* in the *Personnel Management Series*.

1

The implications of human asset-accounting have been stressed by Likert amongst others. Hekimian and Jones' article is the most concise treatment of the subject, although it does not really probe all the possible implications. Caplan also touches on the topic in his book. The analogy of the football club is currently being investigated as part of a project at the London Business School, but has so far not been written up.

2

Alfred's article 'Checkers or choice in manpower management' contrasts the 'Open' and 'Closed' systems of development and describes some examples. An overview of the various systems is provided by Markwell and Roberts' book. On the topic of manpower forecasting, Vether's book is a reliable introduction. Brown, in his recent book on organization, describes some of the formal mechanisms for management development that he recommends.

A good review of the research on pay is provided by Opsahl and Dunnette's article in the *Psychological Bulletin*. This is brought up to date in Campbell *et al.*'s larger work on managerial effectiveness. Jacques' system of differentials is described in his book *Equitable Payment* and discussed by Brown in his book, *Organization*.

3

General approaches to individual development are provided by Schein in his article and by Markwell and Roberts.

This discussion of formal education is based very largely on my article, 'European business'. Revans's views on formal education and its perils are well worth studying and are set out in his book *Developing Managers*. Other studies are reported and commented on in Campbell *et al.*'s review.

A good summary of the evaluation studies of group learning is provided by Morgan, in Rackham *et al.* Campbell *et al.* provide more details and further references. Morgan also provides a good description of the various types of group development methods to be found. Morris' article describes the use of team project learning within companies and business schools, along with other devices, as a way of developing managers for the development activities within organizations – a useful foretaste of possible future trends in management education.

There is, in general, a confusion in this area as to whether the object of development is the group or the individual. It can blur the issue to claim that both happen simultaneously, since there is no clear evidence that they do.

A good discussion of coaching as a mechanism for developing the individual is provided by Levinson. Berlew and Hall's article on the early careers of new recruits is a good study of the effects of high expectations on performance. Schein's studies of the early careers of new graduates is evidence of the possible detrimental effects of socialization if badly handled. Life-planning is one method for clarifying one's personal goals and objectives.

4

There are articles in McFarland which focus on the role of the personnel department. They also give references to other studies. Many studies have looked at the conflict that almost always seems to accompany the role of the personnel function, but few give a really adequate account of its origins. One that does is Ritzer and Trice.

5

The whole topic of organization development should perhaps be given more space than a sub-section. The view I have taken is that organization development is really the whole topic of this book. The role of the manager in instituting change will be discussed in chapter 13. Here we are concerned only with the techniques of O.D. as an alternative to individual development. Warren Burke's attitude is a good summary of the differences. For a fuller treatment of the methods of O.D. one should consult Beckhard's book or Fordyce and Weil's account of the methods used at T.R.W. systems, one of the foremost exponents of O.D. in its traditional form. Paul Hill gives an interesting account of an O.D. programme in Shell, while Paul and Robertson describe the job enrichment programme in I.C.I. Both of these are good examples of changing the way of working in a large organization as a method of improving the effectiveness of the individual and his contribution to the organization.

Most of the writing and research of Chris Argyris has been taken up by the topic of the individual and the organization, with the need to integrate the objectives of the two and to allow for individual psychological development within the constraints of organizational goals. He is more concerned with the damaging consequences of most managerial practices and not especially interested in socialization. His 1964 book is the best statement of his views. Whyte's book remains the best polemic on the danger of socialization and, though now seventeen years old, is still relevant and stimulating reading.

References

ALFRED, T. M. (1967), 'Checkers or choice in manpower management', *Harvard Business Review*, January–February.

ARGYRIS, C. (1964), *Integrating the Individual and Organization*, Wiley.

BECKHARD, R. (1969), *Organization Development: Strategies and Models*, Addison-Wesley.

BERLEW, D., and HALL, D. (1966), 'The socialization of managers: the effects of expectations on performance', *Admin. Sci. Quarterly*, September.

BERRY, D. F. (1968), 'Applied research in motivation performance and assessment', Bath Conference.

BROWN, W. (1971), *Organization*, Heinemann.

BURKE, W. W. (1971), 'A comparison of management development and organization development', *Management Science*.

CAMPBELL, J. P., DUNNETTE, M. D., LAWLER, E. E., and WEIK, E. E. (1970), *Managerial Behaviour, Performance and Effectiveness*, McGraw-Hill.

CAPLAN, E. H. (1971), *Management Accounting and Behavioural Science*, Addison-Wesley.

DUEU, C. (1971), *Management Kinetics*, McGraw-Hill.

FLAMHOLZ, E. (1971), 'Should your organization attempt to value its human resources?', *California Management Review*.

FORDYCE, J. K. and WEIL, R. (1971), *Managing with People*, Addison-Wesley.

HANDY, C. B. (1971), 'Exploding the myth of management education', *European Business*, Spring.

HEKIMIAN, J. S. and JONES, C. H. (1967), 'Put people on your balance sheet', *Harvard Business Review*, January–February.

HILL, P. (1971), *Towards a New Philosophy of Management*, Gower Press.

JACQUES, E. (1961), *Equitable Payment*, Wiley.

LEVINSON, H. (1970), 'A psychologist looks at executive development', in G. W. Dalton, P. R. Lawrence, and L. E. Greina, *Organizational Change and Development*, Irwin and Dorsey.

LIKERT, R. (1967), *The Human Organization: its Management and Value*, McGraw-Hill.

MCFARLAND, D. E. (ed.), *Personnel Management Readings*, Penguin.

MARKWELL, D. S. and ROBERTS, T. J. (1970), *Organization of Management Development Programmes*, Gower Press.

MEYER, H. H., KAY, E. and FRENCH, J. R. P. jnr. (1965), 'Split Roles in Performance Appraisal, *H.B.R.*, January–February.

MORRIS, J. (1971), 'Development management and management development', *Personnel Review*, December.

NICHOLS, R. G. (1967), 'Listening is good business', in Huneryager and Heckman, *Human Relations in Management*, Arnold.

OPSAHL, R. L. and DUNNETTE, M. D. (1966), 'The role of financial compensation in industrial motivation', *Psychological Bulletin*.

PAUL, W. J. and ROBERTSON, K. B. (1970), *Job Enrichment and Employer Motivation*, Gower Press.

RACKHAM, N., HONEY, P. and COLBERT, M. (1971), *Developing Interactive Skills*, Wellens Publishing.

REVANS, R. G. (1971), *Developing Effective Managers*, Longman.

RITZER, G., and TRICE, H. M. (1969), *An Occupation in Conflict: A Study of the Personnel Manager*, Cornell University.

SCHEIN, E. H. (1969), 'Management development as a process of influence', *Industrial Management Review*, May.

TOWNSEND, R. (1970), *Up the Organization*, Michael Joseph.

VETHER, E. (1968), *Manpower Forecasting*, Bureau of Industrial Relations, Univ. of Michigan.

WHYTE, W. H. (1957), *The Organization Man*, Cape.

Chapter 10

1

As will have been readily apparent from the text, Lawrence and Lorsch's *Organization and Environment* has been the main inspiration for at least the first two parts of this chapter, along with many other parts of this book. Their book should be read by anyone seriously interested in the design of organizations, both for their detailed findings and for their demonstrable conclusions, to me most reassuring, that different ways of designing organizations can be equally effective, depending on the circumstances. They are also among the few writers on organizations who have tackled the question 'How do I begin to design an organization?', in a contingency manner, as opposed to the universalists, those who would like to see a dominant theme or philosophy embodied in all organizations, and answer the question by implication only.

Drucker, with his senses attuned to the needs of the practising manager, is one of the exceptions, with a chapter headed 'What kind of structure'. In this he recommends an analysis of key activities, divisions and relations.

Dill gives a good summary of all the approaches to the study of these organizations up to 1965. His summary reveals the vast amount of writing that there has been on this subject, but also lays bare the fundamentally piecemeal approaches of so many of them. Goals, interest groups, participation aspects, internal structure, the organization and society are the principal headings in his review. Likert's classic book is a good example of the working-through of a principle or philosophy of management into the design of the structure, using his concept of 'linking-pins'. Sadler's article is a nice practical example of the problems of designing and implementing the design, in a real-life situation with the need to pay some costs, for instance satisfaction with the work-group, to obtain some benefit, e.g. better overall integration.

2

Diversity in various forms has cropped up in several studies as a determinant of organization design. Weinshall's monograph is primarily concerned with the structural features of design, but he clearly depicts how structure is related to the scope of the design-making process. He cites the various other studies that support his contention, particularly Stopford's. I am not aware of writers who stress the other pole of my continuum 'uniformity'. 'Uniformity' is not a totally successful word. It has undesirable overtones. 'Consistency' and 'regularity' were two others that I have considered, but which equally fail to convey the full meaning required. Similarly diversity, as I use it, enhances more than Lawrence and Lorsch's differentiation. These semantic difficulties epitomize the dilemma of the social scientist when he seeks to use everyday terms to describe a precise feature of organization or of reality. The proliferation of newly-invented terms, with definitions tailored to purpose, is understandable. Unfortunately, these terms, although they gain in precision, lose in ease of use by the non-initiate.

The matrix organization, its features and its problems, is well discussed in Galbraith's book on the topic. His way of looking at organizations as information-processing devices is interesting and full of implications.

3

Corning Glass undertook a detailed implementation of Lawrence and Lorsch right through from diagnosis using the same questionnaires and interview schedules, to implementation. They have described this in a series of papers to the *American Psychological Association* in September 1971. Only the last of these papers, Hundert's on project teams, is referenced here, but his and his colleagues' can be obtained by applying to the Organizational Research and Development Department of Corning Glass, Corning, NY.

4

Job design, and in particular, job enlargement, has become a way of life and even a way of business to a large number of people. A good summary of the implications of job design is provided by Guest's article. Paul and Robertson provide a good account of the systematic application of job enrichment principles to a large organization, and Reif and Schodenbek provide a summary of the experiences of a number of organizations who have tried systematic job enlargement (and, it must be added, were willing to talk of their experiences). For a counterblast, and some useful warnings, Hulin and Blood's article should be studied. Caplow, in his largely sociological treatment of organizations, has a good summary of the effects of the micro-division of labour, while Lawler makes a very readable plea for more individual control over jobs. The literature on this topic is large, often anecdotal and sometimes messianic. The above list is a small cross-section of what is available. Each work cited will give references to more studies.

4.3

The literature on participation is essentially that which was listed in chapter 4 (on leadership). Tannenbaum and Massaryk's article is a good list of the practical problems, written for the manager rather than the theorist.

4.4

Delegation is one of those topics that has fascinated the practitioner and those who write for him, but has been largely ignored by the researchers, or at least incorporated into other topics such as job enlargement or participation. It is, however, in my experience, a different problem from these, and one that is a real and pressing dilemma for many managers. Drucker, inevitably, recognized it back in 1954, and with his original idea of management by objectives, suggested a mechanism for implementing it.

4.5

Trist *et al.*'s study of the Durham Coal Field, is the classic work on the value of the autonomous work group. This, and other Tavistock Studies, is concisely reviewed in Hill's account of their attempt to create these groups in a process technology in Shell U.K. McGregor pleads eloquently for more trials with this form of work, and instances the experiences of non-linear systems where Maslow was particularly impressed by the potential for self-fulfilment that was tied up in the design of the job. In a sense, all these authors are prophets of this philosophy of management. Although ideologically in agreement with them, I felt it necessary to spell out in the chapter the basic conditions for success which explain so many of the failures, of the lack of attempts to implement the concepts.

References

BAVELAS, A., and STRAUSS, G. (1961), 'Group dynamics and inter-group relations', in W. G. Bennis (ed.), *The Planning of Change*, H. Holt.

CAPLOW, T. (1964), *Principles of Organization*, Harcourt, Brace & World.

DILL, W. R. (1965), 'Business organizations', in J. G. March (ed.), *Handbook of Organizations*, Rand McNally.

DRUCKER, P. F. (1954), *The Practice of Management*, Harper.

GALBRAITH, J. R. (1973), *Designing Complex Organizations*, Addison-Wesley.

GUEST, R. (1964), 'Better utilization of skills through job design', *Management of Personnel Quarterly*, Fall.

HARRISON, R., 'Effective organization for start-up', unpublished paper.

HILL, P. (1971), *Towards a New Philosophy of Management*, Gower Press.

HULIN, C. L. and BLOOD, M. R. (1968), 'Job enlargement, individual differences and worker responses', *Psych. Bulletin*.

HUNDERT, A. T. (1971), 'Problems and prospect for project teams in a large bureaucracy', paper presented to *Am. Psych. Assoc.*, September 3.

LAWLER, E. E. (1968), *Motivation and the Design of Jobs*, ASTME-Vectors.

LAWRENCE, P. R. and LORSCH, J. W. (1967), *Organization and Environment*, Harvard.

LIKERT, R. (1961), *New Patterns of Management*, McGraw-Hill.

MCGREGOR, D. (1967), *The Professional Manager*, McGraw-Hill.

PAUL, W. J., and ROBERTSON, K. B. (1970), *Job Enrichment and Employee Motivation*, Gower Press.

REIF, W. E. and SCHODENBEK, P. P. (1966), 'Job enlargement: antidote to apathy', *Management of Personnel Quarterly*.

SADLER, P. (1971), 'Designing an organization structure', *International Mgt. Review*.

STOPFORD, J. M., 'Growth and organizational change in the multinational firm', unpublished doctoral dissertation.

TANNENBAUM, R. and MASSARYK, F. (1950), 'Participation by subordinates in the managerial decision-making process, *Canadian Journal of Economics and Political Science*, August.

TRIST, E. L., HIGGIN, G. W., MURRAY, H. and POLLOCK, A. B. (1963), *Organizational Choice*, Tavistock.

WEINSHALL, T. D. (1970), *Applications of Two Conceptual Schemes of Organization Behaviour, in Case Study and General Organizational Research*, Ashridge.

Chapter 11

1

There has been no single illuminating source for this chapter. Perhaps this is because few authors have treated operating systems as a unit. Alternatively it may be because there has been little total coverage by behavioural scientists which have gone beyond broad principles. Detailed studies there are in plenty, but each on a different aspect of this chapter. Caplan's book provides a useful overview of the major strands of behavioural science that are relevant to accountants. Joan Woodward's conceptualization of information systems I have found revealing and insightful. Stafford Beer's cybernetic view of organizations provides a model which many people find helpful. All cost-accounting texts discuss budgeting and control systems. References to some of them are available in Caplan.

2

Joan Woodward's conceptualization of control systems is, like most conceptualizations in this field, useful for seeing the wood from the trees when looking at an organization, although less useful in detailed implementation. Henderson and Dearden provide a very practical overview of the problem.

3

Argyris' work on budgets, although of some years ago, is still a good account by a behavioural scientist of the impact that budgeting systems have on the organization. Hofstede's book is an interesting account of his investigation of the budgeting process in some European firms.

4

The computer has generated a lot of books. Not all of them are very relevant for our purposes. McRae summarizes the best of them. The McKinsey survey of 1963 is perhaps the most factual. Rosemary Stewart's study of the working of computer systems is the most behaviourally oriented. Wasserman's article on security is useful.

References

ARGYRIS, C. (1952), *The Impact of Budgets on People*, Controllership Foundation.

BEER, S. (1971), *Brain of the Firm*, Penguin.

BLACK, H. (1967), *Accounting in Business Decisions*, Prentice-Hall, New Jersey, U.S.A.

CAPLAN, E. H. (1971), *Management Accounting and Behavioral Science*, Addison-Wesley.

HENDERSON, B. D., and DEARDEN, J. (1966), 'New Systems for Divisional Control', *Harvard Business Review*.

HOFSTEDE, G. (1967), *The Cause of Budget Control*, Van Nostrand, U.S.A.

MCKINSEY & Co. Inc. (1968), *The McKinsey Report on Computer Utilization*, McKinsey.

MCRAE, T. W. (ed.) (1971), *Management Information Systems*, Penguin.

STEDRY, A. C. (1960), *Budget Control and Cost Behaviour*, Prentice-Hall.

STEWART, R. (1970), *How Computers Affect Management*, Macmillan.

WASSERMAN, J. J. (1969), 'Plugging the Leaks in Computer Security', *Harvard Business Review*.

WOODWARD, J. (ed.) (1970), *Industrial Organization: Behaviour and Control*, Oxford University Press.

Chapter 12

This is a different type of chapter. It is not an attempt to re-cast into a consistent conceptual framework the findings and writings of other men. In this chapter I am seeking to share with the reader my own life-long reflections about the management job. I want to link the more theoretical chapters to the immediate concerns of the reader. For this purpose I have assumed the reader to be, in some capacity, a manager.

Chapter 12 is therefore very much a personal anthology. In my more reflective moments, I do not expect that it will be of much use to anyone. As I state in the conclusion other men's anthologies are of limited interest only. I would hope at best to encourage the reader to compile his own.

Two other personal anthologies on the job of a manager have become classics, but are well worth studying: Alfred P. Sloan's story of how he ran General Motors and Peter Drucker's recent book *The Effective Executive*. Sloan's account is long and reads tediously, but is fascinating for its insight into his own job that it reveals, and all of forty years ago. Drucker's book is loaded with pragmatic wisdom and hordes of examples. On a rather different plane, but providing a useful counterbalance, Sir Geoffrey Vickers looks at the problem of judgement, perhaps the key unending task of the manager.

2.3

Leavitt's four-point analysis of change has been the starting-point for this section.

3

Toffler's book *Future Shock* is an alarmist but readable account of the world of over-stimulation and over-rapid change. Descriptive more than prescriptive it provides a useful backcloth for this section.

References

DRUCKER, P. F. (1967), *The Effective Executive*, Heinemann.

LEAVITT, H. J. (1965), 'Applied Organizational Change in Industry', in March J. G. (ed.), *Handbook of Organizations*, Rand McNally.

SLOAN, A. P. (1954), *My Years with General Motors*, Doubleday.

TOFFLER, A. (1970), *Future Shock*, Bodley Head.

VICKERS, G. (1965), *The Art of Judgement*, Chapman and Hall.

Chapter 13

1

Anyone looking into the future of organizations must first look at the literature on the possible future of society. There is a rich and constantly changing selection here; what is in vogue one year will be out of date the next. David Bell's classic book on the post-industrial society still remains very relevant. James Robertson's latest books argue for a rather optimistic steady-state world, with which all might not agree, but in *The Sane Alternative* he reviews the other possible scenarios and thereby provides a useful check-list. Hazel Henderson, in America, has a similar point of view. Higgin presents a more cataclysmic view, seeing the future as a set of possible disaster scenarios, which we shall only with difficulty avoid. Hirsch has a different viewpoint. His important book argues that materialism carries in-built limits which are more social than physical. His argument is not fully worked through but he raises interesting questions. The Club of Rome publications are important in that they try now to balance all the variables and have moved away from the extrapolatory methods of their first study. These studies, however, along with those of others in the 'futures' business, are almost too global to be useful for our purposes here.

2

Schumacher's book *Small is Beautiful* is well known. Much of his influence, however, was due to his talks and writings in small journals in his later years. These are inadequately captured in the two books published after his death. Kuhn's notion of paradigms is important; it is set out in his book on the history of science.

Elliott Jaques has summarized his work on organizations in a major work, *A General Theory of Bureaucracy*, which is serious reading but worthwhile for anyone interested in a full understanding of Jaques' position.

3

There is a great dearth of writing on the future shape of organizations. The general assumption seems to be that they will continue much the same as before, with minor genuflections to the expressed demands of a more sophisticated environment. Of those writing in this vein Mintzberg, in his set of proposed volumes under the general title of *The Theory of Management Policy* (the first, *The Structuring of Organizations*, came out in 1979), is perhaps the most useful. Lindblom's recent book on politics and markets is also full of implications for organizations although these are not spelt out; it is an investigation into the viability of enterprise in modern societies.

Another trend has been to investigate the more political nature of organizations, viewing them as mini states. This, as was argued in chapter 8, is a long-overdue emphasis, but it is not at present as future-orientated as it needs to be. An important but difficult book in this area is Williamson's *Markets and Hierarchies*.

Jonathan Gershuny's book on the post-industrial society is an interesting riposte to David Bell's hypothesis that we are moving into a service society. Gershuny's ideas could be of major importance to organizations.

Fred Hirsch's book on the social limits to growth is an interesting speculation which needs more thought.

The idea of the three forty-eights (section 3.5 (b)) comes from John Hughes, Principal of Ruskin College, Oxford.

4

These ideas are taken further in my book *Gods of Management*, which postulates that a major change in the way organizations see their responsibilities is necessary if society is not to fall in on itself.

Federalism is a little-understood concept. In a small booklet, Derek Sheane has set out what is involved as well as anybody.

References

BELL, D. (1974), *The Coming of Post-Industrial Society*, Heinemann.

GERSHUNY, J. (1979), *After Industrial Society*, Macmillan.

HANDY. C. B. (1979), *Gods of Management*, Pan.

HENDERSON, H. (1979), *Creating Alternative Futures*, Berkeley Publishing Corp.

HIGGINS, R. (1978), *The Seventh Enemy*, Hodder & Stoughton.

HIRSCH, F. (1977), *The Social Limits to Growth*, Routledge & Kegan Paul.

JAQUES, E. (1976), *A General Theory of Bureaucracy*, Heinemann.

KUHN, T. S. (1962), *The Structure of Scientific Revolutions*, University of Chicago Press.

LINDBLOM, C. E. (1977), *Politics and Markets*, Basic Books Inc.

MINTZBERG, H. (1979), *Structuring of Organizations*, Prentice-Hall.

ROBERTSON, J. (1978), *The Sane Alternative*, Robertson.

SCHUMACHER, E. F. (1973), *Small is Beautiful,* Blond & Briggs.
SCHUMACHER, E. F. (1977), *A Guide for the Perplexed,* Cape.
SCHUMACHER, E. F. and GILLINGHAM, P. N. (1977), *Good Work,* Cape.
SHEANE, D. (1976), *Beyond Bureaucracy,* Management Research.
WILLIAMSON, O. E. (1975), *Markets and Hierarchies: Analysis and Antitrust Implications,* The Free Press.

Acknowledgements

For excerpts reproduced in this volume Acknowledgement is made to the following sources:

R. Ardrey, *The Territorial Imperative*, 1967: Collins, Publishers/Atheneum Press, New York

C. Argyris, *Personality and Organization*, 1948: Chapman and Hall Ltd

R. Blake and J. Mouton, 'The Management Grid', *Advanced Management Journal:* The Society for Advancement of Management, New York

E. H. Caplan, *Management Accounting and Behavioral Science*, 1971: Addison-Wesley, Massachusetts

N. Dornbusch, *The Military Academy as an Assimilating Institution*, 1953; University of North Carolina Press.

P. F. Drucker, *The Practice of Management*, 1954: Harper and Row, New York

J. M. Dutton and R. E. Walton, *Interdepartmental Conflict and Co-operation: Two Contrasting Studies*, 1966: The Society for Applied Anthropology, Washington, D.C.

H. Garfinkel, *Studies in Ethnomethodology*, 1967: Prentice-Hall Inc., Englewood Cliffs, New Jersey, U.S.A.

D. Hargreaves, *Social Relations in a Secondary School*, 1967: Routledge & Kegan Paul/Humanities Press, New York

R. Harrison, *What Kind of Organization?*: Development Research Associates

J. Kelly, 'The Organizational Concept of Leadership', 1970: *International Management*

F. Landis, *What Makes Technical Men Happy and Productive?*, 1971: American Society of Mechanical Engineers

P. R. Lawrence and J. W. Lorsch, 'Distribution of Influence in Two Organisations', 1967: *Organisation & Environment*, Harvard

R. Likert, *New Patterns of Management*, 1961: McGraw-Hill, New York

D. Miller, *Using Behavioral Science to Solve Organization Problems*, 1968: International Personnel Management Association

R. L. Peabody, 'Perceptions of Organizational Authority: A Comparative Analysis', *Administrative Science Quarterly*, 1962: Cornell University, U.S.A.

E. H. Porter, 'The Parable of the Spindle', *Harvard Business Review*, May-June 1962: *Harvard Business Review*, Harvard University Graduate School of Business Administration

460 Acknowledgements

D. S. Pugh and D. C. Phesey, 'Some Developments in the Study of Organizations':
Management International Review

N. Rackham, P. Honey and M. Colbert, *Developing Interactive Skills*, 1971:
Wellens Publishing

E. H. Schein, *Process Consultation*, 1969: Addison-Wesley

M. Sherif and C. W. Sherif, *An Outline of Social Psychology*, 1956: Harper &
Row, New York

A. J. M. Sykes and J. Bates, 'A study of conflict between formal company policy
and the interest of informed groups', *Sociological Review*, 1962: *Sociological
Review*, University of Keele

R. Tannenbaum, I. R. Weschler and F. Massaryk, *Leadership and Organisation*,
1961: McGraw-Hill, New York

T. D. Weinshall, *Applications of Two Conceptual Schemes of Organizational Behaviour in Case Study and General Organizational Research*, 1971: Ashridge
Management College, Herts.

Index

FIND OUT MORE ABOUT PENGUIN BOOKS

We publish the largest range of titles of any English language paperback publisher. As well as novels, crime and science fiction, humour, biography and large-format illustrated books, Penguin series include *Pelican Books* (on the arts, sciences and current affairs), *Penguin Reference Books*, *Penguin Classics*, *Penguin Modern Classics*, *Penguin English Library*, *Penguin Handbooks* (on subjects from cookery and gardening to sport), and *Puffin Books* for children. Other series cover a wide variety of interests from poetry to crosswords, and there are also several newly formed series – *Lives and Letters*, *King Penguin*, *Penguin American Library*, and *Penguin Travel Library*.

We are an international publishing house, but for copyright reasons not every Penguin title is available in every country. To find out more about the Penguins available in your country please write to our U.K. office – Dept EP, Penguin Books Ltd, Harmondsworth, Middlesex UB7 0DA – unless you live in one of the following areas:

In the U.S.A.: Dept DG, Penguin Books, 299 Murray Hill Parkway, East Rutherford, New Jersey 07073.

In Canada: Penguin Books Canada Ltd, 2801 John Street, Markham, Ontario L3R 1B4.

In Australia: Marketing Department, Penguin Books Australia Ltd, P.O. Box 257, Ringwood, Victoria 3134.

In New Zealand: Marketing Department, Penguin Books (N.Z.) Ltd, P.O. Box 4019, Auckland 10.

In India: Penguin Overseas Ltd, 706 Eros Apartments, 56 Nehru Place, New Delhi 110019.

Organization Theory
Edited by D. S. Pugh

The editor of this volume of readings defines organization theory as 'the study of the structure, functions and performance of organizations and the behaviour of groups and individuals within them'.

From the point of view of organizational behaviour, the task of management can be considered as the organization of individuals in relation to the physical means and resources to achieve the desired goal. In Part One the continuing activities of task allocation, coordination and supervision, which constitute the organization's structure, are discussed. A theoretical analysis of what managers have to do is given in Part Two. Part Three describes behaviour in organizations. Included here is a section of Elton Mayo's key Hawthorne studies – the human relations approach. Some of the research by Lewin on group dynamics, attitude change and leadership style is also examined.

Management and Motivation
Edited by Victor H. Vroom and Edward L. Deci

The performance of anyone at his job is affected by a combination of ability and motivation. This book brings together papers which represent the main work being done in the study of motivation.

There are three main approaches to the subject. The first is paternalistic in nature and assumes that the more a worker is rewarded, the harder he will work. The second approach assumes that a person will be motivated to work if rewards and penalties are tied directly to his performance. The third approach is that called participative management in which the incentives for effective performance are in the job itself or in the individual's relationship with members of his working team.

Related titles in Penguin Education

Management and the Social Sciences
Tom Lupton

A knowledge of the social sciences is essential for managers. Here Professor Lupton begins by considering some of the early theories of social scientists and managers. The methods and research procedures of social science are illustrated in detail in six studies which clearly bring out the implications of this work for management. These studies are on industrial bureaucracy; assembly-line work; the influence of production technology on the organization; the reasons for resistance to technical and administrative change; the Fawley productivity agreement; and a study of working groups and the effect of their formation on output. Some problems of practical interest to management are then discussed – industrial conflict and cooperation, communication and technical change. The final chapter describes some recent developments in the theory of organizations, and examines their relevance for the practice of management.

Writers on Organizations
D. S. Pugh, D. J. Hickson and C. R. Hinings

Even though all organizations are different, it is useful to study their differences and the ways in which they work. Many prominent management thinkers have made a study of organizations and, in many cases, the impact of their work has been very important.

The authors have focused their attention on five aspects of organizations – the Structure of Organizations, the Functioning of Organizations, the Management of Organizations, People in Organizations and the Organization in Society. In each of these divisions they discuss the contributions made by important writers on the subject. The object of the book is to give an introduction to the views of leading management writers. It was first commissioned by the Administrative Staff College at Henley-on-Thames, and is now published by Penguin Education in a revised and updated form.

Pelicans on Business and Management

An Insight into Management Accounting
John Sizer

During the last decade managements have had to learn to live with high rates of inflation, low levels of profitability, and serious liquidity problems. The more sophisticated techniques developed by management accountants in response to these conditions are described in the second edition of Professor Sizer's best-selling work. It has been extensively revised and extended by almost two hundred pages.

'For managers and management students rather than professional accountants. The author explains the elements of financial and cost accounting and goes on to consider financial planning, investment appraisal, budgetary control and decision making. This is no easy popularisation but a substantial contribution to an important subject' – *The Times Educational Supplement*

Management Thinkers
Edited by A. Tillett, T. Kempner and G. Wills

'British management was backward by the end of the nineteenth century and, with notable exceptions, has never caught up.'

'The Ford Co. from October 1912 to October 1913 hired 54,000 men to maintain an average working force of 13,000. This was a labour turnover of 416 per cent for the year.'

With observations like these this book vividly recalls and presents the problems of industry from the industrial revolution to the present day.

Management Thinkers contains readings from the pioneers of management thought – Frederick Taylor, Henri Fayol, Seebohm Rowntree, Mary Parker Follett, Elton Mayo and C. I. Barnard.

Pelicans on Business and Management

The Management of Industrial Relations
Kevin Hawkins

Many people believe that Britain has too many strikes, and this reflects the excessive power of the trade unions. Indeed, it is often argued that trade union militancy is the major cause of our economic problems. But, as Kevin Hawkins shows in his fascinating and timely examination of industrial relations during the last decade, the situation is much more complex than popular discussion would have it. He challenges the view that there are quick and painless solutions to our problems but suggests certain policy changes which should help to bring about a broad, non-political consensus. Building this consensus will be long and difficult but the implications for managers, trade unionists and politicians will be far reaching.

The Multinationals
Christopher Tugendhat

In recent years vast international companies have developed which dominate the 'commanding heights of the economy' throughout Western Europe and North America. Firms like Alcan, IBM, Ford, Shell and Bayer have annual sales as large as the gross national products of many countries, and their rate of growth is much faster. Inevitably there are tensions between the companies and governments who see control of a vital sector of the economy slipping from their grasp.

Christopher Tugendhat's book, which won a McKinsey Foundation Book Award in 1971, is a detailed examination of the multinationals and the political implications of their position and influence. His theories and principles, supported with examples from the experience of companies and governments, illuminate a major political and economic problem.

'The importance of this book is not in doubt. It will stand the test of years' – Tam Dalyell in the *New Scientist*